WHAT EXPERTS

JEFF BEEDY AND PLUS ...

especially, an athletic game can be an occasion for many lessons indeed — emotional and moral, and too, cognitive of factual. Those of us who were active during our high school and college years in a particular sport well remember those moments when something was said or done that lived long and hard in our memories: a gesture, a nod, an effort of one kind or another, a remark — and suddenly a new sense of things, an awareness of this or that, heretofore absent."

Dr. Robert Coles,
"Foreword," Jeff Beedy's
Positive Learning Using Sports

"Jeff Beedy has been a pioneer in using sports to teach lessons beyond the playground. In Positive Learning Using Sports, *he has put together an amazing resource to help coaches become effective teachers of life as well as their sports. It is an invaluable resource for school leaders who want their sports programs to be the equal of their academic programs in having a lifetime impact on their students"*

Jim Thompson
Founder and Executive Director
Positive Coaching Alliance

"Jeff created the PLUS model.   I have often turned to his now classic book, Sports PLUS, *for ideas and inspiration.   It is used as a basic reference by sport psychologists and youth sport leaders throughout the world including China, South Korea, Africa, Cyprus, and throughout the United States."*

Brenda Light Bredemeier, Ph.D
Pioneer in Sports and development

"I am always amazed and gratified when Jeff Beedy publishes yet another work on how to use sport participation and competition to develop better kids — and to help the adults who teach and coach them. This latest work is as magnificent as the multitude of his previous endeavors. Jeff has been teaching this writer a hardened and too often pessimistic youth sports "culture changer" for well over two decades; and I always learn plenty of new tools to try to help make American organized youth sports more child-centered. Jeff is a true beacon of valuable wisdom. If you're going to invest any time in administrating, coaching and "sidelinewatching" children in sport, please read this book."

Bob Bigelow
Youth Sports Activist
co-author, *Just Let the Kids Play*

"Jeff Beedy — a philosopher, a visionary humanist and a true educator, provides the framework, the guidelines, the rationale and the tools for a new global "investment." An investment that can last over time and space. An investment on character development, civic engagement and human potential through the "New Science of Sport-based Teaching and Learning." Jeff's inspiring and refreshing work reminds us the importance and the need of investment in Human Capital through sport-based value-oriented youth development in a very simple and applicable way. Jeff's work and recommendations will last over time and space, since they blend the universality of Socrates, Plato, Aristotle's pedagogy, philosophy and ontology, revive ancient Olympia's values of holistic human development and civic engagement, merge this ontology with the theoretical foundations of the greatest moral and human development theorist of our days, and showcase how the theory of science of sport-based teaching and learning can become praxis. A great book and a great tool for all youth development "investors" (educators, policy makers, researchers and practitioners). A clear roadmap and robust foundation for "sport"-for-development programming around the globe. Thank you Jeff for this great contribution!!!"

Alexis Lyras, Ph.D
Sport-for-Development and Peace
Georgetown University

SPORTS PLUS

Positive **L**earning

Using **S**ports

SPORTS PLUS

Positive **L**earning **U**sing **S**ports

The New Science of Sport-Based Education

Jeffrey Pratt Beedy, Ed.D.
with Matt Davidson

SPORTS PLUS
Positive Learning Using Sports
The New Science of Sport-Based Education

First paperback edition published in the United States of America, January 2016

ISBN-10: 0-9855223-0-5   ISBN-13: 978-0-9855223-0-8

First printing, 2004
10   9   8   7   6   5   4   3   2

For permission requests to reproduce selections from this book, write to the publisher, subject line: Attention: Permissions Coordinator, jpbeedy@gmail.com

Colophon: This book is set in Minion Pro, Minion Bold, Minion Italic, Minion Bold Italic. The text is set, 12/14.4 x 30.

Author Photo by Karyn Beedy.

Global Children Publishing
235 N. Chesterville Road
Farmington, ME 04938-6223
globalchildrenpublishing.com

TABLE OF CONTENTS

INTRODUCTION

Guiding Philosophical Principles

Educational medium

PLUS understands that sports possess the unique social and educational components to promote collaboration and engage in dialogue and conflict resolution. Children learn best when involved with activities and people they enjoy.

Transferability

PLUS is based on the fact that lessons learned about critical thinking and problem solving from sports are transferable to other areas of a child's life including home and school.

Skills Training

PLUS offers 21st Century leadership skills training to community organizations through online education and train-the-trainers workshops in community settings.

Strengthen local self-reliance

The goal of PLUS is to be regionally inspired, locally supported, and with sustainability and replication as the long-term goals. PLUS seeks to strengthen the capacities of local organizations and promote community self-reliance through sustainable strategies.

Inclusion

PLUS includes children who may be marginalized for reasons of gender, religion, ability, ethnicity, disability or social background.

Integration

PLUS seeks to connect and utilize all aspects of community including classrooms, sports, boarding in the educational process.

Research and practice

PLUS connects outcome goals such as teamwork and innovation to relevant research in 21st Century teaching and learning. Programs can conduct pre-and-post tests to determine growth in outcome goals.

Sustainability

PLUS builds the community's capacity to take full ownership of the program following the active project implementation. The ultimate goal is to hand over the program to the community

Replication

An important goal of PLUS is for schools around the world to replicate the principles of the program in their respective schools.

Foreword From Tom Lickona

When the great scorer comes to write against your name. He
marks not that you won or lost but how you played the game

— Grantland Rice

Like a lot of kids in my generation, I grew up hearing those immortal words of the great sportswriter, Grantland Rice. As I grew older, I understood that he wasn't just talking about the game of sports. He was talking about the game of life.

Do sports teach us how to play well the game of life? It all depends. Most of us know from firsthand observation that sports can build character or undermine it. They can foster fair play or dirty play, honest competition or win-at-all-costs. They can promote teamwork or selfishness, self-control or fits of rage, the ability to win and lose gracefully or neither.

In my lifetime, the negative character effects of competitive sports have, sadly, become ever more common. From Little League to professional athletics, competitive sports have seemed increasingly to bring out the worst, not the best, in players and fans alike. But as the PLUS curriculum makes clear, it doesn't have to be that way. Approached correctly, sports can be an important tool for building the character of our children and helping to rebuild the character of our culture.

Happily, in the past decade, the national character education movement has done much to restore character development to the center of schooling. There has been an explosion of books and materials, federal funding for character education, state mandates, teacher training institutes, a National Schools of Character awards program, and a groundswell of grassroots support for teaching all children virtues such as respect, responsibility, and hard work that are the basis of strong personal character and a decent, democratic society.

While character education continues to gain momentum, two challenges loom large: integrating it into the school's academic curriculum and extending it to the extracurricular program. PLUS, by using problem-posing stories to increase reading skills and stimulate critical thinking, bridges character and academics. By subsequently providing action opportunities to apply lessons from the sports stories to the give-and-take of a real game, PLUS takes character education beyond the classroom into the realm of sports activity. And through guided reflection on both the sports stories and the sport experience, students are helped to find the larger lessons about teamwork, fairness, and perseverance that will serve them well on the playing field of life.

All of us can be grateful that we finally have a program that capitalizes on the character-building potential of sports. Every school in America that is serious about character education should have PLUS in its toolbox.

Tom Lickona
Author, *Educating for Character*
Director, *Center for the 4th and 5th Rs*
(Respect and Responsibility)

A Message From The Founder

It's been thirty years since I arrived at Harvard Graduate School of Education ready to explore the role that sports play in children's development. As an athlete, I enjoyed competing at the highest levels including playing baseball in the Cape Cod League and skiing in the Freestyle Tour. Like many other competitive athletes, I felt sports were awesome. After a few weeks at Harvard, however, I learned not everyone feels this way about sports. I soon learned that some of my new friends had bad experiences playing Little League Baseball or Youth Soccer. Many of these graduate students had and never played a high school sport outside of gym class volleyball. This was certainly an eye-opening moment for me. How much fun was their sport experience? What did they learn? I would soon find out.

What I discovered from my research was that while sports are popular around the globe, the idea of sport as serious scholarly inquiry was widely dismissed. In the early eighties, I found myself as a pioneer in what would soon become a new field in education and youth development. I was surprised to learn that there was little quality research on sports and the developing child. I was a blender of feelings: on the one hand, I believed sports were positive and awesome. On the other hand, I was learning that sports may be positive for those who were good at them, but negative for those who were left out or not highly skilled. I eventually came to the belief that sports are a powerful medium – not unlike school or family– but whether they are positive or negative depends on how the sport experience it's organized. I was fortunate at Harvard to study under Lawrence Kohlberg, Bob Selman, Sesame Street founder, Gerald Lesser and Carol Gilligan, who allowed me to study the moral impact of sport on youth.

Early sport-based research on moral development

In the early eighties, I pioneered a summer camp in Maine called The NewSport Experience. I created the camp as a way to study the impact of sports on the moral development of eight- to twelve-year-old boys. I was fortunate to be able to study with world-renowned moral psychologist Lawrence Kohlberg. I'll never forget the day Dr. Kohlberg flew up to Maine, and facilitated an eight-hour community meeting among the campers and staffers to discuss a theft in a dorm. I was nervous for a week trying to figure what type of activity we could "stage" at camp to show Dr. Kohlberg that we were a moral community. At the last minute there was a theft at the camp and we decided that we would address the theft as a community, with Dr. Kohlberg. What took place in that long meeting with children and adult of all ages demonstrated to me the power and value of community. After a couple of hours of dialogue around "you should lock the doors," "hey should not have left the money out in the open," Dr. Lawrence Kohlberg stood up and said "what role does the community have in getting the money back to the campers who had their money stolen?" At that moment the whole community dialogue shifted to what the role of community is in moral reasoning. That was one of my first glimpses into the intellectual potential of sports. Thank you Larry.

PLUS summer camp and after school program

After completing my thesis in 1988, and as a way to expand to more diverse populations, I founded the PLUS camp (Personal Learning Using Sports) at Milton Academy in 1990. At the time, I was teaching a class with Pulitzer Prize winner Dr. Robert Coles, called *Social Reflections in Literature*. The course prompted me to add literature to the learning environment. In the late 1980s when I was working on my thesis, Brenda Bredemeier and David Shields were studying Kohlberg's work. Bredemeier and Shields were analyzing sports and character development as a branch of sport psychology, but my investigation into how sport can factor into the moral, cognitive, social and emotional development of youth was, heretofore, unexplored. It was in the early nineties that I began to realize we could use the model from our camp to create an after-school program. We brought the sport-based youth development program to inner city Lawrence and Dorchester, Massachusetts, and rural New Hampton, New Hampshire, with success.

Creation of PLUS Curriculum

All these "hands on experiences" led to the archiving and creation of the PLUS Curriculum. Today, after thousands of hours of work, we have formulated our principles and practices into a sport-based curriculum that communities across the country can implement through the comprehensive manual you are about to read. The PLUS Program has benefited from the assembly of a first rate research and development team. Dr. Matt Davidson, Research Director at the Center for the 4th and 5th Rs (Respect & Responsibility) has come on board to help co-author the program, bringing with him the expertise of Kelli Moran-Miller and Dr. Vladimir Khmelkov. Together with longtime staffers Kris Genakos, Cindy Glidden, Adam Tanney, Joe Bowab, Tom Zierk, Gara Field, Steve Davis, Morgan Murphy, Tom Zierk, Jerry Pieh, Andrew Churchill, and Amanda Beedy, we feel that we have assembled a team that is committed to creating a research-based program that is theoretically sound and empirically tested.

PLUS goes global

In 2006, PLUS was invited to Cyprus to examine how sports can be used to bridge peace between the Greek and Turkish families. The groups of children, whose parents retained vivid memories of the tumultuous events of the 1970s and the subsequent division of the island, had previously been forbidden to speak to each other. But to our surprise, by the third night of the camp, the Greek and Turkish children were dancing, singing, and laughing together. Using sports as a neutral medium, the camp brought the next generation of Cypriots together, doing a small part to heal the divide and conflict experienced by their parents.

In 2010, I was hired as the founding headmaster of Korea International School, which is a part of Korea's 2 billion dollar Global Education City on Jeju Island, South Korea. We learned that in Korea it is customary for older boys and girls to "rule over" their younger schoolmates. In an effort to address bullying, we created the Learn to Lead program. Based on the idea that leadership is not intentionally taught in the curriculum we taught the older students how to lead. We figured if we could replace "bullying power" with "leading power" than we could eradicate bullying and create a circle of good. Understanding that the socialization of children begins in kindergarten we taught the older students how to mentor younger students with the goal of creating a continuous cycle of positive leaders. Within a relatively short time we noticed a shift in perspective. Instead of investing time in bullying their younger classmates they where learning how to lead their younger schoolmates in a positive way with the goal of to creating a circle of good where respect trumps bullying.

Montessori and sports

In 2013, I had the pleasure of leading a Montessori Academy in Indian Springs, Al. I spent most of my days observing the teachers and watching the children. The teachers were respectful and very successful in creating a peaceful environment in which to take risks. The students were curious, respectful and curious. I wondered in what ways Maria Montessori's principles of teaching and learning apply to children's sports? Are there things to be learned by studying The Montessori Method and how it applies to youth sports? Certainly Montessori's view of children " as human beings to whom respect is due, superior to us by reason of their innocence and of the greater possibilities of their future" is a fine principle to guide us as teachers. What if youth sport coaches and leaders adhered to this principle when coaching children in Youth Soccer and Little League Baseball? Would our children's sport experiences change for the better? If the Montessori children are so respectful and intrinsically motivated than maybe we could apply some of the Montessori principles to children's sports. It is true that sports are different than school, but both arenas share a common thread — the children.

Summary

The goal of this book is to bring intentionality to children's sports. What is new in this book is the intentional application of research in the fields of human development and psychology to the philosophical and pedagogical design of sport-based activities. It is our responsibility as leaders to design programs where children can have authentic opportunities to be "at the forefront of global change and innovation." Crafting sport-based programs that educate and empower children is what this book is about.

I may not have realized it when I began my doctoral program at Harvard in the early 1980s, but my original thesis charted the cartography of a new domain — sports as moral pedagogy, built on a foundation of research and experience. Today, this field has gained wide attention and continues to attract the interest of more scholars and schools each year. It is with deference to the potential that research in both of these fields will have to better our lives and communities that I offer this book *PLUS Global: The New Science of Sport-based Education.* I believe readers will find that it holds some seminal relevance to these crucial "emerging fields."

Jeff Beedy Ed.D
PLUS Founder
Brewster, Cape Cod
Spring 2015

OVERVIEW

The New Science of Sport-Based Education

What is The New Science of Sport-based Education? It is the intentional synthesis and application of research in the fields of human development and psychology to the philosophical and pedagogical design of sport-based activities. More simply, the new science of sport-based education allows us to move from having to accept the metaphor that "sports build character" to the ability to actually design sport-based activities intentionally that develop targeted educational goals. This approach is new in a couple of important ways. First, this new approach views sports as a legitimate educational medium similar to the classroom. This new field designs sport-based activities in the much same way that a middle school teacher might prepare a biology curriculum with intentional outcome goals. A second reason this approach is new is because until recently, the field of sports and human development were separate fields, one conducted by researchers who viewed sports as inherently bad and the other by coaches who believe sports to be inherently good.

Intentionality

We no longer should argue whether sports are good or bad for children. That statement is too simple and only starts a fight at the dinner table.

The truth is, research over the past 20 years indicates that sports can be a powerful medium for promoting learning and growth. Depending on a number of factors that we will discuss in depth in this book — sports can be good or bad. The research (mostly from the educational domain and not the sport domain) indicates that educational goals such as teamwork, respect or even critical thinking do not happen randomly and programs need to be proactively designed to develop specific goals.

Connecting research to practice: Knowledge synthesizers

Educational programs often lag educational research by as many as 20 years. For example, the work I began in the mid-eighties at Harvard, is just finding its way into some of the more intentional sport-based youth development programs like First Tee, The Magic Bus, and the Olympic Doves Movement. Sport programs that are using this new approach to learning can connect outcome goals (i.e., teamwork) to the relevant research of how teamwork is actually learned in the classroom, at home and on the playing fields. Many of the more advanced sport-based youth development programs that have emerged in the past decade can actually prove their claims through pre- and-post tests. In this sense, programs that employ this new science are knowledge synthesizers — that is, they are drawing from the field of human development and psychology to design the pedagogy and activities of their sport programs and have a way to show what they actually teach.

21st Century skills

In the thirty years since I began my research, I have travelled our larger world, studying how children experience sports and the role sports play in their lives. I have studied children's sport programs in China, South Korea, Cyprus, and throughout the United States. I have started programs in rural Maine and New Hampshire, and in urban areas such as Boston, Chicago, and New Orleans. I have run after-school programs, summer camps, Montessori-based sports programs, and elite high school programs that train Division I- and Olympic-caliber athletes. One thing I have learned is that schools are not the only place children learn. In fact, 21st-century skills are sometimes best learned *outside* the classroom. These skills can be taught effectively in places of passion, conflict, and joy. Youth sports, when properly designed, can serve as 21st-century classrooms. Tony Wagner, in his seminal book, Creating Innovators, lists the following skills as critical for surviving in the 21st Century.

1. Critical thinking and problem-solving

2. Collaboration across networks and leading by influence

3. Agility and adaptability

4. Initiative and entrepreneurialism

5. Effective oral and written communication

6. Accessing and analyzing information

7. Curiosity and imagination

A systems approach to learning

PLUS is a comprehensive, integrated and developmental sport-based educational approach that draws upon longstanding educational theory, including the experiential, social learning, behavioral, and cognitive-developmental learning theories, and research-based educational practice. PLUS is a systems model that encourages children to make connections from their sport experiences to other areas of their lives. Children learn to identify how the principles and skills that make them successful in sports – team play, self- discipline, hard work, belief in oneself, perspective-taking, and decision-making – can also lead to success at home, in school, on the job and in the community. PLUS encourages all community stakeholders – coaches, parents, players, fans and umpires – to adhere to the program's interconnected components. When PLUS is employed in its entirety, the potential for sports to contribute to the positive development of our children is more fully realized.

PLUS Core Principles

Children's sports are played within the context of communities and communities by nature are complicated social systems. A "systems thinking" organizational model is driven by a set of shared operating principles that serve as the template for everything the team does on the field as well as within the community. Core Operating Principles (COP) provide the entire community with a template for interpersonal relationships, team building, hiring, program development, professional development, and staff evaluation. The program's core principles *drive* day-to-day operations, *serve* as a guide for training and evaluating all community stakeholders, *guide* adoption of policies, inform how resources such as the distribution of playing time and positions are allocated. Our operating principles must be *data-driven, specific, action-oriented* and live deep within our learning organization. PLUS is guided by five Core Operating Principles.

Philosophy

The philosophy of our program defines why we are doing what we are doing and what we want to accomplish. In this sense, our program's philosophy drives all of our decisions and serves as a template as we think about issues ranging from distribution of playing time to how we address social and moral issues as a team.

Psychology

This important component of the learning process suggests that we need to be cognizant of how children learn in general, and, specifically, how children learn important program goals such as teamwork and responsibility. The PLUS Model turns to and employs the common theories of how people learn including the Social Learning Theory, The Behavioral Learning Theory and the Cognitive Development Learning Theory.

Pedagogy

How we "teach and coach" can be understood as our pedagogy. If one of our goals is to teach teamwork, for example, it is important to explore the best ways to teach the concept of working together. Our team's pedagogy takes into account our team's philosophy and psychology as well as our program's outcome goals.

Program

All of the activities that we design including practices, team meetings, team orientations, readings and rituals make up what we call our Program. The program activities are the places in which the learning takes place. It is important to expand our vision of what it means to play on our team. Sports can be much more than practices and games. The "coach as teacher" understands that within the program or season there are many ways to bring the team together and provide opportunities for learning.

Process

A great program can validate that it does what it says it does. The new science of sport-based learning provides tools for coaches and teachers to define their programs outcome goals and design pre-and-post tests to determine how successful our program was in promoting our outcome goals. It is one thing to state that "sports are good for everyone" and quite another to announce teamwork as a desired outcome goal and have the ability to demonstrate how well the program did in regards to the goal of advancing our team players' understandings of teamwork.

PLUS Outcome Goals

PLUS focuses on five outcome goals. PLUS defines the following five outcome goals; community, leadership skills, intrinsic motivation, physical health, and moral theme comprehension and literacy. All outcome goals can be measured and evaluated to determine the success of each program.

Community

A sense of community is defined by how each member of the team is known, needed, cared for, and has the opportunity to shape their environment.

21st Century Skills

The PLUS Model employs five critical 21st Century skills: Teamwork, Respect, Responsibility, Fair Play and Perseverance.

Intrinsic, self-referenced motivation

PLUS cultivates a self-referenced approach to motivation (what the research literature calls a "task or mastery orientation"), that is built upon a cyclical pattern of personal goal setting, monitoring, and reformulation. In addition to numerous positive performance outcomes (academic, athletic, and other), research suggests that cultivating an orientation in which a person competes against self- referenced personal achievement (e.g., a better time than before, more right on this test than last time, fewer unnecessary interruptions of the class today than yesterday) tends to promote self-reflection and awareness, to support strong intrinsic motivation, and to reduce helpless response to failure (Nicholls 1984; Duda and Nicholls 1992; Harackiewicz and Elliot 1993; Molden and Dweck 2000).

Physical health

The benefits of physical activity are well-documented. Research suggests that a physically active youngster has a more positive self-image, greater self- confidence, and demonstrates improvement in motor skills, cognitive functioning (Etnier et al., 1997) and health-related fitness. Studies from the American Council on Exercise have shown that physically active children also are more likely to become physically active adults. Thus, developing an interest in sport and physical activity at a young age is something that will likely continue to benefit them later in life.

Literacy and moral theme comprehension

The literacy component of the Sports PLUS Program attempts to accomplish two central goals. First, it attempts to increase students' interest in and appreciation for literature by exposing them to the kinds of stories they like and are interested in – namely, sport stories. Encouraging children to read is much easier when they can read about subjects they care about. Secondly, PLUS seeks to increase students' moral theme comprehension by providing them with a script for considering the important elements regarding the moral of the story. Learning to ask critical comprehension questions of a text allows students to consistently extract the moral of future stories they read or in which they are involved. The ability to identify conflicts, generate solutions, predict outcomes, and consider potential consequences constitutes the critical thinking skills that are developed through the literacy component.

The PLUS Curriculum

The PLUS curriculum consists of over 100 daily activities that develop the five core leadership skills and outcome goals. Chapters three through eight of this book will introduce the potential of sport as an educational medium, outline the philosophy of the PLUS model, describe the importance of creating a positive learning environment, and illustrate the PLUS five outcome goals. The last section of the book will provide the tools needed to run a successful PLUS program and will outline how to use the daily lesson plans. As it leads you through a typical Sports PLUS day, each phase of the PLUS curriculum will be explained in detail. The phases are interrelated, but each plays an integral role within the five Theme Units – Teamwork, Respect, Responsibility, Fair Play, and Perseverance. They are designed to foster positive development while creating a caring, connected community among program participants. The pattern of the Warm-Up, Activity, and Cool-Down sessions provides a consistent structure for introducing those program components necessary for positive development, including team-building activities, reading and sports activities, and time for reflection and goal- setting. Moreover, the predictable rhythm of each Warm-Up, Activity, and Cool-Down session allows the individual components to flow together.

The PLUS Program is organized into 50 sessions – 10 sessions for each of the five Theme Units. Each session is further divided into three, roughly one-hour lessons, equaling 150 individual lessons. Each of the 50 sessions has one of each of the following lessons, in this order: The three lessons in each session are designed to flow together and cover similar content through different methodologies. Although the sessions are ideally done in order and in their entirety, we tried to create resources that could be used to meet the goals of your particular program. What do your students need? How much time do you have? What space is available to you? Some programs will be able to incorporate two lessons from a session back-to-back on the same day. Others may only be able to do one lesson a week. Only you will be able to decide how to use these resources.

Summary

Growing up I always felt there was something magical about sports. I could escape any problem when I was skiing. When pitching, I forgot everything for those three hours. Nothing else did that for me. I still dream about pitching. But that is not really what this book is about. This book is about what we can actually learn from playing sports and how schools and youth programs can be designed to teach important social skills and life lessons. If it is true that educational programs lag behind research by 20 years, it is even more acute in the field of sports. There are many reasons for this including over-zealous parents, professional athletes and a frenzied media. As a Headmaster of a private independent school, I have witnessed the recent trends to shorten the research-to-practice lag and bring our teaching philosophy and pedagogy into the 21st century. Authors including Daniel Pink, Tony Wagner, Daniel Coyle, Thomas Friedman and Howard Gardner are telling us that we live in a new world, that there is a new set of core skills that are necessary to be successful in the new workplace and that our children learn these skills differently. In short, we need to revamp our children's sport programs. This is what this book is all about.

The purpose of this book is to bring our sport-based youth development programs into the 21st century. *Sports Plus: Positive Learning Using Sports: The New Science of Sport-Based Education* suggests that, when intentionally designed for positive development of youth, sports provide a powerful and natural way to help them develop the skills they will need to be happy and productive global citizens

SECTION I

THE PLUS APPROACH

CHAPTER ONE

Tapping the Potential of Sports

We are a nation intensely into sports. Many scholars suggest that, in terms of cultural scope and significance, sports are second only to religion in our country. Sports play a powerful part in molding the character of the nation — especially the character of millions of our nation's youth who participate in organized sports programs. Because of the growing frequency of un-sportsmanlike attitudes and conduct at all levels of athletic competition, many observers have concluded that, contrary to the popular adage, sports do not build good character.

— Beedy and Gough

Introduction

We have all learned lessons from sports — some of the lessons healthy and positive, others, painful and destructive. For some, sport provides powerful opportunities for personal growth and development reinforced by team camaraderie and relationships that last a lifetime. Unfortunately, for others, the experience is negative, marked by emotional scars from unhealthy performance expectations, from unfair or humiliating incidents (such as limited playing time, always being chosen last, or from being picked on during games or in the locker room).

The reality is that sport is one of the most powerful and popular socializing agents in the lives of children. The socialization comes from within our teams through the quality of player-to-player and coach-to-player relationships. It also comes from outside our teams through the media and the culture of professional and high profile sports. Our children emulate sports heroes, mimicking their behavior and speaking their language. Our young athletes participate on teams, watch, read and talk about sports. But as we well know, not all actions they see and language they hear represent the lessons and values we want our youth to exemplify. Fortunately, for the majority, sports are positive, but the goal is not simply to reduce harm. Rather, the goal is to maximize the potential for positive impact on the overall development of our children through the educational medium of sport. Clearly, sport holds great potential for teaching valuable lessons; this cannot be denied. Achieving that potential, however, cannot occur until our efforts are pursued with purposeful design, rather than haphazard assumption.

Sport as the Medium

"Medium" refers to important social developmental pathways that affect a child's overall development. There are many mediums in a child's life including family, school, peer groups, church, and extra curricular activities. Each medium offers different opportunities to learn and develop character. Sport presents a qualitatively different learning experience than other mediums. For example, children face different peer-related challenges in a sport context than they do in school or family life. Sport competition is much different than competition in school or Girl Scouts, for example.

Sport is an undeniably powerful medium for connecting to our children. It provides an authentic social and moral arena within which to teach important values such as respecting others and the importance of working together as a team. Sport provides real-life dilemmas that stimulate cognitive conflict and provide opportunities for proactive resolution through proven educational practices such as modeling and mutual dialogue. However, the medium of sport, in and of itself, is neither positive nor negative. The degree to which sport promotes positive values depends on the quality of the experience, which, in turn, is influenced by the nature of the relationships, the system of governance and the opportunities for positive growth found within the sport environment.

Go To the Youth

In order to deliver positive youth development opportunities, we must first go to the youth; that is, we must identify *their* interests and passions. Sport provides an invaluable medium for reaching youth precisely because for many, sport is their passion. Consider the sheer number of youth who participate in sport: Each year in this country, upwards of thirty million children play some form of organized team sport, and many more play pick-up games with friends and neighbors, brothers and sisters (Lauer, 2002). Sport is especially pervasive in the lives of elementary school children, with the highest participation occurring at around age ten.

According to sports data expert Harvey Lauer, one reason sport is underutilized as an educational medium is that "as a cultural concept, 'sport' is synonymous with 'fun,' 'leisure,' 'recreation' and 'play' — distinctly separated from the more serious work of society." Lauer (2002) goes on to suggest that sport participation is linked to youth development only as a metaphor. He states:

> Because a metaphor by definition is not obligated to explain precisely how, for example, the captaincy of a basketball team translates to leadership in the boardroom, the links between sports participation and the various goals of youth development (i.e., respect, discipline, compassion, perseverance, decision-making, problem solving, etc.) remain vague abstraction (Lauer, 2002, p. 11).

In other words, sport has never been awarded the respect it deserves as an educational medium in traditional classroom learning environments. More often, it is viewed as primarily a physical pursuit. This explains why sport, although a metaphor for teaching character, has never really caught on in the educational sphere — both in practice and in research.

Development as the Aim of Youth Sports

John Dewey, the progressive twenty-first century educator, considered "development as the major aim of education." Sport has unique potential to influence development because of the captive interest of the participants. Sport isn't simply providing safe and enjoyable entertainment activities — although it does that too — rather, sport contributes to the fundamental educational quest for development. From inter-collegiate sports to high school sports, on down through junior high and elementary, education and sport are intertwined in a way that presumes they are educative, so much so that sports are often referred to as co-curricular activities. More specifically, as Stevenson notes, "It is the rationale of character building, of moral development, of citizenship development, of social development that justifies the existence of physical education and athletics (Stevenson, 1985, p. 287).

Recently, there has been much written about the skills children will need to be successful in the 21st century (Tony Wagner 2012). Skills such as the ability to think critically across multiple domains while being able to work collaboratively on a team that is comprised of diverse members are just a few of the skills children will need to compete in the 21st century marketplace. As we proceed in this book we will go in more depth about how to define and measure these critical life skills.

The potential of sport to impact development is so great precisely because it engages the whole person. It does not simply involve physical development; rather, it involves social, cognitive, emotional and moral development. While it seems logical to separate these developmental categories, in reality they are overlapping. They contribute to and inform each other, and must be considered as asserting equal influence upon the end-goal of development. When sport is viewed from this perspective, the idea of "development as the aim of sport" can be understood through the following aspects of human development.

Physical Development — Including the development of strength & coordination, endurance, habits of good nutrition, and a positive attitude towards health.

Social Development — Including teamwork, leadership, conflict resolution, cooperation, and pursuit of shared goals.

Intellectual/Cognitive Development — Including knowledge acquisition, critical thinking & reasoning, perspective taking, and decision-making.

Emotional Development — Including empathy, self-control, perseverance, courage, commitment, and self-esteem.

Moral Development — Including sportsmanship & respect, responsibility, and a sense of fair play (justice).

Physical Development

The potential of sport to promote physical development is easily recognizable. Sports and physical activity have the potential to develop strength, coordination, and endurance, as well as positive nutritional habits and overall health. Learning to hit, throw, and catch a ball help kids develop hand-eye coordination; moving into position on a field promotes agility and balance; and running up and down a court during a game require strength and endurance. Unfortunately, all too often youth sport programs view physical development as a natural bi-product of sport participation, which may or may not necessarily be the case. As Siegel (2002) notes, "For the most part sports have been offered as a product, and effects have been left to…an 'Osmotic Process'" (p. 7). That is, positive effects on physical development require sustained and consistent activities, the standards of which are rarely achieved by most youth sport programs. As Siegel states, "virtually no information regarding how youth sports programs impact fitness exist in the literature" (p. 7). Thus, it is critically important that physical development be planned in an intentional way that ensures youth are developing balance, agility, endurance, strength, and coordination.

Social Development

Because sport is essentially a social undertaking, it also has great potential to promote social development. The development of social skills has recently been linked to future success in life. (Yeager, Paunesku, Walton and Dweck,

White paper, June 2013). Sports involve teams — groups of individuals coming together to participate in shared activities (even individual sports require other individuals to compete). Because preadolescents begin to spend a tremendous amount of time in the company of their peers (more than twice the amount of time spent when they were preschoolers), team sports represent both important and relevant opportunities for learning. During preadolescence children begin to move beyond an egocentric view of the world, to develop a social awareness and understanding of other perspectives. Within the social milieu of team sports, children interact, play, fight, and make friends. The high degree of intra- and interpersonal interaction in sports provides a rich setting to learn about human interaction and responsibility both within groups (teammates) and between groups (opponents).

With so many opportunities to make choices and negotiate perspectives, sport is an ideal context for kids to practice social problem-solving skills. When children are given real decision-making choices and responsibility in their games, they can learn the appropriate skills for resolving conflicts with peers. They have many opportunities for negotiating compromise: Who decides the teams? Who gets to bat first? What are the rules? How is a disputed play decided? How is playing time distributed? Rather than reacting impulsively to situations, children also must learn to solve their problems peacefully by considering their range of choices. In short, children learn that if they do not work out their problems cooperatively, the game will break down, no one gets to play, and everyone loses. Thus, sport offers a rich promised land for positively affecting children's social lives.

Cognitive Development

Sport is as much a cognitive activity as it is a social or physical one. As contest-based games, sport involves thinking through a strategy and reacting to both teammates and opponents. Team members learn to interpret situations and imagine a possible course of action: "If I pass the ball, she might steal the pass." Kids learn to anticipate another player's actions or thoughts in relation to their own when they are challenged to perceive a situation from multiple perspectives. And sports teams, with their various roles, positions, and relationships, do just this. In baseball, for example, while one team is at bat, the other team is in the field. Within each team there are a variety of positions, such as a pitcher, infielder and outfielder. Playing on a team requires players to coordinate different roles and to react accordingly, given their specific role.

The ability to react appropriately in a given situation is related to another important developmental skill – perspective-taking. Research suggests that children's understanding of teams develops from an egocentric or individualistic point of view to one that includes the ability to assume the perspective of others. Young children often interpret events from their own point of view. Watch any group of young children play soccer and you will notice how they all tend to swarm around the ball. Often referred to as "beehive soccer," this tendency reflects the developmental constraints of the early stages of social and cognitive perspective-taking. As children develop, a greater ability to coordinate the perspectives of self and others emerges, allowing for more cooperative and team-building play. The better the team gets at negotiating and organizing, the more complex challenges can be introduced and understood. The better the players become at the challenges, the more developed they become as a unified whole. The better the team functions together as a group, the more games they will win.

The ability to think clearly, objectively, and critically are important life skills; however, to develop these skills through sport, players must share responsibility for organizing the equipment and for distributing playing time, positions and batting order, as well as other important team activities. The coach can, and should, organize and direct the team, but the main objective should be to get the players to think actively about the challenges that sport presents. Applying a little time and attention to the intellectual/cognitive dimensions of sport organization creates the atmosphere required for realizing the true potential of sport.

Emotional Development

Emotional intelligence includes self-awareness and impulse control, persistence, zeal and self-motivation, empathy and social deftness. These are the qualities that mark people who excel in real life: whose intimate relationships flourish, who are the stars in the workplace.

— Goleman, Emotional Intelligence

We all want our children to develop confidence through their activities in and out of school. Confidence grows out of meaningful experiences. How children feel about themselves is an important predictor of performance. Ultimately, a child's level of confidence will influence her motivation to achieve. Teams that function within a positive environment provide all players with equal access to playing time and opportunities for building confidence. This approach addresses the "I was the last one to be picked" problem. This is true for all ages but especially true for younger children. This does not mean removing all challenges — quite the opposite. Creating a positive learning environment is about creating a psychologically and socially safe environment where children feel confident to express their thoughts and develop their skills.

Sport connects to our emotional side in a number of important ways. How did you feel when you were left out of a game? When you made a game winning shot? When you struck out in a big game? Sports engender a wide range of human emotions, and not just those associated with winning and losing. The uncertainty inherent in game competition can bring out strong feelings. Feelings like joy, sorrow, anger, excitement and fear are often stirred when kids play sports. As we all know, it can sometimes be difficult to make rational, sound decisions during emotionally-charged moments. Under stress we can react to situations without thinking; we may not take time to step back and think of the possible consequences for others and ourselves. Nowhere is this more evident than during athletic contests.

Learning to manage and express emotions constructively is an important part of growing up. If children can learn to recognize and understand their feelings within the context of sports, perhaps they can do the same in other aspects of their lives. They may well be able to see how emotional reactions in sports relate to the risks and challenges of their day-to-day experiences.

The ability to recognize, experience, and respond to the feelings of others is another valuable skill. Understanding the feelings and point of view of others requires empathy. Empathy is the affective component of perspective taking. Supporting a teammate who makes a mistake or showing concern for an injured opponent involves the practice of empathy.

Sport provides tremendous potential for developing the psychological and emotional areas of human development.

Moral Development

Moral education is not a new idea. It is, in fact, as old as education itself. Down through history, in countries all over the world, education has had two great goals: to help young people become smart and to help them become good

— Tom Lickona, author, Educating For Character

Moral development frequently is an implicit developmental goal of sport, generally framed within the age-old assumption that "sport builds character." What do we mean when we make this claim? In general, we mean that sports teach children the building blocks of responsible citizenship — respect, responsibility, a sense of fairness. For example, in the early 1900's an American newspaper quoted Notre Dame football coach, Knute Rockne, as saying, "Sportsmanship means fair play. It means having respect for the other person's point of view. It means a real application of the Golden Rule. Fair play and sportsmanship if practiced will go a long way in developing a finer type of citizenship throughout the country." How people treat one another, how a player reacts to a foul when a referee is not looking, how issues of fairness are decided and whether one is truthful to self or others are all opportunities for moral development. In the sports arena, the term "sportsmanship" is most often used to define issues of fairness, caring, justice and honesty. Whatever term we use, the point is that moral values such as respect, responsibility, and honesty (especially in the face of pressure) are among the most valuable lessons we could hope to teach our children. The sport environment provides tremendous opportunities to learn about fairness, sportsmanship, respect, responsibility, and justice in relationship to rules, distribution of playing time, and positions.

People learn moral values such as respect, kindness, and responsibility in a number of ways. First and foremost, youth need opportunities for moral action, authentic opportunities to engage in lived moral development experiences. Sport provides a safe environment to practice living out moral values and for working out moral conflicts. Modeling is another powerful moral development opportunity. Research suggests powerful moral development results for adults who explain and discuss their actions while connecting them to the norms of the group. Discussion of moral values and moral issues, where the facilitator supports and challenges the thinking of youth, provides another proven strategy for promoting moral development. Moral issues are rarely black and white; youth need opportunities to confront the tensions between values such as honesty and respect, responsibility and loyalty. A third way people learn moral values such as responsibility is through rewards and punishment, which gets to the heart of an important moral development question: Why be good? What is rewarded and how it is rewarded can support or undermine an intrinsic desire to do what is right for an internal commitment, rather than for external inducements.

With its team-based relationships, universal rules and the ever present goal of winning, sport is an excellent vehicle for exercising ethical and moral thought. In their book *Character Development and Physical Activity*, Shields and Bredemeier (1985), observe, "The moral tension that participants often experience, for example, between the norms of fair play and the desire to win parallels tension in almost any moral situation. The main difference between sport and everyday life is that moral experience is condensed and exposed in sport." How a player ought to solve a conflict and why a particular course of action is right are important questions presented in sport situations. Sport experiences are full of ethical issues — issues that confront the participant with choices of how he or she should act in a particular set of circumstances.

Sport and the developing child

PLUS seeks to cultivate the total human development of youth — socially, physically, intellectually, emotionally, morally — using sport and sports literature and through the experience of a caring community. Whether used as a "stand alone program" in an after-school program or as a guide to improve an existing youth sport program, PLUS offers a new way of viewing youth sport and development. Similar to the way the British school system operated in the nineteenth century, PLUS strives to realize its vision of "development as the aim of sports" by providing kids with intentionally structured opportunities for active participation in challenges that promote physical, social, moral, intellectual, and emotional development. Utilizing *Structured Play*, for example, PLUS fosters physical development: As kids engage in various relays, tag games, and other physically active games, they gain the skills of physical development (strength, flexibility, endurance, balance, agility, and coordination) in a fun, enjoyable way. During sport play, kids' interest in and appreciation for both traditional and lifetime sports (like basketball, soccer, biking, running, etc.) are nurtured.

In addition to sport and physical activities, the PLUS program also includes reading activities designed to capture children's natural interest in sport and sport heroes. These *Lessons from Literature* draw on sport literature as a unique medium to teach character-based lessons. Many of these reading activities are open-ended, designed to present kids with dilemmas that require them to choose a course of action and then defend that decision. The added value is that the PLUS program encourages children's interest in leisure-time reading, with sports as "the hook," which secures the attention of youth.

As PLUS members move from sport activities to reading activities to "cool-down discussions" the PLUS term for a closing reflection), the kinesthetic and cognitive sense-making experiences interact within the social context of the community experience. Children begin to see and to experience how ideals like teamwork and responsibility look, not only within the program, but also in other areas of their lives such as school and home. The active and hands-on nature of the PLUS program ensures that the lessons and values presented on a daily basis do not remain abstract principles, or lofty ideals. Rather, through reading and journal writing, group activities and discussions, and participation in sports, kids begin to understand PLUS lessons as metaphors for broader life lessons. In this way, these lessons become relevant and related to the kids' own lives. The following chapters present a more in-depth description of the PLUS Model.

CHAPTER TWO

The PLUS Model

"I am always amazed and gratified when Jeff Beedy publishes yet another work on how to use sport participation and competition to develop better kids – and to help the adults who teach and coach them. This latest work is as magnificent as the multitude of his previous endeavors. Jeff has been teaching this writer — a hardened and too-often pessimistic youth sports "culture changer" — for well over two decades; and I always learn plenty of new tools to try to help make American organized youth sports more child-centered. Jeff is a true beacon of valuable wisdom. If you're going to invest any time in administrating, coaching and "sidelinewatching" children in sport, please read this book."

— Bob Bigelow
Co-author of *Just Let the Kids Play*

Concepts of teamwork and leadership are often associated with playing sports. It is even claimed that the Duke of Wellington said, "The war of Waterloo was won on the fields of Eaton." The truth is, as Lauer points out below, there is little proof that there is a connection.

Because a metaphor by definition is not obligated to explain precisely how, for example, the captaincy of a basketball team translates to leadership in the boardroom, the links between sports participation and the various goals of youth development (i.e., respect, responsibility, teamwork, problem solving etc. sic) remain a vague abstraction.

— Lauer 2002

Over the past two decades, there has been a growth of sport-based programs using basketball, soccer, golf and snowboarding as mediums for teaching values such as teamwork, respect, and leadership. Global sport-based organizations such as The Magic Bus, Up2US, The Right to Play, and The First Tee use sports as an intentional medium to promote positive social outcomes and teach skills such as respect and leadership (Beedy, Jeff 2007). However, there has been little research that actually makes a connection "between sport-based programs and the desired outcome goals." In this chapter, we will move beyond the "sports build character" metaphor to introduce a "research-based educational model" for sport-based teaching, learning and measuring.

Intentional outcome goals

It is true there is little connection between developing leadership skills and playing sports. One reason is that sports have long been considered "extra" or "physical." They have not been examined with the same scientific inquiry as learning in the classroom. Sports, for the most part, are considered extracurricular — not co-curricula. Consider how schools view the teaching and measurement of academic learning results. Over the past decade, schools, especially international schools, have determined this connection to be important in the classroom and require teachers to design their curriculum around the school's Expected School-wide Learning Results (ESLERS).

This is not to say that sports should be "more school." Athletics are different. However, if we are going to claim that sports teach desired outcome goals, such as leadership, than we need to develop a teaching and learning system that is linked to the desired outcomes. Sports should be used to strengthen school-wide goals by *teaching for transfer* through a different medium than the classroom.

Understanding by Design

Leadership skills are not developed simply by participating in athletics. Skills like teamwork and respect require an *additional socio-moral curriculum* beyond the teaching of sport skills. There needs to be an *intentional effort* to define the outcome goal (i.e. leadership), a curriculum for teaching it, and an assessment for measuring leadership. It is here where we can learn from the academic side of teaching and learning. In an effort to design curriculums that promote Expected School-wide Learning Results , many schools use a "backwards design" model for curriculum development (Wiggins et al). The goal of *Understanding by Design* (UbD) is to determine first "the big idea" in this case, leadership or teamwork, define how leadership can be measured and work backwards to design a curriculum to teach leadership. Essentially there are three stages of UbD.

1. Identify desired results
2. Determine acceptable evidence
3. Plan learning experiences & instruction

At each of these stages it is important to ask, "What should players know and be able to do to demonstrate leadership? What content standards are addressed explicitly by the unit/practice?" Knowledge needs to have real-world applications. That is, "the ability to lead people who are different" will be an important and necessary skill in the workforce. With the UbD model of curriculum planning understanding goes beyond knowing and doing.

Developing PLUS outcomes

PLUS provides a clear definition of the Expected Community-wide Learning Results (community, 21st Century skills, motivation, physical development and moral theme comprehension). PLUS offers a sport-based curriculum to teach these goals and an assessment tool (Leadership Rubric) for measuring how children are doing on the goals. PLUS provides a clear definition of community wide learning results in both the cognitive and behavioral realms.

PLUS is a community-wide map designed to serve as a template for organizing sport-based activities that develop specific and targeted educational goals and reinforce the PLUS Values of *Teamwork, Respect, Responsibility, Fair Play and Perseverance* — and their accompanying social and emotional skills.

PLUS teaching and learning components

PLUS consists of five integrated components including philosophy, psychology, pedagogy, programs and progress/process (assessment).

Taken together these five components provide a template for developing and evaluating all policies, rules and programs for co-curricula activities. PLUS understands learning occurs everywhere and with every community member. Learning about the value of teamwork, for example, can occur when a student interacts with the team's bus driver as easy as it can on the playing field with a coach. Community leaders can utilize teachable moments as opportunities for teaching important life lessons. The first component focuses on the organization's *philosophy of teaching and learning.*

One: Philosophy of teaching and learning

Webster's dictionary defines philosophy as "a set of principles that guide our practical affairs." Every program needs a philosophy. Our team philosophy allows us to make strategic decisions such as how we will distribute playing time and positions. In what order we will rank winning, personal development, and having fun. How we as coaches and parents will react when confronted with the decision between giving all players equal playing time and winning when a clear choice between the two must be made. We must prepare our philosophy before facing such decisions, so that we know how to deal with situations in which our beliefs compete with each other. Every coach has both the right and the responsibility to carry out his or her team philosophy. It is critical that our philosophy matches our actions.

What is Sports PLUS's philosophy about children and sport?

Consider the following situation and ask what you would do. The players have begun to discuss "who's the best" player on the team. They are comparing how many push-ups each person can do and who can run the fastest. Several students have begun to pick on some of their less talented peers. What should you do? Is this just an example of "kids will be kids?" Should you just ignore the discussion and pretend that you didn't hear it? Should you try to give those who are less talented some kind of an award to highlight their strengths? What are we trying to teach? What values do we want the children in our group to transfer beyond their PLUS experience and into their daily lives? The answers to these important questions — and others — stem from our *philosophy* about children, their development, and the role of competition. By not addressing these questions before we begin a program, we may be sending mixed and confusing messages to the children about what we say we value and what our actions show we value.

Two: Psychology of teaching and learning

How do people learn best? According to Daniel Pink's book *Drive* we are motivated to learn when we experience autonomy, mastery and purpose (Pink, Daniel 2009). We know that we do not learn the same. This is the focus of the Psychology of teaching and learning. What place does role-modeling play in the development of youth? How do we motivate players to improve skills? What types of rewards do we give for good conduct? In a very practical sense, how do we achieve the outcome goals we have set? Setting aside time with players to reflect on and learn from their experiences (how should we deal with a player who throws a bat after striking out?) is an action based on an understanding of what theories and practices guide our actions? To answer these questions we must understand our psychology of teaching and learning.

There are essentially four streams of educational psychology that define how people learn.

1. *The Social Learning Theory* states that people learn through interacting with and observing others.
2. *The Cognitive-Developmental Learning Theory* states that people learn through active dialogue about important issues.
3. The Behavioral Learning Theory suggests that people learn through rewards and consequences

The Adventure Education Learning Model states that people learn through hands-on experiences along with opportunities for reflection.

Taken together, *role modeling, dialogue, consequences and expereince* represent four distinct theories of how children learn within social environments such as sports. Ideally, communities include all ways of learning, modeling, consequences, and dialogue. It is the combination and integration of the major ways people learn that strengthen the teaching and learning process. For example, the *Social Learning Theory* shows us that people learn by watching others. So, in a school environment this would mean that the middle schools students learn about respect by watching how their favorite coach treats his wife. Although this is true, people do learn by watching, the learning is deeper when connected to *dialogue.* So, if these same middle school student's understanding of respect would be strengthened if they were able to engage in dialogue with their parents or dorm master about what 'respect" means. Modeling is a powerful medium for teaching and learning, especially when the students admire the teacher or coach. As we all know, this can be good or bad. If the coach was abusive in his relationship with his wife, and was arrested for domestic violence, than the students would connect a *behavioral consequence* to meaning of respect. However, the process would more likely be positive if the students had an engaged and positive adult they could dialogue with about the idea of respect. Otherwise, the *teachable moment* is potentially lost.

Three: Pedagogy of teaching and learning

> *"You have not taught until they have learned"*
> — Coach Wooden

Pedagogy is how we deliver our teaching and lessons. Our pedagogy should be directly aligned with our philosophy and psychology of teaching and learning. If we believe, for example, that dialogue is how children best than our pedagogy needs to include opportunities for authentic dialogue. See the connection? How do you begin a day or a practice? How do our children enter our respective sport environments? What is on their minds as they jump out of the car or walk in from the streets to join our programs? Each child possesses his or her own emotions and attitudes as they join our respective programs. How can we most respectfully and efficiently transform the collective psychological and social energy of the individual child and harness this energy toward our collective program goals? One way is to introduce a continuous structure or daily rhythm where children gather as a group and allow the coach to be a teacher.

In the PLUS program, we call this daily rhythm the *PLUS Cycle* which consists of a *Warm-up* followed by an *Activity* concluding with a *Cool-down.* This consistent and reoccurring structure provides the youth leaders with continuous opportunities to gather the team, reflect on the process and set new goals. Group dialogue takes place during the *PLUS Cycle.*

The *Warm-up* phase of the cycle allows the coach to quiet the chaos and direct the social and psychological attention of the children toward the goals of the day. The *Activity* phase is the active part of the practice or game during which teachable moments occur. The *Cool-down* meeting provides the team with an opportunity to reflect, dialogue, and set new goals, and to put the *PLUS Cycle* in motion once again. In this way, the *PLUS Cycle* allows the team and coach to transition from one activity to another. Most importantly, the *PLUS Cycle* allows the coach to be a respectful teacher.

Design Developmental Levels

Upwards to 75 million children play organized sports each year. The highest level is at ten-years-old. By fourteen years old, roughly 75% of these children have dropped out of organized sports. The major reason cited is that it is no longer any fun. One way to keep sports fun and healthy is make sure they are developmentally appropriate physically, mentally and socially. What does these mean? Little players play on little fields. This makes sense. It would not make sense to pitch to six-year-olds from major league distances or to use a full-size soccer field for second graders. Smaller and lighter bats allow for smaller children to swing at the ball with a motion that is appropriate to their stage of physical development. Smaller soccer balls and goals match their physical size and ability. As children grow in size and physical strength, their equipment and playing fields can also get larger. This developmental difference occurs in the psychological and social domains as well. The goals, rules, relationships, and discussions need to be appropriate to the children's developmental stages if fun and development are important goals of the program. Activities that are not challenging enough will be boring; too competitive an environment may result in fear, insecurity, and eventually dropping out. If sports are to be a positive experience, adults must understand the particular needs of children at different developmental levels and then coach toward those needs. Finding the right balance is the key.

Four: Programs of teaching and learning

Consider all the places and activities within our sport program where learning takes place and where there are opportunities to teach valuable lessons. The actual games come to mind first. But as we think for a moment it is often the "before practice chat" or "long bus ride home" where deep learning takes place. So as we consider the power of sports as a teaching and learning medium we need to take into account all the activities that make up what we call our "program."

We can begin by asking a few questions. How do our team activities promote our goals? Are we fully aware of all the opportunities to teach important lessons within our sport program? Do we gather players together before a practice to set the tone of our culture and establish goals for the day or do we simply "roll out the balls" and begin? Similarly, do we consider the importance of bus rides, parents meetings, fund-raising car washes, and post-game dugout cleanings? To *account for our activities* is to ensure that everything we do aligns with our outcome goals and principles and that we are taking full advantage of even seemingly mundane activities (loading and unloading the bus) to achieve our stated goals. These are all opportunities to teach what we deem to be important. If we want sports to develop leadership skills than developing in our athletes the intrinsic drive to not only clean the bus but teach the new players that that is part of the teams norms around responsibility. In addition to all the above-mentioned opportunities PLUS Global offers the following sport-based activities.

- Lessons from Literature

- Lessons from the Field

- Lessons from Adventure

- Sports Short and Theme Books

- You Make the Call

- Instant Replays

- Sport Extras

- Quote of the Week

- Respect & Responsibility Huddle

Cultivate culture of programs

As the coach or parent we need to think of the sport experience in a larger sense. We need to consider all the relationships and activities that make up what we refer to as the sport program. The letters we write to the parents. How we handle the parents' behavior on the sidelines. Shopping for equipment. How we treat the referees. Children need to continually witness and experience the act of respect as people conduct their daily affairs. Respect can't simply be taught on Thursday night at a "sportsmanship night" or Saturday morning during a "theme of the week" activity — although those events can be helpful if conducted within a positive learning culture. Children learn values like respect when multiple stakeholders demonstrate respectful actions consistently across the different domains of a child's life. Relationships between role models and youth within the day-to-day activities of the program are the core of a child's learning opportunity. Are the parents supportive or yelling constantly at their children? How does a coach quiet down and bring the team together before a practice? What role do children have in shaping the governance of the team? As adults we can purposefully create a culture that enforces the values we want a sports experience to impart or we can create a culture that erodes them.

It is up to us.

Five: Progress: Measure program outcome goals

Sports should be fun, but that does not mean that sports cannot at the same time be educational. That is not the real question. The real question is that sports, like any positive endeavor, should be *intentional*. That is, if we claim to teach leadership skills than we need a system for teaching and a system for measuring. That is what this section is about. The fifth PLUS component is all about measurement and evaluating our progress.

We measure what we deem to be important. We measure our height and weight and golf score. We want to know how old people are and how much money they have. We want to know the score of the game and how fast the new Saab goes. So, if we propose to teach leadership and teamwork than we need to devise both the curriculum and tools to measure our progress. Essential to the success of any community is not that it adheres to any particular outcome goals per se, but that its stakeholders take time and effort to dialogue and decide upon what it strives to achieve. This planning is a part of the backwards design phase of the curriculum. The PLUS Manual provides a rich curriculum for teaching community, character, intrinsic motivation, physical development and literacy (PLUS Outcome Goals). By having clearly defined Outcome Goals and an aligned curriculum it is easier to measure progress around our goals. The PLUS model utilizes five interconnected program outcome goals to realize its comprehensive youth development program. No single outcome goal is more important than another; in fact, they are integrally linked, always building upon each other. Collectively, they develop the complete person. The program components are constructed around the best science-based research, and specifically tailored to the developmental needs of the population it intends to serve (youth grades 3-6).

PLUS Outcome Goals

PLUS has clearly defined the goals it seeks to achieve. One important way to solidify and operationalize our values is through carefully defined outcome goals or Expected Community-wide Learning Results (ECLERS). In an effort to track your programs progress, it is important to define the outcome goals in ways that can be measured (we will address measuring outcome goals later).

1. The cultivation of a sense of community
2. Development of 21st Century Skills
3. The promotion of intrinsic motivation

4. The promotion of physical development
5. The promotion of literacy appreciation and an enhancement of moral theme comprehension.

Community

Students develop in and through the experience of a caring community — a sense of being known, needed, safe and cared about, along with authentic opportunities for shaping the community. All learning takes place within the context of relationships. Unlike the banking model of education where the adult deposits information or values into the child's account, PLUS

Global views relationships in mutual terms with dialogue as being central to a respectful relationship. PLUS respects children as active learners and views dialogue as a necessary ingredient to the educational process. Both the adult and the child are partners in the development process.

21st Century Leadership Skills

Leadership is defined as the development of the social and emotional skills necessary to make good decisions. The PLUS Model employs five values: Teamwork, Respect, Responsibility, Fair Play and Perseverance.

Intrinsic Motivation

Sustained positive development requires the cultivation of intrinsic motivation that extends beyond the "walls" and duration of the program into all phases of life. PLUS seeks to cultivate a self-referenced approach to motivation (what the research literature calls a "task or mastery orientation"), that is built upon a cyclical pattern of personal goal setting, monitoring, and reformulation. In addition to numerous positive performance outcomes (academic, athletic, and other), research (Carol Dweck, Mindset, 2006) suggests that cultivating an orientation in which a person competes against self-referenced personal achievement (e.g., a better time than before, more right on this test than last time, fewer unnecessary interruptions of the class today than yesterday) tends to promote self-reflection and awareness, to support strong intrinsic motivation, and to reduce helpless response to failure (Nicholls 1984; Duda and Nicholls 1992; Harackiewicz and Elliot 1993; Molden and Dweck 2000).

Physical development

The benefits of physical activity are well documented. Research suggests that a physically active youngster has a more positive self-image, greater self-confidence, and demonstrates improvement in motor skills, cognitive functioning (Etnier et al., 1997) and health-related fitness. Studies from the American Council on Exercise have shown that physically active children also are more likely to become physically active adults. Thus, developing an interest in sport and physical activity at a young age is something that will likely continue to benefit them later in life.

Literacy and moral theme comprehension

The literacy component of the *Sports PLUS* Program attempts to accomplish two central goals. First, it attempts *to increase students' interest in and appreciation for literature* by exposing them to the kinds of stories they like and are interested in — namely, sport stories. Sport stories have this natural attraction for many young people and can help them develop positive attitudes about the pleasures and value of reading. Like a game, these stories stretch the mind and stir the emotions. Most importantly, sports stories are engaging and fun to discuss.

PLUS seeks to increase students' moral theme comprehension by providing them with a script for considering the important elements regarding the moral of the story. Learning to ask critical comprehension questions of a text allows students to consistently extract the moral of future stories they read or in which they are involved. PLUS isn't simply about developing reading motivation and skills; it also views literature as containing rich material for promoting social and cognitive development. Through reading sport stories, children learn to listen, speculate, share and take turns, as they interact socially with others. Sports literature is also an excellent medium for building children's mental muscles. The ability to identify conflicts, generate solutions, predict outcomes, and consider potential consequences constitutes the critical thinking skills that are developed through PLUS's literacy component.

PLUS Leadership Rubric

PLUS offers an evaluation system for measuring these outcome goals. The PLUS Leadership Ladder provides a cognitive and behavioral leadership ladder that can be used to measure each outcome goal. *The Leadership Ladder* provides a cognitive and behavioral leadership ladder that can be used to measure outcome goals. How do we know when our students have developed leadership skills? How can we measure their progress? As teachers and coaches we are often asked the ideal ratio of players to adults? Often, we neglect to realize that this question is based on the assumption that the teachers or coach are the only leaders and the children, by nature are all detractors. When we consider *that our students and players can serve as leaders* — people who can lead their classmates, bring equipment, clean up the classroom, and address issues of disrespect, then the adult-to-child ratio takes on a whole new meaning. To activate the leadership power of our children, we must develop a system that cultivates leaders. The following Leadership ladder links tangible behavioral actions to the abstract notion of leadership:

PLUS Leadership Rubric

5.0 Leading At Level Five team members lead by example and understand how to implement new programs PLUS mentor other community members to advance the mission and objectives of the community. Level 5.0 is a leader and understands how to create a circle of good.

4.0 Contributing At Level Four the team member implements strategies that model a clear understanding of what it takes to be a team member PLUS seeks new opportunities to promote the communities mission and sense of team.

3.0 Participating Words and actions reveal an understanding of what it means to be a team member. Level 3.0 represents the minimal contribution as a positive teammate.

2.0 Observing Will engage in teamwork but needs external consequences in order to comply with mission and objectives. A neutral influence on others

1.0 Detracting Words and actions go against the mission and objectives of the community. Level 1.0 represents negative influence on others and includes bullying, fighting, and lying.

(adapted from Robert Carkuff)

Definable, observable and measurable

The Leadership Ladder provides teachers and coaches with a way to teach and measure important outcome goals. To make values come to life and have meaning for children, they must be made *observable, measurable, and understandable.* This is also true in terms of being able to measure these goals. Words like teamwork, responsibility, and respect are simply too abstract for children to understand (adults too, but for different reasons!). They need to be defined and reinforced through observable behaviors. Asking players to bring their equipment to practice is an example of teamwork, it presents a concrete behavior that can be observed and understood. "if you don`t bring your equipment, you won`t be able to practice the drills with the rest of the team and you won`t be ready for the contribute to the team." Here is a behavior that can be understood by the children; pointed out and reinforced by the coach and in the end measured.

Using Levels to measure all core values

The Leadership Ladder scale can be used to scale any value or outcome goal. The scale provides five levels on which both general and specific behaviors can fall. For example, a child who hurts someone`s feelings is **detracting** in relation to the value of **respect.** On the positive side, a child who reminds her teammate to bring her equipment to practice is demonstrating concern for others and is at the **leader** end of the scale. A person who neither detracts nor actively contributes but only observes is at **level two.**

This scale is a tool to help you provide meaning to the core values. With a common language and commonly understood levels of behavior, your students will be in a better position to engage in meaningful dialogue. This in turn helps children begin to transfer the lessons learned in school, dorm and sports to other situations in life. When both the teacher and the child recognize where a behavior falls on the Leadership scale, the coach and child can then set goals for the child to move up the scale by changing specific behaviors.

5.0 LEADING

At Level Five team members lead by example and understand how to implement new programs PLUS mentor other community members to advance the mission and objectives of the community. Level 5.0 is a leader and understands how to create a circle of good.

4.0 CONTRIBUTING

At Level Four the team member implements strategies that model a clear understanding of what it takes to be a team member PLUS seeks new opportunities to promote the communities mission and sense of team.

3.0 PARTICIPATING

Words and actions reveal an understanding of what it means to be a team member. Level 3.0 represents the minimal contribution as a positive teammate.

2.0 OBSERVING

Will engage in teamwork but needs external consequences in order to comply with mission and objectives. A neutral influence on others.

1.0 DETRACTING

Words and actions go against the mission and objectives of the community. Level 1.0 represents negative influence on others and includes bullying, fighting and lying.

It is easy to be excited and motivated when things are going your way. The ability to keep trying, to give one's best in spite of setbacks, disappointments and opposition is an important ingredient of success. In the long run, perseverence will often win out over talent.

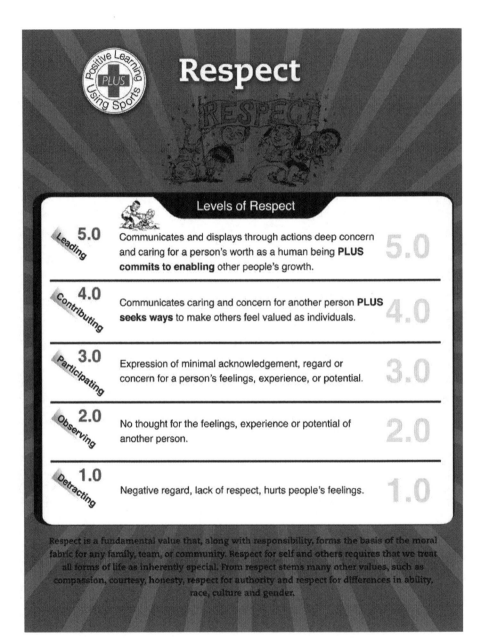

Respect

Levels of Respect

Leading
5.0 Communicates and displays through actions deep concern and caring for a person's worth as a human being **PLUS commits to enabling** other people's growth.

Contributing
4.0 Communicates caring and concern for another person **PLUS seeks ways** to make others feel valued as individuals.

Participating
3.0 Expression of minimal acknowledgement, regard or concern for a person's feelings, experience, or potential.

Observing
2.0 No thought for the feelings, experience or potential of another person.

Detracting
1.0 Negative regard, lack of respect, hurts people's feelings.

Respect is a fundamental value that, along with responsibility, forms the basis of the moral fabric for any family, team, or community. Respect for self and others requires that we treat all forms of life as inherently special. From respect stems many other values, such as compassion, courtesy, honesty, respect for authority and respect for differences in ability, race, culture and gender.

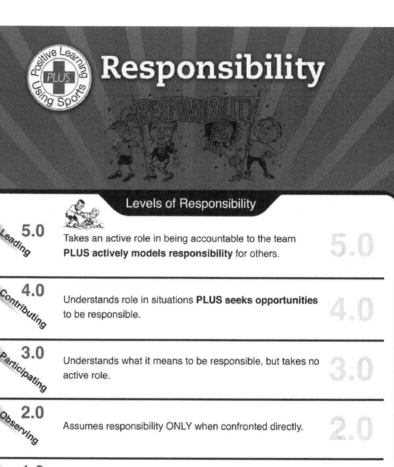

Levels of Responsibility

5.0 Leading
Takes an active role in being accountable to the team **PLUS actively models responsibility** for others.

4.0 Contributing
Understands role in situations **PLUS seeks opportunities** to be responsible.

3.0 Participating
Understands what it means to be responsible, but takes no active role.

2.0 Observing
Assumes responsibility ONLY when confronted directly.

1.0 Detracting
Avoids becoming responsible/accountable. "Here it comes; there I go."

Responsibility is the ACTION side of respect and calls for acting upon one's moral values. Responsibility is the glue that holds the team, family or community together. It is one thing to respect your teammate, and it is another to take responsibility to show that respect in tangible actions. Responsibility is the moral extension of caring. It is the carrying out of our obligation to someone or to something (such as the team) greater than ourselves.

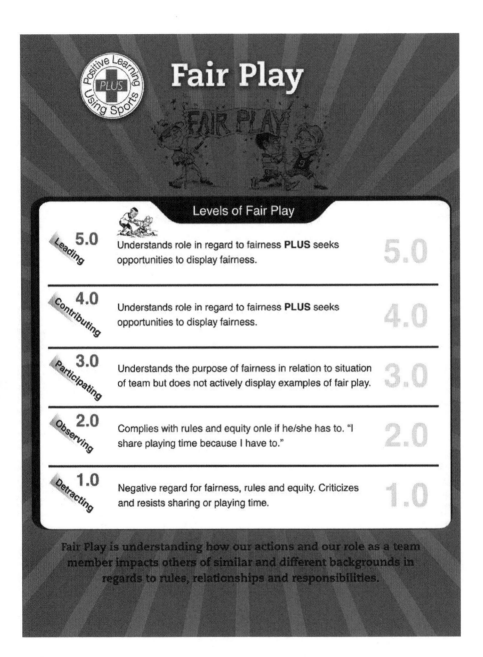

Fair Play

Levels of Fair Play

5.0 Leading
Understands role in regard to fairness **PLUS** seeks opportunities to display fairness.

4.0 Contributing
Understands role in regard to fairness **PLUS** seeks opportunities to display fairness.

3.0 Participating
Understands the purpose of fairness in relation to situation of team but does not actively display examples of fair play.

2.0 Observing
Complies with rules and equity onle if he/she has to. "I share playing time because I have to."

1.0 Detracting
Negative regard for fairness, rules and equity. Criticizes and resists sharing or playing time.

Fair Play is understanding how our actions and our role as a team member impacts others of similar and different backgrounds in regards to rules, relationships and responsibilities.

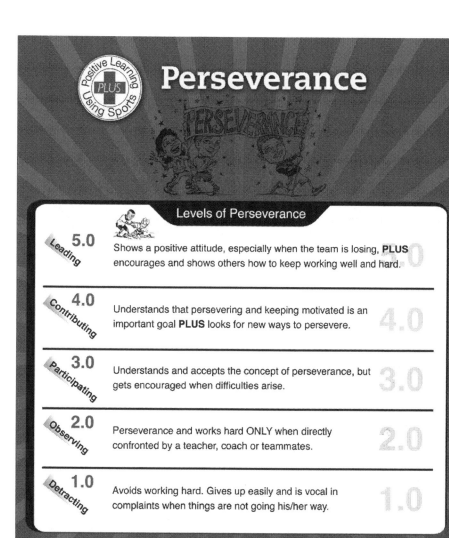

Perseverance

Levels of Perseverance

5.0 Leading
Shows a positive attitude, especially when the team is losing, **PLUS** encourages and shows others how to keep working well and hard.

4.0 Contributing
Understands that persevering and keeping motivated is an important goal **PLUS** looks for new ways to persevere.

3.0 Participating
Understands and accepts the concept of perseverance, but gets encouraged when difficulties arise.

2.0 Observing
Perseverance and works hard ONLY when directly confronted by a teacher, coach or teammates.

1.0 Detracting
Avoids working hard. Gives up easily and is vocal in complaints when things are not going his/her way.

It is easy to be excited and motivated when things are going your way. The ability to keep trying, to give one's best in spite of setbacks, disappointments and opposition is an important ingredient of success. In the long run, perseverance will often win out over talent.

Educate the entire community on PLUS goals

"Anthropologists do agree on three characteristics of culture:
it's not innate, but learned; the various facets of culture are
interrelated — you touch a culture in one place and everything
else is affected; it is shared and in effect defines the boundaries of
different groups."

— Edward T. Hall

What control do we have over our program's philosophy, policies and people? To what degree can we demand respectful behavior on the part of all who are involved? Can we, for example, remove fans who are disrespectful? Who makes the rules of the team? Is there a process for determining the system of governance within the league? Who is in charge of the league policies? Who trains the coaches? What role does the local community play? Where do the children hang out after the games? Where are the playing fields located? How many games do the children play? How is the distribution of playing time and positions decided? Who hires the umpires? Who educates the officials?

PLUS views sports from a systems perspective. Similar to a Swiss watch, there are many interrelated parts that work together to make up the overall sport experience (Senge, Peter). Children learn within this social web of relationships, rules and experiences. The likelihood of positive development is increased when the leaders of a program have control of their entire program and the roles and responsibilities of the diverse stakeholders are clearly defined. When we *synchronize our entire sports systems,* we transform the education process from something haphazard to something intentional.

Creating healthy and sustainable communities requires vision and patience. Learning organizations are by nature complicated social and economic systems. Leaders need to create a community where all stakeholders work in unison. A "systems thinking organization" is driven by a set of shared operating principles that serve as the template for everything the organization does both internally and externally. Core operating principles provide the entire community with a template for team building, hiring, professional development, and staff evaluation. The team's core principles *drive* day-to-day operations, serve as a guide to train and evaluate all community stakeholders, *guide* adoption of policies, *inform* how resources are allocated and ultimately help differentiate one school from another in the competitive market place. Core Operating Principles must be *data-driven, specific, action-oriented* and live deep within our learning organization. When we are the *best at what we do* and can prove it, other areas of institutional advancement such as enrollment and fundraising occur naturally.

Everything we do (or don't do) is interconnected and affects what and how our children learn. If we want our children to learn positive values, then we must actively construct positive program philosophies, demand positive adult role models, and employ positive, consistent practices throughout the entire program. Sports can play a positive role in shaping our children's moral worldview when the surrounding social environment supports the values that we are seeking to impart. If we want our children to learn the importance of "being respectful to one another," all community stakeholders (youth leaders, parents, coaches, players, etc.) must proactively advocate and reinforce this value and all the other values we want children to develop.

Section II

Five Outcome Goals

Chapter Three

Cultivating a Connected and Caring Community

"No significant learning ever took place without a significant relationship."

— James Comer

In general we involve youth in programs to help develop their personal assets; we want to develop their intellectual, physical, and moral functioning. On the one hand, this seems pretty obvious. What may not be quite so obvious is how this actually takes place. There is a growing body of research indicating that if we hope to develop youth, we must attend to the assets of the communities in which they live and dwell. Specifically, the research suggests that the experience of a caring community is a mediating variable in numerous youth development outcomes. That is to say, we cannot simply "fix-the-kids" by pouring values into them; rather, we must simultaneously seek to develop youth as well as the communities they learn and dwell in. On the one hand, this seems fairly obvious; on the other hand, it flies in the face of the "pull yourself up by your own bootstraps, in spite of your community approach" frequently advocated.

Consider, for example, elementary school level research by the *Child Development Project*, which indicates that a sense of the school as a caring community is a leading predictor of a number of positive character qualities, including:

> *Greater liking for school, greater enjoyment of class, greater empathy towards others' feelings, greater concern for others, greater enjoyment of helping others learn, stronger motivation to be kind and helpful to others, more sophisticated conflict resolution skills, more frequent acts of altruistic behavior, higher general self-esteem, higher academic self-esteem, stronger feelings of social competence, less feeling of loneliness in school, less use of tobacco, alcohol, and marijuana, fewer delinquent acts, less victimization (Schaps, Watson et al. 1996, p. 43).*

In this research we see the sense of the school as a caring and supportive community mediating nearly all of the outcomes (intellectual, social, and moral) that character educators might hope to see if effective — findings that also are supported by longitudinal research on adolescents (c.f., Resnick et al., 1997).

Team as a Community

The experience of community is not accidental to youth development; it is essential. Like members of any quality team, children working together in a program need to feel that their efforts and contributions, regardless of their abilities, are recognized, appreciated, and authentically needed. Likewise, a team will not function to its potential without a level of mutual respect, trust, and cooperation among its players and coaches. The creation of a positive, learning culture is central to the PLUS Program; it is within this supportive environment that children learn first-hand the meanings of the PLUS themes — *Teamwork, Respect, Responsibility, Fair Play and Perseverance.*

It is important to remember, however, that the PLUS Culture does not simply develop overnight. Building a respectful community takes time, patience and a good deal of hard work on the part of teachers, staff and students. A sense of connectedness to a caring community won't happen by chance; it probably won't even happen through good intentions.

Community is a lived reality built upon the foundation of human relationships.

Relationships: The Foundation of Community

All learning takes place within the context of a relationship. If pro-social values and skills are the message, then the coach or team leader is the first messenger. Children listen to, respect, and ultimately learn from adults they can trust and believe. In our fast-paced world of cell phones and drive-through fast-food we have a tendency to overlook the importance of quality time and relationships. The PLUS program is based on the idea that coaches and leaders need to develop meaningful relationships with the players if positive learning is to occur.

Human relationships are tricky, sometimes complicated things, especially relationships with youth. Any relationship is a little like a dance: It's a give and take, where sometimes you must lead and sometimes you must follow. Unfortunately, all too often adults assume the lead in their relationships with youth and never quite let go enough to follow. The PLUS program believes that for adults to have meaningful relationships with kids there must be a give and take; adult leaders must be prepared both to lead and to follow. For example, because physical and emotional safety are foundational elements of healthy relationships, there certainly will be times where enforcement of rules must be ironclad. However, because allowing youth to shape the rules and to have input is essential to their ownership of the program, at times, it also will be necessary for leaders to give youth the flexibility and access to change, add, or remove group rules. To be certain, there will be time both to lead and to follow in any mentoring relationship with kids, and effective PLUS Program Leaders must have the flexibility to do both.

If all learning takes place in the context of relationships, the degree to which the learning will be positive depends upon the quality of the relationships. Healthy, caring relationships are the building blocks of a positive learning climate, where all participants, regardless of their abilities, feel both emotionally and physically safe, as well as free from negative criticism and ridicule.

Getting Started — Steps for Cultivating Community

By now, it should be clear that creating a positive learning environment, in which kids experience a sense of community, is central to the PLUS approach to youth development, but how exactly is such an environment cultivated? We know that caring relationships are the building blocks of community, but what exactly do we mean by "community"?

For the PLUS Program the notion of community includes at least four critical elements: (1) being known, (2) being needed, (3) feeling safe and cared for, and (4) having a role in shaping the community. We all learn best in an environment that is supportive and safe. Learning new behaviors and trying new activities presents risks for kids.

These risks become even greater when performing in front of peers. People, kids included, enjoy being a part of a group or team where members treat one another with respect, where an equitable system of governance is of central importance, and where community members feel comfortable, and safe to try on new challenges.

The first step in creating such an environment is to provide kids with ample opportunities to get know one another, both as individuals and as teammates. This is especially important in the first several weeks of the program, when kids are just beginning to learn about and to develop positive relationships with one another. Activities like *Sports Detective* (see Box 3.1) and other introductory exercises are designed to help kids get to know not only the names of their teammates, but also something about them as people — what kinds of things they like and don't like; what their goals are; and how they like to spend their time.

Helping kids get to know one another is an important first step in cultivating a safe, respectful community. The next step is to collectively establish an appropriate game plan for the group with shared norms and values. The Culture Being activity (see Box 3.2) is the first team-building activity in the PLUS program and is designed to begin this process.

During the Culture Being activity, the group decides what specific norms and values will define the group. These norms and values are described in behavioral terms that everyone can understand, measure, and discuss. Identifying specific behaviors enables leaders and kids alike to better understand how to model the value. For example, if the group defined fairness as "all players get to try new positions and share equal playing time," then the leader should make sure to model that behavior. In

Box 3.1

Sports Detective

It's important to know our each other's names, but names don't really tell you much about the person. Even when we think we know someone, we can often be surprised to learn new things. Good teammates get to know one another. They understand what things their teammates like and dislike and what kinds of experiences they have had.

Play

Ask kids to anonymously write something about themselves — something unique or an interesting fact they want their teammates to know — on a piece of paper. (Be sure everybody knows that we're looking for POSITIVE things about themselves). Collect the papers and make a list on a poster or chalkboard.

Ask kids to open their Player Portfolios and copy the list on the appropriate page. Next, each student acts as a detective, searching for people who meet the descriptions provided on the list. As they search for people who fit the descriptions, they first introduce themselves, ask the questions, and then get the signatures of those who fit the descriptions. The goal is to learn something new about, and to get at least one signature from, each person in the group.

A few sample items are listed below to get the group started:

- is left-handed
- has more than one sister or brother
- had a birthday this month
- has a pet bird
- likes to play soccer
- enjoys reading
- can speak a language other than English

R&R Huddle (5 minutes)

<u>Recap</u> by highlighting one or two of the following ideas: After all kids have gotten a signature from everyone else, gather the group together. Were there any surprises? Did you learn anything that you didn't know about a teammate? <u>Reconnect</u> by asking kids to briefly share-out some of the things they learned about each other.

<u>Reset</u> and transition to the next activity.

Box 3.2

Culture Being

The Culture Being is an activity designed to open up kids' minds to the future of their participation in PLUS. The activity produces a poster with words and phrases that are examples of how the participants feel about their environment and how they would liek to shape it. This Being poster should have at least one comment from everyone or have comments upon which everyone strongly agrees.

Play

1. On poster board have the kids decide on an object or shape to represent their group. Some examples are: an outline of a person, a hall, a book, a smiley face, or a schoolhouse.

2. Using the following focus prompts as a guide, facilitate a discussion about yours and the kids' hopes and expectations for their experience in the PLUS program.

   • One thing I hope we can do this year is…

   • One way I want our team/group to look like this…

   • One thing that I think it is important for our team to do is…

   • One thing I don't want to happen this year…

3. After discussin what the kids want and don't want to happen during their time is the PLUS program, invite kids to decorate their shape with all the things they have been talking about. The things kids felt were important to have happen should be written inside of the object. The things the group decided should NOT happen in the PLUS program should be written outside the object.

   • is left-handed

   • has more than one sister or brother

   • had a birthday this month

   • has a pet bird

   • likes to play soccer

   • enjoys reading

   • can speak a language other than English

R&R Huddle (5 minutes)

Recap by highlighting one or two of the following ideas: After all kids have gotten a signature from everyone else, gather the group together. Were there any surprises? Did you learn anything that you didn't know about a teammate?

Reconnect by asking kids to briefly share-out some of the things they learned about each otehr.

Reset and transition to the next activity.

addition to modeling fairness, leaders and kids begin to build a common language for talking about fairness that everyone understands.

Other team-building activities include cooperative games, group projects, and problem-solving exercises. These activities not only play an important role in developing a student's sense of belonging and self-worth, they also help to develop group processing skills. Activities like Respect Posters (see Box 3.3) further kids' understanding of the GoodSport themes and encourage discussion about the importance of living out values such as respect and responsibility.

Cool-Down Rituals (see Box 3.4) create opportunities for kids to share "put-ups" with each other, rather than put-downs, as well as to exchange small signs of enthusiasm, like "High Five's" and group cheers. These opportunities help influence the kinds of social relationships that will develop in the program and will greatly impact kids' experiences, and ultimately, how much they learn.

Creating and maintaining such a learning community is a continuous task. All components of the PLUS program — from the team-building activities to discussion groups — reinforce this effort on a daily basis. The goal is to make sure kids regularly experience all four elements of community — (1) being known, (2) being needed, (3) feeling safe and cared for, and (4) having a role in shaping the community. Without doubt, there will always be issues, incidents and conflicts that will arise. Kids will need to be reminded of the kind of team they have agreed to maintain, and positive and negative behaviors will need to be rewarded in a way that supports the development of intrinsic motivation. Creating a climate of trust and a sense of team will give both leaders and kids the tools and language to deal with conflicts in productive ways.

Over time, and with consistent application of the PLUS Cycle, the various program components will begin to work together systematically. Kids' experience of the PLUS Culture will deepen, as they learn about and internalize the PLUS core values — teamwork, respect, responsibility, fair play, and perseverance. In the next chapter, we focus on PLUS core values and their accompanying social and emotional skills.

Box 3.3

Respect Posters

Materials you will need: poster paper, markers. Optional: dictionaries, magazines, newspapers, scissors, glue.

Break the groups into teams of three or four. Give each team a table to work on (or some open space on the floor), two pieces of paper, a dictionary (or write the definition of teamwork on a chalkbord) and some marekrs).

Play

Each group will use a dictionary to look up the meaning of respect. (Or read it off the board.)

Using this information and their own understanding of teamwork, kids will create a poster that teaches the rest of the gorup what respect means to them. The poster can be anything that the teams choose to represent respect. They can create a Being by tracing the outline of one of their bodies on the poster paper, cut out pictures from magazines if you have a collection to use, or make their own drawing. Encouraate the kids to be creative. Next, have the kids write words and phrases around their drawing to explalin their understanding of respect. They should use their own words to define what respect means, not the words from the dictionary. They also should write words or phrases to illustrate how respct looks and sounds.

Remind kids that this is a team project and they should spend a few minutes planning what they as a team want to create and how they are going to create it. All members of the team should be actively involved in the planning, decision-making, and production of the psoter. Allow 15-20 minutes for the small groups to work.

Once the teams have completed their posters, give each group a few minutes to present its poster to the group and to explain their definition, drawing, words and phrases. If time permits, allow some discussion and questions for each group. Hang the posters around the room and refer back to them as often as necessary throughout the program to reinforce and remind the kids of their commitments. As the unit progresses, and kids' udnerstanding of respect increases, have them add new ideas, words, and phrases to their posters.

Box 3.4

Pass the Put-up

Gather the large group in a circle with a bit of space between each student. Explain to kids the difference between authentic and inauthentic put-ups. For example, sometimes put-ups are actually poorly disguised put-downs. Encourage the kids to look for different kinds of put-ups (e.g., for effort, for respect, etc.). Begin the passing yourself to demonstrate how to "pass a put-up." You can use an imaginary passing motion from any sport — a bounce pass of a basketball, a football pass, a soccer kick, a volleuball bump, etc. Aim the pass at another person in the circle, and as you are passing, give the person a put-up: "Great playing, Robert," "Good work, Kim," etc. The receiving person accepts the pass and says, "Thank you."

This activity may be used frequently to close a session, but for the first few times it is played, ask if anyone has a put-up to share about someone else. After volunteers have shared theirs, be prepared to add a few more to continue modeling how a put-up looks. When this activity has been played a few times and kids have begun to feel more comfortable passing genuine put-ups to each other, the person receiving the pass may quickly pass a put-up to another person, continuing until everyone has received a pass.

CHAPTER FOUR

Development of 21st Leadership Century Skills
and their accompanying social
and emotional skills

We face an exponential increase of readily available information, new technologies that are constantly changing, and more complex societal challenges such as global warming. Thus, work, learning, and citizenship in the 21st century demand thatwe all know how to think — to reason, analyze, weigh evidence, problem solve. These are no longer skills that only the elites in a society must master; they are essential survival skills for all of us.

— Tony Wagner The Achievement Gap

We now live in an innovation-based society and skills such as collaboration, critical thinking, and perspective taking are critical survival skills to be successful in an increasingly global society.

There is a growing movement around the world to enhance the quality and availability of programs that teach these important skills. Whether we define these survival skills as values or 21st Century survival skills the point is these skills will be critical for the future success of our children. Our children need as many opportunities as possible to develop these skills and values. Frequently programs fail to define what, exactly, they mean by character or leadership skills. As indicated in Chapter One, PLUS defines leadership as, **"values in action."** Putting values in action is achieved through attention to the cognitive, affective, and behavioral dimensions of an individual — and always through the interaction between the individual and their environment. What does this mean? It means that we must attend both to the complete moral person — head, heart, and hand — and to the environment in which they live and dwell.

The PLUS Theme Units (Teamwork, Respect, Responsibility, Fair Play and Perseverance) are designed to help kids define and understand our core values in observable and measurable behaviors (what we see as social and emotional skills). "Putting behaviors to values" (e.g., dissing — slang for "disrespecting" — an opponent when they strike out is a behavior associated with disrespect) will allow us to better recognize an "issue of disrespect" when it naturally unfolds during program activities and games. More important, by showing our team members that "organizing the equipment behind the bench without being told" is what we mean by teamwork, we are creating a learning environment where children understand what values such as teamwork actually mean. Teamwork, respect, responsibility, fair play and perseverance form the foundation of the PLUS environment. By defining these values in observable behaviors we will be able to create coaching and teaching techniques that increase the likelihood of "putting values in action" in our team environment.

What Are Values?

The dictionary defines "value" as "that which is desirable or worthy of esteem for its own sake, a quality having intrinsic worth." Values are the "building blocks of character." That is, values might exist in isolation, but character is about values that work together in concert. Here's an example: Your grandmother asks you: "Do you like the tie I got you for Christmas?" Whereas the value honesty would suggest that you tell her the truth ("No. That's the ugliest darn tie I ever saw."), a person of character moderates honesty with charity and prudence ("Grandma, I love the fact that you love me enough to pick out this tie for me. It was very thoughtful. Thank you.").

Character thus represents the collection of values that define an individual. Whether we're describing a community or an individual we describe their enduring mark in terms of values. Most children, however, do not naturally understand the conceptual elements of values. They do not understand abstract concepts. Children need concrete guidelines and examples. Simply yelling, "we need more teamwork" means nothing — or at least different things — to each person who hears it. By defining our values, and then looking at them in behavioral terms, we make it easier for kids to understand the values of which we speak. Developing a common language and behavioral definitions provides everyone with an understanding of what we mean by these values. Thus, we must consciously determine what values are important to our team and then define those values in behavioral terms so that all the stakeholders involved — players, referees, parents, coaches, fans — can understand and accept them, and then all work toward the same goals.

Which Values?

Values are the building blocks of character, and while there are many important values, PLUS attempts to make a developmental match between the values and the needs of youth in this age and developmental range. Towards that end, PLUS focuses on five value themes: teamwork, respect, responsibility, perseverance, and fair play. The PLUS Core values are universal values; they are values, which, despite our individual differences, we all can agree have intrinsic worth, and are good both for us as individuals and for the group as a whole.

The Role of Social & Emotional Skills

If values are the building blocks of character, social and emotional skills are the mortar that holds values together and ensures they are consistently put into action. Let's get philosophical for a moment: In the "Allegory of the Sun" the philosopher Plato said that you can't know the sun completely, because we'll go blind if we attempt to stare at it directly. Instead, he argued, we can only know the sun by viewing as many of its rays as possible.

Like the sun, values are nearly impossible to understand completely since every value is composed of countless particulars, which change based on context and an individual's development and temperament. Social and emotional skills represent the particular rays of values. In order to teach values, in order for youth to realize a vision for character (values in action), we must break values into particular rays, developmentally matched to their needs. So, just as in sport, we must take complex processes (e.g., shooting a jump shot in basketball, setting and tracking progress toward goals, showing respect to our teammates and opponents, etc.) and break them down into composite skills, which can then be scripted out and practiced to ensure competence in different environments.

The legendary basketball coach, John Wooden, taught his Pyramid of Success each fall prior to the season. The Pyramid outlined the values he wanted to define and distinguish the character of his UCLA basketball teams. He did not leave it to chance that his teams would have character; rather, he taught it intentionally and proactively, which ensured the distinguishing mark of UCLA basketball would be lasting and positive (his team's 10 national championships are still unmatched). In pressure situations, teams and individuals must have familiar skills and routines to act upon — whether it's the performance pressure of shooting a big free-throw or the pressure to tell the truth in a difficult situation. We're pretty good at developing the skills and routines needed for performance; we're less effective in developing the skills and routines of character. Social and emotional skills are the processes required for living out values, and we must develop these skills in our children if we want them to perform well in the pressure situations surrounding character.

To this end, the PLUS Program uses a variety of hands-on, experiential activities to bring to life its core values of Teamwork, Respect, Responsibility, Fair Play, and Perseverance. PLUS members learn firsthand what each value looks like during sport and game situations, and then are encouraged to make connections with and learn how they transfer to life at home, in the classroom, and in the neighborhood. The PLUS activities also give kids an opportunity to practice using social and emotional skills in a fun, exciting context. Various reading activities, for example, encourage perspective-taking and decision-making, composite skills of respect and responsibility. (Box 4.1 below outlines the specific social and emotional skills that are taught through the various PLUS activities. Example activities and their corresponding theme unit are included.)

Chapter Five

Promotion of Intrinsic, Self-Referenced Motivation Orientation

Developing good people

"Why be good?" "Why care about these values and skills once this program is over?" "How can I put what I know into action in the face of peer pressure and other competing choices?" These are critical questions that the PLUS approach to motivation seeks to address. The PLUS approach to motivation has three important elements:

1. Cultivate a self-referenced motivation orientation

2. Cultivate intrinsic motivation

3. Cultivate a healthy climate of competition

Self-Referenced Motivation

PLUS attempts to cultivate a self-referenced approach to motivation (what the research literature calls a "task or mastery orientation"), which is built upon a cyclical pattern of personal goal setting, monitoring, and reformulation. In addition to numerous positive performance outcomes (academic, athletic, and other), research suggests that cultivating an orientation where a person competes against self-referenced personal achievement (e.g., a better time than before, more right on this test than last time, fewer unnecessary interruptions of the class today than yesterday) tends to promote self-reflection and awareness, to support strong intrinsic motivation, and to reduce helpless response to failure (Nicholls 1984; Duda and Nicholls 1992; Harackiewicz and Elliot 1993; Molden and Dweck 2000).

What does this look like in practice? Whether youth are attempting to improve at sport, reading, or character, their long-term goals should be broken down into self-referenced, short-term goals, goals based on their past performance and their future potential. The PLUS Program utilizes the *S.M.A.R.T. Goals* goal-setting script (see Box 5.1) to help participants engage in a cyclical process of goal setting, personal monitoring (using checklists, journals, etc.), and then reformulation of goals.

PLUS members have numerous opportunities for goal-setting throughout the day. For example, kids track personal progress during the *Lessons from the Field,* recording Past Personal Bests (PPBs) and setting Future Personal Best Goals (FBGs) in their Player Portfolios. Time also is specifically set aside for goal-setting at the end of each PLUS day. Kids practice using the *S.M.A.R.T. Goals* goal-setting script to set personal and team goals, to track their progress toward those goals in their Player Portfolios, and to set new goals as their goals are reached.

Box 5.1

S.M.A.R.T. Goals

S.M.A.R.T. Goals are:

> Specific — so that it is clear what needs to be accomplished
>
> Measurable — so that progress can be tracked
>
> Achievable — so that goals are challenging, yet attaingable
>
> Relevant — so that achieving our goals will make us better at what we do
>
> Timely — sot hat our goals can be achived within a specific timeframe

---

Through this cyclical process of setting goals, monitoring progress toward those goals, and reformulating new goals, kids acquire the necessary skills to accurately attribute the antecedents of success and failure, and they grow in their intrinsic motivation. Intrinsic motivation, another important aspect of the PLUS approach to motivation, is a critical piece of the "Why be good?" question.

Intrinsic Motivation

Intrinsic motivation is an important topic for character education precisely because it gets to the heart of the question "Why be good?" The PLUS program focuses on cultivating a sense of intrinsic motivation, a state of mind whereby participants care deeply about living out program principles for their own reward, and not in exchange for external inducements. They feel positive when they live out the program message and not positive when they don't. The external inducement to buy-in comes from the "pro-social gang" they have developed through the experience of community within the program — their peers and group leaders. Clearly, the devil is in the details when it comes to rewarding practices and their supportive or detrimental effects on the development of character. However, a wide-body of research suggests that the persistent use of extrinsic motivators — stickers, stars, gum and other forms of behavior inducements — tend to *undermine* intrinsic motivation (c.f., Kohn, 1993; Ryan and Deci, 2000). That is, when the rewards stop, so does the individual's motivation for being good.

The goal of any program is not simply compliance, but transfer across domains. Thus, the PLUS program strives to develop habits of the heart in its participants, an internal commitment to the enjoyment and rewards derived from the activities themselves. Reading about topics you like, playing sports you like, treating people well and being treated well in return: these are rewarding on their own merits, and using external inducements only serves to detract from this motivation.

The PLUS approach uses praise, verbal feedback, and non-contingent group recognition to sustain and develop intrinsic motivation. *Cool-Down Rituals,* for example, close each day and provide time for kids and leaders alike to share praise with one another in the form of "put-ups" and to highlight positive examples of the PLUS values they have noticed throughout the day. During *Respect and Responsibility (R&R) Huddles,* which follow each activity, PLUS leaders highlight teachable moments as they arise and readily offer verbal feedback both to individual kids and to the group as a whole. Kids also have an opportunity to share their perspectives during this time. Finally, each theme unit concludes with a ceremony, during which certificates are presented to the group in recognition of the progress made by group members during that unit.

Extrinsic motivation is not inherently evil, except in how it is used. As Damon (1995) states: "The notion that intrinsic and extrinsic motivation are incompatible, and that educators must choose between them in formulating their strategies for working with students, is just another myth based upon a false dichotomy" (p. 207). Nonetheless, as Bandura argues, "successful socialization requires gradual substitution of symbolic and internal controls for external sanctions and demands" (Bandura 1991, p. 54). Using the strategies described above, the PLUS Program attempts to promote internal controls through a developmental approach to motivation. This effort is further enhanced by PLUS's proactively structured, climate of competition.

Competition

There's no way around it: America is a competitive society. While some see this as a problem, others see it as a strength. It's really neither bad nor good, accepting how it is applied. Utilizing a developmental rationale, the PLUS Program strives to encourage healthy competition by focusing on the specific aspects of success within kids' control, focusing on personal achievement rather than on beating an opponent, and by focusing on the love of winning as opposed to the fear of losing. As David Shields (2001) has argued, it's important that youth learn to view competition as an opportunity for youth to compete *with* each other, not against each other. The idea being that we can only reach our personal best when we challenge and support each other.

The PLUS approach to competition is an important part of the program's effectiveness. Because engaging youth in sport can either support or undermine a healthy approach to competition, the competitive environment must be proactively structured. PLUS games and competitions are specifically designed to build concepts of team and to emphasize personal and group achievement, rather than simply beating an opponent. Tag games challenge kids to work together to make sure their teammates remain in the game. Relays and other speed-oriented activities pit teams against the clock, racing against themselves to better their fastest times. *Lessons from the Field* encourage self-referenced personal achievement and emphasize improvement; kids are recognized for reaching their Future Personal Best Goals rather than for being the "Best at Sit-ups," for example.

Without doubt, competition is central to sport and physical activity. The PLUS approach is not to minimize competition or eliminate it altogether; in fact, many of the sport and physical activities rely upon a climate of healthy competition. Such a climate is vital for helping participants achieve their very best.

It stimulates our motivation to perform difficult tasks: My muscles may be sore and my arms may be tired, but by competing with myself to do one more push-up than last time, I find an inner strength, an intrinsic motivation to push on. The key is to help kids develop that healthy sense of competition whereby they focus not on being the best in the group but on doing the very best they can. The next chapter will focus on the PLUS approach to promoting physical activity and health.

CHAPTER SIX

Promote Physical Activity and Health

"Play, then, is the answer to the puzzle of our existence."

— Dr. George Sheehan
author, *Running & Being*

The benefits of physical activity are well-documented: Research suggests that physically active kids have a more positive self-image, greater self-confidence, and demonstrate improvement in motor skills, cognitive functioning (Etnier et al., 1997) and health-related fitness. Studies from the American Council on Exercise have shown that physically active kids also are more likely to become physically active adults. Thus, developing an interest in sport and physical activity at a young age is something that will likely continue to benefit kids later in life.

While the benefits of sport and physical activity are easily recognizable, physical activity, and sport in particular, remain frequently underutilized mediums through which children can develop physically. More and more kids lack opportunities to participate in physical activity. Physical education classes and extracurricular sports are often the first areas to be cut when schools are struggling financially. Urban youth rarely have the same opportunities to play team sports as their suburban peers. As one study reported, while some 60% of suburban youth play team sports, only 30% of urban youth participate. Further, where they do exist, sports opportunities in the form of club teams and recreational leagues frequently prove cost-prohibitive for many families. For example, to participate in recreational leagues, kids, or their parents, will pay anywhere between $50 and $300. That price tag jumps to $1500 for classic or select club teams (North American Youth Sports Institute, 1997).

The lack of opportunities to engage in physical activity comes at a time when numerous studies have revealed dramatic increases in the prevalence of overweight children; some even suggest that child obesity is reaching epidemic proportion. For example, one study reported that between 1986 and 1998, the number of overweight children increased by more than 50% among whites and more than 120% among African Americans and Hispanics (Strauss & Pollack, 2001). The research suggests that the increase in obese children and adolescents isn't simply a threat to physical health. A particularly troubling study on the health-related quality of life of severely obese children and adolescents indicates that self-perception, mental health, and overall quality of life are deeply impacted by obesity. The study found that "severely obese children and adolescents have lower health-related quality of life than children and adolescents who are healthy and similar quality of life as those diagnosed as having cancer" (Schwimmer, Burwinkle, and Varni, 2003). Clearly, obesity is more than just a physical problem.

Although many after school and youth development programs recognize the importance of physical fitness and health, few have a well-designed research-based physical fitness program capable that meets the physical development needs of kids. As Siegal states, "while many coaches and program directors have had worthy intentions, they have not focused enough on how programs are operationalized to produce desired effects" (p. 7). The PLUS Program recognizes this limitation in many programs attempting to promote physical fitness and well-being in youth, and it attempts to remedy this weakness by proactively structuring a comprehensive physical development protocol that is fun for kids *and* capable of helping them become physically fit.

The PLUS Response

The PLUS Program strives to address the critical need for physical fitness through its fourth program component: the promotion of physical activity and health. While sport and physical activity certainly provide important contributions to the social, moral, intellectual, and emotional aspects of development, this fourth component is designed specifically to promote kids' physical development. The primary objectives of this component are (1) to provide an opportunity for kids to engage in physical activity; (2) to promote kids' overall physical fitness; (3) to help kids develop self-regulations skills through the use of goal-setting, checklists and logs; and (4) to foster an interest in and an appreciation for lifelong physical activity.

To accomplish its objectives, the PLUS Program begins with the premise that kids like to have fun, to play sports, and to be active. As the *President's Council on Physical Fitness and Sports* states, "Rather than encouraging these individuals [overweight or obese individuals] to lose weight it is more appropriate and probably more effective to encourage them to just become physically active. If regular physical activity is performed, physical fitness will improve to the extent possible and lead to positive metabolic changes" (p. 5). Kids need ample time to engage in fun, yet structured physical games and sports activities that foster their physical development in a climate of healthy competition. Each program will be different: Some programs will have access to gyms and fields, while others will not. Kids also will come to the program with a variety of sport interests and skill levels. Thus, the physical activity component is designed to provide just the right balance between structure and flexibility to meet the physical activity needs of a wide range of kids.

During the first block of this component, *Getting Started,* kids learn the importance of getting their bodies physically ready to engage in physical activity. They are introduced to proper stretching techniques, learn to measure and track their resting heart rate, and prepare their body physically through slow jogging, push-ups, sit-ups, lunges, and jumping rope. Through these initial activities, they also develop important self-regulation skills as they record their Past Personal Bests (PPBs) in their Player Portfolios and set Future Personal Best Goals (FBGs). Using checklists and logs, personal progress toward reaching these goals are monitored and recorded in Player Portfolios.

At the core of the physical activity component is the second block, *Structured Play.* Structured play is comprised of two different types of play: *skill play* and *sport play.* Through the various relays, tag games, and other physically active games of *skill play*, kids develop important aspects of physical fitness (strength, flexibility, endurance, balance, agility, and coordination). This time is intentionally structured to maximize kids' development, but the fast pace and great variety help ensure that kids have fun as they develop these skills. During *sport play*, kids' interest in and appreciation for both traditional and lifetime sports (like basketball, soccer, biking, running, etc.) are nurtured. Kids should have some say in what sports they choose to play during this time. The group may choose to play the same sport for several sessions to allow time for dividing into teams and organizing a simple round-robin tournament, or it may prefer to try something new each day. Whatever the group's preference, it is important that all group members are reminded that the primary goal of this time is to *have fun.*

Wrapping Up, the final block of the physical activity component is designed to calm the kids as they wind down from their physical activity and prepare to transition to the next program component. (This time also can be used as a "catch-up time" in case any of the day's activities took longer than expected.)

Physical Activities — A Guide to PLUS Youth Development

The physical activity component of the PLUS Program is designed to promote physical development, but it's important that kids also *have fun.* The sports games and physical activities that comprise this segment of the day should keep kids active and highly involved. Changing the pace, including a variety of both competitive and cooperative games, and giving kids a voice in what they do next are useful strategies for keeping kids engaged and for ensuring this time is fun for them.

As described in the previous chapter, PLUS strives to develop in its participants a healthy sense of competition through a self-referenced, intrinsic motivation orientation. Competition certainly is important, and most of the games and sports activities are intended to be competitive, but the focus should not be on the final outcome. Rather, skill development, personal improvement, and most of all, enjoyment should be the primary focus.

Along with their various skill levels and sports interests, kids also will bring a wide range of previous sport experiences to the program. Kids may have been involved in programs where "winning was everything," where playing time was allotted according to ability, and where star players received more attention than the rest of the team. The PLUS Program strives to create positive learning environment through sport, one in which kids feel physically safe, comfortable interacting with their peers, and confident they will be supported in all their attempts on the playing field. The following research-based recommendations for sport and physical activity are intended to serve as a general guide (along with the specific recommendations included in the theme units) for extending kids' experience of a caring, connected community to the playing field.

PLUS Recommendations for Physical Activity

1. **Sports and physical activity should be structured to promote self-confidence.** The most important aspect of the youth sport experience is how the kids feel about their experience. Above everything else—tournaments, uniforms, winning, positions and playing time—this principle remains paramount: we must create an environment that promotes self-confidence and self-esteem in every player.

2. **Sport and physical activity should NOT be associated with punishment.** Physical activity should never be associated with punishment (e.g., running laps; or withholding opportunities for sport and physical play). No one likes to be punished, and by using physical activity as a punishment, kids begin to associate negative experiences with physical activity. This practice undermines our efforts to promote kids' physical activity.

3. **Program leaders and coaches should provide kids with appropriate feedback.** The type and quantity of feedback kids receive is important. If the only thing kids hear from their coaches is "Good job!" or "Nice try!" that feedback will quickly lose its value. Different situations call for different kinds of feedback: praise should be used for effort and skill;

encouragement should be given when errors are made; and, instruction should follow attempts. Different types of feedback also should be used together (e.g., "You did a great job trying that new dribbling move. Maybe next time you could try kicking the ball with this part of your foot.").

4. **Playing time and positions should be distributed evenly among all players.** For kids in this age group, unequal playing time undermines the development of self-confidence in all players, and thus contradicts PLUS's first principle. The goal of sport and physical activity should be to provide equal access for all kids to opportunities for growth. Just as kids need opportunities to play, they also need opportunities to experience new positions. "Seeing the game" from different positions encourages a respect for and an understanding of all positions on the team. It also promotes kids' intellectual development by giving them important opportunities for perspective-taking and decision-making.

5. **Sport and physical activity should encourage and develop values such as teamwork, respect, responsibility, fairness and perseverance.** The sport environment should be organized to promote the values we deem important. These five fundamental, universal values can and should be taught and promoted through the youth sport experience. Through proactively structured sport activities, kids expand their understanding of these core values and gain opportunities to practice living them out.

6. **Rules and consequences should be clearly spelled out and enforced fairly and consistently.** Team rules should support team values. Clearly specified rules of conduct that are applied fairly and consistently help ensure the development of personal responsibility and consistent behavior among young athletes.

7. **Program leaders and coaches must model the values they want their children to learn.** The behavior of parents and coaches affects the overall development of young people more than any other factor. As role models, we must act in ways that

show we value the very same ideals we are trying to teach our kids. We also must "preach what we practice" by taking time to point out what, exactly, we are modeling.

8. **Winning is important only in that it is the end result of a game.** While competition is inherent in sport and an objective of any game is to win, the efforts of program leaders and parents should reflect that winning and losing are only natural results of any youth sport experience. The greater life lessons of respect, responsibility, fair play, teamwork and perseverance represent the true value of youth sport, lessons which can be realized regardless of the game's final outcome.

9. **Kids should be encouraged to participate in sport and physical activity outside of the program.** If we want our kids to be physically active, we must encourage them to seek out opportunities for physical activity on their own. Ask kids to keep track of their physical activity outside of the PLUS Program in their Player Portfolios, using the activity logs and checklists provided. Highlighting positive, athlete role models, too, will help kids to recognize the intrinsic value of sport and physical activity.

10. **Program leaders and coaches must recognize that kids have developmental differences.** As leaders, we must respect that each child is unique and that kids are at different developmental stages. It is our responsibility to meet kids where they are in the developmental process, to help them realize their personal potential, and to foster both learning and physical activity as part of a lifelong process.

CHAPTER SEVEN

Use of Sport-Based Literature to Increase Moral Theme Comprehension and Overall Literacy Appreciation

"But in reading great literature I become a thousand and yet remain myself."

— C.S. Lewis

For many youth, sports provide numerous aspects of our deepest human needs, especially competence and enjoyment. The PLUS Program attempts to utilize kids' natural interest in sport as a bridge to other topics they need for healthy development, but are frequently less interested in — especially literacy.

The importance of developing basic literacy skills cannot be argued. Not only is reading ability critical for academic development, it also is a basic life skill that is necessary for successful functioning in our society. The elementary years are a critical time for shaping students' literacy development and reading motivation. As children go through school, reading becomes more directly related to academic success, and students with poor reading ability find themselves falling behind in other subjects. If a fourth grader, for example, has a difficult time reading and comprehending material, they will fall behind in other subjects that require them to read and comprehend the subject matter (such as history or science). This becomes a vicious downward spiral as the child becomes discouraged and possibly labeled as a poor student.

Unfortunately, upper elementary students frequently lack important opportunities to develop these vital skills in the classroom, as well as the motivation to work on them independently. In his book, *Raising a Reader,* Paul Kropp points out, "Though most kids are developing the rudiments of reading in primary school, many of them stop developing as readers in grades four and five" Kropp, P. (1996). Fourth graders spend an average of five minutes per day reading in the classroom, which may explain, at least in part, why the National Assessment of Educational Progress reports that 74% of fourth graders cannot read at their own grade level. Further, as children get older, their motivation to read typically diminishes, and they spend less and less time reading for pleasure. One study reported that kids spend less than 1% of their time reading recreationally. Thus, children need additional opportunities to read, as well as greater motivation to read.

Using Sport Stories

The literacy component of the PLUS Program attempts to accomplish two central goals: First, it attempts *to increase kids' interest in and appreciation for literature* by exposing them to different kinds of stories they like and are interested in — namely, sport stories. Encouraging children to read is much easier when they can read about subjects they are interested in and care about. Sport stories have this natural attraction for many kids and can help them develop positive attitudes about the pleasures and value of reading. They include a great deal of action and characters, as well as a recognizable setting and unpredictable outcomes. Like a game, these stories stretch the mind and stir the emotions. Most importantly, sports stories are engaging and fun to discuss. Clearly, the development of reading skills is an important part of the reading equation, but developing a lasting interest and desire in reading is also a critical component in the reading equation.

Second, *PLUS attempts to increase kids' moral theme comprehension* by providing them a script for considering the important elements regarding the moral of the story. Learning to ask critical comprehension questions of a text allows kids to consistently extract the moral of future stories they read or in which they are involved. PLUS isn't simply about developing reading motivation and skills; it also views literature as containing rich material for promoting social and cognitive development. Through reading sport stories, children learn to listen, speculate, share and take turns, as they interact socially with others. Sports literature also is an excellent medium for building children's mental muscles. The ability to identify conflicts, generate solutions, predict outcomes, and consider potential consequences, all constitute critical thinking skills that are developed through PLUS literacy component.

Sports-based literature also has the power to engage kids' moral sensibilities by allowing the reader to get inside the hearts and minds of characters and to experience their successes, struggles, worries, and hopes. Reading and interacting with sport stories, youth better comprehend the moral dimensions of literature, and by extension, of life — a process that is not as simple as reading good books. Research by Narvaez (2001) indicates that "reading moral stories to children does not guarantee that they will understand the moral message or theme as intended by the author" (p.483). In fact, discerning the "moral of the story" requires active engagement of readers, supported by guided reflection, which is exactly what PLUS attempts to accomplish.

The PLUS approach is not simply to give kids the moral of the specific stories covered in the program — although it does that too. Instead, PLUS attempts to teach kids a process, a series of critical questions that they can consistently utilize to understand the essential moral dimensions of any story they encounter. Utilizing a consistent pattern of questions, or moral theme scheme, the program attempts to provide kids with the proverbial fish — the moral of the story — and the fishing pole — a series of questions to consider for every story they read. For example, Box 7.1 contains a sample moral theme scheme questions utilized in the *Sport Shorts and Theme Books*.

Kids gain rich experiences in language through sport books, current events, poems, and quotes from prominent athletes. They improve their language skills as they read on their own and in groups, discuss with others the lessons from the stories they read, and spend time writing in their journals. PLUS unique lesson plans are carefully crafted to develop important skills, such as moral theme comprehension, problem-solving, moral imagination, perspective-taking, and decision-making. Box 7.2 provides some sample questions from an *Instant Replay,* which asks kids to consider the feelings of various stakeholders and to generate different solutions for creating the greatest good for the greatest number of people.

Box 7.1

Moral Theme Scheme Questions

1. Who are the main characters in this story?
2. What is the main problem these characters face?
3. What are some ways that Andy might handle the situation?
4. What would happen if the problem were handled in this way? How would Andy feel?
   How would Jessie feel? How would the other kids feel?
5. If you were Andy, how would you solve the problem?
6. What about your solution would be difficult to do?
7. What if you were Jessie, how would you handle the situation?
8. What might make it difficult to do this?

PLUS literacy component is specifically designed to maximize the benefits of using sport stories to promote kids' cognitive, social, and moral development. The Lessons from Literature refers to the reading activities included in the PLUS program. Each kid receives a personal Player Portfolio on the first day to be used during the Lessons from Literature, as well as in a variety of other activities. The Player Portfolio is designed not only to provide a personal journal for each student with stories, cartoons, and pictures, but also to motivate and encourage kids to write. Where possible, the stories are printed directly into the portfolios and all discussion questions and journal topics are included there. *Lessons from Literature* is comprised of four distinct types of reading activities:

- **Sports Shorts and Theme Books** — short stories and chapter books that present a lesson on a particular value.

- **You Make the Calls** — short scenarios that present a conflict or dilemma and challenge kids to find creative solutions.

Box 7.2

Sample Instant Replay Reflections

1. First, consider how the different characters are feeling and what they are thinking.

   - How is Amanda feeling?

   - How is Vern feeling?

   - What is Kenny thinking?

2. Next, ask the audience if they have any suggestions for how the situation could be resolved. Suggestions could be listed on poster paper.

3. Choosing one solution, say, "OK, let's rewind." Actors then try out different solutions, each time repeating the preceding process.

4. After a few rounds of role-playing, ask kids to sit together in a circle. Lead kids in a discussion about the different solutions, using the following questions as a guide to help them identify the advantages and disadvantges of each solution. (Responses should be written on poster paper by a volunteer.)

   - Is the solution good for the person making the decision?

   - Does the solution help others solve the problem?

   - Is anybody harmed by the solution (physically or emotionally)?

   - Would this be a good solution for everyone in a similar situation to use?

   - Are there any ways to improve this solution? If yes, what are they?

- **Instant Replays** — brief plot descriptions that kids first read and then act out through role-plays.

- **Sports Extras** — magazine articles, news events, and other stories that kids bring to share with the group at the end of each theme unit.

The reading activities follow a similar format (including setting the tone, reading the story, and discussing questions about the story), but each type of activity is specifically designed to promote different skills.

Sport Shorts and Theme Books

These short stories and chapter books include children as the main characters, as well as biographies about athletes and sport-related, historical situations (e.g., Jackie Robinson's breakthrough into baseball). Each story relates directly to the theme unit and is important for developing kids' moral theme comprehension abilities. This type of reading activity can be broken down into three steps:

1. *Set-up* — Set-up guidelines are included at the beginning of each Sport Short or Theme Book to help you set the tone for the story. The stimulating questions and/or brief summaries are related specifically to the story and are designed to get kids thinking about some of the issues the story will raise. This step is very important for focusing the kids' attention on the task at hand.

2. *The Story* — During this step, you will a) read the story aloud as a whole group, and b) have students work through the discussion questions in their Player Portfolios, either in pairs or as a whole group.

3. *Discussion Questions* — Finally, the group will come back together to answer a series of questions called the *8-Question Theme-Scheme*. **Question 1-4** are knowledge questions, asking kids to name the main characters and to identify the problem or challenge they face. Responses should be given in a round-robin format so that several pairs will have an opportunity to share. **Question 5** is a focus prompt that asks kids to identify the lessons learned by the main character. It should be answered in an exhaustive format, allowing kids to continue giving responses until all new answers have been heard. **Question 6-7** are behavior questions, which ask kids to think about what they would do in the main character's situation, and all kids who want to share a response should have an opportunity to

do so. Finally, Question 8 is a focus prompt that kids should complete in their Player Portfolios.

You Make the Call

In this type of reading activity, students are asked to develop creative solutions to realistic social situations. The scenarios are short and present situations with which most children can easily relate. They are intentionally open-ended so that kids can choose an appropriate course of action to resolve the conflict. The You Make the Call reading activities are important for promoting kids' problem-solving and moral imaging skills. These activities, too, can be broken into three steps:

1. *Set-up* — Similar to the Set-up section described above, a few sample questions are included to help you set the tone before breaking kids into small groups of 3 or 4. Once again, the story should be read aloud together as a whole group.

2. *Discussion Questions* — The questions for this type of activity are designed to challenge the kids' thinking about the dilemma presented in the story. The *Knowledge Questions* ask kids to identify the main characters and the primary dilemma. The *Prediction Questions* ask kids to think about possible solutions to the problem, as well as the resulting consequences of taking that solution. The *Behavior Questions* ask kids to think about how they personally would respond if they were faced with a similar dilemma.

3. *Group Share* — Once the Discussion Questions have been completed in small groups, the large group gathers together to talk about the different solutions. Each small group shares the solution(s) they thought of, and their responses are tracked on large poster paper or newsprint. Once all the possible solutions have been laid out, the group as a whole spends a few minutes talking about the consequences of each solution and decides

which solution would be best (i.e., the most good for the most people).

Instant Replay

This type of reading activity is designed as a role-play. Each one presents a sport-related social situation and a cast of characters. Some kids act out the character-parts; others participate from the audience, while you lead the group as director. Instant Replays are important for promoting perspective-taking and decision-making skills and for developing a sense of empathy. The steps for this type of reading activity are as follows:

1. *Set-up* — This step is important for setting the scene, describing the players (or characters), and explaining the plot.
2. *The Play* — After setting the stage, choose a few volunteers to play the different roles. (Typically, an Instant Reply will have only 4 or 5 characters, so it is important that acting responsibilities are rotated so that everyone who wants to will have an opportunity to participate at some point during the year.) With you as director, help the players act out the continuation of the story in front of the group. When an ending of the story has been acted out, call out, "Actors, FREEZE!" Actors will then stand in place as you facilitate a short discussion with the audience, asking them to describe how each character is feeling. Next, ask the audience for possible alternative endings to the story. Choosing one, direct the actors by saying, "OK, let's rewind this!" Actors then try out different solutions, each time concluding with a brief discussion about the character's feelings.
3. *Discussion Questions* — The discussion questions for this activity are designed to help kids identify the advantages and disadvantages of each solution. After a few rounds of role-playing, gather the group into a circle to discuss the different

solutions that were played out, using poster paper or newsprint to track kids' responses.

Sports Extras

This type of reading activity is intended to help kids apply what they are learning during the Lessons from Literature by encouraging them to recognize examples of people in the news who exemplify the core value for that theme unit. At the beginning of each theme unit, kids are encouraged to bring in a newspaper or magazine article to be shared with the class at the end of the theme unit. Prior to presenting their story or article, kids will spend a few moments responding to a few questions about their story in their Player Portfolios. Volunteers then have an opportunity to share their story or article in their own words.

New Knowledge, New Skills, New Worlds

The PLUS Program doesn't claim to be a panacea for the difficult reading challenges facing today's families, schools, and communities. However, it does claim to provide important knowledge (about important values and other life-lessons), to provide important skills (such as how to elicit key thematic elements from a story), and perhaps most importantly, to open kids to new worlds (as they learn about the potential of literature to open our eyes to people and places we may have never known).

The world of sport is a mosaic of people from different time periods, backgrounds and cultures. Many sport stories (both fiction and nonfiction) illustrate athletes who push racial, ethnic, physical or gender barriers. For example, in Jackie Robinson: Bravest Man in Baseball, the reader can go back in time to 1947 with the Brooklyn Dodgers and learn of Jackie's experience of playing in a sport dominated by whites. In Baseball Saved Us, by Ken Mochizuki, we learn how an American boy of Japanese descent endured injustice and racial prejudice during World War II. Through these and other sport stories, children expand their understanding of the experiences and lives of others, and in turn, learn more about themselves.

Section III

Getting Started

Chapter Eight

Getting Started: A Guide to the PLUS Curriculum

Introduction

The first several chapters of this manual introduced the potential of sport as an educational medium, outlined the philosophy of the PLUS Program, described the importance of creating a positive learning environment, and illustrated PLUS's five program components. This chapter will provide the tools needed to run a successful PLUS's program and will outline how to use the daily lesson plans. As it leads you through a typical PLUS day, each phase of the PLUS curriculum will be explained in detail. The phases are interrelated, but each plays an integral role within the five Theme Units — Teamwork, Respect, Responsibility, Fair Play, Perseverance. They are designed to foster positive development while creating a caring, connected community among program participants. The pattern of the *Warm-Up, Activity,* and *Cool-Down* sessions provides a consistent structure for introducing those program components necessary for positive development, including team-building activities, reading and sports activities, and time for reflection and goal-setting. Moreover, the predictable rhythm of each Warm-Up, Activity, and Cool-Down session allows the individual components to flow together.

Below, the PLUS Template is described. It is important that you read this section carefully so that you will be able to effectively use the activities and teaching strategies described in this manual. Sample activities are included to help you become familiar with the various components, and the chapter is designed so that you can easily refer back to it as needed throughout the program. It is critical that leaders understand that the consistency and repetition contained in the organization of the manual is important aspect of the program's effective implementation. PLUS days begin follow a routine, which is required for kids to develop the knowledge and skills contained in the program. Instructors should attempt to follow the activities all the way through each day, resisting the temptations to skip over questions or activities that the program seems to have "already covered." Your faithful implementation of the PLUS Program as a PLUS Leader increases the likelihood that kids leave the program with the knowledge, skills, and commitment to put PLUS into action in all phases of their life.

Warm-Up

Begin the PLUS Cycle

As children step into the PLUS environment, coming straight from the school bus or neighborhood streets, they bring with them a lot of outside energy. The Warm-Up session provides a time for kids to wind down from their previous distractions so they can better focus on the upcoming tasks. It enables you to set the tone, to quiet the chaos and focus the kids' attention. Just as we stretch to prepare our bodies for the physical exertion of an upcoming run, the Warm-Up is designed to prepare kids' mental muscles for the day's activities.

Session Overview. The Session Overview provides an opportunity for you to gather the group together as a team at the outset of each day. Questions, such as "How are you feeling today?" or "What do you want to learn today?", will help draw the kids away from the distractions of the day and into the PLUS culture. Give the group a brief description of the planned activities for the day and encourage the kids to think about the day's goals and challenges.

Quote of the Week. With the exception of the first week, a Quote of the Week will be introduced during the first session of each week. Quotes have a way of helping us think about things in different ways. Analyzing quotes for their deeper meaning helps kids improve their critical thinking and discussion skills. The quotes included in the PLUS manual relate to the specific theme units and are designed to spark discussion and provide ideas for journal writing. They are famous sayings (e.g., "Do unto others as you would have them do unto you.") or quotes from athletes, coaches, and other recognizable persons.

The following 5 steps will help structure the kids' thinking about the Quote of the Week.

1. **Write the Quote of the Week.** Begin by writing the quote on a chalkboard or poster for the whole group to see as they come into the room. You may use the following introductory statement as a guide for introducing the first few quotes: "Many times people say things that help us think about different topics or ideas in different ways. While we are working on the theme of teamwork, we will read a quote from a different person each week to help us understand what others think about values like teamwork. Each time we have a new Quote of the Week we'll spend a few minutes talking about what the quote means and how we might use the ideas in our own group." Ask kids to be on the lookout for interesting quotes from the newspaper, TV or radio that can be brought in and shared with the group.

2. **Think about the Quote as a group.** Read aloud the quote, and with the help of the group, explain it. Ask kids to think about the discussion questions/focus prompts found in their Player Portfolios. Take time to clarify any questions the kids may have. This will ensure that all kids understand what they are being asked to think about.

3. **Pair up to talk about the Quote.** Pair up the kids by having them count off by 2s. (As the program progresses, you may

want to find different ways to pair the kids off so that they will have opportunities to talk with different peers. Encourage kids to pair with someone new each day.) Once the kids are paired off, allow 5-7 minutes for kids to talk about the quote with their partners using the discussion questions/focus prompts in their Player Portfolios. Ask each person to record their ideas in their personal Player Portfolios. Be sure to walk around the groups as the kids discuss in their pairs, taking time to listen, encourage participation, and offer help where needed.

4. **Share answers with the whole group.** Once all the pairs have had a chance to discuss the questions and focus prompts, bring the kids back together as a whole group. Spend a few minutes giving kids an opportunity to share their thoughts on the quote from the pair-discussions. To ensure that everyone who wants to speak has a chance and to make sure everyone is heard, you may want to use a speaking ball or talking tool. Have the group choose any athletic ball or other object to be your talking tool. Explain to the kids that every time you gather as a group to discuss the Quote of the Week, a person may only speak when he is holding this soccer ball, softball ball, etc. It is everyone else's job to listen to the person holding the talking ball, and when that person has finished speaking, she may pass it to the next person. You may decide to go in a circle, starting with a volunteer and then passing the talking ball around in a circle. Give kids the option to pass if they wish.

5. **Reflect individually about the Quote.** After everyone has had a chance to share, conclude the Quote of the Week by having kids spend 3-5 minutes writing individually about the extension questions in their Player Portfolios. Again, you may wish to clarify the question to the entire group before the kids begin to write.

Follow the 5 steps of the Quote of the Week Format each time you introduce a new quote of the week:

1. **Write** the Quote of the Week.

2. **Think** about the Quote as a group.

3. **Pair up** to talk about the Quote.

4. **Share** answers with the whole group.

5. **Reflect** individually about the Quote.

Sometimes an Instructor's Note is included to offer additional guidance.

Other Warm-Up Activities. For days that have no quote of the week, a short warm-up activity will take its place. In the beginning of the program, these brief games serve as ice-breakers designed to help the group get to know each other. For example, the *Toss a Name Game,* played on the very first day, is an easy way for the group to begin learning each other's names. As the program progresses, these simple games continue to be an important means for focusing the group's attention at the start of the day.

Team-Building Activities

Team-building activities follow the brief warm-up activities. Team-building activities serve several purposes: 1) most activities are designed to be semi-active and fun, so they get kids moving after being in school all day; 2) they further kids' understanding of each theme unit's core value (e.g., teamwork) by providing them with hands-on opportunities to explore its meaning; and 3) they help strengthen the group's sense of themselves as a team (e.g., by challenging kids to work together to solve problems).

In Box 8.1 a sample team-building activity from the *Teamwork Unit* illustrates how these activities are laid out in the manual:

Respect and Responsibility (R&R) Huddle

Similar to a time-out in a basketball game, the R&R Huddle serves as an important transition between major activities. Designed as a brief check-in (no more than 5 minutes), its primary purpose is to:

1. **Recap** what just happened by highlighting one or two key points from the activity.

2. **Reconnect** kids back to the theme unit. (Specific focus prompts are often included as a guide.)

3. **Reset** and transition to the next activity using its Set-up guidelines.

In the R&R Huddle, you are the coach talking to your team about their on-court performance, refocusing (or reconnecting) them on the theme unit, and preparing them for the next task.

Activity

The R&R Huddle provides an easy way to transition to the next phase of the day, the Activity. The Activity phase is broken into two parts — Lessons from Literature and Lessons from the Field — each of which plays an important role in drawing out the lessons of sport. Themes that arise in a particular story, such as Teamwork or Perseverance, can be reinforced during the games and sports activities from "the Field". Each section of the Activity phase is described below.

Lessons from Literature

The Lessons from Literature refers to the reading activities included in the PLUS program. Each kid receives a personal Player Portfolio on the first day to be used during the Lessons from Literature, as well as in a variety of other activities. The Player Portfolio is designed not only to provide a personal journal for each student with stories, cartoons, and pictures, but also to motivate and encourage kids to write. Where possible, the stories are printed directly into the portfolios and all discussion questions and journal topics are included there.

Four types of reading activities comprise the Lessons from Literature — Sport Shorts and Theme Books, You Make the Call, Instant Replays, and Sport Extras. The reading activities follow a similar format (including setting the tone, reading the story, and discussing questions about the story), but each type of activity is specifically designed to promote different skills.

Sport Shorts and Theme Books These short stories and chapter books include children as the main characters, as well as biographies about athletes and sport-related, historical situations (e.g., Jackie Robinson's breakthrough into baseball). Each story relates directly to the theme

Box 8.1
Slot Machine

This group problem-solving activity offers another opportunity for the group to work together to solve a problem. You can do this activity in a classroom, but playing this game in your gym or outside on a field affords more options and creativity. Bring the group together in a circle. Break into three teams of 3 or more.

Play

1. The name of the game is Slot Machine. Like any slot machine player, the goal is to get three matching pictures.

2. Each team will go to a corner of the room and create a group gesture to represent teamwork, drawing from what they have lerned about teamwork in previous sessions.

3. Once each team has a gesture, breing the group back together. Line the teams up in a triangle formation. Ask each team to show its gesture.

4. For the rest of the activity, there will be no talking between teams. The goal of the group is for you (the facilitator) to count to three, say go and have all three teams show the same gesture.

5. Play one round — count to three and see what gesture each team shows. This round helps the group to understand the game. Now, send the teams back to their corners, allowing time for the teams to decide which gesture they will use.

6. Come back together. Count to three, and see what gestures are presented.

7. Repeat this process until all three groups get the same gesture (or the group tires of the game).

This problem can be more difficult than it appears. Consider the following:

1. The teams cannot speak to each other, yet they are all trying to do the same thing. They need to develop a system for nonverbal communication.

2. It is not uncommon for one team to forget that the group's goal is to have everyone show the same gesture. This group may become unbending in showing any other gesture than their own (this can be OK if the rest of the teams use this group's gesture, but this doesn't always happen). If one team makes it impossible for the group as a whole to achieve its goal, stop the game and use this as a discussion topic — what responsibility does each small group have to the larger group in accomplishing its goal? What happens when a small group of people are not helping a team achieve its goal?

unit and is important for developing kids' moral theme comprehension abilities. This type of reading activity can be broken down into three steps:

1. ***Set-up*** — Set-up guidelines are included at the beginning of each Sport Short or Theme Book to help you set the tone for the story. The stimulating questions and/or brief summaries are related specifically to the story and are designed to get kids thinking about some of the issues the story will raise. This step is very important for focusing the kids' attention on the task at hand.

2. ***The Story*** — During this step, you will a) read the story aloud as a whole group, and b) have students work through the discussion questions in their Player Portfolios, either in pairs or as a whole group.

3. ***Discussion Questions*** — Finally, the group will come back together to answer a series of questions called the *8-Question Theme-Scheme*. **Questions 1-4** are knowledge questions, asking kids to name the main characters and to identify the problem or challenge they face. Responses should be given in a round-robin format so that several pairs will have an opportunity to share. **Question 5** is a focus prompt that asks kids to identify the lessons learned by the main character. It should be answered in an exhaustive format, allowing kids to continue giving responses until all new answers have been heard. **Questions 6-7** are behavior questions, which ask kids to think about what they would do in the main character's situation, and all kids who want to share a response should have an opportunity to do so. Finally, **Question 8** is a focus prompt that kids should complete in their Player Portfolios.

You Make the Call In this type of reading activity, students are asked to develop creative solutions to realistic social situations. The scenarios are short and present situations with which most children can easily relate. They are intentionally open-ended so that kids can choose an appropriate course of action to resolve the conflict. The You Make the Call reading activities are important for promoting kids' problem-solving and moral imaging skills. These activities, too, can be broken into three steps:

1. **Set-up** — Similar to the Set-up section described above, a few sample questions are included to help you set the tone before breaking kids into small groups of 3 or 4. Once again, the story should be read aloud together as a whole group.

2. **Discussion Questions** — The questions for this type of activity are designed to challenge the kids' thinking about the dilemma presented in the story. The Knowledge Questions ask kids to identify the main characters and the primary dilemma. The Prediction Questions ask kids to think about possible solutions to the problem, as well as the resulting consequences of taking that solution. The Behavior Questions ask kids to think about how they personally would respond if they were faced with a similar dilemma.

3. **Group Share** — Once the Discussion Questions have been completed in small groups, the large group gathers together to talk about the different solutions. Each small group shares the solution(s) they thought of, and their responses are tracked on large poster paper or newsprint. Once all the possible solutions have been laid out, the group as a whole spends a few minutes talking about the consequences of each solution and decides which solution would be best (i.e., the most good for the most people).

Instant Replay This type of reading activity is designed as a role-play. Each one presents a sport-related social situation and a cast of characters. Some kids act out the character-parts; others participate from the audience, while you lead the group as director. Instant Replays are important for promoting perspective-taking and decision-making skills and for developing a sense of empathy. The steps for this type of reading activity are as follows:

1. **Set-up** — This step is important for setting the scene, describing the players (or characters), and explaining the plot.

2. **The Play** — After setting the stage, choose a few volunteers to play the different roles. (Typically, an Instant Reply will have only 4 or 5 characters, so it is important that acting

responsibilities are rotated so that everyone who wants to will have an opportunity to participate at some point during the year.) With you as director, help the players act out the continuation of the story in front of the group. When an ending of the story has been acted out, call out, "Actors, FREEZE!" Actors will then stand in place as you facilitate a short discussion with the audience, asking them to describe how each character is feeling. Next, ask the audience for possible alternative endings to the story. Choosing one, direct the actors by saying, "OK, let's rewind this!" Actors then try out different solutions, each time concluding with a brief discussion about the character's feelings.

3. **Discussion Questions** — The discussion questions for this activity are designed to help kids identify the advantages and disadvantages of each solution. After a few rounds of role-playing, gather the group into a circle to discuss the different solutions that were played out, using poster paper or newsprint to track kids' responses.

Sports Extras This type of reading activity is intended to help kids apply what they are learning during the Lessons from Literature by encouraging them to recognize examples of people in the news who exemplify the core value for that theme unit. At the beginning of each theme unit, kids are encouraged to bring in a newspaper or magazine article to be shared with the class at the end of the theme unit. Prior to presenting their story or article, kids will spend a few moments responding to a few questions about their story in their Player Portfolios. Volunteers then have an opportunity to share their story or article in their own words.

R&R Huddle Once again, the R&R Huddle provides an important transition between the Lessons from Literature and the second part of the Activity section, the Lessons from the Field. As described above, the R&R Huddle is designed as a 5 minute check-in that serves to:

1. **Recap** what just happened by highlighting one or two key points from the discussion.

2. **Reconnect** kids back to the theme unit. (Specific focus prompts are often included as a guide.)

3. **Reset** and transition to the Lessons from the Field.

Lessons from the Field

The second part of the Activity phase is the Lessons from the Field, PLUS's physical activity component. Kids like to have fun. They like to play sports and to be active. Thus, the primary goal of this phase of the PLUS program is to provide kids with an opportunity to engage in fun, yet structured, physical games and sports activities.

PLUS recognizes that each program will be different: Some programs will have access to gyms and fields, while others will not. Kids also will come to the program with a variety of sport interests and skill levels. Thus, the physical activity component is designed to provide just the right balance between structure and flexibility to meet the physical activity needs of a wide range of kids. Below, each aspect of the Lessons from the Field is explained in greater detail.

Block I: Getting Started During Block I, kids will begin to develop important skills for setting physical activity goals and for monitoring their progress toward those goals. The group will stand together in a circle for most of this block, and it is important that you foster a fun, enthusiastic atmosphere by encouraging kids to clap and cheer for one another. Music may also be included to help you set a fun, exciting tone. Kids will divide into pairs and work together during the seven steps of this first block. Each day will follow the same basic format:

1. **Measure resting heart rate** — Kids will learn how to measure their resting heart rate (RHR) on the very first day and will measure it at the beginning of each subsequent day.

2. **Record, check in and set goals** — Next, kids will record their RHR for that day, check back over their Past Personal Best (PPB), and set a new Future Personal Best Goal (FBG). Thus, it is important that kids have their Player Portfolios within easy reach during this block.

3. **Jog** — After setting new goals, kids will spend a few minutes slowly jogging to get their bodies warmed-up for the upcoming physical activities. Jogging can be as done as a lap, or by jogging in place while standing in the circle. You may want to present a few different options and let the group decide as a whole, or let individuals choose for themselves which they would prefer.

4. **Stretch** — Next, spend a few minutes engaged in easy stretching to further loosen muscles and prevent any injuries. You can introduce a lot of variety here, but be sure to target the major muscle groups.

5. **Strength/Endurance** — After warming the body up, the kids will spend about 1 minute doing one or two of the following: sit-ups, push-ups, lunges, or calf raises. For the first couple of sessions, you may need to go over the proper form. By counting how many sit-ups, push-ups, calf raises and/or lunges they can initially do in a set amount of time, kids will set an individual baseline for themselves (PPB) that can be recorded in their Player Portfolios. One member of the pair will do the activity, while the other member will count for and cheer on their partner. Roles will then switch, so that everyone will have an opportunity.

6. **Jump Rope** — Pairs next will spend a few minutes doing a variety of jump rope activities, such as jumping on first one then the other foot or jumping on both feet. Again, one member of the pair will do the jumping while the partner does the counting and cheering. Kids should have 2 or 3 short sessions of jumping rope for 30-45 seconds, before gradually building up to 1-minute sessions.

7. **Track personal progress** — Finally, kids will track their personal progress by recording their achievements during steps 5 and 6. This progress will become their PPB and will inform their future best goals (FBGs).

Block II: Structured Play Block II is designed to allow time for kids to engage in a variety of games and activities. It is divided into two segments:

1. ***Skill Play*** – The goal of this segment is to provide a nice blend of races, relays, and other games that target various muscle groups and promote cardio movement, strength, flexibility, balance, agility and coordination. Each day, you will have the option to choose from a list of 5 or 6 activities. Directions for how to play each of these activities are included in the *Physical Activities Description Appendix.*

2. ***Sport Play*** – During this segment, kids have the opportunity to play any number of different sports. The group should decide as a whole what sports they want to play, but you may choose to give them 4 or 5 options from the list included in the *Sport List Appendix.* You may choose to play the same sport for several sessions to allow time for dividing into teams and organizing a simple round-robin tournament, or you and your group may prefer to try something new each day. It is important that you periodically review the Physical Activity Recommendations from Chapter 6 with the group to make sure everyone understands that the main goal of this time is to have fun.

Block III: Wrapping Up This final block of the Lessons from the Field serves to calm the kids as they wind down from their physical activity and prepare to transition to the final phase of the day. Bring the kids together for a bit of quiet stretching. (This time also can serve as a catch-up time in case any of the activities have taken more time than expected.) The Wrapping Up segment concludes with the final R&R Huddle of the day. Take no more than 5 minutes to:

- **Recap** one or two key moments from the Lessons from the Field.

- **Reconnect** kids back to the theme unit.

- **Reset** and transition kids to the Cool-Down, Reflection time.

Cool-Down

The Cool-Down phase of the program includes the final activities of the day and signals the end of the PLUS day. It has three sections:

Reflection

Most organized youth sport teams end their practice or games with a few didactic yells from the coach: "Don't forget to turn in your uniform. Practice next Thursday night at the baseball field." Kids need an opportunity to wind down from their activities and to reflect on their experiences.

This portion of the Cool-Down allows time to highlight any teachable moments that may have arisen during the day and to make connections between the different sections of the day. It is especially important, during this time, to reconnect the *Lessons from the Field* with the core values of the program and the program as a whole if you have not already done so. Don't assume that kids will naturally make connections; explicitly draw out those connections for them. If you noticed a good example of several kids working together, point it out the group.

This time also provides an opportunity for kids to ask questions and to reflect on the day. For each reflection, a few questions are suggested that you can use to begin a dialogue. Dialogue is important because it stimulates the kids' thinking about issues of fairness, respect, and working together as a team.

Goal-setting

Goal-setting is one of the most important aspects of the PLUS program and opportunities for kids to set personal goals are sprinkled throughout the day. This goal-setting time, however, is set aside each day to give you an opportunity to work with the group to set team and individual goals and to help kids track their progress toward those goals. There is space in the Player Portfolios for kids to keep track of their personal and team goals.

Cool-Down Ritual

This ritual is a great way to consistently bring closure to the day. Suggestions for this final activity are included at the end of each day to help you bring the group together in a fun and supportive way.

Summary

Each PLUS component is designed to support the goals of the program — to create a caring community, to promote core values, to foster intrinsic motivation, to enhance literacy appreciation and moral theme comprehension, and to encourage physical activity. The PLUS framework, outlined above, provides a vital structure to the program. Understanding how all the components interact and relate to one another is critical for running a successful program. Be sure that you become familiar with all of the components before you begin the first curriculum unit. Once you've got a feel for the program components and the structure of the days, PLUS will come to life for you and the kids you serve. Remember: Keep it fun and fair! Enjoy the program!

SECTION IV

SPORT-BASED ACTIVITIES

CHAPTER NINE

The PLUS Youth Development Model

The Sports PLUS Youth Development Program is a comprehensive, integrated and developmental sport-based educational program that draws upon longstanding educational theory and researchbased educational practice that serves school-aged children. The PLUS Philosophy states that sports offer a positive opportunity as an educational medium to teach prosocial values such as teamwork and responsibility. The PLUS Core Principles serve as a guide for training and evaluating all community stakeholders, guide adoption of policies, inform how resources such as the distribution of playing time and positions are allocated.

PLUS 5 Core Operating Principles (COP)

Philosophy

The philosophy of our program defines why we are doing what we are doing and what we want to accomplish. In this sense, our program's philosophy drives all of our decisions and serves as a template as we think about issues ranging from distribution of playing time to how we address social and moral issues as a team and provide opportunities for learning.

Psychology

This important component of the learning process suggests that we need to be cognizant of how children learn in general, and, specifically, how children learn important program goals such as teamwork and responsibility. The PLUS Model turns to and employs the common theories of how people learn including the Social Learning Theory, The Behavioral Learning Theory and the Cognitive Development Learning Theory.

Pedagogy

How we "teach and coach" can be understood as our pedagogy. If one of our goals is to teach teamwork, for example, it is important to explore the best ways to teach the concept of working together. Our team's pedagogy takes into account our team's philosophy and psychology as well as our program's outcome goals.

Program

Basically, all of the activities that we design including practices, team meetings, team orientations, readings and rituals make up what we call our Program. The program activities are the places in which the learning takes place. It is important to expand our vision of what it means to play on our team. Sports can be much more than practices and games. The "coach as teacher" understands that within the program or season there are many ways to bring the team together and provide opportunities for learning.

Proof

Valid sport-based programs seek to prove their validity. The new science of sport-based learning provides tools for coaches and teachers to define their program's outcome goals (i.e., teamwork, respect, responsibility), and design pre-and-post tests to determine how successful their program was in promoting those goals. It is one thing to state that "sports are good for everyone" and quite another to announce teamwork as a desired outcome goal and have the ability to demonstrate how well the program did to advance team players' understandings of teamwork.

PLUS Outcome Goals

If community, for example, is of critical importance, then we can define exactly what community looks like and design distinct activities that promote community. In an effort to design sports to promote overall development, The PLUS Youth Development Model has defined five outcome goals as important: community, character, intrinsic motivation, physical health, and moral theme comprehension and literacy.

Community

A sense of community is defined by how each member of the team is known, needed, cared for, and by their opportunity to shape the environment.

Character

Character is defined as the development of the social and emotional skills necessary to make good decisions. The PLUS Model employs five values: Teamwork, Respect, Responsibility, Fair Play and Perseverance.

Intrinsic Motivation

Sports PLUS seeks to cultivate a selfreferenced approach to motivation (what the research literature calls a "task or mastery orientation"), that is built upon a cyclical pattern of personal goal setting, monitoring, and reformulation.

Health and Physical Development

The benefits of physical activity are well-documented. Research suggests that a physically active child has a more positive self-image, greater self-confidence, and demonstrates improvement in motor skills, cognitive functioning (Etnier et al., 1997) and health-related fitness. Studies from the American Council on Exercise have shown that physically active children also are more likely to become physically active adults.

Literacy and Moral Theme Comprehension

The literacy component of the Sports PLUS Program attempts to accomplish two central goals. First, it attempts to increase childrens' interest in and appreciation for literature by exposing them to the kinds of stories they like and are interested in — namely, sport stories. Secondly, Sports PLUS attempts to increase students' moral theme comprehension by providing them with a script for considering the important elements regarding the moral of the story. Learning to ask critical comprehension questions of a text allows students to consistently extract the moral of future stories they read or in which they are involved.

PLUS Theme Units

The PLUS Program is divided into the following five Theme Units.

- Teamwork

- Respect

- Responsibility

- Fair Play

- Perseverance

PLUS Program Activities

The five theme units Teamwork, Respect, Responsibility, Fair Playand Perseverance are organized into 50 sessions — 10 sessions for each of the five Theme Units. Each session is further divided into three sections Lessons from Literature, Lessons from the Field and Lessons from Adventure. The three lessons in each session are designed to flow together and cover similar content through different methodologies. Although the sessions are ideally presented in order and in their entirety, we tried to create resources that could be used to meet the goals of your particular program. What do your students need? How much time do you have? What space is available to you? Some programs will be able to incorporate two lessons from a session back-toback on the same day. Others may only be able to do one lesson a week. The phases are interrelated, but each plays an integral role within the five Theme Units — Teamwork, Respect, Responsibility, Fair Play, and Perseverance.

- Lessons from Literature

- Lessons from the Field

- Lessons from Adventure

- Sports Short and Theme Books

- You Make the Call

- Instant Replays

- Sport Extras

- Quote of the Week

- Respect & Responsibility Huddle

PLUS Learning Cycle

In the PLUS Approach we call this daily rhythm the PLUS Cycle, which consists of a Warm-up followed by an Activity concluded with a Cool-down. This consistent structure provides the youth leaders with continuous opportunities to gather the team, reflect on the process and set new goals. The PLUS Cycle is where group dialogue takes place.

1. The *Warm-up* phase of the cycle allows the coach to quiet the chaos and direct the social and psychological attention of the children towards the goals of the day.

2. The *Activity* phase is the active part of the practice or game where teachable moments occur.

3. The *Cool-down* meeting provides the team with an opportunity to reflect, dialogue, and set new goals, and to put the PLUS Cycle in motion once again.

Viewed in this way, the PLUS Cycle allows the team and coach to transition from one activity to another. Most importantly, the PLUS Cycle allows the coach to be a respectful teacher.

CHAPTER TEN

Theme Unit 1: Tackling Teamwork

Session 10:
Introduction to Sports PLUS

Overview

Instructor's Notes: *Be sure to review this set of activities before starting this Sports PLUS Session. Directions for how to facilitate each activity are provided, but it is important that you become familiar with them so that you may more effectively lead the group.*

During group discussions, be sure to record all thoughts and ideas on a blackboard or newsprint. Remember that when students are working in their Player Portfolios, spelling, grammar, and penmanship are, relatively speaking, unimportant, so don't dwell on those details or you risk making Sports PLUS into MoreSchool.

The first lessons of the Sports PLUS program concentrate on introducing the group to the theme of Teamwork and on beginning the process of bringing the group together. For most Sports PLUS programs, this represents the first days of a new group. Students may or may not know each other. In programs where they do know each other, there are activities designed to help them to know one another better.

The first days of any new program are critical for setting expectations and developing a positive learning climate. The theme of teamwork offers a good place to begin creating this culture. The goals of the first session are two-fold: to help the group members get to know each other, and to introduce the basic concepts of the program.

This session begins with the *Quote of the Week.* Because this is the first *Quote of the Week,* you will need to spend a few moments explaining the structure and purpose of this activity.

Getting Started

One of the first questions we get from staff is, "How do I get started?" No matter how much you read and study this manual and the lesson plans, the question remains. While we can't predict precisely what you can expect, we offer an outline to follow each day. The outline provides structure and demonstrates how to introduce the schedule, components, activities and tone of the program. Remember that your students may also be a bit apprehensive, not knowing quite what to expect. There will always be some business to attend to on this first day — forms to be completed, attendance, making sure everyone is signed up, etc. You may want to do this immediately, even as each student enters the group. Once this is out of the way, any other specific school or program business or procedures should be taken care of.

Introduction to the Sports PLUS program

Encourage students to sit in a circle. Welcome them to the group and briefly describe the five Sports PLUS values — Teamwork Respect, Responsibility, Fair Play and Perseverance. They will be reading about and discussing each of these values. Even more important, the group will work to create a culture in which behaviors that support these values are practiced. Ask the group what being a respectful group means to them, encouraging them to provide specific examples.

Next explain that the stories, activities, sports, and group discussions will focus on the Sports PLUS themes. Give a general description of the program and the various program components.

Refer to the curriculum outline for brief descriptions:

- **Reading** — You Make the Call, Instant Replay, Sports Shorts, Sports Extras, Theme Books (show the books or give an example of each).
- **Activities** — cooperative problem solving and icebreaker games.
- **Sports** — the various sports you have planned for the program.
- **Player Portfolios** — students will receive their Player Portfolios during the Lessons from Literature.

Finally, give a brief outline of the first day and describe how each subsequent day will be structured:

- The *Warm-up* period starts the day off with a short introduction to the theme and topics of the lesson. It may include an icebreaker or a team-building activity.
- The *Activity* period includes either a reading activity, a physical or sports activity, or an adventure activity.
- The *Cool-down* closes the session with a brief reflection about the day and a forward look to the next session.

Session 1:
Introduction to Sports PLUS
Lessons from Literature

Warm-up	Cool-down
Begin the PLUS Cycle (10-15 min.)	Continue the PLUS Cycle (5-10 min.)
• Session Overview	• Reflection
• Toss A Name Game	• Go-Round

Activity	**Materials**
Lessons from Literature (25-30 min.)	2 poster-sized pieces of paper for each group of 3 or 4 students, markers of assorted colors, one dictionary per group (or you can write the definition of teamwork on a chalkboard or poster; optional: magazines and newspapers — to be cut up), scissors, glue
• Culture Being	

Warm-up

Quote of the Week

Individual glory is insignificant when compared to achieving victory as a team.

— *Dot Richardson*
(Dot Richardson was the captain of the first
United States OLumpic softball team and
is currently an orthopedic surgeon.)

Follow the 5 steps of the Quote of the Week Format:

1. **Write the Quote of the Week:** Bring the group together into a circle, and write the Quote on the blackboard.

2. **Think about the Quote as a group:** Spend two or three minutes talking with the students about what they think the quote means. Ask them to share answers to the following question:

   • Do you agree with what the quote says?

3. **Pair up to talk about the Quote:** Have students separate into pairs. Ask them to spend about five minutes discussing the following questions with their partners. Explain that they will be sharing their answers with the whole group, so they may choose to write their answers in their Player Portfolios. (Be sure to walk around the groups, listen, and offer help where needed.):

   • Can you think of examples of when a team victory is more important than an individual accomplishment?

   • How do you define "team"?

4. **Share answers with the whole group:** Come together as a large group and share the answers from each of the pairs. Everyone who wants to should have an opportunity to share their answers.

5. **Reflect individually about the Quote:** Allow the students two to three minutes to reflect individually by writing a response to the following Journal Questions in their Player Portfolios:

   • Have you ever been a member of a team? If so, when?

   • How will your individual accomplishments in Sports PLUS contribute to the overall success of the group?

Tip

Remember that during a brainstorming session, there is no such thing as a wrong answer. All ideas are listened to and treated with respect. Brainstorming is an excellent strategy to get students thinking, listening to others, using one idea to spark another, etc. Depending on how well your group is working together as a team, you can impose more or less structure and rules on the session. If students are treating one another with a good deal of respect, you might just let the ideas fly, asking a couple of students to write them down. On the other hand, if members of your group have not yet begun to trust each other, or if respect is still an issue the group needs to work on, you might need to impose a more structured approach, such as having students raise their hands before offering an idea.

Brainstorming Procedures

The following steps are an effective way to begin a *brainstorming session*.

- **On Your Mark** — Make the purpose of the session known and decide on the topic. Establish a time limit between five and 15 minutes.

- **Get Set** — Review the rules for brainstorming.

- **Go** — Have each member offer any words, ideas or phrases that are directly related to the topic. Record all ideas so that the whole group can clearly see them. Continue to brainstorm until the team feels it has exhausted all its ideas. Finally, facilitate a discussion that clarifies and addresses all the ideas.

Brainstorming Rules

- Welcome all ideas, no matter how crazy or silly they appear to be.

- Suspend judgment of all ideas. Anyone may ask for a clarification of any idea on the list, but continue to suspend criticism.

- Promote piggybacking of ideas. Do this by encouraging students to generate as many ideas as possible by building on one another's suggestions.

Setup

Why do we need rules in sports? Begin by brainstorming rules for various types of sports and write them on a board or poster. Students will probably think of the rules of a game, how the game is played. Ask them to think of rules of conduct that help to create a good and positive team atmosphere — for example, showing up on time for practice, wearing the right equipment, being supportive of teammates, no put-downs, etc.

Play

1. Separate into small groups of three to four students (you can include staff, too). Go through the guidelines for brainstorming.

2. Have students open their Player Portfolios to the Create Your Own Team sheet in the Teamwork section.

3. Instruct each group to create a team name and then develop a list of four team rules of conduct, along with consequences for breaking each rule. Set a time limit of 10-15 minutes.

4. After students have finished, have each group present its rules and consequences to the whole group. Allow questions and discussion of each team's ideas.

5. Ask students to explain why they chose these rules and what they think might happen to a team that did not have these rules.

Discussion Questions

Reconvene the group and continue to discuss the need for team rules. Select one or two of the questions below to focus the short discussion:

1. What would happen if a team did not have any rules?

2. What are some of the most important rules? Why?

3. Can you think of rules that you think are unfair? Explain.

4. Why do we have to have consequences for rules?

5. How do the consequences fit each rule?

6. Ask the group if they can think of other groups that have rules. What are the rules? Have them discuss why the rules are important to each group.

When you think that the group has an adequate understanding of and commitment to creating rules, ask which of the rules they think should be adopted for the whole group. Write these on a poster and hang it in a prominent place in the room. Add to the list as necessary during the course of your program and refer back to it often to remind students of their commitments.

Once you have a few rules listed, talk about why some rules might be more important than others.

Discuss the difference between the rules of conduct and rules of play. Ask students to think of the corresponding penalties or consequences for breaking some of the rules.

Cool-down

- **R&R Huddle** (5 min.)

- **Recap** by highlighting one or two key points that arose from the discussion.

- **Reconnect** by having the group consider the importance of rules for a safe and enjoyable Sports PLUS experience.

- **Reset** and get ready for the next lesson.

Session 1: **Introduction to Sports PLUS** **Lessons from the Field**	
Warm-up Begin the PLUS Cycle (5 min.) • Session Overview • Touching Base on Teamwork **Activity** Lessons from the Field (25-30 min.) • Sports Activity	**Cool-down** Continue the PLUS Cycle (5-10 min.) • Reflection • Go-Round **Materials** Sports equipment

Warm-up

Touching Base On Teamwork (5 min.)

Ask students to think about the previous lesson. What can they do today to bring the Lessons from Literature into their work together in the sports activity?

Activity

Lessons from the Field
Sports Activity

Block I: Getting Started (15 20 min.)

Block I is given an extended amount of time on this first day so that you can explain the different forms of getting started. You may want to spend the entire time in Block I — see how your time goes.

On the first day, players will learn how to measure their resting heart rates (RHR). They will also set baselines for their RHR, number of sit-ups/push-ups/lunges/calf raises, and number of jumps during jump rope. Each day they will try to improve upon their Past Personal Best (PPB) by achieving their Future Best Goal (FBG) and by tracking progress toward that goal in the physical activities progress chart located in the back of their Player Portfolios. Take one minute to make sure all participants turn to the back of their portfolios and locate the progress charts. Explain to them that they will be using this chart each time you meet to do physical activities. Be sure to emphasize the importance of keeping track of their progress by using the chart.

Stand together in a circle for all *Getting Started* activities (except for jogging). Have players partner up, with one player doing the activity and the partner keeping count and giving encouragement. Be sure that players have their Portfolios handy so that they can record their progress. Encourage them to clap and cheer for their teammates to create an enthusiastic environment. You may also choose to include music.

- **Measure resting heart rate (RHR)** — Spend a few minutes showing players how to find their pulses, either on their necks or wrists. Explain that you will be giving them a few seconds to count how many times their hearts beat. Take a moment to allow them to sit quietly on the floor and find their pulses. Give them 30 seconds to count their heartbeats.

- **Record, check in and set goals** — Allow a couple of minutes for players to record their RHRs in their Player Portfolios.

- **Jog (2-3 min.)** — This can be done as a lap or in place as a circle.

- **Stretch (2-3 min.)** — Be sure to include stretches for the major muscle groups.

- **Strength/Endurance (1 min.)** — On this first day, players will set baseline numbers for the four Strength/Endurance activities (push-ups, sit-ups, lunges, calf raises), but usually, you will only choose one or two. Players will work in pairs. One member of the pair will have 30 seconds to do as many of the activities as they can. Their partner will cheer them on and count for them.

- **Jump Rope (4 min.)** — Again, players will work in pairs, with one person jumping and the other person counting and cheering. They should have three to four sets of 30-45 seconds of jumping rope.

- **Track personal progress** — Have players record their totals for steps five and six in their Player Portfolios. These totals will represent their baseline achievements, or their Past Personal Bests (PPB). Each day, players will check their progress from the previous session and will set a Future Personal Best Goal (FBG) to work toward for next time. Be sure to remind them about setting realistic goals (for example, adding one or two to their baseline, as opposed to ten).

Block II: Structured Play (30 min.)

Skill Play (10 min.)

Choose one or two of the following activities to play today. You can refer back to the Physical Activities Description in the Appendix at the back of the book for instructions on how to run the activities. Encourage players to cheer for each other, and include music if you wish.

- Jump Rope Relay

- Sack Race

- Limbo

- Dribbling Relay

- Standing Broad Jump

- Backwards Run/Walk Relay

Sport Play (10 min.)

Generally, the time allotted for this will be longer. On this first day, consider this time frame as an opportunity to introduce players to the topic, rather than have them actually get into a sport. On a typical day, as a group, you will decide which sport you want to play. Select from the Sports List contained in the Appendix at the back of the book. Be sure to periodically review with the group the Physical Activities Recommendations for Sport from Chapter Six.

Cool-down

If time permits, close the day with a few minutes of stretching while conducting the following R&R Huddle.

- **Recap** one or two key moments from the Lessons from the Field.

- **Reconnect** players back to the theme unit.

- **Reset** and transition players to the Cool-down, Reflection time.

  OR

- **Reflection**

Use this time to highlight teachable moments you observed during the day and to give players an opportunity to share their experiences about Sports PLUS during the day. The following questions can serve as a guide:

- What did you like about today?

- What did you learn today?

- How did we show teamwork today?

- What are one or two ways we can show better teamwork next time?

Session 1: Introduction to Sports PLUS Lessons from Adventure	
Warm-up Begin the PLUS Cycle (5 min.) • Session Overview • Toss A Name Game	**Cool-down** Continue the PLUS Cycle (5-10 min.) • Reflection • Go-Round
Activity Lessons from Adventure (25-30 min.) • Culture Being	**Materials** 10 soft throwable items (stuffed toys, fleece balls, Nerf-type balls . . .)

Warm-up

Toss a Name Game
Setup

Tip

Even players who come from the same school and know each other well can benefit from participating in a name game. It is a nice way to break the ice and bring some action to the program. It is also an opportunity to emphasize that speaking to each other politely is an integral part of the program.

Play

1. Have players form a circle, staff included. Begin setting a fun, cooperative tone —" Can anyone in the group imagine a team where people don't know each other's names? We are going to see what might happen if our team was like that. I'm going to pass the ball to someone without saying their name and that person will pass the ball on to someone else, again without saying their name."

2. Add all the balls and let the passing continue for a minute or two. Quiet the group and ask players how the game felt: "Did it feel a little chaotic? Was anyone passed a ball that they weren't expecting?

    Now we're going to play this game again to make sure we all know who's who here."

3. Say to the group: "This time, I'll start by saying my name and handing the ball to the person next to me. That person will state his or her name and pass the ball to the next person. This goes on until the ball gets back to me. "

4. Say to the group: "Now toss the ball gently to someone across the circle whose name you remember. Before you toss the ball, say that person's name. That person catches the ball, says "Thank you, _____ (person's name)," then tosses the ball on to someone else. This tossing and thanking continues for a few minutes before more balls are added. Eventually all the balls will be in play and everyone will be calling out each other's names. We'll continue this action for a few minutes."

5. Ask the players to toss you all the balls. Now ask who can go around the circle and name everyone. After the second volunteer, mixup the circle. Give every student who wants to the chance to name everyone. The more the names are repeated, the better they will be remembered.

Activity

Lessons from Adventure
Culture Being
(see Player Portfolio)

The Culture Being is an activity designed to engage players in the concept of their future participation in Sports PLUS. Participants in this activity produce a poster with words and phrases that are examples of how they feel about their Sports PLUS environment and how they would like to shape it. This Being poster should have at least one comment from everyone or have comments on which everyone strongly agrees. Use the suggested focus prompts to allow players to generate ideas themselves. The core Sports PLUS principles such as *Respect and Teamwork* need not necessarily be written up. The primary goal of this activity is for players to take ownership of what they come up with. The leader(s) should help make the connection between what players put on paper and what they want to have happen in the group. Keep in mind that it is the process by which they do this — not the result — that matters most.

Play

1. Choose a team name. Bring the group together in a circle. On poster board have the players write suggestions for a team name for their entire Sports PLUS group. Use these ideas to choose a team name. Players then decide on an object or shape to represent their group. Most likely, this object will be representative of their team name (e.g., a tiger for the Tigers; a basketball for the Tossers, etc.), but it does not have to. Some other examples are: an outline of a person, a book, a smiley face, a soccer field, or a dog.

2. Using the following focus prompts as a guide, record players' responses onto a chalk board or newsprint. Be sure to write ALL responses to the focus prompts on the board.

•   One thing I like about being on a team...

•   One way I want our team/group to treat each other is...

•   One thing I don't want to happen on this team is...

- One thing I hope I can do this year is…

- One thing I hope our team can do this year is…

  Help players come up with concrete examples of behaviors by asking, "What does that look like?" Explain to them that "We're a team and because we are a team, it's important for everyone to know what everyone else wants, to help make us come together as one."

  After using these prompts, explain to the players that these ideas are part of what makes up "our team culture." Ask for volunteers to share their answers to the following question:

- What is a team culture? (Use concrete examples from players' responses to the previous questions to help define "culture.")

  Explain to the players that "The things we have been talking about are ways we can help each other to feel good, lift each other up, and take care of one another. If we don't do these things, our culture will begin to break down. It's important to know what makes each other feel good, but it's also important to know what makes each other hurt." Ask for volunteers to share their responses to the following question:

3. What are some things we don't want to happen on this team? List several things, again probing for specific examples.

4. **Using what is now on the board or paper decorate your *Culture Being*.** After discussing what the players want and don't want to happen during their time in the Sports PLUS program, invite them to decorate their shape with all the things they have been talking about. The behaviors that the players felt were important to include should be written inside of the object. The behaviors that the group decided should NOT happen in the Sports PLUS program should be written outside the object. Everyone in the group (adults and players alike) should then sign their names somewhere on the culture being.

Cool-down

- **R&R Huddle** (5 min.)

- **Recap** by asking for a few volunteers to comment about what they learned.

- **Reconnect** by asking the group to raise their hands and "sign the contract." By doing this you are asking the group to agree on the poster and to agree that it is important to carry through with the ideas presented there. You may want to use the "sign the contract" often and allow it to become part of your daily ritual.

- **Reset** by bringing the group together and transitioning to the next activity.

- **Reflection**

Reflection provides a consistent opportunity for you to explicitly draw connections between the program components and teamwork, as well as between teamwork and the rest of the core values. For example, if you noticed several players working together as a group, point it out during *reflection*. If you thought there were specific things the group could do to better practice teamwork, bring these up at this time.

Reflection also is a time for the kids to share their thoughts and experiences with the program for that day. Challenge them with interesting and meaningful questions, such as:

How did you feel when…?

- What did you learn today?

- Is there anything you wished could have been different?

This time should not be lengthy, but it is important to give players regular and consistent opportunities to reflect on and dialogue about their experiences in the Sports PLUS program.

Cool-down Ritual

Go-Round

Ask the players to stand in a circle for one final closing activity. Use a quick go-round format — ask the group what they think about the first day of the Sports PLUS program. Does anyone have any questions? Was it similar to or different from what they expected? Start with the person to your left and go around the circle. Thank them for coming.

Don't forget to collect the Player Portfolios if you haven't already done so.

Homework Assignment

As a fun homework assignment, ask the players and staff to begin looking in local newspapers and magazines, and to listen for stories on the radio and television that present examples of good teamwork. Ask everyone to bring these examples to the group when they find them. The group will be starting a collection of these articles and stories for use throughout the program.

Session 2:
Teamwork Posters

Overview

> **Instructor's Notes:** *Be sure to review this set of activities before starting this Sports PLUS Session. Directions for how to facilitate each activity are provided, but it is important that you become familiar with them so that you may more effectively lead the group.*
>
> *During group discussions, be sure to record all thoughts and ideas on a blackboard or newsprint. Remember that when students are working in their Player Portfolios, spelling, grammar, and penmanship are, relatively speaking, unimportant, so don't dwell on those details or you risk making Sports PLUS into MoreSchool.*

The *Sports Short* reading talks about what it feels like when a game or activity is not very fun, why this happens, and what we can do about it. The focus of this story is to help students develop skills to handle not-so-positive sporting (and other) experiences. Negative experiences can have a lasting impact on children. Helping them to realize that they can control their reactions to those experiences is an important step in positive development.

Whiz Bangin' Day continues to explore the meaning of Teamwork and the process of building a positive team atmosphere for your program. The Adventure lesson begins with a fun energizing activity that helps students reconnect with each other and sets the tone for cooperative fun. *Teamwork Posters* is a great activity to get students thinking about what teamwork means. They will form small groups and create posters to represent their own definitions of teamwork. Encourage students to also consider what they hope to learn about teamwork during the next nine Sports PLUS days.

The Cool-down activity gives the group a chance to gain familiarity and trust in the Sports PLUS cycle, while bringing closure to the day:

Session 2: **Teamwork Posters** **Lessons from Literature**	
Warm-up Begin the PLUS Cycle (10-15 min.)	**Cool-down** Continue the PLUS Cycle (5-10 min.)
• Session Overview	• Reflection
• Toss A Name Game	**Materials**
Activity Lessons from Literature (25-30 min.)	2 poster-sized pieces of paper for each group Sports equipment
• You Make the Call — *One-on-One*	

Warm-up

Quote of the Week

The whole is greater than the sum of its parts.

— Anonymous

Follow the 5 steps of the Quote of the Week Format (See the *Getting Started* Chapter 8 for additional explanation):

1. **Write the Quote of the Week:** Bring the group together into a circle, and write the Quote on the blackboard.

2. **Think about the Quote as a group:** Spend two to three minutes talking with the students about what they think the quote means. Ask them to share answers to the group for the following question:

   • What do you think this quote has to do with teamwork?

3. **Pair up to talk about the Quote:** Have students separate into pairs. Ask them to spend about five minutes discussing the following questions with their partners. Explain that they will be sharing their answers with the whole group, so they may choose to write their answers in their Player Portfolios. (Be sure to walk around the groups, listen, and offer help where needed.):

   • Give an example of when you have seen the quote to be true. Feel to make something up if you don't have a specific example.

   • Why is teamwork important in sports?

4. **Share answers with the whole group:** Come together as a large group and share the answers from each of the pair groups. Everyone who wants to should have an opportunity to share their answers.

5. **Reflect individually about the Quote:** Take two to three minutes for students to reflect individually by writing a

response to the following Journal Questions in their Player Portfolios:

- How do you help contribute to the success of the group?

- In what activities besides sports is teamwork important?

Activity

Lessons from Literature
You Make the Call
One-on-One
(see Player Portfolio)

Key Concepts

- Fairness
- Respect
- Teamwork

Setup

Bring the group together to sit in a circle. If there is time, use one or two of the following questions to help set the tone before reading the story:

- Have you ever been told that you couldn't participate in something?

- If you were excluded from an activity, what are some ways you might handle that situation?

Next, read the story aloud and with enthusiasm to the whole group.

Discussion Questions:

Separate students into groups by having them count off by threes (or fours depending on the group size). Spend a couple of minutes distributing their Player Portfolios and pencils. Ask one or two volunteers to help.

Using their Player Portfolios, have students discuss and write answers to the following questions in their small groups. It is important to remember that spelling, grammar, and penmanship are NOT important during this activity.

1. Who are the main characters in this story?

2. What is the main problem these characters face?

3. What is Marshall's suggestion for solving the problem?

4. Marshall suggests one way to solve the problem so that no one feels left out. What are some other ways that the problem might be handled?

5. What would happen if the problem were handled in that way?

   • How would Jim feel?

   • How would Marshall feel?

   • How would Steffon feel?

6. If you were Marshall, what solution would you choose to handle the situation?

7. What do you think would be difficult about speaking up if you were Marshall?

8. If you were Steffon, what are two ways that you might respond to Marshall's suggestion?

Group Share:

1. After the small groups have had time to discuss each question, gather the groups together to sit in one large circle.

2. Ask each small group to share their suggestions for solving the problem, using students' answers to number 4 above. (As suggestions are given, you or a volunteer should write them on poster paper for all to see.)

3. Once all the different solutions have been laid out, spend a few minutes discussing the consequences of each solution, using students' answers to question number 5 as a guide.

4. As a group, choose the best solution (i.e., the most good for the most people).

5. Finally, as a group, complete the following two focus prompts on poster paper.

- One thing we can take from this story is that we should...

- We should be careful not to...

Cool-down

- **R&R Huddle** (5 min.)

- **Recap** with one or two key points from the previous discussion. Consider the following ideas: Being a good teammate involves helping out and supporting other members of the team. But what happens if someone isn't a member of our team. Should we try to help and support them? When someone is feeling left out, do you think it is important to try to include them? Why or why not?

- **Reconnect** with the following focus prompt: One thing I can do to make sure I am including others in a game or an activity is...

- **Reset** and get ready for the next lesson.   .

Session 2: Introduction to Sports PLUS Lessons from the Field	

Warm-up
Begin the PLUS Cycle (5 min.)
   • Session Overview
   • Touching Base on Teamwork
Activity
Lessons from the Field (25-30 min.)
   • Sports Activity
	Cool-down
	Continue the PLUS Cycle (5-10 min.)
	   • Reflection
	Materials
	Sports equipment

Warm-up

Touching Base On Teamwork (5 min.)

Ask players to think about the previous lesson. What can they do today to bring the Lessons from Literature into their work together in the sports activity?

Activity

Lessons from the Field—Sports Activity

Block I: Getting Started (5 min.)

On the first day, players will learn how to measure their resting heart rates (RHR). They will also set baselines for their RHR, number of sit-ups/pushups/lunges/calf raises, and number of jumps during jump rope. Each day they will try to improve upon their Past Personal Best (PPB) by achieving their Future Best Goal (FBG) and by tracking progress toward that goal in the physical activities progress chart located in the back of their Player Portfolios. Take one minute to make sure all participants turn to the back of their portfolios and locate the progress charts. Explain to them that they will be using this chart each time you meet to do physical activities. Be sure to emphasize the importance of keeping track of their progress by using the chart.

Stand together in a circle for all Getting Started activities (except jogging). Have players partner up, with one player doing the activity and the partner keeping count and giving encouragement. Be sure players have their Portfolios handy so that they can record their progress. Encourage them to clap and cheer for their teammates to create an enthusiastic environment. You may also choose to include music.

- **Measure resting heart rate (RHR)** — Spend a few minutes showing players how to find their pulses, either on their necks or wrists. Explain that you will be giving them a few seconds to count how many times their hearts beat. Take a moment to allow them to sit quietly on the floor and find their pulses. Give them 30 seconds to count their heartbeats.

- **Record, check in and set goals** — Allow a couple of minutes for players to record their RHRs in their Player Portfolios.

- **Jog** (2-3 min.) — This can be done as a lap or in place as a circle.

- **Stretch** (2-3 min.) — Be sure to include stretches for the major muscle groups.

- **Strength/Endurance** (1 min.) — On this first day, players will set baseline numbers for the four Strength/Endurance activities (push-ups, sit-ups, lunges, calf raises), but usually, you will only choose one or two. They will work in pairs. One member of the pair will have 30 seconds to do as many of the activities as they can. Their partner will cheer them on and count for them.

- **Jump Rope** (4 min.) — Again, players will work in pairs, with one person jumping and the other person counting and cheering. They should have three to four sets of 30-45 seconds of jumping rope.

- **Track personal progress** — Have players record their totals for steps five and six in their Player Portfolios. These totals will represent their baseline achievements, or their Past Personal Bests (PPB). Each day, playerswillcheck their progress from the previous session and will set a Future Personal Best Goal (FBG) to work toward for next time. Be sure to remind them about setting realistic goals (for example, adding one or two to their baseline, as opposed to 10).

Block II: Structured Play (30 min.)

Skill Play (10 min.)

Choose one or two of the following activities to play today. You can refer back to the *Physical Activities Description Appendix* for instructions on how to run the activities. Encourage players to cheer for each other, and include music if you wish.

- 3-legged Race

- Water Balloon Toss

- Sprint/stride Runs

- Crab Walk

- Kick Up Your Heels Relay

Sport Play (20 min.)

As a group, decide which sport you want to play today. Select from the sport list contained in the *Sports List Appendix*. Be sure to periodically review with the group the Physical Activities Recommendations for Sport from Chapter Six.

Cool-down

If time permits, close the day with a few minutes of stretching while conducting the following R&R Huddle.

- **Recap** one or two key moments from the Lessons from the Field.

- **Reconnect** players back to the theme unit.

- **Reset** and transition players to the Cool-down, Reflection time.

  OR

- **Reflection**

Use this time to highlight teachable moments you observed during the day and to give players an opportunity to share their experiences about Sports PLUS during the day. The following questions can serve as a guide:

- What did you like about today?

- What did you learn today?

- How did we show teamwork today?

- What are one or two ways we can show better teamwork next time?

Whiz, Bang!

Bring the group together in a circle (standing). Begin the game by cupping your hands together as if hiding a small object. Tell the group, "I am holding in my hands a small energy orb. We are going to pass this orb around the circle so we can all share the energy. However, before we get started, I need to share with you the rules for passing our orb."

Play

Tell the group that there are a couple of ways to pass the imaginary orb — they can Whiz the orb or Bang it. To Whiz it, simply wave your hand towards the person to your right or left while saying "[Receiver's name], Whiz."

The person receiving the whiz can choose to Whiz it on in the same direction or Bang it back. To Bang the orb, place your palm flat and rigid in front of the imaginary orb and loudly say, "[Receiver's name], Bang!" This sends the orb back to the person who Whizzed it. This person now has the choice to Whiz it on in the opposite direction or Bang it back to the Banger.

Play the game for a few minutes, making sure everyone understands the directions. To make the game more fun, add some new methods for passing the energy:

- **Kerplink, Kerplunk** — to Kerplink, you'll send the orb across the circle as if shooting it into a hoop, saying, "[Receiver's name], Kerplink." The receiver will hold out his or her arms like a hoop and say "Kerplunk" as he or she receives the energy.

- **Whoosh, Aaah** — To Whoosh, send the energy to anyone in the circle with both hands in an underhanded motion, and say "[Receiver's name], Whoosh." The receiver will say "Aaah" as he or she captures the energy by cupping his or her hands.

If the group enjoys this activity, play it again and have players invent new ways to pass and catch the orb, and don't forget the sound effects.

Session 2: Teamwork Posters Lessons from Adventure	

Warm-up	Cool-down
Begin the PLUS Cycle (5 min.)	Continue the PLUS Cycle (5-10 min.)
• Session Overview	• Reflection
• Whiz, Bang!	• Go-Round
Activity	**Materials**
Lessons from Adventure (25-30 min.)	10 soft throwable items (stuffed toys, fleece balls, Nerf-type balls . . .)
• Teamwork Posters	

Activity

Lessons from Adventure
Teamwork Posters

Setup

Separate the groups into teams of three or four. Give each team a table to work on (or some open space on the floor), two pieces of paper, a dictionary (or write the definition of teamwork on a chalkboard) and some markers.

Play

1. Each group will use a dictionary to look up the meaning of teamwork. (Or read it off the board.)

2. Using this information and their own understanding of teamwork, players will create a poster to teach the rest of the group what teamwork means to them. The poster can be anything that the groups choose to represent teamwork. They can create a Being by tracing the outline of one of their bodies on the poster paper, cut out pictures from magazines if you have a collection to use, or make their own drawing. Encourage players to be creative.

3. Next, have players write words and phrases around their drawings to explain their understanding of teamwork. They should use their own words to define what teamwork means, not the words from the dictionary. They should also write words or phrases to illustrate how teamwork looks and sounds.

4. Remindplayers that this is a team project and they should spend a few minutes planning what they as a team want to create and how they are going to create it. All members of the team should be actively involved in the planning, decision-making, and production of the poster. Allow 15-20 minutes for the small groups to work.

5. Once the teams have completed their posters, give each group a few minutes to present their poster to the larger group and to explain their definitions, drawings, words and phrases. If time permits, allow some discussion and questions for each group.

6. Hang the posters around the room and refer back to them as often as necessary throughout the program to reinforce and remind players of their commitments. As the unit progresses, and their understanding of teamwork increases, have players add new ideas, words, and phrases to their posters.

7. Hang the "Sports PLUS Leader to Detractor Poster" for Teamwork. Reflect on the five-point scale and the connections between this scale and the players' posters. Utilize this scale to guide your reflections in all phases of the program.

Cool-down

- **R&R Huddle** (5 min.)

- **Recap** one or two important themes from the activity.

- **Reconnect** the themes to the topic of teamwork.

- **Reset** and transition to the next activity.

S.M.A.R.T. Goals
(see Player Portfolio)

Learning how to set and work toward goals is an important personal skill for anyone to have. Having a goal keeps us on task, gives us a clear direction, and helps us to monitor our progress. The S.M.A.R.T. Goal process provides an easy and understandable way to assess our goal-setting strategies. S.M.A.R.T. Goals are:

- Specific
- Measurable
- Achievable
- Relevant
- Timely

Explain what each letter means using the following descriptions as a guide to facilitate discussion:

Specific

First of all, a goal should be *specific* so that it is clear what needs to be accomplished. A basketball player who wants to become a better defender should carefully define his or her goal by choosing specific aspects of the game that he or she can improve. For example, holding the player that he or she is guarding to under eight points or making three steals per game are specific ways to be a better defender. A student who wants to become a better reader should choose specific goals like finishing a challenging book or making a grade of B or better on the next reading quiz.

Afterdescribingtheletter "S" askplayers to respond to the following questions in their Player Portfolios:

- Give one or two examples of goals that are NOT specific.
- Now try to make those goals more specific.

Ask for a few volunteers to share what they wrote. If goals are not specific enough, find ways to make them more specific.

Measurable

Secondly, goals should be *measurable*. Using the example of the basketball player above, keeping track of the opponent's points or counting the number of steals made in a game are ways to measure progress. When choosing a goal, ask yourself, "What are the ways you will be able to measure your progress?"

After describing the letter "M", ask players to choose one or two of the goals mentioned above and respond to the following question in their Player Portfolios:

• What is one way that I could measure that goal?

Ask for volunteers to share what they wrote. If necessary, work together as a group to make goals more measurable.

Achievable

Thirdly, goals should be *achievable* — setting goals that have little or no likelihood of being met will only lead to frustration and probably giving up. A beginning reader who sets a goal of reading Tolstoy's *War and Peace* will most likely fail. A beginning runner has little chance of completing a marathon, or running a mile in fewer than four minutes. The key to goalsetting is to set goals that are neither impossible to reach nor too easily met. Goals should be challenging enough that they require hard work to achieve them, but they should not be so high that accomplishing them is unrealistic. In short, goals should be challenging, yet achievable. When choosing a goal, ask yourself, "Will accomplishing this goal be a challenge for me?" and "Can I realistically expect to achieve this goal?"

After describing the letter "A", ask players to write responses to the following questions in their Player Portfolios:

• What are two examples of goals that are NOT achievable?

• Write examples of two goals that you could achieve?

Ask for volunteers to share what they wrote.

Relevant

Goals should be *relevant*. In keeping with the Sports PLUS values, goals must be worthy of our time and effort and should in some way make us better at what we do. Setting goals that do little to help us develop as people or that have negative consequences (e.g., learning how to hot-wire a car) are unworthy of our time and effort. When choosing a goal, ask yourself, "Is the goal I am setting relevant and meaningful to me? Is it a worthwhile pursuit?"

After describing the letter "R", ask players to list three goals in their Player Portfolios that are relevant to them.

Timely

Finally, when setting goals, keep in mind the *time frame* within which they should be accomplished. Some have said that goals are dreams with a timeline. Having an appropriate timeline to work within helps us to track progress toward achieving our goals and enables us to measure our true success. For example, setting a goal to read a book is very different than setting a goal to complete a book in one month. Students whosegoalistoreadachallengingbookwithinamonth will benefit from tracking their progress through the book as the days and weeks go by to ensure they are on schedule and are likely to achieve success. When choosing a goal, ask yourself, "How much time will it take to achieve my goal?" "When, specifically, will I take time to work on it?" and, "When can I reasonably expect to complete my goal?"

After describing the letter "T", ask players to select two or three of their goals and respond to the following question in their Player Portfolios:

- What is an appropriate timeline for this goal?

Ask for volunteers to share what they wrote. If necessary, work together as a group to help players choose an appropriate timeline.

1. After reviewing each description, explain to the players that goal-setting is an important part of the Sports PLUS program. Each day, you will be setting goals both individually and as a group to get practice at choosing goals that are S.M.A.R.T. Ask players to begin thinking about one or two

   S.M.A.R.T. Goals that would be important for the team. Let them know that during the goalsetting portion of the next session, you will be working together as a group to set one or two team goals for this theme unit.

Cool-down Ritual

Go-Round

Ask the players to stand in a circle for one final closing activity. Use a quick go-round format — ask each student to say one thing he or she has learned about teamwork today. Have them start with the person to their left and go around the circle. Thank them for coming.

Don't forget to collect the Player Portfolios if you haven't already done so.

Session 3:
Teamwork and the Player contract

Overview

Instructor's Notes: *Be sure to review this set of activities before starting this Sports PLUS Session. Directions for how to facilitate each activity are provided, but it is important that you become familiar with them so that you may more effectively lead the group.*

During group discussions, be sure to record all thoughts and ideas on a blackboard or newsprint. Remember that when students are working in their Player Portfolios, spelling, grammar, and penmanship are, relatively speaking, unimportant, so don't dwell on those details or you risk making Sports PLUS into MoreSchool.

The *Instant Replay* asks students to think about how a team and the coach can help players address their emotions when they are hurt and must leave the game. The complexity of the situation unfolds as the students are also asked to think of the point of view of the players who come in as substitutes. This activity helps them develop perspective-taking skills.

Slot Machine challenges three groups to work together toward success. In addition to bringing up important topics, such as working together for the good of the whole team and respecting the team goal over individual accomplishments, this activity challenges students to create a symbol to represent their understanding of teamwork.

Session 3: Teamwork and the Play Contract Lessons from Literature	
Warm-up Begin the PLUS Cycle (10-15 min.) • Session Overview • Quote of the Week **Activity** Lessons from Literature (25-30 min.) • Instant Replay — *The Chargers*	**Cool-down** Continue the PLUS Cycle (5-10 min.) • Reflection **Materials** Copies of *The Chargers,* nametags for all major characters and any minor characters

Warm-up

Quote of the Week

The most important measure of how good a game I played was how much better I'd made my teammates play.

— Bill Russell, former NBA Player

Instructor's Note

Bill Russell is one of the most legendary defensive players in basketball history. At six feet and ten inches, Russell dominated the NBA with his tremendous shot-blocking and rebounding abilities. Only Wilt Chamberlain gathered more rebounds than Russell did during an NBA career. While at the University of San Francisco, Russell helped his team win 57 out of 58 games between 1954 and 1956, before joining the Boston Celtics. As the Celtics' center, Russell led his team to 11 NBA championships in 13 years. From 1966 to 1969, he worked as a player-coach for the Celtics and became the first African-American head coach of any major league professional sports team.)

> — *World Book Encyclopedia,*
> *Contributor: Bob Logan, B.S., Sportswriter,*
> *(Arlington Heights, IL) Daily Herald.*

Follow the 5 steps of the Quote of the Week Format (See the Getting Started chapter for additional explanation):

1. **Write the Quote of the Week:** Bring the group together into a circle, and write the Quote on the blackboard.

2. **Think about the Quote as a group:** Spend two or three minutes talking with students about what they think the quote means. Ask them to share answers to the group for the following statement:

   - Think of a time you helped your teammates play better and complete the following sentence. One thing I did to help my teammates play better was...

3. **Pair up to talk about the Quote:** Have students separate into pairs. Ask them to spend about five minutes discussing the following questions with their partners. Explain that they will be sharing their answers with the whole group, so they may choose to write them in their Player Portfolios. (Be sure to walk around the groups, listen, and offer help where needed.):

   - Why do you think it was important to Bill Russell that he made his teammates better players?

   - What are some ways Bill Russell might have helped his teammates become better players?

   - How can helping your individual teammates help your team to play better as a whole?

4. **Share answers with the whole group:** Come together as a large group and share the answers from each of the pair

groups. Everyone who wants to should have an opportunity to share their answers.

5. **Reflect individually about the Quote:** Take two to three minutes for students to reflect individually by writing their responses to the following Journal Question and Prompts in their Player Portfolios:One way I can help my teammates to play better the next time we play a sport is by...

Activity

Lessons from Literature
Instant Replay:
The Chargers
(see Player Portfolio)

Setup

Bring the students together into a circle and read *The Scene, The Players,* and *The Plot* aloud to the whole group. If possible, this activity should be done either on a field or in a gym with the appropriate sport equipment.

The Play

1. After reading *The Scene,* the player descriptions, and *The Plot,* ask for volunteers to play the different key roles. Since there are a limited number of spots, be sure to rotate this responsibility each time so that everyone who wants to will have an opportunity to participate at some point during the year. (You may choose to keep a record of which students have had a turn as a major player.) You may also wish to give others minor roles in the role play (e.g., additional players on both teams and a referee). Give each actor a nametag to help the audience know who is who.

2. Once all the roles have been assigned, ask actors to re-read the descriptions of their characters. Explain to the audience (the rest of the group) that they will need to watch carefully so that they can make suggestions when you ask for the audience input.

3. With you playing Director, re-read The Plot aloud to the group and help the role players act out the rest of the story in front of the group.

4. After the actors have performed one version of the plot, say to them, "Actors, FREEZE!" The actors will then stand in place as you facilitate a short discussion with the audience and the other role players about how each character is feeling and what they are thinking. {When the questions are not about their character, role players can sit down and participate in the discussion.) You may use the questions below as a guide:

   • How is Jessie feeling?

   • How is Tony feeling?

   • What is Rachel thinking?

5. Ask the audience if they have any suggestions for how the situation could be resolved. Suggestions should be listed on poster paper. Choosing one solution, say, "OK, let's rewind and try this idea!" Role players then act out different solutions, each time repeating the preceding process.

Discussion Questions:

After a few rounds of role playing, ask all students to sit together in a circle. Use the following questions to lead them in a discussion about the advantages and disadvantages of each solution (responses should be written on poster paper by a volunteer):

   • Is the solution good for the person making the decision?

   • Does the solution help others solve the problem?

   • Is anybody harmed by the solution (physically or emotionally)?

   • Would this be a good solution for everyone in a similar situation to use?

   • Are there ways to improve this solution? If yes, what are they?

Cool-down

- **R&R Huddle** (5 min.)

- **Recap** one or two key points that arose during the discussion or use the following discussion piece as a guide: Explain to the students that sometimes the best way to understand another person is to put ourselves in their shoes and try looking at the situation from their perspective. This isn't always easy, but it will help us understand why a person may be acting a certain way, and it may help us to act differently towards them.

- **Reconnect** students with the following question: What is one thing you learned about teamwork from this Lesson from Literature activity?

- **Reset** and get ready for the next lesson.

Session 3: Teamwork and the Play contract Lessons from the Field	
Warm-up Begin the PLUS Cycle (5 min.) • Session Overview • Touching Base on Teamwork	**Cool-down** Continue the PLUS Cycle (5-10 min.) • Reflection • Goal-setting
Activity Lessons from the Field (25-30 min.) • Sports Activity	**Materials** Sports equipment

Warm-up

Touching Base On Teamwork (5 min.)

Ask students to think about the previous lesson. What can they do today to bring the Lessons from Literature into their work together in the sports activity?

Activity

Lessons from the Field
Sports Activity

Block I: Getting Started (5 min.)

On the first day, players will learn how to measure their resting heart rates (RHR). They will also set baselines for their RHR, number of sit-ups/pushups/lunges/calf raises, and number of jumps during jump rope. Each day they will try to improve upon their Past Personal Best (PPB) by achieving their Future Best Goal (FBG) and by tracking progress toward that goal in the physical activities progress chart located in the back of their Player Portfolios. Take one minute to make sure all participants turn to the back of their portfolios and locate the progress charts. Explain to them that they will be using this chart each time you meet to do physical activities. Be sure to emphasize the importance of keeping track of their progress by using the chart.

Stand together in a circle for all *Getting Started* activities (except for jogging). Have players partner up, with one player doing the activity and the partner keeping count and giving encouragement. Be sure that players have their Portfolios handy so that they can record their progress. Encourage them to clap and cheer for their teammates to create an enthusiastic environment. You may also choose to include music.

- **Measure resting heart rate (RHR)** — Spend a few minutes showing players how to find their pulses, either on their necks or wrists. Explain that you will be giving them a few seconds to count how many times their hearts beat. Take a moment to allow players to sit quietly on the floor and find their pulses. Give them 30 seconds to count their heartbeats.

- **Record, check in and set goals** — Allow a couple of minutes for players to record their RHRs in their Player Portfolios.

- **Jog (2-3 min.)** — This can be done as a lap or in place as a circle.

- **Stretch (2-3 min.)** — Be sure to include stretches for the major muscle groups.

- **Strength/Endurance (1 min.)** — On this first day, players will set baseline numbers for the four Strength/Endurance activities (push-ups, sit-ups, lunges, calf raises), but usually, you will only choose one or two. They will work in pairs. One member of the pair will have 30 seconds to do as many of the activities as they can. Their partner will cheer them on and count for them.

- **Jump Rope (4 min.)** — Again, players will work in pairs, with one person jumping and the other person counting and cheering. They should have three to four sets of 30-45 seconds of jumping rope.

- **Track personal progress** — Have players record their totals for steps five and six in their Player Portfolios. These totals will represent their baseline achievements, or their Past Personal Bests (PPB). Each day, playerswillcheck their progress from the previous session and will set a Future Personal Best Goal (FBG) to work toward for next time. Be sure to remind them about setting realistic goals (for example, adding one or two to their baseline, as opposed to 10).

Block II: Structured Play (30 min.)

Skill Play (10 min.)

Choose one or two of the following activities to play today. You can refer back to the *Physical Activities Description Appendix* for instructions on how to run the activities. Encourage players to cheer for each other, and include music if you wish.

- Tug o' War

- Long Distance Musical Chairs

- Star Jumps

- Clothes Relay

- Jump Rope Games

Sport Play (20 min.)

As a group, decide which sport you want to play today. Select from the sport list contained in the *Sports List Appendix.* Be sure to periodically review the Physical Activities Recommendations for Sport from Chapter Six.

Cool-down

If time permits, close the day with a few minutes of stretching while conducting the following R&R Huddle.

- **Recap** one or two key moments from the Lessons from the Field.

- **Reconnect** players back to the theme unit.

- **Reset** and transition players to the Cool-down, Reflection time.

  OR

- **Reflection**

Use this time to highlight teachable moments you observed and to give players an opportunity to share their experiences about Sports PLUS during the day. The following questions can serve as a guide:

- What did you like about today?

- What did you learn today?

- How did we show teamwork today?

- What are one or two ways we can show better teamwork next time?

Goal-setting

Keeping the *S.M.A.R.T. Goals* script in mind, spend a few minutes working together as a group to set one or two goals related to Teamwork.

Session 3: **Teamwork and the Player Contract** **Lessons from Adventure**	
Warm-up Begin the PLUS Cycle (5 min.) <ul><li>Session Overview</li><li>Player Contract Introduction</li></ul>	**Cool-down** Continue the PLUS Cycle (5-10 min.) <ul><li>Reflection</li><li>High Five</li></ul>
Activity Lessons from Adventure (25-30 min.) <ul><li>Slot Machine</li></ul>	**Materials** None

Warm-up

Player Contract Introduction

(see Player Portfolio)

Revisit the two previous sessions and recap some of the learning and discussion from the *Create Your Own Team* and *Teamwork Posters* activities.

- Ask players if they remember some of the ways teams come together, how individuals support the team, and how the team supports its individual members. What are some of the rules we agreed are necessary to forming and maintaining a good team?

- How can some of the things that make a successful sports team help make this group successful?

Have players turn to the Player Contracts page xx of their Player Portfolios.

Explain that the purpose of the contract is to help them understand the kind of expectations the Sports PLUS program has for all team members. The formality of agreeing to and then signing the contract lets players know how important these expectations are and how seriously they should be taken.

Introduce the contract by having a general discussion about what a contract is and why people use them.

- What are some different kinds of contracts?

- Why do athletes have contracts with teams they play for?

- What sorts of things do these contracts cover?

- Discuss with the group what they think the contract means and how they think having one for our team could make the program fun and enjoyable for both themselves and staff.

- Ask the players what kind of culture they would like to have in their group and how each of them can take responsibility for achieving it.

- Go through the first few points of the contract, discussing what each individual point means, what sorts of behaviors each covers and what kinds of incidents might come under each point.

- Before ending the discussion, ask players to think about the contract and its importance in making their group one in which all members will feel comfortable, safe and valued.

- They should be ready to conclude the discussion and sign the contract at the next group session.

Activity

Lessons from Adventure
Slot Machine
(see Player Portfolio)

This group problem-solving activity offers another opportunity for the group to work together to solve a problem.

You can do this activity in a classroom, but playing this game in your gym or outside on a field affords more options and creativity.

Bring the group together in a circle. Separate into three teams of three or more.

Play

1. The name of the game is Slot Machine. Like any slot machine player, the goal is to get three matching pictures.

2. Each team will go to a corner of the room and create a group gesture to represent teamwork, drawing from what they have learned about teamwork in previous sessions.

3. Once each team has a gesture, bring the group back together. Line the teams up in a triangle formation. Ask each team to show its gesture.

4. For the rest of the activity, there will be no talking among teams. The goal of the group is for you (the facilitator) to count to three, say, "Go!" and have all three teams exhibit the same gesture.

5. Play one round — count to three and see what gesture each team shows. This round helps the group to understand the game. Now, send the teams back to their corners, allowing time for them to decide which gesture they will use.

6. Come back together. Count to three, and see what gestures are presented.

7. Repeat this process until all three groups get the same gesture (or the group tires of the game).

This problem can be more difficult than it appears.

Consider the following:

1. The teams cannot speak to each other, yet they are all trying to do the same thing. They need to develop a system for non-verbal communication.

2. It is not uncommon for one team to forget that the group's goal is to have everyone show the same gesture. This group may become unbending in showing any other gesture than their own (this can be OK if the rest of the teams use this group's gesture, but this doesn't always happen). If one team makes it impossible for the group as a whole to achieve its

goal, stop the game and use this as a discussion topic — what responsibility does each small group have to the larger group in accomplishing its goal? What happens when a small group of people are not helping a team to achieve its goal?

Cool-down

- **R&R Huddle** (5 min.)

- **Recap** by highlighting one or two key points from the activity.

- **Reconnect** using the following focus prompt, which players can complete in their Player Portfolios: The Slot Machine game was difficult because...

- **Reset** and transition to the next activity.

Cool-down Ritual

High Five

Bring the group together in a circle. Ask each person to think of one thing they have learned about teamwork today. Invite volunteers to share what they thought of and ask for comments to each response. Next, have players share what they learned with their neighbors and exchange high fives. Finally, face the center of the circle and have a group high five.

Remind players to be on the hunt for articles and stories about teamwork to share with the group.

Session 4: Duck-asteroids

Overview

Instructor's Notes: *Be sure to review this set of activities before starting this Sports PLUS Session. Directions for how to facilitate each activity are provided, but it is important that you become familiar with them so that you may more effectively lead the group.*

During group discussions, be sure to record all thoughts and ideas on a blackboard or newsprint. Remember that when students are working in their Player Portfolios, spelling, grammar, and penmanship are, relatively speaking, unimportant, so don't dwell on those details or you risk making Sports PLUS into MoreSchool.

After the opening quote, this session begins with your first *Instant Replay,* so it will be important to review what an Instant Replay is with the students. Expect to have many questions and the need to patiently repeat the instructions. Be sure to move slowly through it this first time.

In this session, the group finishes and signs the *Player Contract,* which establishes a set of norms that the group agrees to abide by for the rest of the program. It helps young people learn to set and manage limits and contributes to the group's growing sense of community. *Asteroid Tag* is an energetic tag game that enables students to have some simple fun while subtly raising questions about teamwork.

Pass the Put-Up closes the lesson, while fostering positive self-esteem and mutual respect among your Sports PLUS team members

---

Session 4: **Duck-Asteroids** **Lessons from Literature**	
Warm-up Begin the PLUS Cycle (5 min.)	**Cool-down** Continue the PLUS Cycle (5-10 min.)
• Session Overview	• Reflection
• Player Contract Introduction	• High Five
Activity Lessons from Adventure (25-30 min.)	**Materials** None
• Slot Machine	

Warm-up

Quote of the Week

Getting good players is easy. Getting 'em to play together is the hard part.

— *Casey Stengel*

Follow the 5 steps of the Quote of the Week Format (See the Getting Started chapter for additional explanation):

1. **Write the Quote of the Week:** Bring the group together into a circle, and write the Quote on the blackboard.

2. **Think about the Quote as a group:** Spend two to three minutes talking with students about what they think the quote means. Ask them to share answers to the group for the following question:

   • Why is it hard to get players to work together

3. **Pair up to talk about the Quote:** Have students separate into pairs. Ask them to spend about five minutes discussing the following questions with their partners. Explain that they will be sharing their answers with the whole group, so they may choose to write their answers in their Player Portfolios. (Be sure to walk around the groups, listen, and offer help where needed.):

   • What can a coach or teacher do to help students work together?

   • Give one example of what you can do to make it easier to work together

4. **Share answers with the whole group:** Come together as a large group and share the answers from each of the pair groups. Everyone who wants to should have an opportunity to share their answers.

5. **Reflect individually about the Quote:** Take two to three minutes for students to reflect individually by writing a

response to the following Journal Question in their Player Portfolios:

- What do you think is the most important thing you can do to help your teammates work together?

Activity

Lessons from Literature
Instant Replay
The Ducks
(see Player Portfolio)

Key Concepts

- Teamwork
- Decision-making
- Respect

Setup

Bring students together into a circle and use the following discussion as a guide to help set the tone: "One of the things that working together as a team means is that the team takes care of its members and the members take care of the team. Another way to look at this is that sometimes the team does something to help out an individual player, and at other times individual players help the entire team. Sometimes these situations mean that we, as individuals, must give up something or make a sacrifice."

Next, read *The Scene, The Players,* and *The Plot* aloud to the whole group. If possible, this activity should be done either on a field or in a gym with the appropriate sport equipment.

The Play

1. After reading *The Scene,* the player descriptions, and *The Plot,* ask for volunteers to play the different key roles. There are a limited number of spots. Be sure to rotate this responsibility each time so that everyone who wants to will have an opportunity to participate at some point during the year. (You may choose to keep a record of which students have had a turn

as a major player.) You may also wish to give others minor roles in the role play (e.g., additional players on both teams and a referee). Give each actor a nametag to help the audience know who is who.

2. Once all the roles have been assigned, ask actors to re-read the descriptions of their characters. Explain to the audience (the rest of the group) that they will need to watch carefully so that they can make suggestions when you ask for the audience input.

3. With you playing Director, re-read *The Plot* aloud to the group and help the role players act out the rest of the story in front of the group.

4. After the actors have performed one version of the plot, say to them, "Actors, FREEZE!" The actors will then stand in place as you facilitate a short discussion with the audience and the other role players about how each character is feeling and what they are thinking. (When the questions are not about their character, role players can sit down and participate in the discussion.) You may use the questions below as a guide:

   • How is Amanda feeling?

   • How is Vern feeling?

   • What is Kenny thinking?

5. Ask the audience if they have any suggestions for how the situation could be resolved. Suggestions should be listed on poster paper. Choosing one solution, say, "OK, let's rewind and try this idea!" Role players then act out different solutions, each time repeating the preceding process.

Discussion Questions:

After a few rounds of role playing, ask all students to sit together in a circle. Use the following questions to lead them in a discussion about the advantages and disadvantages of each solution (responses should be written on poster paper by a volunteer):

   • Is the solution good for the person making the decision?

- Does the solution help others solve the problem?

- Is anybody harmed by the solution (physically or emotionally)?

- Would this be a good solution for everyone in a similar situation to use?

- Are there ways to improve this solution? If yes, what are they?

Cool-down

- **R&R Huddle** (5 min.)

- **Recap** one or two key points that arose during the discussion or use the following discussion piece as a guide: Explain to the students that sometimes the best way to understand another person is to put ourselves in their shoes and try looking at the situation from their perspective. This isn't always easy, but it will help us understand why a person may be acting a certain way, and it may help us to act differently towards them.

- **Reconnect** students with the following question: What is one thing you learned about teamwork from this Lesson from Literature activity?

- **Reset** and get ready for the next lesson.

Session 4: Duck-Asteroids Lessons from the Field	

Warm-up
Begin the PLUS Cycle (5 min.)
 	
  • Session Overview
 	
  • Touching Base on Teamwork
	Cool-down
	Continue the PLUS Cycle (5-10 min.)
	
	  • Reflection
	
	  • Goal-setting

Activity Lessons from the Field(25-30 min.) • Sports Activity	**Materials** Sports equipment

Warm-up

Touching Base On Teamwork (5 min.)

Ask players to think about the previous lesson. What can they do today to bring the Lessons from Literature in their work together in the sports activity.

Activity

Lessons from the Field
Sports Activity

Block I: Getting Started (5 min.)

On the first day, players will learn how to measure their resting heart rates (RHR). They will also set baselines for their RHR, number of sit-ups/pushups/lunges/calf raises, and number of jumps during jump rope. Each day they will try to improve upon their Past Personal Best (PPB) by achieving their Future Best Goal (FBG) and by tracking progress toward that goal in the physical activities progress chart located in the back of their Player Portfolios. Take one minute to make sure all participants turn to the back of their portfolios and locate the progress charts. Explain to them that they will be using this chart each time you meet to do physical activities. Be sure to emphasize the importance of keeping track of their progress by using the chart.

Stand together in a circle for all Getting Started activities (except for jogging). Have players partner up, with one player doing the activity and the partner keeping count and giving encouragement. Be sure that they have their Portfolios handy so that they can record their progress. Encourage them to clap and cheer for their teammates to create an enthusiastic environment. You may also choose to include music.

- **Measure resting heart rate (RHR)** — Spend a few minutes showing players how to find their pulses, either on their necks or wrists. Explain that you will be giving them a few seconds to count how many times their hearts beat. Take a moment to allow the players to sit quietly on the floor and find their pulses. Give them 30 seconds to count their heartbeats.

- **Record, check in and set goals** — Allow a couple of minutes for players to record

- **Jog (2-3 min.)** — This can be done as a lap or in place as a circle.

- **Stretch (2-3 min.)** — Be sure to include stretches for the major muscle groups.

- **Strength/Endurance (1 min.)** — On this first day, players will set baseline numbers for the four Strength/Endurance activities (push-ups, sit-ups, lunges, calf raises), but usually, you will only choose one or two. They will work in pairs. One member of the pair will have 30 seconds to do as many of the activities as they can. Their partner will cheer them on and count for them.

- **Jump Rope (4 min.)** — Again, players will work in pairs, with one person jumping and the other person counting and cheering. They should have three to four sets of 30-45 seconds of jumping rope.

- **Track personal progress** — Have players record their totals for steps five and six in their Player Portfolios. These totals will represent their baseline achievements, or their Past Personal Bests (PPB). Each day, players will check their progress from the previous session and will set a Future Personal Best Goal (FBG) to work toward for next time. Be sure to remind them about setting realistic goals (for example, adding one or two to their baseline, as opposed to 10).

Block II: Structured Play (30 min.)

Skill Play (10 min.)

Choose one or two of the following activities to play today. You can refer back to the *Physical Activities Description Appendix* for instructions on how to run the activities. Encourage players to cheer for each other, and include music if you wish.

- Log Rolling

- Water Balloon Volleyball

- Jumping Distances

- Beanbag Horseshoes

- Gorilla Walk

Sport Play (20 min.)

As a group, decide which sport you want to play today. Select from the sport list contained in the *Sports List Appendix.* Be sure to periodically review with the group the Physical Activities Recommendations for Sport from Chapter Six.

Cool-down

If time permits, close the day with a few minutes of stretching while conducting the following R&R Huddle.

- **Recap** one or two key moments from the Lessons from the Field.

- **Reconnect** players back to the theme unit.

- **Reset** and transition players to the Cool-down, Reflection time.

  OR

- **Reflection**

Use this time to highlight teachable moments you observed during the day and to give players an opportunity to share their experiences about Sports PLUS during the day. The following questions can serve as a guide:

- What did you like about today?

- What did you learn today?

- How did we show teamwork today?

- What are one or two ways we can show better teamwork next time?

Goal-setting

Use this time to track the group's progress toward the team goals you set last time and to start the players thinking about one or two individual goals related to Teamwork they would like to set during the next session.

Session 4: **Duck-Asteroids** **Lessons from Adventure**	

Warm-up
Begin the PLUS Cycle (5 min.)
 	
  • Session Overview
 	
  • Sign Player Contract
	Cool-down
	Continue the PLUS Cycle (5-10 min.)
	
	  • Reflection
	
	  • Pass the Put-up

Activity Lessons from Adventure (25-30 min.) • Asteroids	**Materials** Soft, throwable balls (Nerf-type), one per person; Player Portfolios

Warm-up

Player Contract Review and Signing

Conclude discussion about Player Contract from the previous session. Recap some of what players said during the previous session about why signing this contract is important.

- Ask players if they have any additional thoughts or comments.

- Has anyone thought about the kind of environment they want for the group?

- Why would this kind of environment be a good place to be?

- What are some of the things each member of the group can do to make this happen?

- Finish discussing the remaining points of the contract and relate them to the ideas players have for making the group a positive place to be.

---

official Sports PLUS contract

I, _____, agree to a one-year deal with the Sports PLUS Team!

As a member of this team, I agree to the following terms and conditions:

I agree to be **Team Player** and to work together with my teacher/coach and teammates, both on and off the field. _____

I agree to **Respect** myself and others — parents, teachers, teammates, and opponents.

I agree to be **Responsible** — to attend all group meetings, be on time, and be prepared. I understand that my actions are important because others depend on me. _____

I agree to **Play Fair** and to follow the rules at all times. _____

I agree to **Persevere** and to give my best possible effort, even if I make mistakes or struggle. _____

I understand that it is a privilege to participate in Sports PLUS. I also understand that poor behavior and irresponsible actions can jeopardize my membership at any time.

Player's name

Parent's name

Teacher/coach

- When you think the players understand the significance and purpose of the contract, have some kind of signing ceremony.

- Ask players to open their Player Portfolios. You can preside like a judge and ask them to "Repeat after me..." Or you can simply lead them in reading aloud as a group each statement of the Player Contract, allowing time to initial each statement as it is read.

- Refer to this contract whenever necessary to add items, reinforce lessons, and remind players of what they have agreed to.

Activity

Lessons from Adventure
Asteroid Tag

This simple and fun tag game variation is always a crowd pleaser. You can play this game indoors or out. In an inside setting, it is best to have a relatively open space. If you are working in a small, indoor space, make this a walking only game. If your classroom space doesn't allow for this type of activity, play it at the beginning of the sport session.

Play

1. As a whole group, set up an in-bounds area.

2. Bring the group into a circle, and give each person a ball.

3. Have players count off by threes to form groups of three. Team members must work together to protect each other. (If there are not enough balls to go around, allot one ball for each group.)

4. The rules of the game are this: Team members are trying to tag members of the other teams by making contact with the ball — below the *shoulders* only! When you are hit with a ball, you are rooted to the floor and must squat down in that place. Team members can help you get back in the game by passing you a ball once you have been hit.

5. Once a few groups have lost all their team members, end the round and begin a new one. Continue playing until players become tired.

6. Begin play by having each student toss up their balls at least six feet in the air.

7. On the count of three…one, two, three, OK, play!"

Instructor's Note

One possible variation is to have players pair off as partners. Each pair must lock arms and work together to tag other players. Once one member of a pair is tagged, the pair is out and must squat down. This variation may be followed by the three-member group version to illustrate for players how modifying the rules of a game can affect their experience.

Cool-down

- **R&R Huddle** (5 min.)

- **Recap** and ask players to briefly share their experiences. Highlight one or two of the following questions: Was this a fun game? What were some of the things you liked about playing it? What were some of the things that you didn't like?

- **Reconnect** and focus the discussion on players' experience of team and teamwork. Consider one or two of the following questions as a guide:

1. Was it hard to think about your teammates while you were playing?

    - What were some examples of teamwork you noticed during the game?

    - What was hard about being a good teammate?

    - What was easy? (If you tried the variation, ask players to compare their experiences during each of the different versions:

- Which version did you like better? Why? Was it easy or difficult to work together when your arms were locked with your partner's? In which version were you able to stay in the game longer? Why do you think this was?)

- Reset and transition to the next activity.

Cool-down Ritual

Pass the Put-up

Gather the large group in a circle with a bit of space between each student. Explain to players the difference between authentic and inauthentic put-ups. For example, sometimes put-ups are actually poorly disguised put-downs. Encourage players to look for different kinds of put-ups (e.g., for effort, for respect, etc.). Begin the passing to demonstrate how to "pass a put-up." You can use an imaginary passing motion from any sport — a bounce pass of a basketball, a football pass, a soccer kick, a volleyball bump, etc. Aim the pass at another person in the circle, and as you are passing, give the person a put-up: "Great playing, Robert," "Good work, Kim," etc. The receiving person accepts the pass and says "Thank you."

This activity may be used frequently to close a session, but for the first few times it is played, ask if anyone has a put-up to share about someone else. After volunteers have shared theirs, be prepared to add a few more to continue modeling how a put-up looks.

When this activity has been played a few times and players have begun to feel more comfortable passing genuine put-ups to each other, the person receiving the pass may quickly pass a put-up to another person, continuing until everyone has received a pass.

Session 5:
Getting to Know Your Teammates

Overview

Instructor's Notes: *Be sure to review this set of activities before starting this Sports PLUS Session. Directions for how to facilitate each activity are provided, but it is important that you become familiar with them so that you may more effectively lead the group.*

During group discussions, be sure to record all thoughts and ideas on a blackboard or newsprint. Remember that when students are working in their Player Portfolios, spelling, grammar, and penmanship are, relatively speaking, unimportant, so don't dwell on those details or you risk making Sports PLUS into MoreSchool.

The *Quote of the Week* from Michael Jordan is an effective way to focus this session on the importance of teamwork for success in sports or in any endeavor.

A great team must have members who are willing to make sacrifices for the good of the team. Individuals must be responsible to their teammates, and the group must remember to take care of individual players. The *You Make the Call* for today gives students a chance to read, discuss, and write about these issues.

Name Tag and Sports Detective are great team-building activities that even those who come from the same school and know each other well can enjoy.

The Cool-down ritual allows you to "check in" with everyone before ending the session and to reinforce the notion of *Sports PLUS* as a positive, safe environment for all.

Session 5: Getting to Know Your Teammates Lessons from Literature	
Warm-up Begin the PLUS Cycle (10-15 min.) • Session Overview • Quote of the Week **Activity** Lessons from Literature (25-30 min.) • You Make the Call — *Kickball Trouble*	**Cool-down** Continue the PLUS Cycle (5-10 min.) • Reflection **Materials** Copies of *Kickball Trouble*

Warm-up

Quote of the Week

Me? I'd rather have five guys with less talent who are willing to come together as a team than five guys who consider themselves stars and aren't willing to sacrifice.

— Michael Jordan

Instructor's Note

This quote is good for exploring how individuals can contribute to the overall success of the team but that no one person can make the team succeed by his or her self. It also addresses the idea that there are many different ways individual players can lead their team, and that it is not always the best or most skilled player who leads a team, but rather, it is the player who can help the team play at its highest level.)

Follow the five steps of the Quote of the Week Format (See the *Getting Started* chapter for additional explanation):

1. **Write the Quote of the Week:** Bring the group together into a circle, and write the Quote on the blackboard.

2. **Think about the Quote as a group:** Spend two or three minutes talking with students about what they think the quote means. Ask them to share answers to the group for the following question:

   • Why do you think Michael Jordan would prefer "five guys with less talent" to five stars who "aren't willing to sacrifice"?

3. **Pair up to talk about the Quote:** Have students separate into pairs. Ask them to spend about five minutes discussing the following questions with their partners. Explain that they will be sharing their answers with the whole group, so they may choose to write their answers in their Player Portfolios. (Be sure to walk around the groups, listen, and offer help where needed.):

   • What does Michael Jordan want his teammates to do when he says "sacrifice"?

   • Why is it sometimes difficult to sacrifice for the team?

   • What are some ways that teammates can sacrifice for the team?

4. **Share answers with the whole group:** Come together as a large group and share the answers from each of the pair groups. Everyone who wants to should have an opportunity to share their answers.

5. **Reflect individually about the Quote:** Take two or three minutes for students to reflect individually by writing a response to the following Journal Prompt in their Player Portfolios:

   • Three ways that I can sacrifice to help my team are

     1. _____

     2. _____

     3. _____

Activity

Lessons from Literature
You Make the Call
Kickball Trouble
(see Player Portfolio)

Key Concepts

- Problem-solving
- Managing emotions
- Teamwork

Setup

Bring the group together to sit in a circle. Read the story aloud and with enthusiasm to the whole group.

Discussion Questions:

Separate students into groups by having them count off by threes (or fours depending on the group size). Spend a couple of minutes distributing their Player Portfolios and pencils. Ask one or two volunteers to help.

Using their Player Portfolios, have students discuss and write answers to the following questions in their small groups. It is important to remember that spelling, grammar, and penmanship are NOT important during this activity.

1. Who are the main characters in this story?

2. What is the main problem these characters face?

3. What are some ways that Andy might handle the situation?

4. What would happen if the problem were handled in this way?

   - How would Andy feel?

   - How would Jessie feel?

   - How would the other children feel?

5. If you were Andy, what solution would you choose to handle the situation?

6. What about your solution would be difficult?

7. If you were Jessie, how would you handle the situation?

8. What might make it difficult to do this?

Group Share:

- After the small groups have had time to discuss each question, gather the groups together to sit in one large circle.

- Ask each small group to share their suggestions for solving the problem, using students' answers to number three above. (As suggestions are given, you or a volunteer should write them on poster paper for all to see.)

- Once all the different solutions have been laid out, spend a few minutes discussing the consequences of each solution, using students' answers to question number four as a guide.

- As a group, choose the best solution (i.e., the most good for the most people).

- Finally, as a group, complete the following two focus prompts on poster paper.

  1. One thing we can take from this story is that we should…

  2. We should be careful not to…

Cool-down

- **R&R Huddle** (5 min.)

- **Recap** one or two key points that arose during the discussion.

- **Reconnect** using one or two of the focus prompts above.

- **Reset** and get ready for the next lesson.

Session 5: **Getting to Know Your Teammates** **Lessons from the Field**	

Warm-up
Begin the PLUS Cycle (5 min.)
   • Session Overview
   • Touching Base on Teamwork
Activity
Lessons from the Field(25-30 min.)
   • Sports Activity
	Cool-down
	Continue the PLUS Cycle (5-10 min.)
	   • Reflection
	   • Goal-setting
	Materials
	Sports equipment

Warm-up

Touching Base On Teamwork (5 min.)

Ask students to think about the previous lesson. What can they do today to bring the *Lessons from Literature* into their work together in the sports activity?

Activity

Lessons from the Field
Sports Activity

Block I: Getting Started (5 min.)

On the first day, players will learn how to measure their resting heart rates (RHR). They will also set baselines for their RHR, number of sit-ups/pushups/lunges/calf raises, and number of jumps during jump rope. Each day they will try to improve upon their Past Personal Best (PPB) by achieving their Future Best Goal (FBG) and by tracking progress toward that goal in the physical activities progress chart located in the back of their Player Portfolios. Take one minute to make sure all participants turn to the back of their portfolios and locate the progress charts. Explain to them that they will be using this chart each time you meet to do physical activities. Be sure to emphasize the importance of keeping track of their progress by using the chart.

Stand together in a circle for all *Getting Started* activities (except for jogging). Have players partner up, with one player doing the activity and the partner keeping count and giving encouragement. Be sure that they have their Portfolios handy so that they can record their progress. Encourage them to clap and cheer for their teammates to create an enthusiastic environment. You may also choose to include music.

- **Measure resting heart rate (RHR)** — Spend a few minutes showing players how to find their pulses, either on their necks or wrists. Explain that you will be giving them a few seconds to count how many times their hearts beat. Take a moment to allow them to sit quietly on the floor and find their pulses. Give them 30 seconds to count their heartbeats.

- **Record, check in and set goals** — Allow a couple of minutes for players to record their RHRs in their Player Portfolios.

- **Jog (2-3 min.)** — This can be done as a lap or in place as a circle.

- **Stretch (2-3 min.)** — Be sure to include stretches for the major muscle groups.

- **Strength/Endurance (1 min.)** — On this first day, players will set baseline numbers for the four Strength/Endurance activities (push-ups, sit-ups, lunges, calf raises), but usually, you will only choose one or two. They will work in pairs. One member of the pair will have 30 seconds to do as many of the activities as they can. Their partner will cheer them on and count for them.

- **Jump Rope (4 min.)** — Again, players will work in pairs, with one person jumping and the other person counting and cheering. They should have three to four sets of 30-45 seconds of jumping rope.

- **Track personal progress** — Have players record their totals for steps five and six in their Player Portfolios. These totals will represent their baseline achievements, or their Past Personal

Bests (PPB). Each day, playerswillcheck their progress from the previous session and will set a Future Personal Best Goal (FBG) to work toward for next time. Be sure to remind them about setting realistic goals (for example, adding one or two to their baseline, as opposed to 10).

Block II: Structured Play (30 min.)

Skill Play (10 min.)

Choose one or two of the following activities to play today. You can refer back to the *Physical Activities Description Appendix* for instructions on how to run the activities. Encourage players to cheer for each other, and include music if you wish.

- Wheelbarrow Race

- Sashay Relay

- Chinese Jump Rope

- Beanbag Walk Relay

- Hula Hoop Challenge Course

- Over, Under, Over, Under

Sport Play (20 min.)

As a group, decide which sport you want to play today. Select from the sport list contained in the *Sports List Appendix*. Be sure to periodically review with the group the Physical Activities Recommendations for Sport from Chapter Six.

Cool-down

If time permits, close the day with a few minutes of stretching while conducting the following R&R Huddle.

- **Recap** one or two key moments from the Lessons from the Field.

- **Reconnect** players back to the theme unit.

- **Reset** and transition players to the Cool-down, Reflection time.

OR

- **Reflection**

Use this time to highlight teachable moments you observed during the day and to give players an opportunity to share their experiences about Sports PLUS during the day. The following questions can serve as a guide:

- What did you like about today?

- What did you learn today?

- How did we show teamwork today?

- What are one or two ways we can show better teamwork next time?

Session 5: Getting to Know Your Teammates Lessons from Adventure	
Warm-up Begin the PLUS Cycle (5 min.) • Session Overview • Sports Detective	**Cool-down** Continue the PLUS Cycle (5-10 min.) • Reflection • Put on the Back
Activity Lessons from Adventure (25-30 min.) • Name Tag	**Materials** Player Portfolios

Warm-up

Sports Detective

(see Player Portfolio)

It's important to know each other's names, but names don't really tell much about a person. Even when we think we know someone, we can often be surprised to learn new things. Good teammates get to know one another. They understand what their teammates like and dislike and what kinds of experiences they have had.

Play

Ask players to anonymously write something about themselves — something unique or an interesting fact they want their teammates to know — on a piece of paper. (Be sure to emphasize that we're looking for POSITIVE things about themselves). Collect the papers and make a list on a poster or chalkboard.

Ask players to open their Player Portfolios and copy the list on the appropriate page. Next, each player acts as a detective, searching for people who meet the descriptions provided on the list. As they search for people who fit the descriptions, they first introduce themselves, ask the questions, and then get the signatures of those who fit the descriptions. The goal is to learn something new about, and to get at least one signature from, each person in the group.

A few sample items are listed below to get the group started:

- is left-handed

- has more than one sister or brother

- had a birthday this month

- has a pet bird

- likes to play soccer

- enjoys reading

- can speak a language other than English

- **R&R Huddle** (5 min.)

- **Recap** by highlighting one or two of the following ideas: After all players have collected signatures from everyone, gather the group together. Were there any surprises? Did you learn anything that you didn't know about a teammate?

- **Reconnect** by asking players to briefly share some of the things they learned about each other.

- **Reset** and briefly transition to the next activity using the discussion below as a guideline.

Activity

Lessons from Adventure

Name Tag

This is a fun game to play after the players have learned one other's names.

Explain to players that this is a competition of the group against its own best time. Remind them that they will have to take good care of their teammates as the game begins with everyone closing their eyes and moving slowly and carefully around. (If you think your group is not ready for this activity because of the potential for fooling around and someone getting bumped, save this until a later session when more trust and caring has developed.) Explain and demonstrate the "Bumpers Up" position. This means that hands are held at chest level, palms out, about a foot in front of you. Your hands become bumpers to gently guide you through the group, all the members of which also have their bumpers up.

Play

1. On your command, everyone closes their eyes and puts their bumpers up. One person — you, another staff, or a designated student — keeps their eyes open but also wanders around with the group.

2. Your next command is for the players to slowly wander about among their teammates, "bumpers up." (You may want to have several staff helping to guide errant players if they wander away from the group.)

3. When the group is thoroughly mixed, say, "STOP!" (Everyone keeps their eyes closed and remains in position.) Now place your hand on someone's shoulder, and say that person's name.

4. That person opens his or her eyes and taps the nearest person, saying his or her name. (If they can't think of the person's name, they can go to the next closest person.)

5. After tagging someone, the tagger should raise one hand.

6. The action continues until everyone is tagged and all hands are raised. Keep time and play several rounds to see if the group can improve its time. (If the group manages this task easily, challenge them to use both first and last names, or even middle names.)

- **R&R Huddle** (5 min.)

- **Recap** and focus the discussion on how well the players cared for each other when their eyes were closed.

- **Reconnect** using one or two of the following questions: How does a good team take care of its members? How do we, as individuals, let our teammates know that we do not feel so safe? What should our teammates then do?

- **Reset** and transition to the next activity.

Cool-down

Cool-down Ritual

A Pat on the Back

Bring the group together in a circle, shoulder to shoulder. Ask each person to put his or her right hand on the back of the person to the right and the left hand on that of the person to the left. The group then very gently raises and lowers their hands on the backs of their neighbors (light pats) saying, "Thanks for a great day. I just thought you all deserved a good pat on the back!"

Session 6:
T.E.A.M.

Overview

Instructor's Notes: *Be sure to review this set of activities before starting this Sports PLUS Session. Directions for how to facilitate each activity are provided, but it is important that you become familiar with them so that you may more effectively lead the group.*

During group discussions, be sure to record all thoughts and ideas on a blackboard or newsprint. Remember that when students are working in their Player Portfolios, spelling, grammar, and penmanship are, relatively speaking, unimportant, so don't dwell on those details or you risk making Sports PLUS into MoreSchool.

The *Sports Short* illustrates that a team must learn how to get along, despite differences and problems, if it is going to achieve its goals.

The Adventure lesson begins with a short energizing game that requires quick thinking. The introduction of the *T.E.A.M. Problem-solving Model* enables students to practice solving problems in the context of a group. Students begin to understand the challenges of solving problems within a group, while developing skills to meet this challenge. Building upon the lessons from last session, this activity provides a great opportunity for them to apply the T.E.A.M problem-solving model in action as they wrestle with the dilemmas presented in a story and create their own models.

Session 6: T.E.A.M Lessons from Literature	

Warm-up
Begin the PLUS Cycle (10-15 min.)
 	
  • Session Overview
 	
  • Quote of the Week
 	
Activity
Lessons from Literature (25-30 min.)
 	
  • Sports Short — *Bouncers,*
    Fly Balls, Butterfingers, and
    Victories
	Cool-down
	Continue the PLUS Cycle (5-10 min.)
	
	  • Reflection
	
	Materials
	Copies of Bouncers, Fly Balls, Butterfingers, and Victories

Warm-up

Quote of the Week

> *I am a member of a team, and I rely on the team, I defer to it and sacrifice for it, because the team, not the individual, is the ultimate champion.*
>
> — Mia Hamm

Follow the five steps of the Quote of the Week Format (See the *Getting Started* chapter for additional explanation):

1. **Write the Quote of the Week:** Bring the group together into a circle, and write the Quote on the blackboard.

2. **Think about the Quote as a group:** Spend two or three minutes talking with students about what they think the quote means. Ask them to share answers to the group for the following question:

- Do you agree with Mia that the team "is the ultimate champion?" Why or why not?

3. **Pair up to talk about the Quote:** Have students separate into pairs. Ask them to spend about five minutes discussing the following questions with their partners. Explain that they will be sharing their answers with the whole group, so they may choose to write their answers in their Player Portfolios. (Be sure to walk around the groups, listen, and offer help where needed.):

   - Can you think of any examples from our Sports PLUS time that connects with the quote?

   - How is "deferring" to the team an aspect of working together?

4. **Share answers with the whole group:** Come together as a large group and share the answers from each of the pair groups. Everyone who wants to should have an opportunity to share their answers.

5. **Reflect individually on the Quote:** Allow two to three minutes for students to reflect individually by writing a response to the following Journal Question in their Player Portfolios:

   - Think about an example that could occur in the next Lessons from the Field session that would fit with the quote from Mia Hamm. Write a few sentences to describe what that might look like.

Activity

Lessons from Literature
Sport Short
Bouncers, Fly Balls, Butterfingers and Victories
(see Player Portfolio)

Key Concepts

- Problem-solving

- respect
- competition
- cooperation

Setup

Bring the group together to sit in a circle. Use the following questions to help facilitate a short, five or six minute discussion to help set the tone before reading the story. (Be sure to record students' answers on the board or on poster paper.)

- Have you ever been in a game that wasn't fun?

- What were some of the things that made the game not fun?

- What are some things we could do to make the game more fun?

The Story

Read the story aloud and with enthusiasm to the whole group.

Discussion Questions:

Spend a couple of minutes distributing students' Player Portfolios and pencils. (Ask for one or two volunteers to help.) Work together as a whole group to answer the following questions. Write the questions and focus prompts on a blackboard or newsprint.

Questions one to four should be answered in a round-robin format, with one student answering one question. Try to include those who may not always participate. (If answers for questions three and four are imprecise or need further elaboration, ask if anyone has anything to add.)

1. Who are the main characters in this story?

2. What is the problem or challenge they face?

3. How does each character handle the problem?

4. What happened then?

The following focus prompt should be answered in an exhaustive format. Continue allowing students to give responses until no new answers are given.

1. The main characters learned they should…

For questions six and seven, allow all students an opportunity to share their answers, regardless of whether or not the answers are original.

2. When would it be important in your life to… [insert answer from previous statement]?
3. One thing that might make doing this difficult is…

Finally, ask students to write their responses to the following prompt in their Player Portfolios.

4. One specific way I might support my teammates or avoid "put downs" is…

Cool-down

- **R&R Huddle** (5 min.)

- **Recap** one or two key key points that arose during the discussion.

- **Reconnect** by asking volunteers to briefly share what they wrote for question number eight above.

- **Reset** and get ready for the next lesson.

Session 6: T.E.A.M. Lessons from the Field	

Warm-up
Begin the PLUS Cycle (5 min.)
 	
  • Session Overview
 	
  • Touching Base on Teamwork
 	
Activity
Lessons from the Field(25-30 min.)
 	
  • Sports Activity
	Cool-down
	Continue the PLUS Cycle (5-10 min.)
	
	  • Reflection
	
	  • Goal-setting
	
	Materials
	Sports equipment

Warm-up

Touching Base On Teamwork (5 min.)

Ask students to think about the previous lesson. What can they do today to bring Lessons from Literature into their work in the sports activity?

Activity

Lessons from the Field
Sports Activity

Block I: Getting Started (5 min.)

On the first day, players will learn how to measure their resting heart rates (RHR). They will also set baselines for their RHR, number of sit-ups/pushups/lunges/calf raises, and number of jumps during jump rope. Each day they will try to improve upon their Past Personal Best (PPB) by achieving their Future Best Goal (FBG) and by tracking progress toward that goal in the physical activities progress chart located in the back of their Player Portfolios. Take one minute to make sure all participants turn to the back of their portfolios and locate the progress charts. Explain to them that they will be using this chart each time you meet to do physical activities. Be sure to emphasize the importance of keeping track of their progress by using the chart.

Stand together in a circle for all *Getting Started* activities (except for jogging). Have players partner up, with one player doing the activity and the partner keeping count and giving encouragement. Be sure they have their Portfolios handy so that they can record their progress. Encourage them to clap and cheer for their teammates to create an enthusiastic environment. You may also choose to include music.

- **Measure resting heart rate (RHR)** — Spend a few minutes showing players how to find their pulses, either on their necks or wrists. Explain that you will be giving them a few seconds to count how many times their hearts beat. Take a moment to allow players to sit quietly on the floor and find their pulses. Give them 30 seconds to count their heartbeats.

- **Record, check in and set goals** — Allow a couple of minutes for players to record their RHRs in their Player Portfolios.

- **Jog (2-3 min.)** — This can be done as a lap or in place as a circle.

- **Stretch (2-3 min.)** — Be sure to include stretches for the major muscle groups.

- **Strength/Endurance (1 min.)** — On this first day, players will set baseline numbers for the four Strength/Endurance activities (push-ups, sit-ups, lunges, calf raises), but usually, you will only choose one or two. They will work in pairs. One member of the pair will have 30 seconds to do as many of the activities as they can. Their partner will cheer them on and count for them.

- **Jump Rope (4 min.)** — Again, players will work in pairs, with one person jumping and the other person counting and cheering. They should have three to four sets of 30-45 seconds of jumping rope.

- **Track personal progress** — Have players record their totals for steps five and six in their Player Portfolios. These totals will represent their baseline achievements, or their Past Personal Bests (PPB). Each day, players will check their progress from the previous session and will set a Future Personal Best Goal (FBG) to work toward for next time. Be sure to remind them about setting realistic goals (for example, adding one or two to their baseline, as opposed to 10).

Block II: Structured Play (30 min.)

Skill Play (10 min.)

Choose one or two of the following activities to play today. You can refer back to the *Physical Activities Description Appendix* for instructions on how to facilitate the activities. Encourage players to cheer for each other, and include music if you wish.

- Circle Bonanza

- Balloon-a-thon

- Passing Medicine Balls

- Twister

- Jump Rope Games

- Leap Frog Relay

Sport Play (20 min.)

As a group, decide which sport you want to play today. Select from the sport list contained in the *Sports List Appendix*. Be sure to periodically review the Physical Activities Recommendations for Sport from Chapter Six.

Cool-down

If time permits, close the day with a few minutes of stretching while conducting the following R&R Huddle.

- **Recap** one or two key moments from the Lessons from the Field.

- **Reconnect** players back to the theme unit.

- **Reset** and transition players to the Cool-down, Reflection time.

OR

- **Reflection**

Use this time to highlight teachable moments you observed during the day and to give players an opportunity to share their experiences about Sports PLUS during the day. The following questions can serve as a guide:

- What did you like about today?

- What did you learn today?

- How did we show teamwork today?

- What are one or two ways we can show better teamwork next time?

Goal-setting

Use this time to help players track progress toward their individually chosen goals, as well as toward team goals. As goals from earlier sessions are reached, guide players in setting additional individual and team goals related to *Teamwork*.

Session 6: T.E.A.M. Lessons from Adventure	

Warm-up
Begin the PLUS Cycle (5 min.)
  • Session Overview
  • Bumpity, Bump, Bump
	Cool-down
	Continue the PLUS Cycle (5-10 min.)
	  • Reflection
	  • Alphabet Go-Round

Activity Lessons from Adventure (25-30 min.) • T.E.A.M. Problem-Solving Model	**Materials** Poster of the T.E.A.M. model

Warm-up

Bumpity, Bump, Bump!

This is a fun warm-up game that is also a silly name-refresher.

Play

1. Bring the group together in a circle with you standing in the center.

2. The goal of the person in the center is to get out of the center. You do this by pointing at any person in the circle, loudly stating, "Left!" or "Right!" and then exclaiming, "Bumpity bump bump!"

3. If the person you have pointed to cannot name the person to his or her right (or left, if you said left) before you finish saying "Bumpity bump bump," that person goes to the circle center.

4. Play a practice round and then get started.

5. You may add a third and fourth command of "Me!" and "You!" In these cases, the person you pointed to must say either your or his or her own name.

6. If your group knows each other's names well, use middle or last names instead.

Variation

One variation is to challenge the person pointed at to come up with a word that starts with the same letter as the name of the person next to him (e.g., Jumpin' Joe, Silly Sarah, Excited Emily). If you choose to incorporate this variation, remind players that we care about our teammates and that we should avoid negative descriptors.

Instructor's Note

One possible variation is to have players pair off as partners. Each pair must lock arms and work together to tag other players. Once one member of a pair is tagged, the pair is out and must squat down. This variation may be followed by the three-member group version to illustrate for players how modifying the rules of a game can affect their experience.

Activity

Lessons from Adventure
T.E.A.M. Problem-Solving Model,
(see Player Portfolio)

One important objective of the Sports PLUS program is to help players develop good problem-solving skills. The T.E.A.M. problem-solving model provides a strategy to work out problems. It promotes thoughtful decision making by encouraging players to associate how they think with how they act. Equally important, players learn how the themes of the program come into play when they are faced with choices in their real lives.

The acronym T.E.A.M. not only reminds players of the steps involved in the strategy but also reinforces the importance of cooperating with others. In Sports PLUS programs, all are encouraged to be team players and to learn what this means, not only in sports, but also in everyday-life situations. Players should also be encouraged to use the T.E.A.M. strategy in their day-to-day experiences, both in and out of the group.

Below is a description of the model followed by steps involved and suggestions for how to use it. You can make an activity out of this introduction by creating a poster with the team model on it and have the players decorate it.

Setup

Introduce the T.E.A.M. model by going through each step with the group. Explain what each step is and what it accomplishes. Discuss how each step of the model leads to the next step and finally to a solution.

Step 1 **Take a Time-out** requires players to first stop, then think before they take action. Too often players react to situations without thinking. Impulsivereactions, especially when a person is frustrated, angry, or upset, usually make for bad decisions. Remind players to "keep their cool" and to assess the situation at hand. The familiar sports time-out signal is an excellent visual reminder that encourages players to stop and think about what they are doing.

Step 2 **Examine the Problem** asks players to identify the problem. Ask them to gather information and look for clues to define the situation that exists. In other words — what information is needed to define the problem? Players can try to answer the five Ws — the who, what, where, when, and why of the situation. At times they will discover that there may not be enough information to answer all the questions. Encourage them to see the problem from different angles, reminding them that a crucial part of examining any problem is to consider the intentions and motives of everyone involved.

Step 3 **Add Alternative Solutions** requires players to brainstorm different ways to solve the problem they have identified. Point out that there are no simple either/or solutions to most real problems. When brainstorming, players are asked to think of as many solutions as possible. Ask players to choose the most promising options and consider the pros and cons of each one. (Make sure players know what pro and con mean.) What are the consequences of each option? Are they safe? Challenge players to predict what others might do or say as a result of each option. Ask them to imagine, from a variety of different perspectives, how they would feel if the option was chosen.

Step 4 **Make a Game Plan** asks players to choose the best option available (the one with the most pros and the least cons) to reach their goals. Have players support their decision with solid reasons. They then design a plan with steps to reach their goal(s) and take action. Depending on the situation, the plan could involve one step or many steps to reach the desired outcome(s). After the plan is implemented, have players check their results. "Have our goals been reached?"

(It's a good idea to make a poster of the model or to write the basic steps on a board.) Players also receive a copy of the model in their Player Portfolios, for quick reference and to use as a problem-solving worksheet.

T.E.A.M. Summary

Step 1:   Take a Time-out — Stop and think before you take action.

Step 2:   Examine the Problem — What is the situation? Gather information to define the problem. State your goal to solve the problem.

Step 3:   Add Alternative Solutions — What are the options or alternatives? Explore alternatives and consider the pros and cons of each.

Step 4:   Make a Game Plan — Decide the best courses of action to take and make a plan to reach your goal(s).

Problem-solving strategies are not easy, especially for young people. Reminding players to take a timeout and think is an important first step. Of course, in real-life situations, the decision-making process happens quickly, but with repeated practice, they can learn to internalize the strategies and move quickly through the steps. Remember, practice builds competence and confidence!

Play

After a brief overview of the T.E.A.M. strategy and review of each step, bring the group together into a circle to solve an actual problem from the *You Make the Call* reading activity.

1. Spend a few minutes reviewing the story from the last session, *Kickball Trouble.*

2. Take about five minutes to consider the following questions:

    • Have you ever been in a situation like the one described in the story we read last time?

    • What is something we learned about today that would be helpful if a situation like this occurs in school?

3. Separate the large group into four or five equally-sized, smaller groups. Ask each group to make up a situation similar to the one that happened in the story. Have players use the T.E.A.M.

problem-solving strategy and the worksheet in their Player Portfolios to come up with a solution for the problem they create.

4. After 10-12 minutes, bring the small groups back together into a circle. Ask each group to choose a delegate toshare the problem and their T.E.A.M.-solution with the entire group.

- **R&R Huddle** (5 min.)

- **Recap** one or two key points from the activity.

- **Reconnect** to the theme unit.

- **Reset** andtransition to the next activity.

Cool-down

Cool-down Ritual

Alphabet Go-round

Try this fun, creative way to do a group go-round. Form a circle with the whole group. You or a volunteer can begin the go-round. The catch here is that the group is trying to make a sentence or statement one word at a time, with each word coming from the next person in the circle. (Allow players to pass if they get stuck or ask for help in coming up with a word.) Each word offered must begin with the same letter of the alphabet as their first names. Don't worry about grammar or if the statement gets confused or nonsensical—the point is to have some fun in closing out the day.

Session 7:
The Playing Field

Overview

Instructor's Notes: *Be sure to review this set of activities before starting this Sports PLUS Session. Directions for how to facilitate each activity are provided, but it is important that you become familiar with them so that you may more effectively lead the group.*

During group discussions, be sure to record all thoughts and ideas on a blackboard or newsprint. Remember that when students are working in their Player Portfolios, spelling, grammar, and penmanship are, relatively speaking, unimportant, so don't dwell on those details or you risk making Sports PLUS into MoreSchool.

This series of lessons begins with a straightforward *Quote of the Week* that emphasizes the importance of teamwork. The *You Make the Call* for this session gives students a chance to read, discuss, and write about the importance of being a responsible teammate, even in difficult situations.

Lessons from the Field gives students an opportunity to practice what they've learned about teamwork. Be on the lookout for teachable moments and be prepared to debrief based on how well they transfer these elements of teamwork.

This series of lessons ends with *The Playing Field,* a great activity for developing trust and for exploring the relationship and importance of good communication between a player and a coach and among individual teammates.

Finally, during the Cool-down, students begin to think about constructing their own sports card for the next session.

Session 7: The Playing Field Lessons from Literature	
Warm-up Begin the PLUS Cycle (10-15 min.) • Session Overview • Quote of the Week **Activity** Lessons from Literature (25-30 min.) • You Make the Call — *The Championship Meet*	**Cool-down** Continue the PLUS Cycle (5-10 min.) • Reflection **Materials** Copies of *The Championship Meet*

Warm-up

Quote of the Week
(see Player Portfolio)

A super team is better than a superstar.

— Larry Boyle[1]
Larry Boyle was a long time teacher and
swimming & diving coach at
Deerfield Academy in Deerfield, MA

Follow the five steps of the Quote of the Week Format (See the Getting Started chapter for additional explanation):

1. **Write the Quote of the Week:** Bring the group together into a circle, and write the Quote on the blackboard.

2. **Think about the Quote as a group:** Spend two to three minutes talking with students about what they think the quote means. Next ask them to share out answers to the group for the following question:

   • Have you ever seen a team that didn't play well, even though it had a lot of superstars on it? What are some reasons that such a team might not play well?

3. **Pair up to talk about the Quote:** Have students separate into pairs. Ask them to spend about five minutes discussing the

following questions with their partners. Explain that they will be sharing their answers with the whole group, so they may choose to write their answers in their Player Portfolios. (Be sure to walk around the groups, listen, and offer help where needed.):

- What is the difference between a super team and a superstar?

- What do you think is more important: Being the best player on a team or making your teammates play better? Explain your answer.

4. **Share answers with the whole group:** Come together as a large group and share the answers from each of the pair groups. Everyone who wants to should have an opportunity to share their answers.

5. **Reflect individually about the Quote:** Take two to three minutes for students to reflect individually by writing a response to the following Journal Question in their Player Portfolios:

- What are two or three things that make becoming a super team difficult?

- Two things I can do to make my team a super team are…

Activity

Lessons from Literature
You Make the Call
One-on-One
(see Player Portfolio)

Key Concepts

- Teamwork
- Respect
- Self-sacrifice
- Fairness

Setup

Bring the group together to sit in a circle. If there is time, use one or two of the following questions to help set the tone before reading the story:

> *"Sometimes the desire to win makes it difficult, if not impossible, to ensure that all players receive equal playing time. This often presents a dilemma for the coaches and players."*

- What are some ways that a team can go about deciding how to handle a problem like this?

- Where else besides sports teams might a problem like this occur?

Read the story aloud and with enthusiasm to the whole group.

Discussion Questions:

Separate students into groups by having them count off by threes (or fours depending on the group size). Spend a couple of minutes distributing their Player Portfolios and pencils. Ask one or two volunteers to help.

Using their Player Portfolios, have students discuss and write answers to the following questions in their small groups. It is important to remember that spelling, grammar, and penmanship are NOT important during this activity.

1. Who are the main characters in this story?

2. What is the main problem these characters face?

3. What are some possible ways that the team can solve their dilemma?

4. What would happen if the problem were solved in this way?

   - How would Melanie feel?

   - How would Janetta feel?

   - How might the other team members feel?

5. If you were on the Carver School track team what are two different ways you might sovle the problem?

6. What might make your decision difficult?

7. What solution would you choose to handle the situation if you were Janetta? What about if you were Melanie?

Group Share:

- After the small groups have had time to discuss each question, gather the groups together to sit in one large circle.

- Ask each small group to share their suggestions for solving the problem, using students' answers to number three above. (As suggestions are given, you or a volunteer should write them on poster paper for all to see.)

- Once all of the solutions have been laid out, spend a few minutes discussing the consequences of each solution, using students' answers to question number four as a guide.

- As a group, choose the best solution (i.e., the most good for the most people).

- Finally, as a group, complete the following two focus prompts on poster paper.

- One thing we can take from this story is that we should…

- We should be careful not to…

Cool-down

- **R&R Huddle** (5 min.)

- **Recap** using one or two key discussion points or focus on the discussion below as a guide:

  1. Being a member of a team sometimes requires personal sacrifice for the good of the team.

  2. Sometimes a team must give something up in order to treat

its members fairly and with respect. Situations like the one in this story are not easy to solve and, in the end, someone must make a difficult decision.

- **Reconnect** students with one or two of the following questions:

    1. How can a strong sense of teamwork help a group of individuals work through a problem like this?

    2. Do you think a team that did not practice good teamwork will have a harder time solving this problem than a team that did? Why or why not?

    3. Reset and give information about the next lesson.

Session 7: The Playing Field Lessons from the Field	
Warm-up Begin the PLUS Cycle (5 min.) • Session Overview • Touching Base on Teamwork **Activity** Lessons from the Field(25-30 min.) • Sports Activity	**Cool-down** Continue the PLUS Cycle (5-10 min.) • Reflection • Goal-setting **Materials** Sports equipment

Warm-up

Touching Base On Teamwork (5 min.)

Ask students to think about the previous lesson. What can they do today to bring the Lessons from Literature into their work together in the sports activity?

Activity

Lessons from the Field
Sports Activity

Block I: Getting Started (5 min.)

On the first day, players will learn how to measure their resting heart rates (RHR). They will also set baselines for their RHR, number of sit-ups/push-ups/lunges/calf raises, and number of jumps during jump rope. Each day they will try to improve upon their Past Personal Best (PPB) by achieving their Future Best Goal (FBG) and by tracking progress toward that goal in the physical activities progress chart located in the back of their Player Portfolios. Take one minute to make sure all participants turn to the back of their portfolios and locate the progress charts. Explain to them that they will be using this chart each time you meet to do physical activities. Be sure to emphasize the importance of keeping track of their progress by using the chart.

Stand together in a circle for all Getting Started activities (except for jogging). Have players partner up, with one player doing the activity and the partner keeping count and giving encouragement. Be sure they have their Portfolios handy so that they can record their progress. Encourage them to clap and cheer for their teammates to create an enthusiastic environment. You may also choose to include music.

- **Measure resting heart rate (RHR)** — Spend a few minutes showing players how to find their pulses, either on their necks or wrists. Explain that you will be giving them a few seconds to count how many times their hearts beat. Take a moment to allow players to sit quietly on the floor and find their pulses. Give them 30 seconds to count their heartbeats.

- **Record, check in and set goals** — Allow a couple of minutes for players to record their RHRs in their Player Portfolios.

- **Jog (2-3 min.)** — This can be done as a lap or in place as a circle.

- **Stretch (2-3 min.)** — Be sure to include stretches for the major muscle groups.

- **Strength/Endurance (1 min.)** — On this first day, players will set baseline numbers for the four Strength/Endurance activities (push-ups, sit-ups, lunges, calf raises), but usually, you will only choose one or two. They will work in pairs. One member of the pair will have 30 seconds to do as many of the activities as they can. Their partner will cheer them on and count for them.

- **Jump Rope (4 min.)** — Again, players will work in pairs, with one person jumping and the other person counting and cheering. Players should have three to four sets of 30-45 seconds of jumping rope.

- **Track personal progress** — Have players record their totals for steps five and six in their Player Portfolios. These totals will represent their baseline achievements, or their Past Personal Bests (PPB). Each day, players will check their progress from the previous session and will set a Future Personal Best Goal (FBG) to work toward for next time. Be sure to remind them about setting realistic goals (for example, adding one or two to their baseline, as opposed to 10).

Block II: Structured Play (30 min.)

Skill Play (10 min.)

Choose one or two of the following activities to play today. You can refer back to the *Physical Activities Description Appendix* for instructions on how to run the activities. Encourage players to cheer for each other, and include music if you wish.

- Balance Tag

- Bowling

- High Skipping Relay

- Hopscotch

- Shuttle Run Relay

Sport Play (20 min.)

As a group, decide which sport you want to play today. Select from the sport list contained in the *Sports List Appendix*. Be sure to periodically review with the group the Physical Activities Recommendations for Sport from Chapter Six.

Cool-down

If time permits, close the day with a few minutes of stretching while conducting the following R&R Huddle.

- **Recap** one or two key moments from the Lessons from the Field.

- **Reconnect** players back to the theme unit.

- **Reset** and transition players to the Cool-down, Reflection time.

   OR

- **Reflection**

Use this time to highlight teachable moments you observed during the day and to give players an opportunity to share their experiences about Sports PLUS during the day. The following questions can serve as a guide:

- What did you like about today?

- What did you learn today?

- How did we show teamwork today?

- What are one or two ways we can show better teamwork next time?

Session 7: The Playing Field Lessons from Adventure	
Warm-up Begin the PLUS Cycle (5 min.) • Session Overview • Car and Driver **Activity** Lessons from Adventure (25-30 min.) • The Playing Field	**Cool-down** Continue the PLUS Cycle (5-10 min.) • Reflection • Mental Video • Playing Cards — Extension activity **Materials** One blindfold per each pair of players, boundary markers, assorted obstacles, (e.g., sports balls, tennis rackets, stuffed animals, ropes, traffic cones, etc.)

Warm-up

Touching Base on Teamwork

Ask students to think about the importance of pairs working together in the context of a larger team. How have they seen this come to life during earlier lessons? How is communication helpful when working on a team? What does good communication look like?

Warm-up Activity — Car and Driver

This activity will get students warmed up to the process of working and communicating with a partner.

Setup

Lay out a "course" with rope or cones. Gather students to listen to the instructions. Help each student find a partner.

Play

Tell students that in this activity they will get to practice being a driver of a very expensive car.

Show students the "course" and ask each pair to gather in the course area.

Ask students to choose who will be the car and who will be the driver first. The person who is the driver should stand behind the car with his or her hands on the car's shoulders.

The goal of the activity is for the drivers to safely negotiate traffic and drive their car through the course.

After a few minutes, ask students to switch roles. Be sure to talk about safety considerations!

Activity

Lessons from Adventure
The Playing Field

This activity is designed to build trust and foster communication between partners. One person in each pair is the "coach" and the other is the "player." Players coach their blindfolded partners (or have players close their eyes) through a field of obstacles. The coach learns the difficulty of communicating with a player who is "in the game," and the players learn skills to better listen to and understand the coach.

Setup

The best place to do this activity is in the gym, but it can also be done in a classroom, a hallway or outside. Set up the "playing field" ahead of time. Using the boundary markers, create a rectangle about eight to 10 feet wide and 20—25 feet long. Spread the obstacles around in the area so that there is no clear path through the field.

Play

Introduce the activity in the following way: "Today we are thinking about the roles we all play on a team. Both the coach and the players have important roles. This game will help us to practice these roles." Depending on the size of your field, you can have a number of pairs in the field at one time adding to the difficulty of the activity.

1. Have players partner up.

2. Bring the group to one end of the "playing field."

3. One partner will wear the blindfold (or close his or her eyes). This person will try to get from one end of the field you have set up to the other without touching any of the obstacles. The other partner will coach the blindfolded student through the field.

4. Coaches may not enter the field or touch the player. They must stay outside of the boundary markers. They may go along the sidelines.

5. Coaches count the number of touches the player makes with the obstacles as the player navigates the field. The goal is to have no touches.

6. After the first partner has passed through the field, have players switch roles. Challenge them to get even fewer touches than they did the last time.

• **R&R Huddle** (5 min.)

• **Recap** by looking at how well each pair did in meeting the goal of the game. Use one or two of the following questions as a guide:

1. How many touches did you have going through the field? What made not touching the obstacles so hard? What did you do that made it easier?

2. How well did the players listen to their coaches? (Be sure to let both players and coaches answer this question to see if there are any differences of opinion.) What was hard about being a player? (e.g., wearing a blindfold, not being able to see the obstacles, other players playing at the same time)

3. How did the coaches communicate with the players? What was hard about being a coach? (e.g., players not understanding directions, lots of noise from other coaches and players, etc.)

4. Could there be someone else on a team besides the coach who might help you through the obstacles?

- **Reconnect** players to other situations they might face in their daily lives by asking them to complete the following focus prompts:

    1. One thing I learned from this activity that will help me to be a better listener is…

    2. One thing I learned from this activity that will help me to be a better teacher/coach is…

- **Reset** and transition to the next activity.

Cool-down

Cool-down Ritual

Mental Video

This is a nice way to transition from the program allowing players to mentally review the learning from the past few sessions. If you have space, bring the group into a circle and have everyone sit down. Have them close their eyes and assume their best meditation position. The point is to get really comfortable.

Once everyone has settled down, ask players to imagine that they have a video playing in their mind. The tape is of the past meetings in this group. Have them imagine that they are reviewing this tape. Tell them to hit the pause button when they come to a particularly good example of the group coming together as a team. These moments can come from any kind of activity during the program, from opening activities, to group discussions, to the sports activities. Remind players to be very still and quiet during this time so that they do not disturb others.

As players finish reviewing their tapes, ask them to open their eyes but remain still and quiet until everyone else is finished. Give the group a few minutes todo their review, and if necessary give them a 10-second countdown before everyone opens their eyes. Ask for volunteers to describe the moments they paused on, the moments that they felt the group pulled together and displayed good teamwork. Allow as many players to speak as would like to before ending.

End of Session Extension:

Homework: Sports cards activity

Explain to the group that during the next session they will be making their own trading cards—of themselves. Talk briefly about what information is typically found on trading cards. Ask players to share what cards, if any, they collect. Encourage the group to bring several cards to the next session so they can be used as examples.

Players will need a picture of themselves for this activity. If you have the capability to take individual pictures, you might think of taking photos during the sports session, focusing on the action poses often found on sports cards. If this is a difficult task, just have them do their best to find a suitable photo of themselves at home.

Goal-setting

Use this time to help players track progress toward their individually chosen goals, as well as toward team goals. As goals from earlier sessions are reached, guide players in setting additional individual and team goals related to *Teamwork*.

Session 8:
All Stars

Overview

> **Instructor's Notes:** *Be sure to review this set of activities before starting this Sports PLUS Session. Directions for how to facilitate each activity are provided, but it is important that you become familiar with them so that you may more effectively lead the group.*
>
> *During group discussions, be sure to record all thoughts and ideas on a blackboard or newsprint. Remember that when students are working in their Player Portfolios, spelling, grammar, and penmanship are, relatively speaking, unimportant, so don't dwell on those details or you risk making Sports PLUS into MoreSchool.*

This session begins with *The Sports Short.* This *Lesson from Literature* illustrates that teamwork often is more valued than simply being a star and that even a star player may not be an all-star if they don't exhibit teamwork.

Sometimes simple activities, like Copy Cat, present metaphors to help us explore more complex issues. All-Star Sports Cards encourages students to think about who they are and how they want others to see them. You may want to prepare the material for this ahead of time to minimize setup time.

During the Cool-down, students learn more about each other's role models.

Session 8:
All Stars
Lessons from Literature

Warm-up	Cool-down
Begin the PLUS Cycle (10-15 min.)	Continue the PLUS Cycle (5-10 min.)
• Session Overview	• Reflection
• Quote of the Week	**Materials**
Activity	Copies of *All-Star Sports Team*
Lessons from Literature (25-30 min.)	
• Sports Short — *All-Star Sports Team*	

Warm-up

Quote of the Week

Michael, if you can't pass, you can't play

— Coach Dean Smith to Michael Jordan
in his first year at UNC

Follow the five steps of the Quote of the Week Format (See the Getting Started chapter for additional explanation):

1. **Write the Quote of the Week:** Bring the group together into a circle, and write the Quote on the blackboard.

2. **Think about the Quote as a group:** Spend two to three minutes talking with students about what they think the quote means. Ask them to share answers with the group for the following question:

   • What does this quote have to do with teamwork?

3. **Pair up to talk about the Quote:** Have students separate into pairs. Ask them to spend about five minutes discussing the following questions with their partners. Explain that they will be sharing their answers with the whole group, so they may choose to write their answers in their Player Portfolios. (Be sure to walk around the groups, listen, and offer help where needed.):

   • Michael Jordan is an "all star" — why is it important for him to pass the ball to his teammates?

   • Do you think this quote applies to our Sports PLUS group? Why or why not?

4. **Share answers with the whole group:** Come together as a large group and share the answers from each of the pair groups. Everyone who wants to should have an opportunity to share their answers.

5. **Reflect individually about the Quote:** Take two to three minutes for students to reflect individually by writing a response to the following Journal Question in their Player Portfolios:

   • Describe an example of the quote's meaning that relates to the world outside of sports.

Activity

Lessons from Literature
Sports Short:
All-Star Sports Team

Key Concepts

- Perseverance
- Teamwork
- Respect

Setup

Bring the group together to sit in a circle. Use the following questions to help facilitate a short, five to six minute discussion to help set the tone before reading the story. (Be sure to record their answers on the board or on poster paper.)

"Being a member of a team means that you sometimes have to think first of what the team needs before your own needs."

- Can you think of a time playing sports or in school when you were given an opportunity to vote for an All-Star—someone to represent your team or group?

- What things seemed important when thinking about the kind of person you would want to represent you?

- Who deserves such an honor and what kinds of qualities would they have?

The Story

Read the story aloud and with enthusiasm to the whole group.

The All-Star Team
(see Player Portfolio)

Discussion Questions:

Spend a couple of minutes distributing students' Player Portfolios and pencils. (Ask for one or two volunteers to help.) Work together as a whole group to answer the following questions. Write the questions and focus prompts on a blackboard or newsprint.

Questions one through four should be answered in a round-robin format, with one student answering one question. Try to include those who may not always participate. (If answers for questions three and four are imprecise or need further elaboration, ask if anyone has anything to add.)

1. Who are the main characters in this story?

2. What is the problem or challenge they face?

3. How does each character handle the problem?

4. What happened then?

The following focus prompt should be answered in an exhaustive format (i.e., continue letting students give responses until no new answers are given.)

5. Don learned he should…

For questions six and seven, allow all students an opportunity to share their answers, regardless of whether or not the answers are original.

6. When would it be important in your life to… [insert answer from previous statement]?

7. One thing that might make doing this difficult is…

Finally, ask students to write their responses to the following prompt in their Player Portfolios.

8. One specific way I might show teamwork is by…

Cool-down

- **R&R Huddle** (5 min.)

- **Recap** with one or two key points that arose from the discussion.

- **Reconnect** using one or two of the following questions: Sometimes we all have to put aside our own desires for the good of a team. What are some situations where you might have to do this at school? At home?

- **Reset** and get ready for the next lesson.

Session 8: AllStars Lessons from the Field	

Warm-up
 Begin the PLUS Cycle (5 min.)
 	
  • Session Overview
 	
  • Touching Base on Teamwork
 	
Activity
 Lessons from the Field(25-30 min.)
 	
  • Sports Activity
	Cool-down
	 Continue the PLUS Cycle (5-10 min.)
	
	  • Reflection
	
	  • Goal-setting
	
	Materials
	 Sports equipment

Warm-up

Touching Base On Teamwork (5 min.)

Ask students to think about the previous lesson. What can they do today to bring the Lessons from Literature into their work together in the sports activity?

Activity

Lessons from the Field
Sports Activity

Block I: Getting Started (5 min.)

On the first day, players will learn how to measure their resting heart rates (RHR). They will also set baselines for their RHR, number of sit-ups/pushups/lunges/calf raises, and number of jumps during jump rope. Each day they will try to improve upon their Past Personal Best (PPB) by achieving their Future Best Goal (FBG) and by tracking progress toward that goal in the physical activities progress chart located in the back of their Player Portfolios. Take one minute to make sure all participants turn to the back of their portfolios and locate the progress charts. Explain to them that they will be using this chart each time you meet to do physical activities. Be sure to emphasize the importance of keeping track of their progress by using the chart.

Stand together in a circle for all Getting Started activities (except for jogging). Have players partner up, with one player doing the activity and the partner keeping count and giving encouragement. Be sure they have their Portfolios handy so that they can record their progress. Encourage them to clap and cheer for their teammates to create an enthusiastic environment. You may also choose to include music.

- **Measure resting heart rate (RHR)** — Spend a few minutes showing players how to find their pulses, either on their necks or wrists. Explain that you will be giving them a few seconds to count how many times their hearts beat. Take a moment to allow them to sit quietly on the floor and find their pulses. Give them 30 seconds to count their heartbeats.

- **Record, check in and set goals** — Allow a couple of minutes for players to record their RHRs in their Player Portfolios.

- **Jog (2-3 min.)** — This can be done as a lap or in place as a circle.

- **Stretch (2-3 min.)** — Be sure to include stretches for the major muscle groups.

- **Strength/Endurance (1 min.)** — On this first day, players will set baseline numbers for the four Strength/Endurance activities (push-ups, sit-ups, lunges, calf raises), but usually, you will only choose one or two. They will work in pairs. One member of the pair will have 30 seconds to do as many of the activities as they can. Their partner will cheer them on and count for them.

- **Jump Rope (4 min.)** — Again, players will work in pairs, with one person jumping and the other person counting and cheering. They should have three to four sets of 30-45 seconds of jumping rope.

- **Track personal progress** — Have players record their totals for steps five and six in their Player Portfolios. These totals will represent their baseline achievements, or their Past Personal Bests (PPB). Each day, playerswillcheck their progress from

the previous session and will set a Future Personal Best Goal (FBG) to work toward for next time. Be sure to remind them about setting realistic goals (for example, adding one or two to their baseline, as opposed to 10).

Block II: Structured Play (30 min.)

Skill Play (10 min.)

Choose one or two of the following activities to play today. You can refer back to the *Physical Activities Description Appendix* for instructions on how to run the activities. Encourage players to cheer for each other, and include music if you wish.

- Hula Hoop Marathon
- Train
- Ball Bowling
- Limbo
- Locomotion Relay

Sport Play (20 min.)

As a group, decide which sport you want to play today. Select from the sport list contained in the *Sports List Appendix.* Be sure to periodically review the Physical Activities Recommendations for Sport from Chapter Six.

Cool-down

If time permits, close the day with a few minutes of stretching while conducting the following R&R Huddle.

- **Recap** one or two key moments from the Lessons from the Field.
- **Reconnect** players back to the theme unit.

- **Reset** and transition players to the Cool-down, Reflection time.

  OR

- **Reflection**

Use this time to highlight teachable moments you observed during the day and to give players an opportunity to share their experiences of Sports PLUS during the day. The following questions can serve as a guide:

- What did you like about today?

- What did you learn today?

- How did we show teamwork today?

- What are one or two ways we can show better teamwork next time?

Goal-setting

Use this time to help players track progress toward their individually-chosen goals, as well as toward team goals. As goals from earlier sessions are reached, guide players in setting additional individual and team goals related to **Teamwork.**

Session 8: All Stars Lessons from Adventure	
Warm-up Begin the PLUS Cycle (5 min.) • Session Overview • Copy Cat	**Cool-down** Continue the PLUS Cycle (5-10 min.) • Reflection • High Five
Activity Lessons from Adventure (25-30 min.) • All-Star Sports Cards	**Materials** Card stock, cut into an appropriate size for trading cards (4 per person), crayons, colored materials, scissors, cardboard/posterboard markers, glue, tape, photos of players, laminting paper or machine, or large strips of clear plastic tape.

Warm-up

Copy Cat

Open the day with a brief discussion about role models. What is a role model? What are some qualities that you might look for in a role model? Explain to the players that we will be spending some time talking about our heroes later on today, but for right now, we are going to do an activity that has to do with role models. Tell the group that this is a silent activity in which concentration, observation, and subtlety are important to success.

Play

1. Have the large group form a circle.

2. Tell players that they need to select one person in the circle to be their personal idol. It is very important, however, that this person does not know that he or she is your idol.

3. Once everyone has chosen an idol, have everyone look down at the floor.

4. Count down from five. When you get to one, have the players look up and mimic exactly what their idol is doing. Remind

the players not to look directly at their idol so they don't know they are being watched.

5. Instruct players that as their idol changes facial expression, posture, movement, they should do exactly the same.

What often happens in this activity is that everyone ends up in the same pose. It can be fun trying to figure out who is the ultimate leader, the one who initiated the pose. Play a few rounds and then bring the group together into an R&R Huddle.

*   **R&R Huddle** (5 min.)

*   **Recap** using the following questions as a guide: How did you choose your idol? Why? Did anyone follow you? How did this feel?

*   **Reconnect** players by highlighting one or two of the following questions:

    1. What does it mean to be a role model?

    2. How do we choose people to follow?

    3. What is the difference between being a role model and being a famous person? Are all famous people role models?

    4. Who are some famous role models? What about famous people who are not good role models?

*   **Reset** and transition to the next activity.

Activity

**Lessons from Adventure
All-Star Sports Cards**

Materials

Card stock, cut into size for trading cards (4 per person), crayons, colored materials, scissors, cardboard/posterboard markers, glue, tape, photos of players, laminating paper or machine, or large strips of clear plastic tape.

Ask players if they collect sports cards. Which cards are their favorites? You or your players should bring in sports cards to share. List the kind of information that can be found on a typical sports card.

Sample List:

1. Player's name and number

2. Height & weight

3. Position

4. Team

5. Date and place of birth

6. School or college attended

7. Statistics

Inform the group that they will be making their own sports cards, featuring themselves as the allstars.

Play

1. Design the cards: Decide what information is going to be on the front and back of the cards. Each student should create his or her own design, laying it out on scrap paper first if they want. Encourage them to think about the type of information they might like to share with the rest of the group. Use trading cards as examples. Some examples may be:

   • My favorite/lucky number is…

   • My favorite sports are…

   • I like sports because…

   • My favorite book is…

- My favorite movie is…

- Something unique about me is…

- I write with my left/right hand.

- My eyes are…

- One thing I am proud of is…

2. Once they know what information they are going to put on the cards, they can begin. Be sure to have extra materials for players who want to start over. If possible, laminate the cards.

3. After players have finished making their sports cards, ask them to exchange their card with someone else. Spend several minutes exchanging cards until everyone has had a chance to exchange with everyone else. Or spend a few minutes at the end of each day exchanging cards with a new person. While exchanging, ask players to look for all the things they have in common and how they differ.

4. Don't forget to have staff create their own cards.

- **R&R** Huddle (5 min.)

- **Recap** with the following questions: What did you learn about yourself while making the card? What did you learn about your other group members?

- **Reconnect** players using the following questions and prompts as guides: How might differences among the team members be an advantage to our group? One thing I can do at school (on my sport team) to be a good role model is …? It is important to … when being a role model for others.

- **Reset** and transition to the next activity.

Variations

One possible variation is to have players pair off as partners. Each pair must lock arms and work together to tag other players. Once one member of a pair is tagged, the pair is out and must squat down. This variation may be followed by the three-member group version to illustrate for players how modifying the rules of a game can affect their experience.

1. Help players read the different types of statistical information on the cards they bring in. Quiz them on how to calculate information such as batting average and shooting percentage. Sports statistics provide a fun way for them to learn and practice basic math skills. Remember that there are box scores in the sports section of your local newspaper every day.

2. A good source for sports cards is *Sports Illustrated for Kids.* These cards feature female and male athletes. They also contain personal information such as the athlete's favorite music, food, and hobbies.

3. An excellent book for incorporating math skills with baseball is called *Baseball Math,* by Christopher Jenison, (1995) GoodYear Books: Glenview Illinois.

4. If materials are a problem or if you don't think all of the players will be able to bring in pictures of themselves, a good alternative is to have the players work together to create a poster about their own role models. They can add quotes from their role models or insert descriptions of the particular qualities they admire about their role models.**Cool-down**

Reflection

Gather the group into a circle to talk about some of the things they learned about being a good role model today. What are two or three qualities we might look for in a good role model? How do we choose our role models? Invite players to go around the circle and share with the group who their personal role models are. Challenge the group to remember their teammates' role models because it will be important for the closing activity.

Cool-down Ritual

Bumpity, Bump Role Model Activity

This version of Bumpity Bump focuses on players getting to know each other a little bit more. A goal of the game is that each person will learn everyone else's role model.

1. Have players stand up in a circle with you at the center.

2. You will point at any person in the circle and say "Left!" or "Right!"

3. The person you have pointed to must say the name of the role model for the person on the left (or right, if you have said "right"). If he or she can't remember, the person says who his or her role model is, and moves to the middle of the circle. If they do get the name right, they go to the middle and do the next round of pointing. Go around once as a warm-up and continue to play a few times, switching spots each time.

4. Close the activity and the day by having the group sit down in the circle.

5. Ask for volunteers to explain why they've chosen their particular role models. What are one or two qualities they admire in this person? Do you see these qualities in yourself or your friends? What are some specific examples? Allow time for sharing.

Session 9:
Team Charades

Overview

> **Instructor's Notes:** *Be sure to review this set of activities before starting this Sports PLUS Session. Directions for how to facilitate each activity are provided, but it is important that you become familiar with them so that you may more effectively lead the group.*

During group discussions, be sure to record all thoughts and ideas on a blackboard or newsprint. Remember that when students are working in their Player Portfolios, spelling, grammar, and penmanship are, relatively speaking, unimportant, so don't dwell on those details or you risk making Sports PLUS into MoreSchool.

This session begins by asking students to create their own *Quote of the Week,* a great opportunity to personalize the lessons they have learned about Teamwork and to express their understanding of Teamwork. *Create Your Own Story* gives students a chance to use their imaginations while drawing on their understanding of how teamwork can be lived out. Finally, *Team Charades* reminds students about the characteristics of a good team and what constitutes teamwork.

Session 9: Team Charades Lessons from Literature	
Warm-up Begin the PLUS Cycle (10-15 min.) • Session Overview • Quote of the Week **Activity** Lessons from Literature (25-30 min.) • Create Your Own Story	**Cool-down** Continue the PLUS Cycle (5-10 min.) • Reflection **Materials** Player Portfolios

Warm-up

Quote of the Week

(see Player Portfolio)

The best way to cheer yourself up is to cheer everybody else up
— Mark Twain
World Book Encyclopedia, Contributor:

Alan Gribben, Ph.D.,
Professor and Head, Department of English,
Auburn University, Montgomery.

Instructor's Note

Before separating into groups, you may want to ask students if they know who Mark Twain was. Spend a few minutes explaining who he was using the following as a guide:

Mark Twain (1835-1910), was the pen name of Samuel Langhorne Clemens, one of the major authors of American fiction. Twain is also considered the greatest humorist in American literature. Twain's varied works include novels, travel narratives, short stories, sketches, and essays. His writings about the Mississippi River, such as *The Adventures of Tom Sawyer, Life on the Mississippi,* and *The Adventures of Huckleberry Finn,* have been especially popular among modern readers . (*World Book Encyclopedia,* Contributor: Alan Gribben, Ph.D., Professor and Head, Department of English, Auburn University, Montgomery.) One possible variation is to have players pair off as partners. Each pair must lock arms and work together to tag other players. Once one member of a pair is tagged, the pair is out and must squat down. This variation may be followed by the three-member group version to illustrate for players how modifying the rules of a game can affect their experience.

Follow the five steps of the Quote of the Week Format (See the Getting Started chapter for additional explanation):

1. **Write the Quote of the Week:** Bring the group together into a circle, and write the Quote on the blackboard.

2. **Think about the Quote as a group:** Spend two to three minutes talking with student about what they think the quote means. Ask them to share answers with the group for the following question:

   - How can you cheer yourself up by cheering someone else up?

3. **Pair up to talk about the Quote:** Have students separate into pairs. Ask them to spend about five minutes discussing the following questions with their partners. Explain that they will

be sharing their answers with the whole group, so they may choose to write their answers in their Player Portfolios. (Be sure to walk around the groups, listen, and offer help where needed.):

- What are some examples of when it might be important to cheer up other people?

- Why do you think it might be important to your team as a whole to help cheer up teammates who are feeling down?

4. **Share answers with the whole group:** Come together as a large group and share the answers from each of the pair groups. Everyone who wants to should have an opportunity to share their answers.

5. **Reflect individually about the Quote:** Take two or three minutes for students to reflect individually by writing a response to the following Journal Question in their Player Portfolios:

- How can helping others to feel better assist a team in reaching its goal?

- Do you think it's important to help others feel better even when it doesn't involve helping a team to accomplish a goal? Why or why not?

Activity

Lessons from Literature
Create Your Own Story

The following activity encourages students' creativity andsolidifies their understanding of teamwork. By having students create their own stories involving teamwork, they will draw upon personal knowledge and examples of teamwork, as well as exemplary role models. This activity also encourages them to understand the benefits of teamwork and to transfer that understanding into a new context. It is important to remember that spelling, grammar, and penmanship are NOT important during this activity.

Setup

Bring the group together into a circle and explain the activity as you pass out students' Player Portfolios. Use the following description as a guide:

> *"Today during Lessons from Literature, we will be creating our own story about* Teamwork. *You may choose to work individually or with up to three other students. It may be helpful to create a story about some conflict or problem that is worked out using teamwork. Think of things that may have occurred on your own sports teams or during the Lessons from the Field this theme unit. You also may choose to write a story about some of the characters in an* Instant Replay *or to create a different ending for one of the stories we've read. Spend a few minutes looking over your Player Portfolios to begin getting some ideas."*

Play

Offer guidance as students separate into groups. Make sure that no one feels left out, but do let the students choose their own groups. Walk around the room offering help and suggestions as needed.

Once students have finished writing their stories, give them an opportunity to illustrate them if they would like. (Some students may find it easier to draw a picture before writing an accompanying story. This may help spur their imaginations. Let this be an option for those who want it.)

Explain to students that they will have an opportunity to share their stories with the group on the next Sports PLUS day if they wish to do so. They can finish illustrating their stories at home if necessary.

Discussion Questions:

After students have had an opportunity to write and illustrate their stories, bring the whole group back together in a circle for a brief reflection on the following questions. Let everyone share who wants to do so.

- What stories or examples of teamwork did you use to create your story?

- What are some of the problems that your main characters faced in your stories?

- How do your main characters solve their dilemma?

Cool-down

- **R&R Huddle** (5 min.)

- **Recap** one or two key points from the discussion.

- **Reconnect** students to the theme unit.

- **Reset** and get ready for the next lesson.

Session 9: Team Charades Lessons from the Field	
Warm-up Begin the PLUS Cycle (5 min.) • Session Overview • Touching Base on Teamwork	**Cool-down** Continue the PLUS Cycle (5-10 min.) • Reflection • Goal-setting
Activity Lessons from the Field(25-30 min.) • Sports Activity	**Materials** Sports equipment

Warm-up
Touching Base On Teamwork (5 min.)

Ask students to think about the previous lesson. What can they do today to bring the Lessons from Literature into their work together in the sports activity?

Activity

Lessons from the Field
Sports Activity

Block I: Getting Started (5 min.)

On the first day, players will learn how to measure their resting heart rates (RHR). They will also set baselines for their RHR, number of sit-ups/pushups/lunges/calf raises, and number of jumps during jump rope. Each day they will try to improve upon their Past Personal Best (PPB) by achieving their Future Best Goal (FBG) and by tracking progress toward that goal in the physical activities progress chart located in the back of their Player Portfolios. Take one minute to make sure all participants turn to the back of their portfolios and locate the progress charts. Explain to them that they will be using this chart each time you meet to do physical activities. Be sure to emphasize the importance of keeping track of their progress by using the chart.

Stand together in a circle for all *Getting Started* activities (except for jogging). Have players partner up, with one player doing the activity and the partner keeping count and giving encouragement. Be sure they have their Portfolios handy so that they can record their progress. Encourage them to clap and cheer for their teammates to create an enthusiastic environment. You may also choose to include music.

- **Measure resting heart rate (RHR)** — Spend a few minutes showing players how to find their pulses, either on their necks or wrists. Explain that you will be giving them a few seconds to count how many times their hearts beat. Take a moment to allow them to sit quietly on the floor and find their pulses. Give them 30 seconds to count their heartbeats.

- **Record, check in and set goals** — Allow a couple of minutes for players to record their RHRs in their Player Portfolios.

- **Jog (2-3 min.)** — This can be done as a lap or in place as a circle.

- **Stretch (2-3 min.)** — Be sure to include stretches for the major muscle groups.

- **Strength/Endurance (1 min.)** — On this first day, players will set baseline numbers for the four Strength/Endurance activities (push-ups, sit-ups, lunges, calf raises), but usually, you will only choose one or two. They will work in pairs. One member of the pair will have 30 seconds to do as many of the activities as they can. Their partner will cheer them on and count for them.

- **Jump Rope (4 min.)** — Again, players will work in pairs, with one person jumping and the other person counting and cheering. They should have three to four sets of 30-45 seconds of jumping rope.

- **Track personal progress** — Have players record their totals for steps five and six in their Player Portfolios. These totals will represent their baseline achievements, or their Past Personal Bests (PPB). Each day, playerswillcheck their progress from the previous session and will set a Future Personal Best Goal (FBG) to work toward for next time. Be sure to remind them about setting realistic goals (for example, adding one or two to their baseline, as opposed to 10).

Block II: Structured Play (30 min.)

Skill Play (10 min.)

Choose one or two of the following activities to play today. You can refer back to the *Physical Activities Description Appendix* for instructions on how to run the activities. Encourage players to cheer for each other, and include music if you wish.

- Softball Throw

- Round and Round the Hoops Go

- Drum Major Walk

- Hoop Monster

- Gorilla Walk

Sport Play (20 min.)

As a group, decide which sport you want to play today. Select from the sport list contained in the *Sports List Appendix*. Be sure to periodically review with the group the Physical Activities Recommendations for Sport from Chapter Six.

Cool-down

If time permits, close the day with a few minutes of stretching while conducting the following R&R Huddle.

- **Recap** one or two key moments from the Lessons from the Field.

- **Reconnect** players back to the theme unit.

- **Reset** and transition players to the Cool-down, Reflection time.

   OR

- **Reflection**

Use this time to highlight teachable moments you observed during the day and to give players an opportunity to share their experiences about Sports PLUS during the day. The following questions can serve as a guide:

- What did you like about today?

- What did you learn today?

- How did we show teamwork today?

- What are one or two ways we can show better teamwork next time?

Goal-setting

Use this time to help players track progress toward their individually chosen goals, as well as toward team goals. As goals from earlier sessions are reached, guide players in setting additional individual and team goals related to Teamwork.

Session 9: Team Charades Lessons from Adventure	
Warm-up Begin the PLUS Cycle (5 min.) • Session Overview • Hustle Bustle	**Cool-down** Continue the PLUS Cycle (5-10 min.) • Reflection • Impulse Go-Round
Activity Lessons from Adventure (25-30 min.) • Team Charades	**Materials** Charade cards — 8 per group of players; paper, pencils, pens, crayons, markers

Warm-up

Hustle Bustle

This is a quick activity that allows students to learn names and to think about the nature of competition.

Setup

Gather the group into a circle.

Play

1. Ask each student to say their name as you go around the circle to the right.

2. Ask students to guess how fast they think they can do exactly the same thing: each person saying their own first name, in order, around the circle.

3. Do a first round, keeping track of how long it takes. Consider this Team A's first time.

4. Tell the group to go again, trying to beat their original time.

5. Next, have the group try the same task, but this time going around to the left. Consider this Team B. Have the group try a few times in this new direction.

6. For a final round, attempt Team A and Team B at the same time. Which will be faster?

7. Finish by asking students if they found themselves holding alliegences to Team A or Team B. Why or why not?

Activity

Lessons from Adventure
Team Charades

This variation of charades has small groups competing against each other to be the fastest.

Separate the group into small teams of four or five players.

Have the groups spread around the room so they are all the same distance from you—at least ten feet away if possible.

Tip

Remember that during a brainstorming session, there is no such thing as a wrong answer. All ideas are listened to and treated with respect. Brainstorming is an excellent strategy to get students thinking, listening to others, using one idea to spark another, etc. Depending on how well your group is working together as a team, you can impose more or less structure and rules on the If the members of your group have never played charades, you will need to give the group some basic charades coaching: signals for number of words, syllables, sounds like, etc. Before beginning the game, do some practice rounds. If during the game a player gets stuck, offer some help or a new card. If the player is really stuck, offer a skip card.

Play

1. The goal is for each team to complete eight charades as quickly as possible. The first team to complete eight charades wins.

2. Each team sends a person to get a card from you. That person goes back to his or her team and acts out the charade. As soon

as his or her team guesses correctly, the team quickly sends a new person for the next card. Each player should act out at least two cards.

3. Give the teams a minute or two to strategize and set up an order for acting.

4. On a "GO!" signal, each team sends up their first representative.

5. The categories for the charades are: Team Sports, Sports PLUS Values and Sports Legends. Encourage the teams to set up signals to identify the categories before you start.

6. You will need eight cards for each group. It is OK to have some of the same cards for each group.

Some ideas for the cards

- Team Sports: Soccer, Basketball, Hockey, Baseball, Football, Softball.

- Sports PLUS Values: Teamwork, Perseverance, Fair Play, Respect and Responsibility.

- Legendary Athletes

- **R&R Huddle** (5 min.)

- **Recap** by asking players about their experience during the activity: What was fun about the activity? What made it difficult?

- **Reconnect** players to the theme unit. What did this activity teach us about teamwork?

- **Reset** and transition to the next activity using the Setup discussion as a guideline.

Cool-down

Cool-down Ritual

Impulse Go-Round

Try an Impulse go-round format to close out the day. With the whole group in a large circle, holding hands, start an impulse while at the same time saying one word that describes how you are feeling about the team. To do an impulse, simply squeeze the hand of the person next to you. That person squeezes the hand of the next person while making their statement and so on around the circle until the impulse gets back to where it started.

Session 10:
Team Certificates

Overview

> **Instructor's Notes:** *Be sure to review this set of activities before starting this Sports PLUS Session. Directions for how to facilitate each activity are provided, but it is important that you become familiar with them so that you may more effectively lead the group.*

> *During group discussions, be sure to record all thoughts and ideas on a blackboard or newsprint. Remember that when students are working in their Player Portfolios, spelling, grammar, and penmanship are, relatively speaking, unimportant, so don't dwell on those details or you risk making Sports PLUS into MoreSchool.*

Sports Extras is the Lessons from Literature activity for this session, and for the last session of each theme unit. During Sports Extras, students will present the articles, quotes, or stories they have been collecting to illustrate teamwork, or a lack of teamwork. During this session, empower students to run the *Team Certificates* and *Sports Extras* activities. By deciding how the activities are run and ensuring they abide by their own rules, students practice living out the value of Teamwork. Be sure to take notes on any issues that may arise (e.g., sharing).

These issues may provide a valuable transition into the next theme unit, Respect

This Lesson from Adventure section begins with Impulse, an activity similar to the *Go-Round* from the previous cool-down ritual. This game can be simple entertainment, but it also is a good cooperative game where students work together as a unit to achieve an intrinsic goal. The brief tour of the teamwork posters from the second session is followed by *Team Certificates.*

Allow plenty of time for the closing activities today. *Hopes and Fears* in a Hat enables students to express their feelings candidly about the program to the group. Following this activity, students will present the teammate awards they created earlier in the day.

Session 10: **Team Certificates** **Lessons from Literature**	
Warm-up Begin the PLUS Cycle (10-15 min.)	**Cool-down** Continue the PLUS Cycle (5-10 min.)
• Session Overview	• Reflection
• Quote of the Week	**Materials**
Activity Lessons from Literature (25-30 min.)	What students have gathered for *Sports Extras*
• Sports Extras	

Warm-up

Quote of the Week

Individual comittment to a group effort; that's what makes a team work.

— Vincent Lombardi

Follow the five steps of the Quote of the Week Format (See the *Getting Started* chapter for additional explanation):

1. **Write the Quote of the Week:** Bring the group together into a circle, and write the Quote on the blackboard.

2. **Think about the Quote as a group:** Spend two or three minutes talking with students about what they think the quote means. Ask them to share answers with the group for the following question:

   • Can you give an example of when this quote has come to life during our Sports PLUS sessions?

3. **Pair up to talk about the Quote:** Have students separate into pairs. Ask them to spend about five minutes discussing the following question with their partners. Explain that they will be sharing their answers with the whole group, so they may choose to write their answers in their Player Portfolios. (Be sure to walk around the groups, listen, and offer help where needed.):

   • The next theme we will explore together is respect. How is respect an ingredient of something "that makes a team work?"

4. **Share answers with the whole group:** Come together as a large group and share the answers from each of the pair groups. Everyone who wants to should have an opportunity to share their answers.

5. **Reflect individually about the Quote:** Take two or three minutes for students to reflect individually by writing a response to the following Journal Question in their Player Portfolios:

   • Can you give an example of how your individual efforts have had an impact on making this team "work?"

Activity

Lessons from Literature
Sports Extras

This is an important activity to conclude each theme unit. Students may work alone or in small groups. At the start of the unit, they were asked to look for actual events and stories of people in the news or in history who exemplify the core value for that theme unit. They should be reminded frequently throughout the theme unit to be on the lookout for examples of the core Sports PLUS values in magazines and newspapers. They can ask a parent or guardian if they are unsure where to find an article. If possible, provide students access during the Sports PLUS program to youth-oriented magazines, such as *Sports Illustrated for Kids.* A certain area of the room can be designated as the "Sports Extras Area," in which students can store their articles and stories as they find them.

Setup

Bring the group together to form a circle. Explain the next activity as you hand out the Player Portfolios and pencils. Use the following description as a guide:

> "Today you will have an opportunity to share a story about Teamwork with the rest of the group. You may choose either to share the article you brought in or to share the story you wrote during 'Create Your Own Story.'"

Ask students to spend a few minutes writing answers to the pre-work questions in their Player Portfolios:

- Who is the main character in your story?

- What happened to the main character? Or what did the main character do?

- In what way is this story an example of Teamwork?

- One thing the main character learned is that he or she should…

- This story teaches us that we should…

After students have had some time to answer the questions in their portfolios, ask for volunteers to share their stories in their own words. Let everyone who wants to share do so.

Cool-down

- **R&R Huddle** (5 Min.)

- **Recap** by asking students: What do these articles teach us about Teamwork?

- **Reconnect** students to the theme unit using the following focus prompt: One way these exam- ples of teamwork help us to be a better team is by...

- **Reset** and get ready for the next lesson.

Session 10: Team Certificates Lessons from the Field	
Warm-up Begin the PLUS Cycle (5 min.) • Session Overview • Touching Base on Teamwork	**Cool-down** Continue the PLUS Cycle (5-10 min.) • Reflection • Goal-setting
Activity Lessons from the Field(25-30 min.) • Sports Activity	**Materials** Sports equipment

Warm-up

Touching Base On Teamwork (5 min.)

Ask students to think about the previous lesson. What can they do today to bring to life the Lessons from Literature into their work together in the sports activity?

Activity

Lessons from the Field
Sports Activity

Block I: Getting Started (5 min.)

On the first day, players will learn how to measure their resting heart rates (RHR). They will also set baselines for their RHR, number of sit-ups/pushups/lunges/calf raises, and number of jumps during jump rope. Each day they will try to improve upon their Past Personal Best (PPB) by achieving their Future Best Goal (FBG) and by tracking progress toward that goal in the physical activities progress chart located in the back of their Player Portfolios. Take one minute to make sure all participants turn to the back of their portfolios and locate the progress charts. Explain to them that they will be using this chart each time you meet to do physical activities. Be sure to emphasize the importance of keeping track of their progress by using the chart.

Stand together in a circle for all *Getting Started* activities (except for jogging). Have players partner up, with one player doing the activity and the partner keeping count and giving encouragement. Be sure they have their Portfolios handy so that they can record their progress. Encourage them to clap and cheer for their teammates to create an enthusiastic environment. You may also choose to include music.

- **Measure resting heart rate (RHR)** — Spend a few minutes showing players how to find their pulses, either on their necks or wrists. Explain that you will be giving them a few seconds to count how many times their hearts beat. Take a moment to allow them to sit quietly on the floor and find their pulses. Give them 30 seconds to count their heartbeats.

- **Record, check in and set goals** — Allow a couple of minutes for players to record their RHRs in their Player Portfolios.

- Jog (2-3 min.) — This can be done as a lap or in place as a circle.

- Stretch (2-3 min.) — Be sure to include stretches for the major muscle groups.

- **Strength/Endurance (1 min.)** — On this first day, players will set baseline numbers for the four Strength/Endurance activities (push-ups, sit-ups, lunges, calf raises), but usually, you will only choose one or two. They will work in pairs. One member of the pair will have 30 seconds to do as many of the activities as they can. Their partner will cheer them on and count for them.

- **Jump Rope (4 min.)** — Again, players will work in pairs, with one person jumping and the other person counting and cheering. They should have three to four sets of 30-45 seconds of jumping rope.

- **Track personal progress** — Have players record their totals for steps five and six in their Player Portfolios. These totals will represent their baseline achievements, or their Past Personal Bests (PPB). Each day, playerswillcheck their progress from the previous session and will set a Future Personal Best Goal (FBG) to work toward for next time. Be sure to remind them about setting realistic goals (for example, adding one or two to their baseline, as opposed to ten).

Block II: Structured Play (30 min.)

Skill Play (10 min.)

Choose one or two of the following activities to play today. You can refer back to the *Physical Activities Description Appendix* for instructions on how to run the activities. Encourage players to cheer for each other, and include music if you wish.

- Water Fill Relay

- Beanbag Walk Relay

- Pac-Man/Ms. Pac-Man Tag

- Chase Ball

- Clothes Relay

Sport Play (20 min.)

As a group, decide which sport you want to play today. Select from the sport list contained in the *Sports List Appendix.* Be sure to periodically review with the group the Physical Activities Recommendations for Sport from Chapter Six.

Cool-down

If time permits, close the day with a few minutes of stretching while conducting the following R&R Huddle.

- **Recap** one or two key moments from the Lessons from the Field.

- **Reconnect** players back to the theme unit.

- **Reset** and transition players to the Cool-down, Reflection time.

  OR

- **Reflection**

Use this time to highlight teachable moments you observed during the day and to give players an opportunity to share their experiences about Sports PLUS during the day. The following questions can serve as a guide:

- What did you like about today?

- What did you learn today?

- How did we show teamwork today?

- What are one or two ways we can show better teamwork next time?

Goal-setting

Use this time to track the group's progress toward their individual and team goals and to start players thinking about one or two team goals related to Respect that will be set during the next session.

Session 10: Team Certificates Lessons from Adventure	
Warm-up Begin the PLUS Cycle (5 min.) • Session Overview • Impulse **Activity** Lessons from Adventure (25-30 min.) • Team Certificates/Teamwork Posters Revisited	**Cool-down** Continue the PLUS Cycle (5-10 min.) • Reflection • Presentation of Certificate • Hopes and Fears in a Hat **Materials** Teamwork posters: 3" x 5" notecards — enough for at least 4 per person in the group; marking pens; a hat or something similar in which to put the note cards

Warm-up

Impulse

Gather the whole group into a circle — teachers and staff included. Have everyone hold hands to create a completely connected circle. Explain to players that it is not always necessary to communicate verbally with our teammates. You are going to show them how the whole team can check in without saying a word.

Tell them that they are going to squeeze the hand of a person next to them and when that person receives the hand squeeze, they will pass it on to the next person, and so on all the way around the circle until the squeeze gets back to them. Try it a couple of times going in different directions. (Remind players that excessively hard squeezing hurts and is not a good example of taking care of their teammates.) If the group is into competition, time how quickly they can send an impulse all the way around the circle. Or begin two impulses, going in opposite directions, and see which gets back first. Watch for the surprise and sometimes moment of confusion as someone halfway around gets two squeezes at the same time.

Variation

This activity can easily be morphed into a relay race. Ask the group to form a line. Start the impulse on one end, and when it reaches the end, the last student will run around a cone, do a set of jumping jacks, or whatever the group decides. When that person finishes, he or she will head to the front of the line and start the next impulse. This continues until everyone has had a turn, each time going for a new record.

Activity

Lessons from Adventure
Team Certificates

During this activity, players will create a "Team Certificate" to signify their completion of the first Sports PLUS theme unit. There are several ways this could be done, and players should have some voice in the decision. Possibilities include:

- Players work in small groups to make certificates for other small groups.

- The whole team works together to make one giant team certificate (e.g., making handprints to spell out Teamwork).

Play

1. Gather the group into a circle, and explain the purpose of the next activity — "To create certificates that signify our completion of the first Sports PLUS theme unit."

2. Describe one or two possible ways that this can be done, and ask players if they have any other ideas. As a group, decide what you are going to do, and create the certificate(s).

3. When the certificate(s) are finished, gather the group to vote on the two people who have given their best effort to show Teamwork during this theme unit. Voting can be done either by a show of hands, applause for nominated candidates, or by writing names on slips of paper. (In the case of a tie, allow multiple winners.)

4. Once the decision has been made, explain that the people chosen will be the "Masters of Ceremonies" for the presentation of the Team Certificate(s) at the end of the day.

Teamwork Posters Revisited

If time allows, take a brief tour of the teamwork posters that were created during the second session. Stop at each poster and discuss what is represented on it and what it says about teamwork. Ask players to comment on how they think the group is doing with being good teammates to each other and with creating a good team. Draw on what is on the posters to help players give specific examples of teamwork they noticed throughout the theme unit. Ask if anyone has anything they would like to add to the posters to update them (e.g., adding new insights and ideas they have learned over the course of the theme unit).

- **R&R Huddle** (5 min.)

- **Recap** one or two points from the previous discussion about the Teamwork Posters.

- **Reconnect** players to the theme unit.

- **Reset** and transition to the next activity.

Cool-down

Reflection
Hopes/Fears in a Hat

Setup

Give two note cards to each person in the group. Ask players to think about their Sports PLUS experience so far and to mentally picture what they are excited for and hope will happen. Ask what they are nervous about or fear will happen during the experience ahead.

Play

Playes should write their hopes on one note card and their fears on the other note card. They do not need to put their names on the cards. Ask them to fold the cards in half and place them in the hat. Mix up the cards and then pass them around the circle, with each person taking one card at a time until all the cards are taken. Go around the circle, with each person taking a turn sharing what was written on the cards in their hand. If time allows, you may choose to discuss what was on each card as a group. Continue this process—reading and discussing— until all the cards are read.

After sharing all the cards, place them in a spot that is visible to all group members (e.g., tacked to a wall). Players may revisit the cards periodically throughout the program to remember what was written on them. Are our hopes being realized? What do we need to do to make sure they are realized? What about our fears? Are they still present? What can we do to change them?

Cool-down Ritual

Presentation of Team Certificates

Have the twoplayerschosenas Masters of Ceremonies (MC) present the certificates. If certificates were created for different small groups, the MCs should call each group up one by one and formally present the certificate with a handshake and congratulations. If the group decided on one giant certificate, the MCs can hang it somewhere in the group meeting room. (You may need to help them accomplish this task.)

CHAPTER ELEVEN

Theme Unit 2: Rolling into Respect

Session 11:
Respect Posters

Overview

Instructor's Notes: *Be sure to review this set of activities before starting this Sports PLUS Session. Directions for how to facilitate each activity are provided, but it is important that you become familiar with them so that you may more effectively lead the group.*

During group discussions, be sure to record all thoughts and ideas on a blackboard or newsprint. Remember that when students are working in their Player Portfolios, spelling, grammar, and penmanship are, relatively speaking, unimportant, so don't dwell on those details or you risk making Sports PLUS into MoreSchool.

The focus of the first Respect session is on transitioning to a new value, Respect, and defining this value in the context of what the group has already learned about Teamwork. Look for ways to build on Teamwork to help students better understand and apply Respect.

The Quote of the Week initiates dialogue on Respect by giving us a definition of Respect. The You Make the Call activity asks players to consider how to respond when an adult, in this case the coach, sends confusing signals about respect and hard play. Students then create a Respect Poster that asks them to demonstrate their present understanding of respect.

Be sure to remind students to be on the look out for articles and stories about respect that they can present during the Sports Extras.

Session 11: **Respect Posters** **Lessons from Literature**	

Warm-up
Begin the PLUS Cycle (10-15 min.)
 	
   • Session Overview
 	
   • Quote of the Week
Activity
Lessons from Literature (25-30 min.)
 	
   • You Make the Call — *A Big Hit*
	Cool-down
	Continue the PLUS Cycle (5-10 min.)
	
	   • Reflection
	Materials
	Copies of *A Big Hit*

Warm-up

Quote of the Week

"I judge a person's worth by the kind of person he is in life—by the way he treats his fellow man, by the way he wants to be treated, and by the way he respects people around him."

— Calvin Murphy, former NBA guard

Follow the five steps of the Quote of the Week Format (see Chapter Eight: *Getting Started* for additional explanation):

1. **Write the Quote of the Week:** Bring the group together into a circle, and write the Quote on the blackboard.

2. **Think about the Quote as a group:** Spend two or three minutes talking with the students about what they think the quote means. Ask students to share answers to the group for the following question:

    *   Calvin Murphy says he judges people based on how they treat others. Why do you think he doesn't say that he judges people by how much money they make or how good they are on the basketball court?

3. **Pair up to talk about the Quote:** Have students separate into pairs. Ask them to spend about five minutes discussing the following questions with their partners. Explain that they will be sharing their answers with the whole group, so they may choose to write their answers in their Player Portfolios. (Be sure to walk around the groups, listen, and offer help where needed.):

    *   What are some ways that you can be respectful of others around you?

4. **Share answers with the whole group:** Come together as a large group and share the answers from each of the pair groups. Everyone who wants to should have an opportunity to share their answers.

5. **Reflect individually about the Quote:** Take two or three minutes for students to reflect individually by writing a response to the following Journal Question in their Player Portfolios:

    *   Why is it important to respect others regardless of whether they have a lot of money or are good at sports?

    *   When someone shows me respect it makes me feel…

Activity

Lessons from Literature
You Make the Call
(see Player Portfolio)

Key Concepts

- Sportsmanship
- Respecting Others
- Playing Hard

Setup

Bring the group together to sit in a circle. If there is time, use one or two of the following questions to help set the tone before reading the story:

- How can the desire to win become more important than having fun, more important than playing fairly, or more important than respecting our opponents?

- What are some examples of when this can happen both on and off the field?

- Have you ever wanted to win so badly that you lost sight of having fun, playing fairly, and respecting your opponents?

Next, read the story aloud and with enthusiasm to the whole group.

Discussion Questions:

Separate the students into groups by having them count off by threes (or fours depending on the group size). Spend a couple of minutes distributing students' Player Portfolios and pencils. Ask one or two volunteers to help.

Using their Player Portfolios, have students discuss and write answers to the following questions in their small groups. It is important to remember that spelling, grammar, and penmanship are NOT important during this activity.

1. Who are the main characters in this story?

2. What is the main problem these characters face?

3. What are some possible ways that Mitch and the rest of the team could respond to Coach Jackson?

4. What might happen if they responded this way?

5. If you were Mitch, what are one or two other ways that you might handle the situation?

6. What do you think would be difficult about speaking up if you were Mitch? If you were one of the other members of the Warriors?

7. Which solution would you want to use if you were Mitch?

Group Share:

- After the small groups have had time to discuss each question, gather the groups together to sit in one large circle.

- Ask each small group to share their suggestions for solving the problem, using students' answers to number three above. (As suggestions are given, you or a volunteer should write them on poster paper for all to see.)

- Once all the different solutions have been laid out, spend a few minutes discussing the consequences of each solution, using students' answers to question number four as a guide.

- As a group, choose the best solution (i.e., the most good for the most people).

- Finally, as a group, complete the following two focus prompts on poster paper.

  1. One thing we can take from this story is that we should…

  2. We should be careful not to…

Cool-down

- **R&R Huddle** (5 min.)

- **Recap** by highlighting one or two key points from the previous discussion. You might, for example, consider the following ideas: Learning to have a competitive spirit is a good thing. It can make you try hard to improve your skills. Learning to work hard in school to constantly improve and to meet new and greater challenges brings success. But if you always compare yourself with others and see winning as the only goal, you will most likely be disappointed whenever you are bested by someone else.

- **Reconnect** using the following ideas as a guide: One way to respect an opponent is by understanding that he or she simply wants the same thing you do. Learning to compete more against yourself, to measure success by your own improvements and efforts, means that the final score is not so important after all. Complete this sentence: One thing I can do to make sure I am respecting my opponent in a game or an activity is...

- **Reset** and get ready for the next lesson.

Session 11: **Respect Posters** **Lessons from the Field**	
Warm-up Begin the PLUS Cycle (5 min.) • Session Overview • Reviewing Respect	**Cool-down** Continue the PLUS Cycle (5-10 min.) • Reflection • Goal-setting
Activity Lessons from the Field (25-30 min.) • Sports Activity	**Materials** Sports Equipment

Warm-up

Reviewing Respect (5 min.)

Ask players to think about the previous lesson. What can they do today to bring the Lessons from Literature into their work together in the sports activity?

Activity

Lessons from the Field
Sports Authority

Block I: Getting Started (5 min.)

Stand together in a circle for all *Getting Started* activities (except jogging). Have players partner up, with one player doing the activity and the partner keeping count and giving encouragement. Be sure players have their Portfolios handy so that they can record their progress. Encourage them to clap and cheer for their teammates to create an enthusiastic environment. You may also choose to include music.

- **Measure resting heart rate (RHR)** — Spend a few minutes showing players how to find their pulses, either on their necks or wrists. Explain that you will be giving them a few seconds to count how many times their hearts beat. Take a moment for the players to sit quietly on the floor and to find their pulses. Give them 30 seconds to count their heartbeats.

- **Record, check in and set goals** — Allow a couple of minutes for players to record their RHRs in their Player Portfolios. Walk around the circle and help players double the number if needed.

- **Jog (2-3 min)** — This can be done as a lap or in place as a circle.

- **Stretch (2-3 min)** — Be sure to include stretches for the major muscle groups.

- **Strength/Endurance (1 min)** — Choose one or two of the Strength/Endurance activities (push-ups, sit-ups, lunges, calf raises). Players will work in pairs. One member of the pair will have 30 seconds to do as many of the activities as he or she can. Their partners will cheer them on and count for them.

- **Jump Rope (4 min)** — Again, players will work in pairs, with one person jumping and the other person counting and cheering. Players should have three to four sets of 30-45 seconds of jumping rope.

- **Track personal progress** — Have players record their totals for steps five and six in their Player Portfolios. These totals will represent players' Past Personal Bests (PPB). Players should check their progress from the previous session and set a Future Personal Best Goal (FBG) to work toward for next time. Be sure to remind players about setting realistic goals (for example, adding one or two to their PPB, as opposed to 10).

Block II: Structured Play (30 min.)

Skill Play (10 min.)

Choose one or two of the following activities to play today. You can refer back to the *Physical Activities Description Appendix* for instructions on how to run the activities. Encourage players to cheer for each other, and include music if you wish.

- Long Distance Musical Chairs

- Water Balloon Volleyball

- Line Jumping

- Slides

- Hopscotch

Sport Play (20 min.)

As a group, decide which sport you want to play today. Select from the sport list contained in the *Sports List Appendix.* Be sure to periodically review with the group the Physical Activities Recommendations for Sport from Chapter Six.

Cool-down

If time permits, close the day with a few minutes of stretching while conducting the following R&R Huddle.

- **Recap** one or two key moments from the Lessons from the Field.

- **Reconnect** players back to the theme unit.

- **Reset** and transition players to the Cool-down, Reflection time.

  OR

- **Reflection**

Use this time to highlight teachable moments you observed during the day and to give players an opportunity to share their experiences about Sports PLUS during the day. The following questions can serve as a guide:

- What did you like about today?

- What did you learn today?

- What are some ways you were respectful today?

- In what ways can we be more respectful next time?

Goal-setting

Keeping the *S.M.A.R.T.* goals script in mind, spend a few minutes working together as a group to set one or two team goals related to Respect.

Session 11: Respect Posters Lessons from Adventure	
Warm-up Begin the PLUS Cycle (5 min.) • Session Overview • Line Ups	**Cool-down** Continue the PLUS Cycle (5-10 min.) • Reflection • Go-Round
Activity Lessons from Adventure (25-30 min.) • Respect Posters	**Materials** 2 poster-sized pieces of paper for each group of three or four students, different colored markers, one dictionary per group (if dictionaries are unavailable, write the definition of respect on a chalkboard or poster), magazines, newspapers for cutting, glue

Warm-up

Line Ups

Setup

Gather players to listen to the instructions.

Play

1. Tell players that you will be calling out a variety of topics. They are to organize themselves, without talking, in a line, from smallest to biggest or least to greatest.

2. Possible categories:

   - Height

   - Age (could just be order of birthdays)

   - Number of articles of clothing

   - Number of pets

   - Number of siblings

3. Ask players to strategize in between rounds. What can they do differently?

Activity

Lessons from Adventure
Respect Posters
(see Player Portfolio)

Defining Respect

Begin by having a large group discussion of the meaning of the word Respect. This can be a brainstorming discussion, with someone keeping track of ideas on a poster or chalkboard. (You might consider using focus prompts to guide the discussion, such as: "Respect means…," "Respect is important because…," "One way we show respect is…." Once you think the group has some ideas, form small groups of four or five players.

This hands-on activity helps players come up with concrete examples of different aspects of respect and allows them to share with each other what they know about respectful behavior. The group also benefits from having visual reminders of what they have defined as respect.

Setup

Separate the groups into teams of three or four. Give each team a table or some open space on the floor, poster paper, a dictionary if available, and some markers.

Play

1. Each group will use a dictionary to look up the meaning of respect. If dictionaries are unavailable, write the definition on the chalkboard.

2. Using this information, and their own understanding of respect, players will create a poster to teach the rest of the group what respect means to them. For this activity, have a volunteer from each group lie down on the poster paper and have someone trace the outline of their body on the paper. Or let the groups choose to create something else to represent respect rather than a Being.

3. Groups then write words and phrases inside the body of their Being that represent their definitions and examples of respect. Players should use their own words to define what respect means along with the dictionary definition. They should write words or phrases that show what respect looks and sounds like. On the outside of their Being, they should write words and behaviors that show the opposite of respect (i.e., examples of disrespect).

4. Remind the players that this is a team project and they should spend a few minutes planning what they, as a team, want to create and how they are going to create it. All members of the team should be actively involved in the planning, decision-making, and production of the poster. Allow 15-20 minutes for the small groups to work.

5. Once the groups have completed their posters, spend a few minutes presenting them to the group and explaining definitions, drawings, words, and phrases. If time permits, allow some discussion and a question period for each group.

6. Hang the posters around the room and refer to them as often as necessary throughout the program to reinforce and remind players of their commitments. As the unit progresses, and players' understanding of respect increases, have them add new ideas, words and phrases to their posters.

7. Hang the "Sports PLUS Leader to Detractor Poster" for Respect. Reflect on the 5-point scale and the connections between this scale and the players' posters. Utilize this scale to guide your reflections in all phases of the program.

   - **R&R Huddle** (5 minutes)

   - **Recap** by highlighting one or two important points from the activity.

   - **Reconnect** by reminding the group of why respect is so important and how the posters will help the group.

   - **Reset** and transition to the next activity.

Cool-down

Reflection

Use this time to highlight teachable moments you observed during the day and to give players an opportunity to share their experiences with Sports PLUS. The following questions can serve as a guide:

- What did you like about today?

- What did you learn today?

- What are some ways you were respectful today?

- In what ways can we be more respectful next time?

Cool-down Ritual

Go-Round

End this first day with a simple group go-round. Bring the group together in a circle. Begin with your own summary of the day—what the group has done, what you think the group has learned. Ask each person to think of one thing they know about respect. Go around the circle giving everyone a chance to answer.

Homework Assignment

As a fun homework assignment, ask the students and staff to begin looking in local newspapers and magazines, and to listen for stories on the radio and television that show examples of respect. Ask everyone to bring these examples to group when they find them. The group will continue adding to the collection of articles and stories they gathered for teamwork and will use them in the program.

Session 12:
Contract Renewal (with an Eye on Respect)

Overview

> **Instructor's Notes:** *Be sure to review this set of activities before starting this Sports PLUS Session. Directions for how to facilitate each activity are provided, but it is important that you become familiar with them so that you may more effectively lead the group.*
>
> *During group discussions, be sure to record all thoughts and ideas on a blackboard or newsprint. Remember that when students are working in their Player Portfolios, spelling, grammar, and penmanship are, relatively speaking, unimportant, so don't dwell on those details or you risk making Sports PLUS into MoreSchool.*

This session begins with a quote that speaks to how to find success while respecting those around us. *Baseball Saved Us* is a moving story that raises questions about the fairness of the Japanese internment during WW II. The main character struggles to maintain respect for himself and confidence in his ability to play baseball while those around him are disrespectful and doubting.

The Adventure lesson begins with a casual warm-up to help players better know each other. The *Respect Relay* is a fun and challenging activity that helps players explore their understanding of respect.

The day ends with players reviewing the principles and rules they have previously committed to and then signing the Respect line of the contract.

Session 12: **Contract Renewal (with an Eye on Respect)** **Lessons from Literature**	
Warm-up Begin the PLUS Cycle (10-15 min.) • Session Overview • Quote of the Week **Activity** Lessons from Literature (25-30 min.) • Theme Book — *Baseball Saved Us*	**Cool-down** Continue the PLUS Cycle (5-10 min.) • Reflection **Materials** Copies of *Baseball Saved Us*

Warm-up

Quote of the Week
You can stand tall without standing on someone. You can be a victor without having victims.

— Harriet Woods

Instructor's note

Briefly mention that Harriet Woods was a politician and activist from Missouri. Share an example of how politics and sports are similar. Finally, you may need to define the word victor for your group.

Follow the five steps of the Quote of the Week Format (see Chapter Eight: *Getting Started* for additional explanation):):

1. **Write the Quote of the Week:** Bring the group together into a circle, and write the Quote on the blackboard.

2. **Think about the Quote as a group:** Spend two or three minutes talking with the students about what they think the quote means. Ask students to share answers to the group for the following question:

   • Do you agree with this quote from Harriet Woods? Why or why not?

3. **Pair up to talk about the Quote:** Have students separate into pairs. Ask them to spend about five minutes discussing the following questions with their partners. Explain that they will be sharing their answers with the whole group, so they may choose to write their answers in their Player Portfolios. (Be sure to walk around the groups, listen, and offer help where needed.):

   • Give an example of what it means to "stand tall."

   • How does this quote relate to the theme of respect for others?

4. **Share answers with the whole group:** Come together as a large group and share the answers from each of the pair groups. Everyone who wants to should have an opportunity to share their answers.

5. **Reflect individually about the Quote:** Take two or three minutes for students to reflect individually by writing a response to the following Journal Question in their Player Portfolios:

   • What can help you "stand tall?" What gets in the way of you "standing tall?"

Activity

Lessons from Literature
Theme Book
Baseball Saved Us
(see Player Portfolio)

by Ken Mochizuki

Setup

Gather the students together into a circle and read the summary below:

"In 1942, while the Unites States was at war with Japan (World War II), the U.S. Army moved all people of Japanese descent away from the West Coast. They were sent to internment camps in the middle of American deserts up until 1945. The reason, the U.S. government said, was because it could not tell who might be loyal to Japan. None of these immigrants from Japan—or their children, who were American citizens—were ever proven to be dangerous to America during World War II. In 1988, the U.S. government admitted that what it did was wrong." (Mochizuki, Ken. *Baseball Saved Us.*)

Baseball Saved Us is the story of a young Japanese-American boy who is put into an internment camp with his family. Living in the camp was really hard and relationships between family members began to suffer. The main character's father suggested that the community work together to set up a baseball league to help boost the spirits of those in the camp until they were released. All the while, the main character, who is small and only a modest player, struggles to find confidence in his game. Difficulties do not end for the main character after he leaves the camp. He finds that once he is mainstreamed back into society he encounters disrespect from many boys, which affects his self-esteem.

The Story

Read the story aloud and with enthusiasm to the whole group. Be sure to show the pictures to the students as you read.

Discussion Questions:

Spend a couple of minutes distributing students' Player Portfolios and pencils. (Ask for one or two volunteers to help.) Write the questions and focus prompts on a blackboard or newsprint.

Work together as a whole group to answer the following questions. Questions one through four should be answered in a round-robin format, with one student answering one question. Try to include students who may not always participate. (If answers for questions three and four are imprecise or need further elaboration, ask if anyone has anything to add.)

1. Who is the main character in this story?

2. What are the problems or challenges he faces?

3. How does he handle the problem?

4. What happened then?

The following focus prompt should be answered in an exhaustive format. Continue letting students give responses until no new answers are given.

5. The main character learned he should…

For questions six and seven, allow all students an opportunity to share their answers, regardless of whether or not the answers are original.

6. When would it be important in your life to… [insert answer from previous statement]?

7. One thing that might make doing this difficult is…

Finally, ask students to write their responses to the following prompt in their Player Portfolios.

8. One specific way I might show respect to my teammates is by…

Cool-down

- **R&R Huddle** (5 min.)

- **Recap** one or two key points that arose during the discussion.

- **Reconnect** by asking volunteers to briefly share what they wrote for question number eight above.

- **Reset** and get ready for the next lesson.

<table>
<tr><td colspan="2">

Session 12:
Contract Renewal (with an Eye on Respect)
Lessons from the Field
</td></tr>
<tr><td>

Warm-up
  Begin the PLUS Cycle (5 min.)

  - Session Overview

  - Reviewing Respect

Activity
  Lessons from the Field (25-30 min.)

  - Sports Activity
</td><td>

Cool-down
  Continue the PLUS Cycle (5-10 min.)

  - Reflection

  - Goal-setting

Materials
  Sports Equipment
</td></tr>
</table>

Warm-up

Reviewing Respect (5 min.)

Ask players to think about the previous lesson. What can they do today to bring the Lessons from Literature into their work together in the sports activity?

Activity

Lessons from the Field
Sports Activity

Block I: Getting Started (5 min.)

Stand together in a circle for all Getting Started activities (except for jogging). Have players partner up, with one player doing the activity and the partner keeping count and giving encouragement. Be sure that players have their Portfolios handy so that they can record their progress. Players will try to improve upon their Past Personal Best (PPB) by achieving their Future Best Goal (FBG) and by tracking progress toward that goal in their Player Portfolios.

Encourage players to clap for and cheer on their teammates to create an enthusiastic environment. You also may choose to include music.

- **Measure resting heart rate (RHR)** — Spend a few minutes showing players how to find their pulses, either on their necks or wrists. Explain that you will be giving them a few seconds to count how many times their hearts beat. Take a moment for the players to sit quietly on the floor and to find their pulses. Give them 30 seconds to count their heartbeats.

- Record, check in and set goals — Allow a couple of minutes for players to record their RHRs in their Player Portfolios. Walk around the circle and help players double the number if needed.

- **Jog (2-3 min)** — This can be done as a lap or in place as a circle.

- **Stretch (2-3 min)** — Be sure to include stretches for the major muscle groups.

- **Strength/Endurance (1 min)** — Choose one or two of the Strength/Endurance activities (push-ups, sit-ups, lunges, calf raises). Players will work in pairs. One member of the pair will have 30 seconds to do as many of the activities as he or she can. Their partners will cheer them on and count for them.

- **Jump Rope (4 min)** — Again, players will work in pairs, with one person jumping and the other person counting and cheering. Players should have three to four sets of 30-45 seconds of jumping rope.

- **Track personal progress** — Have players record their totals for steps five and six in their Player Portfolios. These totals will represent players' Past Personal Bests (PPB). Players should check their progress from the previous session and set a Future Personal Best Goal (FBG) to work toward for next time. Be sure to remind players about setting realistic goals (for example, adding one or two to their PPB, as opposed to 10).

Block II: Structured Play (30 min.)

Skill Play (10 min.)

Choose one or two of the following activities to play today. You can refer back to the *Physical Activities Description Appendix* for instructions on how to run the activities. Encourage players to cheer for each other, and include music if you wish.

- Dribble Relay

- Sack Race

- Twister

- 3-legged Race

- Hula Hoop Challenge Course

Sport Play (20 min.)

As a group, decide which sport you want to play today. Select from the sport list contained in the *Sports List Appendix*. Be sure to periodically review with the group the Physical Activities Recommendations for Sport from Chapter Six.

Cool-down

If time permits, close the day with a few minutes of stretching while conducting the following R&R Huddle.

- **Recap** one or two key moments from the Lessons from the Field.

- **Reconnect** players back to the theme unit.

- Reset and transition players to the Cool-down, Reflection time.

  OR

- **Reflection**

Use this time to highlight teachable moments you observed during the day and to give players an opportunity to share their experiences about Sports PLUS during the day. The following questions can serve as a guide:

- What did you like about today?

- What did you learn today?

- What are some ways you were respectful today?

- In what ways can we be more respectful next time?

Goal-setting

Use this time to track the group's progress toward the team goals you set last time and to start the players thinking about one or two individual goals related to Respect they would like to set during the next session.

Session 12:
Contract Renewal (with an Eye on Respect)
Lessons from Adventure

Warm-up	Cool-down
Begin the PLUS Cycle (5 min.)	Continue the PLUS Cycle (5-10 min.)
• Session Overview	• Reflection
• Peek A Who?	• Contract Renewal
Activity	**Materials**
Lessons from Adventure (25-30 min.)	Large blanket or sheet that cannot be seen through; four large flip charts or sheets of poster paper hung around the room with the following headings on them—two that read "Respect Yourself," and two that read "Respect Others," different colored markers at each station; cones or other objects to create a simple obstacle course
• Respect Relay	

Warm-up

Peek a Who?

This follow-up game is good for groups who already know each other well and will help to reinforce names. It also provides a fun challenge to the group

1. Divide the group in half (see Tip on the following page). Ask each team to sit on the floor across from each other.

2. Tell your players, "This is a fun name-review game. I am going to hold up this blanket like a curtain. One team will sit behind each side of the curtain." You'll need a volunteer to hold up the other side of the divider.

3. Next tell the players, "To begin, I will ask each team to send one person to sit right in front of the curtain. The two team members will be sitting facing each other with the curtain between them. When we drop the curtain, the first person to say the other person's name "wins" that person to his or her side. There is no helping from the rest of the team! If anyone says the name of a person other than the one up at the curtain, that side loses the round."

4. Play one sample round so everyone understands. Remind the group that some simple strategies may be useful—like making sure the other team doesn't hear or see you while you send teammates up to the curtain.

5. Play a few rounds (maybe five or more depending on the level of enthusiasm).

6. Continue play with some rule changes—each team sends up two people — first team to guess both names wins; have teams say first, middle and last names; or have the players sit back to back and have each person's team describe the other person without using his or her name. The person at the curtain

has to guess who is sitting behind them based on the group's description.

Tip

A fun way to divide a group in two is to give directions like, "Go to the right of the room if you are right-handed; go to the left if you are a lefty." Let the group separate. Now tell them to, "Go to the back of the room if you are under 10 [or an age that you think will evenly split the group]. Go to the front if you are 10 or over 10." Let the group separate. Now tell them "Go to the back of the room if your phone number ends in 1 through 5, go to the front if it ends in 6 through 0." See how the group is divided. If you are pretty much two even groups, begin the game. If necessary, move some people around. Play around with the group-splitting questions you ask. Anything goes.

Activity

Respect Posters
(see Player Portfolio)

Setup

Before you begin, hang the four large pieces of poster or art paper in different parts of the room. Make sure the players will be able to reach the paper to write on it. While there are four posters, there are only two statements. This is simply to speed up the activity and allow players time to be directly involved. Each team only visits two different posters. Set up the cones or other objects so that players will have a clear path to run around.

Divide the group into four smaller groups.

Play

1. Assign each team to one of the posters.

2. Each team will be given three to five minutes to write as many responses as possible to complete the phrase,

   • "Respecting Yourself sounds like or looks like...," or "Respecting Others looks like, sounds like…"

3. The team must work as a relay team. Each person on the team has a turn with the marker and writes something on the poster. After writing a statement, each player must run around a cone before handing off the marker to a teammate. The team repeats the relay pattern until time is up. Teammates can help each other if someone gets stuck.

4. After five minutes or so, yell "Switch!" at which point each team moves to a different poster with a different statement.

5. Remind players that they should be practicing respectful behavior.

Discussion

Bring the players back together as a large group. Hang the posters in a place where everyone can see them. Spend some time discussing each poster. Create two new posters as a group with simple statements of what the group sees as the most important ideas about respecting yourself and others. Finally, if time permits, allow the players an opportunity to decorate the posters.

Leave these posters hanging in the after-school space for the remainder of the program.

• **R&R Huddle** (5 minutes)

• **Recap** by highlighting one or two key discussion points.

• **Reconnect** with one or two of the following focus prompts:

   – Respecting yourself is important because…

   – Respecting others is important because…

• **Reset** and transition to the next activity.

Cool-down

Cool-down Ritual

Player Contract Renewal

This is a good time to revisit the Player Contract that the players first developed in the Teamwork Unit. Have players take their contracts out of their portfolios. The next value on the list is Respect. Spend some time in a whole group discussion reviewing what the group knows so far about respect and how it exists in their group. Refer to the posters created during this session. Move the discussion into what each player can do to be a respectful teammate. The following discussion questions are intended as suggestions to start and guide the discussion.

- What do you think respect means?

- Can anyone give an example of respectful behavior you have seen in this group? From school... from home... from your neighborhood?

- Why is respect important to our group?

- What can each of us commit to in order to maintain a respectful group?

Once you think the group has a good understanding of why respect is important and how to be a respectful teammate, have a Player Contract Signing Ceremony. Remind players that by signing the Respect line on their contract, they are making a commitment to themselves and their teammates.

Session 13:
A Good Class

Overview

Instructor's Notes: *Be sure to review this set of activities before starting this Sports PLUS Session. Directions for how to facilitate each activity are provided, but it is important that you* *become familiar with them so that you may more effectively lead the group.*

During group discussions, be sure to record all thoughts and ideas on a blackboard or newsprint. Remember that when students are working in their Player Portfolios, spelling, grammar, and penmanship are, relatively speaking, unimportant, so don't dwell on those details or you risk making Sports PLUS into MoreSchool.

This session begins with a discussion about one of the most well-known adages about respect, the Golden Rule. Your challenge, as the facilitator, will be to help the players learn to apply the quote, rather than just recognize it. The *You Make the Call* activity brings up the themes of respecting the rules, the equipment, and taking responsibility for mistakes.

The team-building activity has three groups trying to work together to achieve success. It is a simple activity, but it fosters some good discussion topics. It brings up working together for the good of the whole team and respecting the team goal rather than individual accomplishments

---

Session 13:
A Good Class
Lessons from Literature

Warm-up	**Cool-down**
Begin the PLUS Cycle (10-15 min.)	Continue the PLUS Cycle (5-10 min.)
• Session Overview	• Reflection
• Quote of the Week	**Materials**
Activity	Copies of *A Good Class*
Lessons from Literature (25-30 min.)	
• You Make the Call — *A Good Class*	

Warm-up

Quote of the Week

Do unto others as you would have them do unto you.

— The Golden Rule

Follow the five steps of the Quote of the Week Format (See the Getting Started chapter for additional explanation):

1. **Write the Quote of the Week:** Bring the group together into a circle, and write the Quote on the blackboard.

2. **Think about the Quote as a group:** Spend two or three minutes talking with the students about what they think the quote means. Ask students to share answers to the group for the following:

   - Explain what this quote means by putting it into your own words.

3. **Pair up to talk about the Quote:** Have students separate into pairs. Ask them to spend about five minutes discussing the following questions with their partners. Explain that they will be sharing their answers with the whole group, so they may choose to write their answers in their Player Portfolios. (Be sure to walk around the groups, listen, and offer help where needed.):

   - Sometimes, when someone mistreats us, we want to "get even." Tell your partner about a time when you were playing sports when being kind to someone was difficult.

   - What are two ways that you can make sure you respect others the way you would want them to respect you when playing sports?

4. **Share answers with the whole group:** Come together as a large group and share the answers from each of the pair groups. Everyone who wants to should have an opportunity to share their answers.

5. **Reflect individually about the Quote:** Take two or three minutes for students to reflect individually by writing a response to the following Journal Question in their Player Portfolios:

   - Take a few minutes to think and write about ways outside of sports that you can respect others the way you would want them to respect you. Think about your family, your school, and your community.

Activity

Lessons from Literature
You Make the Call
A Good Class
(see Player Portfolio)

Key Concepts

- respect
- teamwork
- honesty
- responsibility

Setup

Bring the group together to sit in a circle. If there is time, use one or two of the following questions to help set the tone before reading the story:

- How does respect help create a climate that is safe and fair for groups to work in?

- Why might it be hard to respect yourself if you know you have done something wrong and haven't tried to improve the situation?

Read the story aloud and with enthusiasm to the whole group.

Discussion Questions:

Separate the students into groups by having them count off by threes (or fours depending on the group size). Spend a couple of minutes distributing students' Player Portfolios and pencils. Ask one or two volunteers to help.

Using their Player Portfolios, have students discuss and write answers to the following questions in their small groups. It is important to remember that spelling, grammar, and penmanship are NOT important during this activity.

1. Who are the main characters in this story?

2. What is the main problem these characters face?

3. What are some ways that the class could respond to the situation? What are some ways that Ben and Wilson might respond?

4. What would happen if the team responded in that way?

   • How would Ben and Wilson feel?

   • How would Coach Amthor feel?

   • How would the other team members feel?

5. If you were Ben or Wilson, what are one or two other ways that you might handle this situation? If you were another member on the team, what might you do?

6. What do you think would be difficult about speaking up if you were Ben or Wilson? What about if you were another member of the team?

7. Which solution would you want to use if you were Ben or Wilson?

Group Share:

• After the small groups have had time to discuss each question, gather the groups together to sit in one large circle.

• Ask each small group to share their suggestions for solving the problem, using students' answers to number three above. (As suggestions are given, you or a volunteer should write them on poster paper for all to see.)

- Once all the different solutions have been laid out, spend a few minutes discussing the consequences of each solution, using students' answers to question number four as a guide.

- As a group, choose the best solution (i.e., the most good for the most people).

- Finally, as a group, complete the following two focus prompts on poster paper.

  1. One thing we can take from this story is that we should...

  2. We should be careful not to...

Cool-down

- **R&R Huddle** (5 min.)

- **Recap** with one or two key points from the previous discussion.

- **Reconnect** by highlighting one or two responses to the two focus prompts above.

- **Reset** and get ready for the next lesson.

Session 13: A Good Class Lessons from the Field	
Warm-up Begin the PLUS Cycle (5 min.)	**Cool-down** Continue the PLUS Cycle (5-10 min.)
• Session Overview	• Reflection
• Reviewing Respect	• Goal-setting
Activity Lessons from the Field (25-30 min.)	**Materials** Sports Equipment
• Sports Activity	

Warm-up

Reviewing Respect (5 min.)

Ask players to think about the previous lesson. What can they do today to bring the Lessons from Literature into their work together in the sports activity?

Activity

Lessons from the Field
Sports Activity

Block I: Getting Started (5 min.)

Stand together in a circle for all Getting Started activities (except for jogging). Have players partner up, with one player doing the activity and the partner keeping count and giving encouragement. Be sure that players have their Portfolios handy so that they can record their progress. Players will try to improve upon their Past Personal Best (PPB) by achieving their Future Best Goal (FBG) and by tracking progress toward that goal in their Player Portfolios.

Encourage players to clap for and cheer on their teammates to create an enthusiastic environment. You also may choose to include music.

- **Measure resting heart rate (RHR)** — Spend a few minutes showing players how to find their pulses, either on their necks or wrists. Explain that you will be giving them a few seconds to count how many times their hearts beat. Take a moment for the players to sit quietly on the floor and to find their pulses. Give them 30 seconds to count their heartbeats.

- **Record, check in and set goals** — Allow a couple of minutes for players to record their RHRs in their Player Portfolios. Walk around the circle and help players double the number if needed.

- **Jog (2-3 min)** — This can be done as a lap or in place as a circle.

- **Stretch (2-3 min)** — Be sure to include stretches for the major muscle groups.

- **Strength/Endurance (1 min)** — Choose one or two of the Strength/Endurance activities (push-ups, sit-ups, lunges, calf raises). Players will work in pairs. One member of the pair will have 30 seconds to do as many of the activities as he or she can. Their partners will cheer them on and count for them.

- **Jump Rope (4 min)** — Again, players will work in pairs, with one person jumping and the other person counting and cheering. Players should have three to four sets of 30-45 seconds of jumping rope.

- **Track personal progress** — Have players record their totals for steps five and six in their Player Portfolios. These totals will represent players' Past Personal Bests (PPB). Players should check their progress from the previous session and set a Future Personal Best Goal (FBG) to work toward for next time. Be sure to remind players about setting realistic goals (for example, adding one or two to their PPB, as opposed to 10).

Block II: Structured Play (30 min.)

Skill Play (10 min.)

Choose one or two of the following activities to play today. You can refer back to the Physical Activities Description Appendix for instructions on how to run the activities. Encourage players to cheer for each other, and include music if you wish.

- Water Balloon Toss
- Chinese Jump Rope
- Ball Bowling
- Leap Frog Relay
- Crab Walk

Sport Play (20 min.)

As a group, decide which sport you want to play today. Select from the sport list contained in the Sports List Appendix. Be sure to periodically

review with the group the Physical Activities Recommendations for Sport from Chapter Six.

Cool-down

If time permits, close the day with a few minutes of stretching while conducting the following R&R Huddle.

- **Recap** one or two key moments from the Lessons from the Field.

- **Reconnect** players back to the theme unit.

- **Reset** and transition players to the Cool-down, Reflection time.

  OR

- **Reflection**

Use this time to highlight teachable moments you observed during the day and to give students an opportunity to share their experiences about Sports PLUS. The following questions can serve as a guide:

- What did you like about today?

- What did you learn today?

- What are some ways you were respectful today?

- In what ways can we be more respectful next time?

Goal-setting

Use this time to help students track progress toward their individually chosen goals, as well as toward team goals. As goals from earlier sessions are reached, guide students in setting additional individual and team goals related to *Respect.*

Session 13: A Good Class Lessons from Adventure	
Warm-up Begin the PLUS Cycle (5 min.) • Session Overview • Transformer Tag	**Cool-down** Continue the PLUS Cycle (5-10 min.) • Reflection • Put on the Back
Activity Lessons from Adventure (25-30 min.) • Slot Machine	**Materials** None

Warm-up

Transformer Tag

This is a fairly active game. If you have space in your room or even in a hallway, great; otherwise, you may want to save this for the sport component of the day or even reverse the order of your session. You can have a fast walking only rule to keep things in semi-control.

Play

This is a game involving teams; the only thing is you won't know who is on your team until the last second.

1. Show players the two basic hand positions for this tag game, either one hand on the top of your head, or one hand on your bottom.

2. After showing the basic team positions, allow a few moments for reflecting which position students will want to choose.

3. Begin the game by shouting, "DECLARE!" at which point everyone must assume one of the team hand positions.

4. One team, heads or bottoms, has to tag the members of the other team. (Don't declare who chases whom until you shout "DECLARE!")

5. As players are tagged, they become transformed into members of the other team and chase their former teammates until everyone is on the same side.

6. Play as many rounds as appropriate, as long as the game remains fun.

Variation

Depending on the group size, you may invite players to come up with additional hand signals after the first round. This would enable the group to divide into three or more smaller groups. Each group could have different roles. Get the players involved and come up with some fun variations to this simple game.

- **R&R Huddle** (5 minutes)

- **Recap** by asking the players to describe how it felt to change from one team to another very quickly.

- **Reconnect** by pointing out that in sports, each team has the same goals, and this is one of the reasons we should respect our opponents.

- **Reset** and transition to the next activity.

Activity

Lessons from Adventure
Slot Machine
(see Player Portfolio)

This group problem-solving activity offers another opportunity for the group to work together to solve a problem.

You can do this activity in a classroom, but playing this game in your gym or outside on a field allows more options and creativity.

Bring the group together in a circle. Separate into three teams of three or more.

Play

1. The name of the game is Slot Machine. The goal is to get three matching pictures.

2. Each team will go to a corner of the room and create a group gesture to represent respect, drawing on what they have learned about respect in previous sessions.

3. Once each team has a gesture, bring the group back together. Have the teams line up in a triangle formation. Ask each team to show its gesture.

4. For the rest of the activity, there will be no talking among teams. The goal of the group is for you (the facilitator) to count to three, say Go and have all three teams show the same gesture.

5. Play one round — count to three and see what gesture each team shows. This round helps the group to understand the game. Now, send the teams back to their corners, allowing time for the teams to decide which gesture they will use.

6. Come back together. Count to three, and see what gestures are presented.

7. Repeat this process until all three groups get the same gesture (or the group tires of the game).

This problem can be more difficult than it appears:

1. The teams cannot speak to each other, yet they are all trying to do the same thing. They need to develop a system for nonverbal communication.

2. It is not uncommon for one team to forget that the group's goal is to have everyone show the same gesture. This group may become unbending in showing any other gesture than their own (this can be OK if the rest of the teams use this group's gesture, but this doesn't always happen). If one team makes it impossible for the group as a whole to achieve its

goal, stop the game and use this as a discussion topic—what responsibility does each small group have to the larger group in accomplishing its goal? What happens when a small group of people are not helping a team to achieve its goal?

- **R&R Huddle** (5 min.)

- **Recap** using the following focus prompt: The Slot Machine game was difficult because...

- **Reconnect** by asking players to complete the following sentence in their Player Portfolios: The best part of the activity was...

- **Reset** and transition to the next activity.

Cool-down

Cool-down Ritual

Pat on the Back

Try a group pat on the back today, especially if the group did a good job respecting and taking care of one another. Form a large circle. Have everyone put their arms over the shoulders of the player next to them. On your signal, everyone gives the two players next to them a pat on the back. Ask for any volunteers who want to offer a respectful comment to the group.

Session 14:
Trust

Overview

Instructor's Notes: *Be sure to review this set of activities before starting this Sports PLUS Session. Directions for how to facilitate each activity are provided, but it is important that you become familiar with them so that you may more effectively lead the group.*

During group discussions, be sure to record all thoughts and ideas on a blackboard or newsprint. Remember that when students are working in their Player Portfolios, spelling, grammar, and penmanship are, relatively speaking, unimportant, so don't dwell on those details or you risk making Sports PLUS into MoreSchool.

This session's Lesson from Literature is from the theme book *Teammates*. Teammates is the story of how major league baseball became integrated when Jackie Robinson signed with the Brooklyn Dodgers in 1947. It describes the racial prejudice Robinson faced from his teammates and baseball fans and the support offered by his white teammate, Pee Wee Reese. The issues raised in this book may provide a background for discussion in future sessions.

The Lessons from Adventure section begins with a trust activity called Trust Circle. It is an activity that requires the group members to trust one another and to make every effort to take care of one another. If, after reading the instructions, you don't think your group is ready for this activity, save it for another time.

The session closes with the humorous game "Thank You."

Session 14:
Trust
Lessons from Literature

Warm-up	Cool-down
Begin the PLUS Cycle (10-15 min.)	Continue the PLUS Cycle (5-10 min.)
• Session Overview	• Reflection
• Quote of the Week	**Materials**
Activity	Copies of *Teammates*
Lessons from Literature (25-30 min.)	
• Theme — *Teammates*	

Warm-up

Quote of the Week

I'm not concerned with your liking me or disliking me. All I ask is that you respect me as a human being.
— Jackie Robinson

Follow the five steps of the Quote of the Week Format (See the Getting Started chapter for additional explanation):

1. **Write the Quote of the Week:** Bring the group together into a circle, and write the Quote on the blackboard.

2. **Think about the Quote as a group:** Spend two or three minutes talking with the students about what they think the quote means. Ask them to share answers to the group for the following question:

    *   What's the difference between liking someone and respecting someone?

3. **Pair up to talk about the Quote:** Have students separate into pairs. Ask them to spend about five minutes discussing the following questions with their partners. Explain that they will be sharing their answers with the whole group, so they may choose to write their answers in their Player Portfolios. (Be sure to walk around the groups, listen, and offer help where needed.):

    *   How do you act if you are being respectful? What does being respectful look like?

    *   Have you ever been disrespectful to your coach? Have you ever been a good teammate? How?

4. **Share answers with the whole group:** Come together as a large group and share the answers from each of the pair groups. Everyone who wants to should have an opportunity to share their answers.

5. **Reflect individually about the Quote:** Take two or three minutes for students to reflect individually by writing a response to the following Journal Question in their Player Portfolios:

   - How does treating your teammates respectfully help the team? Is the same true when you treat your classmates respectfully? Why or why not?

Activity

Lessons from Literature
Theme Book
Teammates
(see Player Portfolio)

by Peter Golenbock

Setup

Gather the students together into a circle and read the summary below:
   Teammates is the story of how major league baseball became integrated. In 1947 Jackie Robinson signed with the Brooklyn Dodgers where he faced tremendous racial prejudice from his teammates and baseball fans. The story also describes the support given Robinson by one of his white teammates, Pee Wee Reese.

The Story

Read the story aloud and with enthusiasm to the whole group. Be sure to show the pictures to the students as you read.

Discussion Questions:

Spend a couple of minutes distributing students' Player Portfolios and pencils. (Ask for one or two volunteers to help.) Write the questions and focus prompts on a blackboard or newsprint.Work together as a whole group to answer the following questions:

   Questions one through four should be answered in a round-robin format, with one student answering one question. Try to include students who may not always participate. (If answers for questions three and four are imprecise or need further elaboration, ask if anyone has anything to add.)

1. Who are the main characters in this story?

2. What is the problem or challenge they face?

3. How does each character handle the problem?

4. What happened then?

The following focus prompt should be answered in an exhaustive format. Continue letting students give responses until no new answers are given.

5. Pee Wee Reese learned that he should…

6. Jackie Robinson learned that he should…

For questions six and seven, allow all students an opportunity to share their answers, regardless of whether or not the answers are original.

7. When would it be important in your life to… [insert answer from previous statement]?

8. One thing that might make doing this difficult is…

9. Finally, ask the students to write their responses to the following prompt in their Player Portfolios.

   • One specific way I might show respect to my teammates is by…

Cool-down

• **R&R Huddle** (5 min.)

• **Recap** one or two key points that arose during the discussion.

• **Reconnect** by asking volunteers to briefly share what they wrote for question number nine above.

• **Reset** and get ready for the next lesson.

Session 14: **Trust** **Lessons from the Field**	

Warm-up
Begin the PLUS Cycle (5 min.)
 	
  • Session Overview
 	
  • Reviewing Respect
	Cool-down
	Continue the PLUS Cycle (5-10 min.)
	
	  • Reflection
	
	  • Goal-setting

Activity Lessons from the Field (25-30 min.) • Sports Activity	**Materials** Sports Equipment

Warm-up

Reviewing Respect (5 min.)

Ask players to think about the previous lesson. What can they do today to bring the Lessons from Literature into their work together in the sports activity?

Activity

Lessons from the Field—Sports Activity

Block I: Getting Started (5 min.)

Stand together in a circle for all *Getting Started* activities (except for jogging). Have players partner up, with one player doing the activity and the partner keeping count and giving encouragement. Be sure that players have their Portfolios handy so that they can record their progress. Players will try to improve upon their Past Personal Best (PPB) by achieving their Future Best Goal (FBG) and by tracking progress toward that goal in their Player Portfolios.

Encourage players to clap for and cheer on their teammates to create an enthusiastic environment. You also may choose to include music.

- **Measure resting heart rate (RHR)** — Spend a few minutes showing players how to find their pulses, either on their necks or wrists. Explain that you will be giving them a few seconds to count how many times their hearts beat. Take a moment for the players to sit quietly on the floor and to find their pulses. Give them 30 seconds to count their heartbeats.

- **Record, check in and set goals** — Allow a couple of minutes for players to record their RHRs in their Player Portfolios. Walk around the circle and help players double the number if needed.

- **Jog (2-3 min)** — This can be done as a lap or in place as a circle.

- **Stretch (2-3 min)** — Be sure to include stretches for the major muscle groups.

- **Strength/Endurance (1 min)** — Choose one or two of the Strength/Endurance activities (push-ups, sit-ups, lunges, calf raises). Players will work in pairs. One member of the pair will have 30 seconds to do as many of the activities as he or she can. Their partners will cheer them on and count for them.

- **Jump Rope (4 min)** — Again, players will work in pairs, with one person jumping and the other person counting and cheering. Players should have three to four sets of 30-45 seconds of jumping rope.

- **Track personal progress** — Have players record their totals for steps five and six in their Player Portfolios. These totals will represent players' Past Personal Bests (PPB). Players should check their progress from the previous session and set a Future Personal Best Goal (FBG) to work toward for next time. Be sure to remind players about setting realistic goals (for example, adding one or two to their PPB, as opposed to 10).

Block II: Structured Play (30 min.)

Skill Play (10 min.)

Choose one or two of the following activities to play today. You can refer back to the Physical Activities Description Appendix for instructions on how to run the activities. Encourage players to cheer for each other, and include music if you wish.

- Chase Ball Jumping Distances

- Tug o' War

- Jump Rope Relay

- Backwards Walk/Run Relay

Sport Play (20 min.)

As a group, decide which sport you want to play today. Select from the sport list contained in the *Sports List Appendix*. Be sure to periodically review with the group the Physical Activities Recommendations for Sport from Chapter Six.

Cool-down

If time permits, close the day with a few minutes of stretching while conducting the following R&R Huddle.

- **Recap** one or two key moments from the Lessons from the Field.

- **Reconnect** players back to the theme unit.

- **Reset** and transition players to the Cool-down, Reflection time.

  OR

- **Reflection**

Use this time to highlight teachable moments you observed during the day and to give players an opportunity to share their experiences about Sports PLUS during the day. The following questions can serve as a guide:

- What did you like about today?

- What did you learn today?

- What are some ways you were respectful today?

- In what ways can we be more respectful next time?

Goal-setting

Use this time to help players track progress toward their individually chosen goals, as well as toward team goals. As goals from earlier sessions are reached, guide players in setting additional individual and team goals related to Respect.

Session 14: **Trust** **Lessons from Adventure**	
Warm-up Begin the PLUS Cycle (5 min.) • Session Overview • Trust Circle	**Cool-down** Continue the PLUS Cycle (5-10 min.) • Reflection • Thank you very much
Activity Lessons from Adventure (25-30 min.) • Robot Tag	**Materials** None

Warm-up

Trust Circle

Setup

If you don't think your players are able to take their responsibilities seriously and participate in this activity safely, don't use it at this time. Trust Circle asks that players make a commitment to take good care of one another and display respect for the safety of all members of the group. It is a good activity for exploring the concepts of making commitments to and trusting each other, and respecting teammates. It is also a lot of fun.

Activity

1. Ask the players to form a large circle.

2. Have everyone put bumpers up—arms extended in front of the chest, elbows bent, palms out acting as bumpers.

3. Give these instructions: "When I say 'Cross,' everyone slowly walks across the circle and takes a place on the side opposite from where they are now. This means we will all be crossing through the middle at the same time, so we have bumpers up. Show respect for your teammates' safety by moving slowly and carefully. There will be some bumping and jostling, but if we are careful, we will arrive safely."

4. Give the "Cross!" command and see how the group does taking care of one another. If at any time anyone is acting in an unsafe manner, call a halt to the activity and discuss why it isn't working. Do a few rounds, and if you think the group can do it safely, tell them that the new challenge is to make the crossing with their eyes closed. This will require a good deal of trust and extra attention to going slowly and being aware of others' safety. If you are at all unsure of the group's ability to do this in a safe manner, do not attempt it.

Variation

If you are unsure of your group's ability to do the activity safely with their eyes closed, an additional challenge is to time the group after a few practice rounds to see if they can do things more quickly. Remind the group that crossing the circle quickly does not necessarily involve moving more quickly; rather, it involves extra alertness and awareness of where everyone else is and also it may require that individuals step aside to make way for teammates.

- **R&R Huddle** (5 minutes)

- **Recap** using one or two of the following questions: How did it feel to cross the circle and be bumped into? Did you trust your teammates to take care of you? Was it comfortable or uncomfortable? Was it difficult to do with closed eyes?

- **Reconnect** using one of the following questions or focus prompts as a guide: How do you think we did as a group? One way we could have done better is... In what other areas in our lives must we trust our friends, classmates, family members?

- **Reset** and transition to the next activity.

Activity

Lessons from Adventure
Robot Tag
(see Player Portfolio)

This is a variation on the tag game Everybody's It. You won't need a large space, just some enthusiastic players.

Setup

Mark the boundaries. If you have a large space, allow for running. If you are indoors, make this a walking tag game. The boundary should not be too large or else you'll end the tag game with two players running endlessly away from each other. Make it so they'll have no place to run!

Play

1. Bring the group together in a circle.

2. Tell the players, "This is the scenario: you are all robots. You must place one hand behind your back. This hand is your on-off button. Your other hand will be extended in front of you, palm down. The goal is to turn the other robots off by tagging their buttons—their hands—while not getting turned off yourself. Extended hands must remain in front of players at all times.

3. Players who are tagged on the palm are frozen from the waist down. They can continue to try to push the buttons of other robots who walk or run by.

4. A round ends when there is only one robot left walking.

- **R&R Huddle** (5 min.)

- **Recap** when only one person is left walking. Bring the group together to form a circle and use the following questions to get the discussion started: Raise your hand if you were one of the first people tagged. How did you like the game? Did anyone feel frustrated that they couldn't move once they had been tagged?

- **Reconnect** with the following discussion as a guide: Help the group to understand that every person was out for themselves and that there was no teamwork involved. Ask the group if they have any suggestions for modifying the game to incorporate more teamwork. If the group has some trouble coming up with ideas, offer one of the suggestions below:

  – Include a couple of "humans" who cannot be turned off, but who can unfreeze others.

  – Include a "special robot" who can unfreeze everyone, but who can only be unfrozen by a pair of unfrozen robots working together.

- **Reset** and transition to the next activity.

Cool-down

Cool-down Ritual

Thank you very much

Try this simple closing activity to send everyone off with a smile on their face. Ask the group if they know who Elvis Presley was. Ask if anyone can imitate the way he said, "Thank you, thank you very much!" Ask for volunteers, but if no one steps forward, you will have to provide your best imitation of Elvis. After a demonstration, have the group give a group imitation. Next, offer a few positive statements to the group on their ability to be respectful to each other during the last few sessions. After each statement, the group will respond with "Thank you, thank you very much" in their best Elvis voices.

Session 15:

Stereotypes

Overview

> **Instructor's Notes:** *Be sure to review this set of activities before starting this Sports PLUS Session. Directions for how to facilitate each activity are provided, but it is important that you become familiar with them so that you may more effectively lead the group.*
>
> *During group discussions, be sure to record all thoughts and ideas on a blackboard or newsprint. Remember that when students are working in their Player Portfolios, spelling, grammar, and penmanship are, relatively speaking, unimportant, so don't dwell on those details or you risk making Sports PLUS into MoreSchool.*

This session's *Instant Replay* activity encourages players to think about how they can apply their learning in a new situation. In this role-play, the players explore how to handle a situation in which a boy does not want to pass the ball to a girl. This is a good follow-up to the Teammates book and discussion from the previous session.

The *Lessons from the Field* may be an important time to put into action the concept of respect. While players are playing or practicing, be sure to make note of positive, respectful behaviors, which you may then bring up during the Cool-down.

This session also uses a team-building activity, Group Juggle, in which the group must work together to attain success. Watch how the players treat, speak to, and behave toward each other during this activity. Look for examples of both respectful and disrespectful behavior. The focus of this initiative is on respectful communication and teamwork.

Session 15: Stereotypes Lessons from Literature	
Warm-up	**Cool-down**
Begin the PLUS Cycle (10-15 min.)	Continue the PLUS Cycle (5-10 min.)
• Session Overview	• Reflection
• Quote of the Week	**Materials**
Activity	Copies of *Recess Hoops;* name tags for all major characters and any minor characters
Lessons from Literature (25-30 min.)	
• Instant Replay — *Recess Hoops*	

Warm-up

Quote of the Week
(see Player Portfolio)

I had to fight hard against loneliness, abuse, and the knowledge that any mistake I made would be magnified because I was the only black man out there, but I never cared about acceptance as much as I cared about respect

— Jackie Robinson

Instructor's note

This quote builds upon the learning from Teammates. It can effectively bring out thoughts and discussion of stereotypes, particularly racism, but you may wish to define some potentially tricky words such as:

- Loneliness
- Magnified
- Acceptance

Follow the five steps of the Quote of the Week Format (See the *Getting Started* chapter for additional explanation):

1. **Write the Quote of the Week:** Bring the group together into a circle, and write the Quote on the blackboard.

2. **Think about the Quote as a group:** Spend two or three minutes talking with the students about what they think the quote means. Ask students to share their answers to the following questions

   • What is the difference between "acceptance" and "respect?"

   • Why is it important to show respect to others, even if they don't show respect to you?

   • Why might being black have magnified (made bigger) any mistake that Jackie Robinson made?

3. **Pair up to talk about the Quote:** Have students separate into pairs. Ask them to spend about five minutes discussing the following questions with their partners. Explain that they will be sharing their answers with the whole group, so they may choose to write their answers in their Player Portfolios. (Be sure to walk around the groups, listen, and offer help where needed.):Tell your partner about a situation when you made a mistake that felt magnified (seemed like a big deal) or about a time when you felt singled out because you were different from the people around you. How did you feel when this happened? What made you feel this way?

   • One way that you can still show respect to someone who might not respect you is by...

4. **Share answers with the whole group:** Come together as a large group and share the answers from each of the pair groups. Everyone who wants to should have an opportunity to share their answers.

5. **Reflect individually about the Quote:** Take two or three minutes for students to reflect individually by writing a response to the following Journal Question in their Player Portfolios: (Instructor's Note: Before asking this journal question, you may wish to preface it by reminding the students that we are all different from each other in some way, whether those differences are as simple as liking different flavors of ice cream or are bigger, like practicing different religions. If time allows, you may wish to allow volunteers to share their answers to the journal questions with the group. Encourage students to identify why they think their proposed action will be respectful.)

   • Picture someone in your own community who is somehow different. Write about one or two ways that you can make sure to respect a person who may be different this week.

Activity

Lessons from Literature
Instant Replay
Recess Hoops
(see Player Portfolio)

Key Concepts

• Stereotyping
• Respect
• Courage

Setup

Bring the students together into a circle and set the tone:

"Sometimes people make assumptions about others based upon what group they think a person belongs to. Have you ever seen someone excluded or put down simply because they were not in the same group? How did you handle that situation?"

Read the story and the character descriptions aloud to the whole group ***Recess Hoops, Player Portfolio.***

The Play

1. After reading *The Scene,* the player descriptions, and *The Plot,* ask for volunteers to play the different key roles. There are a limited number of spots. Be sure to rotate this responsibility each time so that everyone who wants to will have an opportunity to participate at some point during the year. (You may choose to keep a record of which students have had a turn as a major player.) You may also wish to give other students minor roles in the role-play (e.g., additional players on both teams and a referee). Give each actor a name tag to help the audience know who is who.

2. Once all the roles have been assigned, ask actors to re-read the descriptions of their characters. Explain to the audience (the rest of the group) that they will need to watch carefully so that they can make suggestions when you ask for the audience input.

3. With you playing Director, re-read *The Plot* aloud to the group and help the role-players act out the rest of the story in front of the group.

4. After the actors have performed one version of the plot, say to them, "Actors, FREEZE!" The actors will then stand in place as you facilitate a short discussion with the audience and the other role-players about how each character is feeling and what they are thinking. {When the questions are not about their characters, role-players can sit down and participate in the discussion.) You may use the questions below as a guide:

   • How is Rachel feeling?

   • How is Stan feeling?

   • What is Michael thinking?

   • What is Kobee thinking?

5. Ask the audience if they have any suggestions for how the situation could be resolved. Suggestions should be listed on poster paper. Choosing one solution, say, "OK, let's rewind and try this idea!" Role-players then act out different solutions, each time repeating the preceding process.

Discussion Questions

After a few rounds of role-playing, ask all players to sit together in a circle. Use the following questions to lead students in a discussion about the advantages and disadvantages of each solution (responses should be written on poster paper by a volunteer):

- Is the solution good for the person making the decision?

- Does the solution help others solve the problem?

- Is anybody harmed by the solution (physically or emotionally)?

- Would this be a good solution for every one in a similar situation to use?

- Are there any ways to improve this solution? If yes, what are they?

Cool-down

- **R&R Huddle** (5 min.)

- **Recap** one or two key points that arose during the discussion or use the following question as a guide:

    Stan seems to think that girls can't play sports. Can you think of any examples that might prove him wrong?

- **Reconnect** students with the following question:

    What is wrong with stereotyping people? Where else in your lives can you find examples of stereotyping? What is one thing you learned from this lesson from literature activity?

- **Reset** and get ready for the next lesson.

Session 15: **Stereotypes** **Lessons from the Field**	

Warm-up
Begin the PLUS Cycle (5 min.)
 	
   • Session Overview
 	
   • Reviewing Respect
 	
Activity
Lessons from the Field (25-30 min.)
 	
   • Sports Activity
	Cool-down
	Continue the PLUS Cycle (5-10 min.)
	
	   • Reflection
	
	   • Goal-setting
	
	Materials
	Sports Equipment

Warm-up

Reviewing Respect (5 min.)

Ask players to think about the previous lesson. What can they do today to bring the Lessons from Literature into their work together in the sports activity?

Activity

Lessons from the Field—Sports Activity

Block I: Getting Started (5 min.)

Stand together in a circle for all *Getting Started* activities (except for jogging). Have players partner up, with one player doing the activity and the partner keeping count and giving encouragement. Be sure that players have their Portfolios handy so that they can record their progress. Players will try to improve upon their Past Personal Best (PPB) by achieving their Future Best Goal (FBG) and by tracking progress toward that goal in their Player Portfolios.

Encourage players to clap for and cheer on their teammates to create an enthusiastic environment. You also may choose to include music.

- **Measure resting heart rate (RHR)** — Spend a few minutes showing players how to find their pulses, either on their necks or wrists. Explain that you will be giving them a few seconds to count how many times their hearts beat. Take a moment for the players to sit quietly on the floor and to find their pulses. Give them 30 seconds to count their heartbeats.

- **Record, check in and set goals** — Allow a couple of minutes for players to record their RHRs in their Player Portfolios. Walk around the circle and help players double the number if needed.

- **Jog (2-3 min)** — This can be done as a lap or in place as a circle.

- **Stretch (2-3 min)** — Be sure to include stretches for the major muscle groups.

- **Strength/Endurance (1 min)** — Choose one or two of the Strength/Endurance activities (push-ups, sit-ups, lunges, calf raises). Players will work in pairs. One member of the pair will have 30 seconds to do as many of the activities as he or she can. Their partners will cheer them on and count for them.

- **Jump Rope (4 min)** — Again, players will work in pairs, with one person jumping and the other person counting and cheering. Players should have three to four sets of 30-45 seconds of jumping rope.

- **Track personal progress** — Have players record their totals for steps five and six in their Player Portfolios. These totals will represent players' Past Personal Bests (PPB). Players should check their progress from the previous session and set a Future Personal Best Goal (FBG) to work toward for next time. Be sure to remind players about setting realistic goals (for example, adding one or two to their PPB, as opposed to 10).

Block II: Structured Play (30 min.)

Skill Play (10 min.)

Choose one or two of the following activities to play today. You can refer back to the *Physical Activities Description Appendix* for instructions on how to run the activities. Encourage players to cheer for each other, and include music if you wish.

- Passing a Medicine Ball

- Standing Broad Jump

- Star Jumps

- Balance Tag

- Bowling

Sport Play (20 min.)

As a group, decide which sport you want to play today. Select from the sport list contained in the Sports List Appendix. Be sure to periodically review with the group the Physical Activities Recommendations for Sport from Chapter Six.

Cool-down

If time permits, close the day with a few minutes of stretching while conducting the following R&R Huddle.

- **Recap** one or two key moments from the *Lessons from the Field.*

- **Reconnect** players back to the theme unit.

- **Reset** and transition players to the Cool-down, Reflection time.

  OR

- **Reflection**

Use this time to highlight teachable moments you observed during the day and to give students an opportunity to share their experiences about Sports PLUS. The following questions can serve as a guide:

- What did you like about today?

- What did you learn today?

- What are some ways you were respectful today?

- In what ways can we be more respectful next time?

Goal-setting

Use this time to help players track progress toward their individually chosen goals, as well as toward team goals. As goals from earlier sessions are reached, guide players in setting additional individual and team goals related to *Respect*.

Session 15: **Introduction to Sports PLUS** **Lessons from Adventure**	
Warm-up Begin the PLUS Cycle (5 min.) • Session Overview • How Do You Do	**Cool-down** Continue the PLUS Cycle (5-10 min.) • Reflection • Go-Round
Activity Lessons from Adventure (25-30 min.) • Group Juggle	**Materials** Soft, throwable balls (Nerf-type), one per person; Player Portfolios

Warm-up

How Do You Do?

This warm-up gives your participants a chance to run around while practicing respectful behaviors.

Setup

Gather your group in a circle, with one player in the middle. Tell players that in this activity they should get in touch with their inner politeness.

Play

1. Instruct the player in the middle to select a player in the circle and greet them by shaking their hand and saying, "How do you do?" The player picked should respond by saying, "Fine, thanks!" This exchange should be repeated three times, while continuing to shake hands.

2. As soon as the third exchange of "How do you do?" and "Fine, thanks!" is finished, the player from the middle and the player who was selected take off around the outside of the circle, at a fast walk. When these two people meet roughly half way around the circle, they should stop and do one exchange of "How do you do?/Fine, thanks!" and then continue on their way.

3. Each player is trying to get back to the vacated spot in the circle as quickly as possible, i.e., before the other player.

4. Whoever returns first stays put; the other player then becomes the player in the middle.

5. As a means for engaging other players, as the two people walk quickly around the outside of the circle, players may greet them by giving them a high five or shaking their hands. The people on the outside of the circle must stop, however briefly, and return the greeting.

6. Remind players to be safe — fast walking is a must to prevent collisions.

7. Consider creating a rule that a player can only be in the middle twice in a row.

Activity

Lessons from Adventure

Group Juggle

This quick problem-solver also serves as a nice group gathering game.

Setup

Spend a minute or two reviewing the focus of the previous four sessions for this theme unit. Share with the group that today you will continue focusing on the theme of "Respecting Others." One good way to think and learn about respecting others is to work together as a group to solve problems.

Play

1. Bring the group together in a small circle. You can do this activity with one large group or separate the group into two. This can then be a competition between the groups.

2. Ask everyone in the circle to raise their right hands.

3. Begin by tossing the ball to a player across the circle from you. Once this player has caught the ball, he or she can lower his or her hand and toss the ball across the circle to someone new.

4. Players must remember who tossed them the ball and to whom they threw it. No one may toss the ball to the player next to them.

5. Once everyone has received the ball once — this is your group juggle pattern. Toss the ball around once more in the same pattern—making sure people know who tosses to whom.

6. The group goal is to juggle (that is pass from the first player to the last) as quickly as possible. Or try to add as many balls (up to ten) as the players think they can handle without dropping them. The rules are: a ball must be tossed at least two feet; the balls must be tossed in the same order; once the first ball is

tossed to the second player, the next ball can be added; if a ball is dropped, the group begins again with one ball.

7. Have the group set a goal, then begin.

- **R&R Huddle** (5 min.)

- **Recap** using one or more of the following questions to understand the players' experience during the activity:

    - What was our group goal? How did we decide upon that goal? Was everyone happy with the goal?

    - How did the group solve the problem? Was everyone involved? Did anyone feel left out? Why? How can we do better next time?

- **Reconnect** by asking players to give examples of respectful and disrespectful behavior from the activity. What are some things we can do to help make sure disrespectful behavior doesn't happen?

- **Reset** and transition to the next activity using the *Setup* as a guideline.

Cool-down

Reflection

Bring the group together in a circle and try the following closing activity. Ask for volunteers to name a group or a kind of person who gets stereotyped. Other players then add a characteristic we use to describe that stereotyped group of people. After the characteristic is named, the rest of the group either agrees with the statement by nodding their heads or disagrees by shaking their heads. For example, if someone said, "smart kids," someone else might offer, "nerdy," as a stereotyping characteristic. There would then be lots of nodding and shaking of heads. When players agree or disagree with a particular stereotype, challenge them to articulate why. Encourage them to look for counter examples.

If you have time, briefly discuss some of the following focus prompts or write them on a poster and save them for a discussion in your next session:

- One mistake I could make if I stereotype someone is…

- When others stereotype me, I feel…

- When I stereotype a person, that person may feel…

This activity leads nicely into the next session when the players will make collages showing examples of stereotyping from magazines.

Cool-down Ritual

Go-Round

Bring the group together into a circle and ask players to share one thing they learned about stereotypes today.

Session 16:
Stereotypes Revisited

Overview

> **Instructor's Notes:** *Be sure to review this set of activities before starting this Sports PLUS Session. Directions for how to facilitate each activity are provided, but it is important that you become familiar with them so that you may more effectively lead the group.*
>
> *During group discussions, be sure to record all thoughts and ideas on a blackboard or newsprint. Remember that when students are working in their Player Portfolios, spelling, grammar, and penmanship are, relatively speaking, unimportant, so don't dwell on those details or you risk making Sports PLUS into MoreSchool.*

The Moccasin Goalie is a story about a young hockey player who is excluded from a team because of a disability. The story raises important questions about fairness, respect, and even perseverance and courage. The Adventure Warm-up is a group discussion activity that asks students to think about what they have learned in previous Sports PLUS days about teamwork and respect. It encourages students to think about how the

Sports PLUS values relate to and support each other. During the Stereotype Collage, students expand their understanding of the problems with stereotypes by creating posters in small groups to illustrate different forms of stereotypes and then presenting them to the whole group. Finally, Mental Video is a great exercise to encourage students (and staff) to quietly reflect on their experiences of the day and program.

Session 16: **Stereotypes Revisited** **Lessons from Literature**	

Warm-up
  Begin the PLUS Cycle (10-15 min.)
 	
  • Session Overview
 	
  • Quote of the Week
 	
Activity
  Lessons from Literature (25-30 min.)
 	
    • Theme Book — *The Moccasin Goalie*
	Cool-down
	  Continue the PLUS Cycle (5-10 min.)
	
	  • Reflection
	
	Materials
	  Copies of *Fly Balls, Butterfingers, and Victories*

Warm-up

Quote of the Week

To me, we must learn to spell the word RESPECT. We must respect the rights and properties of our fellowman. And then learn to play the game of life, as well as the game of athletics... if you can take that and put it into practice in the community in which you live, then, to me you have won the greatest championship.

— Jesse Owens

Follow the five steps of the Quote of the Week Format (See the *Getting Started* chapter for additional explanation):

8. **Write the Quote of the Week:** Bring the group together into a circle, and write the Quote on the blackboard.

9. **Think about the Quote as a group:** Spend two or three minutes talking with the students about what they think the quote means. Next ask students to share answers to the group for the following question:

   - What does it mean to "play the game of life?"

10. **Pair up to talk about the Quote:** Have students separate into pairs. Ask them to spend about five minutes discussing the following questions with their partners. Explain that they will be sharing their answers with the whole group, so they may choose to write their answers in their Player Portfolios. (Be sure to walk around the groups, listen, and offer help where needed.):

    - Why do you think Jesse Owens was interested in respect on and off the field?

    - Give an example of how you could put "respect" into action in the community to make a difference.

11. **Share answers with the whole group:** Come together as a large group and share the answers from each of the pair groups. Everyone who wants to should have an opportunity to share their answers.

12. **Reflect individually about the Quote:** Take two or three minutes for students to reflect individually by writing a response to the following Journal Question in their Player Portfolios:

    - What is one thing you can do to bring what you have learned about respect into your community?

Activity

Lessons from Literature
Theme Book
The Moccasin Goalie
(see Player Portfolio)

by William Roy Brownridge

Instructor's note

There are many ways that the vocabulary words can be incorporated into this lesson if you have the time and desire to do so. You can brainstorm a definition for each word as a group. The group can write sentences using the words. Or if the group is large, separate into two groups and split up the words. The sub-groups can report back to the entire group with their definitions.

Prairies	Impatient	Crippled
Moccasins	Anxiously	Disappointment

Setup

Gather the students together into a circle and read the summary below:

Danny is a young boy who lives on the prairie with his family. It is very cold on the prairie during the winter, but Danny doesn't mind it, because when the weather turns cold, he gets to play hockey—his favorite pastime. Even though Danny has a crippled leg and foot that prevents him from wearing skates, he can play goalie very well in his moccasins. He plays anytime and anywhere he can with his four best friends (Anita, Marcel, Petou, and dog Bingo), that is, until the town ice rink is ready and the official hockey league begins. Marcel is chosen to play on a team, but Danny, Anita, and Petou are excluded for various reasons— Danny because he can't skate. Danny is heartbroken. The story describes Danny's struggle to maintain confidence in himself.

The Story

Read the story aloud and with enthusiasm to the whole group. Be sure to show the pictures to the students as you read.

Discussion Questions:

Spend a couple of minutes distributing students' Player Portfolios and pencils. (Ask for one or two volunteers to help.) Write the questions and focus prompts on a blackboard or newsprint.

Work together as a whole group to answer the following questions:

Questions one through four should be answered in a round-robin format, with one student answering one question. Try to include students who may not always participate. (If answers for questions 3 and 4 are imprecise or need further elaboration, ask if anyone has anything to add.)

1. Who is the main character in this story?

2. a.) What is the problem or challenge the main character faces?

    b.) What similar challenge do two other characters face?

3. How do the characters handle these challenges?

4. What happened then?

The following focus prompt should be answered in an exhaustive format. Continue letting students give responses until no new answers are given.

5. The main character learned he should…

6. One important lesson we can take from this story is…

For questions seven and eight, allow all students an opportunity to share their answers, regardless of whether or not the answers are original.

7. When would it be important in your life to… [insert answer from statement six]?

8. One thing that might make doing this difficult is…

Finally, ask the students to write their responses to the following prompt in their Player Portfolios.

9. One specific way I might …[insert answer from statement six] to others is by…

Additional Questions

1. Have you or someone you know ever been excluded from joining an activity because of a certain disability? How did it make you feel? How can remembering that feeling help you to be inclusive to others the next time you play sports?

2. Sometimes even adults make mistakes and do not act as respectfully as they should. Danny's coach, Mr. Matteau, waits until he is desperate for a goalie to include Danny in the team. How do you think Mr. Matteau could have included Danny in the beginning?

3. Often it is easy to think of our friends when we are feeling down and need someone to lean on, but sometimes when things are going great we can forget about our friends, like when Danny wins the championship game and becomes a hero. What do you think is Danny's best accomplishment in the story: Overcoming his fears and just playing? Helping his team win? Remembering to include his friends when he is the hero of the moment? Why did you make the choice you did?

Cool-down

- **R&R Huddle** (5 min.)

- **Recap** by summarizing one or two key points from the discussion.

- **Reconnect** by asking for a few volunteers to complete this sentence: One thing I learned about stereotypes from this story...

- **Reset** and get ready for the next lesson.

Session 16: Stereotypes Revisited Lessons from the Field	

Warm-up
  Begin the PLUS Cycle (5 min.)
  • Session Overview
  • Reviewing Respect
Activity
  Lessons from the Field (25-30 min.)
  • Sports Activity
	Cool-down
	  Continue the PLUS Cycle (5-10 min.)
	  • Reflection
	  • Goal-setting
	Materials
	  Sports Equipment

Warm-up

Reviewing Respect (5 min.)

Ask players to think about the previous lesson. What can they do today to bring the Lessons from Literature into their work together in the sports activity?

Activity

Lessons from the Field
Sports Activity

Block I: Getting Started (5 min.)

Stand together in a circle for all Getting Started activities (except for jogging). Have players partner up, with one player doing the activity and the partner keeping count and giving encouragement. Be sure that players have their Portfolios handy so that they can record their progress. Players will try to improve upon their Past Personal Best (PPB) by achieving their Future Best Goal (FBG) and by tracking progress toward that goal in their Player Portfolios.

Encourage players to clap for and cheer on their teammates to create an enthusiastic environment. You also may choose to include music.

- **Measure resting heart rate (RHR)** — Spend a few minutes showing players how to find their pulses, either on their necks or wrists. Explain that you will be giving them a few seconds to count how many times their hearts beat. Take a moment for the players to sit quietly on the floor and to find their pulses. Give them 30 seconds to count their heartbeats.

- **Record, check in and set goals** — Allow a couple of minutes for players to record their RHRs in their Player Portfolios. Walk around the circle and help players double the number if needed.

- **Jog (2-3 min)** — This can be done as a lap or in place as a circle.

- **Stretch (2-3 min)** — Be sure to include stretches for the major muscle groups.

- **Strength/Endurance (1 min)** — Choose one or two of the Strength/Endurance activities (push-ups, sit-ups, lunges, calf raises). Players will work in pairs. One member of the pair will have 30 seconds to do as many of the activities as he or she can. Their partners will cheer them on and count for them.

- **Jump Rope (4 min)** — Again, players will work in pairs, with one person jumping and the other person counting and cheering. Players should have three to four sets of 30-45 seconds of jumping rope.

- **Track personal progress** — Have players record their totals for steps five and six in their Player Portfolios. These totals will represent players' Past Personal Bests (PPB). Players should check their progress from the previous session and set a Future Personal Best Goal (FBG) to work toward for next time. Be sure to remind players about setting realistic goals (for example, adding one or two to their PPB, as opposed to 10).

Block II: Structured Play (30 min.)

Skill Play (10 min.)

Choose one or two of the following activities to play today. You can refer back to the *Physical Activities Description Appendix* for instructions on how to run the activities. Encourage players to cheer for each other, and include music if you wish.

- Over, Under, Over, Under

- Shuttle Run Relay

- Round and Round the Hoops Go

- Sprint/Stride Runs

- Sashay Relay

Sport Play (20 min.)

As a group, decide which sport you want to play today. Select from the sport list contained in the *Sports List Appendix. Be* sure to periodically review with the group the Physical Activities Recommendations for Sport from Chapter Six.

Cool-down

If time permits, close the day with a few minutes of stretching while conducting the following R&R Huddle.

- **Recap** one or two key moments from the Lessons from the Field.

- **Reconnect** players back to the theme unit.

- **Reset** and transition players to the Cool-down, Reflection time.

  OR

- **Reflection**

Use this time to highlight teachable moments you observed during the day and to give players an opportunity to share their experiences about Sports PLUS during the day. The following questions can serve as a guide:

- What did you like about today?

- What did you learn today?

- What are some ways you were respectful today?

- In what ways can we be more respectful next time?

Goal-setting

Use this time to help players track progress toward their individually chosen goals, as well as toward team goals. As goals from earlier sessions are reached, guide players in setting additional individual and team goals related to *Respect*.

Session 16: **Stereotypes Revisited** **Lessons from Adventure**	
Warm-up Begin the PLUS Cycle (5 min.) • Session Overview • Add On	**Cool-down** Continue the PLUS Cycle (5-10 min.) • Reflection • Mental Video
Activity Lessons from Adventure (25-30 min.) • Stereotype Collage	**Materials** Paper (large, white, construction weight), glue, scissors, markers (enough for everyone), lots of magazines and newspapers

Warm-up

Add On

Bring the group together in a circle (sitting in chairs or on the floor). Explain to the group, "We will be playing a game called Add On. If you can think of something to add to what the person speaking is saying, raise your hand. The speaker will finish and give you a high five. Then it will be your turn to speak."

Play

1. Begin by asking the players to answer the following: "We have been talking about two kinds of respect. Can anyone tell me what they are?" (Respect for Self, Respect for Others)

2. "What are some of the things we have learned about respect?" Continue the game (with prompting from you), encouraging the group to think of the many activities and discussions they have had around the ideas of teamwork and respect.

3. "How is respect related to what we've been talking about concerning stereotypes?"

This short warm-up will help to get the juices flowing for the next activity during which the group will make a collage.

Activity

Lessons from Adventure

Stereotype Collage

Have players separate into groups of four or five. Using pictures from magazines and newspapers, ask players to create collages showing as many different kinds of stereotypes as they can find.

Have each group present their poster and describe the different kinds of stereotyping they have included on it. Or hang the posters around the room and do a tour, with each group explaining their poster and answering questions. Encourage players to use the following focus prompts as a guide:

- We chose this picture because…

- In this example, stereotyping is a _____ (fill in the blank using bad or good) thing because…

- One lesson we can learn from this example is…

Give each player an opportunity to talk about a picture or a story.

- **R&R Huddle** (5 min.)

- **Recap** by summarizing one or two key points from the discussion.

- **Reconnect** by asking for a few volunteers to complete this sentence: One thing I learned about stereotypes today is…

- **Reset** and transition to the next activity.

Cool-down

Reflection

In a large group, discuss some of the things the players have learned about stereotyping. Ask how stereotyping is related to respect and how it can lead to disrespect of others.

Goal-setting

Use this time to help players track progress toward their individually chosen goals, as well as toward team goals. As goals from earlier sessions are reached, guide players in setting additional individual and team goals related to Respect.

Cool-down Ritual

Mental Video

This is a nice way to transition from the program, allowing players to mentally review the learning from the past few sessions. If you have space, bring the group into a circle and have everyone sit down. Have players close their eyes and assume their best meditation pose; they can even lie down if they want. The point is to get really comfortable.

Once everyone has settled down, ask players to imagine that they have a video playing in their mind. The tape is of the past sessions in this group. Have them imagine that they are reviewing this tape. Tell them to hit the pause button when they come to a particularly good example of the group coming together as a team. These can come from any kind of activity during the program, from opening activities, to group discussions, to the sports activities. Remind players to be very still and quiet during this time so that they do not disturb others.

As players finish reviewing their tapes, ask them to open their eyes but remain still and quiet until everyone else is finished. Give the group a few minutes to do their review, and if necessary give them a 10 second countdown to opening their eyes. Ask for volunteers to describe the moments they paused on, the moments when they felt the group pulled together and displayed good teamwork. Allow as many players to speak as want to before ending the session.

Session 17: Feelings

Overview

Instructor's Notes: *Be sure to review this set of activities before starting this Sports PLUS Session. Directions for how to facilitate each activity are provided, but it is important that you become familiar with them so that you may more effectively lead the group.*

During group discussions, be sure to record all thoughts and ideas on a blackboard or newsprint. Remember that when students are working in their Player Portfolios, spelling, grammar, and penmanship are, relatively speaking, unimportant, so don't dwell on those details or you risk making Sports PLUS into MoreSchool.

This session introduces the connection between expressing emotions and acting respectfully. Disrespectful behavior is often the result of people expressing frustration or excitement in inappropriate ways. It is important for children to learn to identify their emotions in various situations and then have skills (and vocabulary) to express these emotions in a respectful way.

The Theme Book reading is a moving book about respect, acceptance, and love that centers on a girl named Kate and a boy named Timmy with Down's Syndrome who become friends. The importance of helping each child feel he or she is known, needed, cared for, and has the opportunity to shape his or her environment is raised powerfully in this book. Allow yourself plenty of time to comfortably read this book and discuss its questions.

The Feelings Charades game is a fun way to get players thinking about the vocabulary of emotions. Be sure to prepare the Feeling Cards ahead of time by writing one emotion word (e.g., angry, sad, happy, joyful, etc.) on each card. Playing charades is an active, energizing way to begin introducing emotional expression.

The Player Portfolio entry asks players to try using a new emotion word—use a card to tell a story about a time when you had trouble telling someone how you felt. A group go-round brings the conversation from the vocabulary of emotions to the life-skill of expressing emotions.

Session 17: Feelings Lessons from Literature	
Warm-up Begin the PLUS Cycle (10-15 min.) • Session Overview • Quote of the Week **Activity** Lessons from Literature (25-30 min.) • Theme Book — *What's Wrong With Timmy*	**Cool-down** Continue the PLUS Cycle (5-10 min.) • Reflection **Materials** Copies of *What's Wrong With Timmy*

Warm-up

Quote of the Week

(see Player Portfolio)

Ability may get you to the top, but it takes character to keep you there.

— John Wooden
— Michael Jordan

Instructor's note

Born in 1910, John Wooden was one of the most successful college basketball coaches of all time. With the UCLA Bruins, Wooden coached his teams to 10 NCAA championships between 1964 and 1975, including a record-setting seven in a row (1967-1973), and four undefeated seasons. Many of his players were all-Americans including Kareem Abdul-Jabbar, Lew Alcindor, Lucius Allen, Gail Goodrich, Bill Walton, and Sidney Wicks. Using his well-known Pyramid of Success, he taught his players the principles necessary to succeed both on and off the court. He is one of only two people to be inducted into the Basketball Hall of Fame as both a player and a coach. (*World Book Encyclopedia:* Bob Logan, B.S., Sportswriter, (Arlington Heights, IL) Daily Herald.)

Follow the five steps of the Quote of the Week Format (See the Getting Started chapter for additional explanation):

1. Write the Quote of the Week: Bring the group together into a circle, and write the Quote on the blackboard.

2. Think about the Quote as a group: Spend two or three minutes talking with the students about what they think the quote means. Ask the students to share answers to the group for the following question:

   • What do you think John Wooden means by "get you to the top"?

   • Some people get cocky when they win. When they get cocky, they forget about their teammates and forget to be respectful. Do you think this helps them stay on top or do you think it hurts them? Why?

3. Pair up to talk about the Quote: Have students separate into pairs. Ask them to spend about five minutes discussing the following questions with their partners. Explain that they will be sharing their answers with the whole group, so they may

choose to write their answers in their Player Portfolios. (Be sure to walk around the groups, listen, and offer help where needed.):

- What do you think "character" means?

- Why do you think "character" is important to stay "on top"?

- How is "ability" different from "character?"

4. Share answers with the whole group: Come together as a large group and share the answers from each of the pair groups. Everyone who wants to should have an opportunity to share their answers.

5. Reflect individually about the Quote: Allow two or three minutes for students to reflect individually by writing a response to the following Journal Question in their Player Portfolios:

- Think of your favorite sport. What skills does your sport require to be successful? (Dribbling skills, quickness, strength, coordination, etc.)

- Now think of the Sports PLUS values we've talked about — teamwork and respect. What values do you think are required to be successful in your favorite sport? How might practicing these same values (putting them into action) make you both a better teammate and a more successful player?

- Why do you think practicing these values is important off the field?

Activity

Lessons from Literature
Theme Book
What's Wrong With Timmy
(see Player Portfolio)

by Maria Shriver

Instructor's note

It is important to set a tone of respect before reading this story. Take a few minutes to talk with the students about Down's Syndrome and ask if anyone in the group knows anyone with Down's Syndrome. How do they know that person? Why is that person special and important? What qualities make people respect that person? Thank students for the respectful dialogue and ask them to show the same level of respect and maturity when listening to the theme book.

Vocabulary

There are many ways the vocabulary words can be incorporated into the lesson. You can brainstorm a definition for each word as a group. The group can write sentences using the words. Or if the group is large, separate into two groups and split up the words. The sub-groups can report back to the entire group with their definitions.

Disabilities	Special Needs	Institution
Unique	Anxious	Polio
Retarded	Mission	

Setup

Gather the students together into a circle and read the summary below:

This is the story of eight-year-old Kate who meets an eight-year-old boy with Down's syndrome at the park. After initially feeling uncomfortable around him, Kate's mom helps her to realize she has more in common with her new acquaintance than she thought at first. The book explores common reactions to disabled people and shows a way to move past looking at differences by emphasizing what all people share in common.

What's Wrong with Timmy? includes a discussion of acceptable terminology to use when talking about developmentally-disabled people. Be prepared for questions concerning why some children are born with differences.

The Story

Read the story aloud and with enthusiasm to the whole group. Be sure to show the pictures to the students as you read.

Discussion Questions

Spend a couple of minutes distributing students' Player Portfolios and pencils. (Ask for one or two volunteers to help.) Write the questions and focus prompts on a blackboard or newsprint.

Work together as a whole group to answer the following questions. Questions one through four should be answered in a round-robin format, with one student answering one question. Try to include students who may not always participate. (If answers for questions 3 and 4 are imprecise or need further elaboration, ask if anyone has anything to add.)

1. Who are the main characters in this story?

2. What is the problem or challenge they face?

3. How does each character handle the problem?

4. What happened then?

The following focus prompt should be answered in an exhaustive format. Continue letting students give responses until no new answers are given.

5. Kate learned that she should…

6. Timmy learned…

For questions seven and eight, allow all students an opportunity to share their answers, regardless of whether or not the answers are original.

7. When would it be important in your life to… [insert answer from previous statement]?

8. One thing that might make doing this difficult is…

Finally, ask the students to write their responses to the following prompt in their Player Portfolios.

9. One specific way I might …[insert answer from previous statement] to others is by…

Additional Questions

1. Before we read *What's Wrong with Timmy?* we talked about what we might have in common with someone who has special needs. In the book, Kate's mom says Timmy "loves his family, he wants friends, he dreams about who he wants to be when he grows up...just like you. Timmy is a lot like you. That's why it's so important to treat him like any other kid." What are some things you have in common with Timmy?

2. What is the Golden Rule? Does Kate follow the Golden Rule? What are some other ways we can treat each other respectfully?

3. When Kate first met Timmy, he was thrilled to be bouncing the basketball better than he had been able to before. He was focusing on what he could do rather than what he couldn't do. That's something we can all learn from Timmy. What is more important to you, winning a game or getting better at a sport? Why?

4. When Kate first saw Timmy from a distance, she noticed that he was different. But when she took the time to get closer and meet him, what did she notice? ("She noticed Timmy's eyes were green like hers. He had a big smile like her friend Eduardo and big white teeth like her girlfriend Tanya.") How can our feelings and opinions sometimes change when we take the time to get to know someone? Have you ever seen someone who was dressed differently than you? How did your feelings change after you met them or played with them? What are two or three things we can learn from that experience?

Cool-down

- **R&R Huddle** (5 min.)

- **Recap** one or two key points that arose during the discussion.

- **Reconnect** by asking volunteers to briefly share what they wrote for question number nine above.

- **Reset** and get ready for the next lesson.

Reflection

Use this time to allow students to reflect on what they have learned today using the following journal reflections as a guide. The reflections are printed in students' Player Portfolios. Read each journal question aloud to the group and then ask students to choose one to write about in their Portfolios.

1. A wise person once said that we are judged by how we treat others. Write about how you could treat your family, teacher or coach with more respect. What is your plan? Be specific.

2. Timmy says he sometimes feels lonely or sad when kids tease him. Do you remember what his mom told him to do? "Be strong inside. Ignore them and keep going. Don't look back." What do you do when you're lonely or sad? Could you learn a new way from Timmy? Write about how you might react the next time you're feeling sad or lonely or what you might do if you see someone who is being left out of the fun.

3. Kate asked her mom why Timmy is different. Her mom says no one is perfect and "all we have to do is be ourselves and God will help us make a big difference in the world." Write about how Timmy is making a difference in the world. Is Timmy making a difference in the way Kate looks at special needs kids? Have you ever thought about how you could make a difference in the world? Think about it and write some details.

4. Kate is learning that even though we are all different, each of us has something to offer those around us. Think of your teammates or the members of your group and write about what each one of them contributes to your group. Try to think about what is unique or different about them.

Session 17: Feelings **Lessons from the Field**	

Warm-up
  Begin the PLUS Cycle (5 min.)
 	
  • Session Overview
 	
  • Reviewing Respect
	Cool-down
	  Continue the PLUS Cycle (5-10 min.)
	
	  • Reflection
	
	  • Goal-setting

Activity
  Lessons from the Field (25-30 min.)
 	
  • Sports Activity
	Materials
	  Sports Equipment

Warm-up

Reviewing Respect

Ask players to think about the previous lesson. What can they do today to bring the Lessons from Literature into their work together in the sports activity?

Activity

Lessons from the Field—Sports Activity

Block I: Getting Started (5 min.)

Stand together in a circle for all Getting Started activities (except for jogging). Have players partner up, with one player doing the activity and the partner keeping count and giving encouragement. Be sure that players have their Portfolios handy so that they can record their progress. Players will try to improve upon their Past Personal Best (PPB) by achieving their Future Best Goal (FBG) and by tracking progress toward that goal in their Player Portfolios.

Encourage players to clap for and cheer on their teammates to create an enthusiastic environment. You also may choose to include music.

- **Measure resting heart rate (RHR)** — Spend a few minutes showing players how to find their pulses, either on their necks or wrists. Explain that you will be giving them a few seconds to count how many times their hearts beat. Take a moment for the players to sit quietly on the floor and to find their pulses. Give them 30 seconds to count their heartbeats.

- **Record, check in and set goals** — Allow a couple of minutes for players to record their RHRs in their Player Portfolios. Walk around the circle and help players double the number if needed.

- **Jog (2-3 min)** — This can be done as a lap or in place as a circle.

- **Stretch (2-3 min)** — Be sure to include stretches for the major muscle groups.

- **Strength/Endurance (1 min)** — Choose one or two of the Strength/Endurance activities (push-ups, sit-ups, lunges, calf raises). Players will work in pairs. One member of the pair will have 30 seconds to do as many of the activities as he or she can. Their partners will cheer them on and count for them.

- **Jump Rope (4 min)** — Again, players will work in pairs, with one person jumping and the other person counting and cheering. Players should have three to four sets of 30-45 seconds of jumping rope.

- **Track personal progress** — Have players record their totals for steps five and six in their Player Portfolios. These totals will represent players' Past Personal Bests (PPB). Players should check their progress from the previous session and set a Future Personal Best Goal (FBG) to work toward for next time. Be sure to remind players about setting realistic goals (for example, adding one or two to their PPB, as opposed to 10).

Block II: Structured Play (30 min.)

Skill Play (10 min.)

Choose one or two of the following activities to play today. You can refer back to the *Physical Activities Description Appendix* for instructions on how to run the activities. Encourage players to cheer for each other, and include music if you wish.

- Balance Tag

- Hoop Monster

- High Skipping Relay

- Softball Throw

- Train

Sport Play (20 min.)

As a group, decide which sport you want to play today. Select from the sport list contained in the *Sports List Appendix.* Be sure to periodically review with the group the Physical Activities Recommendations for Sport from Chapter Six.

Cool-down

If time permits, close the day with a few minutes of stretching while conducting the following R&R Huddle.

- **Recap** one or two key moments from the Lessons from the Field.

- **Reconnect** players back to the theme unit.

- **Reset** and transition players to the Cool-down, Reflection time.

  OR

- **Reflection**

Use this time to highlight teachable moments you observed during the day and to give players an opportunity to share their experiences about Sports PLUS during the day. The following questions can serve as a guide:

- What did you like about today?

- What did you learn today?

- How did we show respect today?

- What are one or two ways we can show better respect next time?

Goal-setting

Use this time to help players track progress toward their individually chosen goals, as well as toward team goals. As goals from earlier sessions are reached, guide players in setting additional individual and team goals related to *Respect*.

<table>
<tr>
<td colspan="2">Session 17:
Feelings
Lessons from Adventure </td>
</tr>
<tr>
<td>Warm-up
Begin the PLUS Cycle (5 min.)<ul><li>Session Overview</li><li>Emotions Tag</li></ul>Activity
Lessons from Adventure (25-30 min.)<ul><li>Feelings Charades</li></ul></td>
<td>Cool-down
Continue the PLUS Cycle (5-10 min.)<ul><li>Reflection</li><li>Feelings Go-Round</li></ul>Materials
Feelings Note Cards (You will need to prepare these cards ahead of time by writing one emotion word, such as "happy" "angry" "excited" "sad," on each card.) and extra blank cards</td>
</tr>
</table>

Warm-up

Emotions Tag

This activity is very similar to Transformer Tag, played earlier. Instead of having players display "heads" or "tails," they will show a feeling as they move around the play space.

Setup

Hand out a feeling card to each player. Ask them to look at the feelings on their cards. Can they imagine expressing that feeling by making actions with their bodies? Tell them that in this tag game they will be moving around while demonstrating an emotion.

Play

1. Tell the players that when you say, "Go," they are to start moving around the play area while showing their emotions. Provide an example.

2. As they move around, the goal is to try to tag other players. When someone is tagged, he or she becomes the emotion of the person who tagged them. For example, if a player was demonstrating "happy" but was tagged by someone demonstrating "bored," the "happy" person then becomes "bored."

3. Continue play until either everyone becomes the same emotion or only a few emotions remain.

4. Remind the players to use safe and gentle tags.

5. Consider starting the activity with only three or four different emotions, instead of using a different card for each player. As the game progresses, add more cards.

6. End by asking the players to think about how sometimes a feeling can be "infectious." Have they ever started to feel what people around them are feeling?

Activity

Lessons from Adventure

Feelings Charades and Portfolio Writing

This fast-paced relay game is played in teams and is a variation of the old classic, Charades.

Play

1. Spread out the Feelings Cards you have prepared with the word-side up.

2. Ask players to choose a word that they don't know. Go around the circle sharing words and working as a group to define them.

3. Ask players to try to think of other words that can be used to describe different emotions. Write these on the blank cards.

4. Next, separate the group into two teams to play a game of Feelings Charades: One team member draws a card and acts out the word on the card (without talking) as the other team members try to guess the emotion word being acted out.

5. After several rounds, bring the whole group back together again. Once again, look through each of the words on the cards and decide as a group if the word describes feeling good (happy, joyful) or if it describes feeling badly (angry, sad).

6. Finally, ask players to open their Player Portfolios to the Feelings Charades activity. Choosing one of the words on the cards, ask them to write two or three sentences about a time when they felt the emotion on the card.

- **R&R Huddle** (5 min.)

- **Recap** by asking players to share any new words they learned. "Did anyone learn a word they didn't know during this activity?"

- **Reconnect** *b*y asking for volunteers to briefly share their writing with the group.

- **Reset** and transition to the next activity.

Cool-down

Cool-down Ritual

Feelings Go-round

Do a large group go-round and have players choose a new word they learned during this session to describe how they are feeling or how they felt at some point during this session. Invite players to share why they chose the word they did, but remind them that they do not have to. Go around the circle a couple of times and give players the chance to offer several different words.

Session 18:
Respect for Self

Overview

Instructor's Notes: *Be sure to review this set of activities before starting this Sports PLUS Session. Directions for how to facilitate each activity are provided, but it is important that you become familiar with them so that you may more effectively lead the group.*

During group discussions, be sure to record all thoughts and ideas on a blackboard or newsprint. Remember that when students are working in their Player Portfolios, spelling, grammar, and penmanship are, relatively speaking, unimportant, so don't dwell on those details or you risk making Sports PLUS into MoreSchool.

This session introduces the connection between expressing emotions and acting respectfully. Disrespectful beThis session begins with a Sports Short activity that discusses how being a winner and winning a game are not always the same thing. It also provides an opportunity to talk about extrinsic motivation. The Lessons from Adventure start with a quiet warm-up activity that encourages players to do some reflection. The team-building activity encourages energy and excitement from the players with a rousing tag game.

The closing Cool-Down presents an opportunity for children to assemble quietly and end the day where they began—with some thoughtful self-reflection.

Session 18: **Respect for Self** **Lessons from Literature**	
Warm-up Begin the PLUS Cycle (10-15 min.) • Session Overview • Quote of the Week **Activity** Lessons from Literature (25-30 min.) • Sports Short — *The Close Call*	**Cool-down** Continue the PLUS Cycle (5-10 min.) • Reflection **Materials** Copies of *The Close Call*

Warm-up

Quote of the Week

Sportsmanship for me is when a guy walks off the court and you really can't tell whether he won or lost, when he carries himself with pride either way.

— Jim Courier

Follow the five steps of the Quote of the Week Format (See the Getting Started chapter for additional explanation):

1. **Write the Quote of the Week:** Bring the group together into a circle, and write the Quote on the blackboard.

2. **Think about the Quote as a group:** Spend two or three minutes talking with the students about what they think the quote means. Next ask students to share answers to the group for the following question

   • Make a connection between this quote and the topic of this session: respect for self.

3. **Pair up to talk about the Quote:** Have students separate into pairs. Ask them to spend about five minutes discussing the following question with their partners. Explain that they will be sharing their answers with the whole group, so they may choose to write their answers in their Player Portfolios. (Be

sure to walk around the groups, listen, and offer help where needed.):

- What does it mean to carry yourself with pride? What does that look like? Be prepared to actually show the group what it looks like!

4. **Share answers with the whole group:** Come together as a large group and share the answers from each of the pair groups. Everyone who wants to should have an opportunity to share their answers.

5. **Reflect individually about the Quote:** Take two or three minutes for students to reflect individually by writing a response to the following Journal Question in their Player Portfolios:

- Share an example of when you've carried yourself with pride. Was it in a Sport PLUS moment or a different area of your life?

Activity

Lessons from Literature
Sports Short
The Close Call
(see Player Portfolio)

Key Concepts
- Respect for self
- Respect for others
- Fair play

Setup

Bring the group together to sit in a circle. Use the suggestion below to help facilitate a short, five or six minute discussion to help set the tone before reading the story. (Be sure to record students' answers on the board or on poster paper.)

"Respecting others as individuals is an important aspect of respect, but there is another very important side of respect, and that is respect for yourself. A lot goes into respecting yourself—being honest, working hard in school and making good decisions."

- What are some things that can happen if you don't have respect for yourself (i.e., self-respect)?

- What are some ways that you can practice self-respect?

- As we read the story, think about the decision with which Leo is faced and see if you can predict how he might feel depending on the decision he makes.

The Story

Read the story aloud and with enthusiasm to the whole group.

Discussion Questions:

Spend a couple of minutes distributing students' Player Portfolios and pencils. (Ask for one or two volunteers to help.) Work together as a whole group to answer the following questions. Write the questions and focus prompts on a blackboard or newsprint.

Questions one through four should be answered in a round-robin format, with one student answering one question. Try to include students who may not always participate. (If answers for questions three and four are imprecise or need further elaboration, ask if anyone has anything to add.)

1. Who are the main characters in this story?

2. What is the problem or challenge Leo faces?

3. How does Leo handle the problem?

4. What happened then?

The following focus prompt should be answered in an exhaustive format. Continue letting students give responses until no new answers are given.

5. Leo learned that he should...

For questions six and seven, allow all students an opportunity to share their answers, regardless of whether or not the answers are original.

6. When would it be important in your life to… [insert answer from previous statement]?

7. One thing that might make doing this difficult is…

Finally, ask students to write their responses to the following prompt in their Player Portfolios.

8. One specific way I might respect my opponents or avoid "put downs" is by…

9. One specific way I might respect myself is by…

Cool-down

- **R&R Huddle** (5 min.)

- **Recap** one or two key points that arose during the discussion.

- **Reconnect** by asking volunteers to briefly share what they wrote for questions number eight and number nine above.

- **Reset** and get ready for the next lesson.

Session 18: Respect for Self Lessons from the Field	

Warm-up
Begin the PLUS Cycle (5 min.)
  • Session Overview
  • Reviewing Respect
Activity
Lessons from the Field (25-30 min.)
  • Sports Activity
	Cool-down
	Continue the PLUS Cycle (5-10 min.)
	  • Reflection
	  • Goal-setting
	Materials
	Sports Equipment

Warm-up

Reviewing Respect

Ask players to think about the previous lesson. What can they do today to bring the Lessons from Literature into their work together in the sports activity?

Activity

Lessons from the Field
Sports Activity

Block I: Getting Started (5 min.)

Stand together in a circle for all *Getting Started* activities (except for jogging). Have players partner up, with one player doing the activity and the partner keeping count and giving encouragement. Be sure that players have their Portfolios handy so that they can record their progress. Players will try to improve upon their Past Personal Best (PPB) by achieving their Future Best Goal (FBG) and by tracking progress toward that goal in their Player Portfolios.

Encourage players to clap for and cheer on their teammates to create an enthusiastic environment. You also may choose to include music.

- **Measure resting heart rate (RHR)** — Spend a few minutes showing players how to find their pulses, either on their necks or wrists. Explain that you will be giving them a few seconds to count how many times their hearts beat. Take a moment for the players to sit quietly on the floor and to find their pulses. Give them 30 seconds to count their heartbeats.

- **Record, check in and set goals** — Allow a couple of minutes for players to record their RHRs in their Player Portfolios. Walk around the circle and help players double the number if needed.

- **Jog (2-3 min)** — This can be done as a lap or in place as a circle.

- **Stretch (2-3 min)** — Be sure to include stretches for the major muscle groups.

- **Strength/Endurance (1 min)** — Choose one or two of the Strength/Endurance activities (push-ups, sit-ups, lunges, calf raises). Players will work in pairs. One member of the pair will have 30 seconds to do as many of the activities as he or she can. Their partners will cheer them on and count for them.

- **Jump Rope (4 min)** — Again, players will work in pairs, with one person jumping and the other person counting and cheering. Players should have three to four sets of 30-45 seconds of jumping rope.

- **Track personal progress** — Have players record their totals for steps five and six in their Player Portfolios. These totals will represent players' Past Personal Bests (PPB). Players should check their progress from the previous session and set a Future Personal Best Goal (FBG) to work toward for next time. Be sure to remind players about setting realistic goals (for example, adding one or two to their PPB, as opposed to 10).

Block II: Structured Play (30 min.)

Skill Play (10 min.)

Choose one or two of the following activities to play today. You can refer back to the Physical Activities Description Appendix for instructions on how to run the activities. Encourage players to cheer for each other, and include music if you wish.

- Distance Running

- Ball Bowling

- Pac-Man Tag

- Drum Major Walk

- Chase Ball

Sport Play (20 min.)

As a group, decide which sport you want to play today. Select from the sport list contained in the *Sports List Appendix.* Be sure to periodically

review with the group the Physical Activities Recommendations for Sport from Chapter Six.

Cool-down

If time permits, close the day with a few minutes of stretching while conducting the following R&R Huddle.

- **Recap** one or two key moments from the Lessons from the Field.

- **Reconnect** players back to the theme unit.

- **Reset** and transition players to the Cool-down, Reflection time.

  OR

- **Reflection**

Use this time to highlight teachable moments you observed during the day and to give players an opportunity to share their experiences about Sports PLUS today. The following questions can serve as a guide:

- What did you like about today?

- What did you learn today?

- What are some ways you were respectful today?

- In what ways can we be more respectful next time?

Goal-setting

Use this time to help players track progress toward their individually chosen goals, as well as toward team goals. As goals from earlier sessions are reached, guide players in setting additional individual and team goals related to Respect.

Session 18: Respect for Self Lessons from Adventure	
Warm-up Begin the PLUS Cycle (5 min.) • Session Overview • Go-Round	**Cool-down** Continue the PLUS Cycle (5-10 min.) • Reflection • Mental Video
Activity Lessons from Adventure (25-30 min.) • Giants, Wizards and Elves	**Materials** Rope and cones

Warm-up

Go-Round

Bring the group together in a circle. Ask the players to close their eyes and to think back through this session and remember one time that someone treated them with respect. Ask players to say one word or a short phrase that describes how this made them feel at the time. Anyone who wants to speak may do so at any time, but have everyone keep their eyes closed. See how they handle two players beginning to speak at the same time.

Activity

Lessons from Adventure
Giants, Wizards & Elves

Setup

Place a rope or other marker horizontally across your play area. Create an "end zone" using cones approximately 25 feet from the center line. Divide your group into two halves, one on either side of the middle line.

Play

1. Tell players that this activity will be like a "super-sized" group version of "rock, paper, scissors" where each team will show one of three characters.

2. Demonstrate the three characters, each time asking players to practice them with you.

   - Start with Giants. Giants stand as tall as possible, with their arms outstretched over their heads, while making loud roaring sounds.

   - Next are the Wizards. Wizards stand with one foot forward and an arm extended forward toward the other team. In the hand of the extended arm is an imaginary wand. The Wizards move the wand around while saying, "Shazam!"

   - Finally, the Elves. The Elves crouch down, bending their knees, and scrunching their hands open and closed, make a high-pitched "Eee — eee — eee" sound.

3. Similar to "rock, paper, scissors" each of the characters "beats" one of the other ones. Tell players that Giants beat Wizards, Wizards beat Elves, and Elves beat Giants. Remind players of this circular hierarchy often, as it can be confusing the first few times this game is played.

4. Now you are ready to explain the remaining instructions. Ask players to come up to the line and then take one large step back, so that each team is about two or three feet back from the center line. Tell players that when you say "Go," each team will collectively show, at the same time, one of the three characters. Explain to the players, "If your team shows a character that 'beats' the character shown by the other team, your team chases and tries to tag members of the other team before they reach their end zone. If, however, you are on a team whose character is 'beat,' you should turn and run quickly for your end zone. If someone gets tagged before reaching their end zone, they join the other team."

5. Before each round, give the groups a few minutes to collectively decide on one of the three characters.

6. In the case of a "tie," have players reach out and shake each other's hands across the line and then go back and choose another character.

7. Continue play until all players are on one team or time/energy runs out.

- **R&R Huddle** (5 min.)

- **Recap** by asking the players to describe how it felt to change from one team to another.

- **Reconnect** by pointing out that, in sports, each team has the same goals, and this is one of the reasons we should respect our opponents.

- **Reset** and transition to the next activity.

Cool-down

Mental Video

This is a nice way to transition from the program allowing players to mentally review the learning from the past few sessions. If you have space, bring the group into a circle and have everyone sit down. Have players close their eyes and assume their best meditation pose; the point is to get really comfortable.

Once everyone has settled down, tell players to imagine that they have a video playing in their mind. The tape is of the past sessions in this group. Have them imagine that they are reviewing this tape. Tell them to hit the pause button when they come to a particularly good example of the group respecting each other. These can come from any kind of activity during the program, from opening activities, to group discussions, to the sports activities. Remind players to be very still and quiet during this so that they do not disturb others.

As players finish reviewing their tapes, ask them to open their eyes but remain still and quiet until everyone else is finished. Give the group a few minutes to do their review, and, if necessary, give them a 10-second countdown to everyone opening their eyes. Ask for volunteers to describe the moments they paused on, the moments when the group demonstrated good respect. Allow as many players to speak as want to before ending the session.

Session 19:
Reflecting on Respect

Overview

Instructor's Notes: *Be sure to review this set of activities before starting this Sports PLUS Session. Directions for how to facilitate each activity are provided, but it is important that you become familiar with them so that you may more effectively lead the group.*

During group discussions, be sure to record all thoughts and ideas on a blackboard or newsprint. Remember that when students are working in their Player Portfolios, spelling, grammar, and penmanship are, relatively speaking, unimportant, so don't dwell on those details or you risk making Sports PLUS into MoreSchool.

In this session players begin by creating their own quote of the week, a great opportunity for them to personalize and own the lessons they have learned on respect.

The *Create Your Own Story* activity takes the learning opportunity of *Create Your Own Quote* one step further by giving players the chance to use their imagination while drawing on their understanding of how respect can be lived out.

The team-building activity, *Balloon Trolley,* is a fun (possibly laughter-filled) game that prioritizes the need for teamwork and respect.

Session 19: **Reflecting on Respect** **Lessons from Literature**	
Warm-up Begin the PLUS Cycle (10-15 min.) • Session Overview • Quote of the Week **Activity** Lessons from Literature (25-30 min.) • Create Your Own Story	**Cool-down** Continue the PLUS Cycle (5-10 min.) • Reflection **Materials** Player Portfolios, paper, pencils, pens, crayons

Warm-up

Create a Quote of the Week

The goal of this activity is to allow students to engage their creativity, to work collectively, and to reflect on the themes of respect.

Separate students into small groups and give each group five to ten minutes to create its own "Quote of the Week" about respect. Students can look through stories and previous quotes in their Portfolios for ideas, but their quotes should be in their own words. Encourage them to write their quotes on pieces of poster board that will then be hung on the wall. Make supplies, such as markers, available for decorating the posters because some students will find this part of the activity particularly enjoyable.

After students have finished, ask groups to take turns sharing their quotes.

Allow a few minutes to discuss each one, during which time you should encourage the students who are listening to ask questions once the group presenting has finished.

When the students have finished asking questions of the group, conclude the activity by asking three questions of your own:

• What does your quote mean?

• When is it important to live this quote?

• One way I can live this quote during Sports PLUS is...

- One way I can live this quote at school is…

- One way I can live this quote at home is…

Activity

Create Your Own Story

The following activity encourages students' creativity and solidifies their understanding of respect. By having students create their own stories involving respect, they will draw upon personal knowledge as well as role models who exemplify respect. This activity also encourages students to understand the benefits of respect and to transfer that understanding into a new context. It is important to remember that spelling, grammar, and penmanship are NOT important during this activity.

Setup

Bring the group together into a circle and explain the next activity as you pass out students' Player Portfolios. Use the following description as a guide:

"Today during Lessons from Literature, we will be creating our own story about Respect. You may choose to work individually or with up to three other students. It may be helpful to create a story about some conflict or problem that is then worked out using respect. Think of things that may have occurred on your own sports teams or during the Lessons from the Field this theme unit. You also may choose to write a story about some of the characters in an Instant Replay or to create a different ending for one of the stories we've read. Spend a few minutes looking back over your Player Portfolios to begin getting some ideas."

Play

Offer guidance as the students separate into groups. Make sure that no one feels left out, but do let the students choose their own groups. Walk around the room offering help and suggestions as needed.

Once students have finished writing their stories, give them an opportunity to illustrate their story if they choose to do so. (Some students may find it easier to draw a picture before writing an accompanying story. It may help spur their imaginations. Let this be an option for those who want it.)

Explain to the students that they will have an opportunity to share their stories with the group on the next Sports PLUS day if they wish to do so. Students can finish illustrating their stories at home if necessary.

Discussion Questions:

After students have had an opportunity to write and illustrate their stories, bring the whole group back together in a circle for a brief reflection on the following questions. Let everyone share who wants to do so.

- What stories or examples of respect did you use to create your story?

- What are some of the problems that your main characters faced?

- How do your main characters solve their dilemma?

Cool-down

- **R&R Huddle** (5 min.)

- **Recap** one or two key points from the discussion.

- **Reconnect** students to the theme unit.

- **Reset** and get ready for the next lesson.

Session 19: Reflecting on Respect Lessons from the Field	

Warm-up
Begin the PLUS Cycle (5 min.)
 	
  • Session Overview
 	
  • Reviewing Respect
 	
Activity
Lessons from the Field (25-30 min.)
 	
  • Sports Activity
	Cool-down
	Continue the PLUS Cycle (5-10 min.)
	
	  • Reflection
	
	  • Goal-setting
	
	Materials
	Sports Equipment

Warm-up

Reviewing Respect

Ask players to think about the previous lesson. What can they do today to bring the Lessons from Literature into their work together in the sports activity?

Activity

Lessons from the Field—Sports Activity

Block I: Getting Started (5 min.)

Stand together in a circle for all *Getting Started* activities (except for jogging). Have players partner up, with one player doing the activity and the partner keeping count and giving encouragement. Be sure that players have their Portfolios handy so that they can record their progress. Players will try to improve upon their Past Personal Best (PPB) by achieving their Future Best Goal (FBG) and by tracking progress toward that goal in their Player Portfolios.

Encourage players to clap for and cheer on their teammates to create an enthusiastic environment. You also may choose to include music.

- **Measure resting heart rate (RHR)** — Spend a few minutes showing players how to find their pulses, either on their necks or wrists. Explain that you will be giving them a few seconds to count how many times their hearts beat. Take a moment for the players to sit quietly on the floor and to find their pulses. Give them 30 seconds to count their heartbeats.

- **Record, check in and set goals** — Allow a couple of minutes for players to record their RHRs in their Player Portfolios. Walk around the circle and help players double the number if needed.

- **Jog (2-3 min)** — This can be done as a lap or in place as a circle.

- **Stretch (2-3 min)** — Be sure to include stretches for the major muscle groups.

- **Strength/Endurance (1 min)** — Choose one or two of the Strength/Endurance activities (push-ups, sit-ups, lunges, calf raises). Players will work in pairs. One member of the pair will have 30 seconds to do as many of the activities as he or she can. Their partners will cheer them on and count for them.

- **Jump Rope (4 min)** — Again, players will work in pairs, with one person jumping and the other person counting and cheering. Players should have three to four sets of 30-45 seconds of jumping rope.

- **Track personal progress** — Have players record their totals for steps five and six in their Player Portfolios. These totals will represent players' Past Personal Bests (PPB). Players should check their progress from the previous session and set a Future Personal Best Goal (FBG) to work toward for next time. Be sure to remind players about setting realistic goals (for example, adding one or two to their PPB, as opposed to 10).

Block II: Structured Play (30 min.)

Skill Play (10 min.)

Choose one or two of the following activities to play today. You can refer back to the *Physical Activities Description Appendix* for instructions on how to run the activities. Encourage players to cheer for each other, and include music if you wish.

- Circle Bonanza

- Hula Hoop Marathon

- Hopscotch

- Balloon-a-thon

- Slides

Sport Play (20 min.)

As a group, decide which sport you want to play today. Select from the sport list contained in the *Sports List Appendix*. Be sure to periodically

review with the group the Physical Activities Recommendations for Sport from Chapter Six.

Cool-down

If time permits, close the day with a few minutes of stretching while conducting the following R&R Huddle.

- **Recap** one or two key moments from the Lessons from the Field.

- **Reconnect** players back to the theme unit.

- **Reset** and transition players to the Cool-down, Reflection time.

  OR

- **Reflection**

Use this time to highlight teachable moments you observed during the day and to give players an opportunity to share their experiences about Sports PLUS. The following questions can serve as a guide:

- What did you like about today?

- What did you learn today?

- What are some ways you were respectful today?

- In what ways can we be more respectful next time?

Goal-setting

Use this time to help players track progress toward their individually chosen goals, as well as toward team goals. As goals from earlier sessions are reached, guide players in setting additional individual and team goals related to Respect.

Session 19:
Reflecting on Respect
Lessons from Adventure

Warm-up	Cool-down
Begin the PLUS Cycle (5 min.)	Continue the PLUS Cycle (5-10 min.)
• Session Overview	• Reflection
• Blob Tag	• Go-Round
Activity	**Materials**
Lessons from Adventure (25-30 min.)	12 inch or larger balloons, Player Portfolios, large construction-type paper, markers
• Balloon Trolley	

Warm-up

Blob Tag

Setup

Designate a large play area, about the equivalent of half of a basketball court for 15 players. Gather players together for instructions. Ask for two volunteers.

Play

1. Ask the two volunteers to hold hands or link elbows. Tell the group that these two will be part of an ever-growing "blob." Their job is to move around the play space, trying to tag other players.

2. When players are tagged, they become part of the "blob." As a new player is added to the blob, the blob should say, "AND THE BLOB GROWS!" The tagged player joins the blob by holding the hand of one of the end members of the blob.

3. For a tag to count, all members of the blob must be holding hands. If the hand-holding link is broken, a tag does not count.

4. Continue playing until everyone has become part of the blob!

5. For safety reasons, do not allow players to run through the blob, either under or through the hands of the blob. This is not a version of "Red Rover."

Activity

Lessons from Adventure

Balloon Trolley

In this activity, players use balloons placed between their backs and stomachs to create a "trolley" and move from point A to point B without dropping a balloon.

Setup

Bring the group together in a circle. Take a few minutes to remind the group of what they have learned in the past sessions about Teamwork and Respect. Explain that the next activity will give them an opportunity to practice working together as a team.

Give each player a balloon to blow up, or have staff blow them up before the session begins.

Play

1. Set up a course for the group to walk through (adding some obstacles to walk over, around and under will add to the difficulty). Show the course to the group.

2. The group needs to get from the beginning of the course to the end as a trolley—everyone being linked together by a balloon pressed between one player's back and the other player's front— without dropping any balloons.

3. You can make this activity more or less difficult by: a) having different consequences for dropping a balloon (hardest is to start over if you drop, easiest is to just count the number of drops), or b) if you don't think your group will be able to stick together as a whole, do the activity in twos or threes, then try again as a whole group.

- **R&R Huddle** (5 min.)

- **Recap** using a quick go-round with the group:

  - How did we work as a team?

  - One thing that is really hard about this activity is…

- **Reconnect** with the following focus prompts:

  - One thing we did really well as a team is…

  - Respect was important in this activity because…

- **Reset** and transition to the next activity.

Cool-down

Cool-down Ritual

Go-round

Ask players to respond to three questions in their Player Portfolios: 1) What did you know about Respect before this unit began? 2) What do you know now? 3) What can you do to practice what you have learned about Respect outside this group? Ask players to separate into pairs and share their responses with a partner. When pairs have finished sharing, ask for volunteers to share what their partners had to say. Let as many players share as time allows.

Session 20:
Respect Certificates

Overview

Instructor's Notes: *Be sure to review this set of activities before starting this Sports PLUS Session. Directions for how to facilitate each activity are provided, but it is important that you become familiar with them so that you may more effectively lead the group.*

During group discussions, be sure to record all thoughts and ideas on a blackboard or newsprint. Remember that when students are working in their Player Portfolios, spelling, grammar, and penmanship are, relatively speaking, unimportant, so don't dwell on those details or you risk making Sports PLUS into MoreSchool.

This final Respect session follows the Sports PLUS format for the closing of a theme unit. The Respect Posters Revisited allows players to revisit the commitments they made to themselves and each other in the beginning of the theme unit.

As much as possible, empower players to run the *Respect Certificates* and Sports Extras activities. By deciding how the activities are run and abiding by their own rules, players practice living out the value of respect. Be sure to take notes on any issues that may arise (e.g., sharing). These issues may provide a valuable transition into the next theme unit, Responsibility.

Session 20: **Respect Certificates** **Lessons from Literature**	
Warm-up Begin the PLUS Cycle (10-15 min.)	**Cool-down** Continue the PLUS Cycle (5-10 min.)
• Session Overview	• Reflection
• Quote of the Week	**Materials**
Activity Lessons from Literature (25-30 min.)	Student-found material for Sports Extras
• Sports Extras	

Warm-up

Quote of the Week

If you want to be respected by others the great thing is to respect yourself. Only by that, only by self-respect will you compel others to respect you.

— Fyodor Dostoyevsky

Instructor's note

Briefly explain that Dostoyevsky was a Russian author during
the late 19th century.

Follow the five steps of the Quote of the Week Format (See the Getting
Started chapter for additional explanation):

1. **Write the Quote of the Week:** Bring the group together into a
   circle, and write the Quote on the blackboard.

2. **Think about the Quote as a group:** Spend two or three
   minutes talking with the students about what they think the
   quote means.

3. **Pair up to talk about the Quote:** Have students separate into
   pairs. Ask them to spend about five minutes discussing the
   following questions with their partners. Explain that they will
   be sharing their answers with the whole group, so they may
   choose to write their answers in their Player Portfolios. (Be
   sure to walk around the groups, listen, and offer help where
   needed.)

4. **Share answers with the whole group:** Come together as
   a large group and share the answers from each of the pair
   groups. Everyone who wants to should have an opportunity to
   share their answers.

5. **Reflect individually about the Quote:** Take two or three
   minutes for students to reflect individually by writing a
   response to the following Journal Question in their Player
   Portfolios:

   • How can I respect myself today?

Activity

Lessons from Literature

Sports Extras

This is an important activity for the conclusion of each theme unit. Students may work alone or in small groups. At the start of the unit, students were asked to look for actual events and stories of people in the news or in history who exemplify the core value for that theme unit. Students should be reminded frequently throughout the theme unit to be on the lookout for examples of the core Sports PLUS values in magazines and newspapers. They can ask a parent or guardian if they are unsure of where to find an article. If possible, provide access during the Sports PLUS program to magazines, such as Sports Illustrated for Kids. A certain area of the room can be designated as the "Sports Extras Area," in which students can store their articles and stories as they find them.

Setup

1. Bring the group together to form a circle. Explain the next activity as you pass out the Player Portfolios and pencils. Use the following description as a guide:.

   - "Today you will have an opportunity to share a story about Respect with the rest of the group. You may choose either to share the article you brought in or to share the story you wrote during 'Create Your Own Story.'"

2. Ask students to spend a few minutes writing answers to the pre-work questions in their Player Portfolios:

   - Who is the main character in your story?

   - What happened to the main character? Or what did the main character do?

   - In what way is this story an example of Respect?

   - One lesson the main character learned is that he or she should…

- This story teaches us that we should...

3. After students have had some time to answer the questions in their portfolios, ask for volunteers to share their stories in their own words. Let everyone who wants to share do so.

Cool-down

- **R&R Huddle** (5 min.)

- **Recap** by asking students: What do these articles teach us about Respect?

- **Reconnect** students to the theme unit using the following focus prompt: One way these examples of Respect help us be a better team is by...

- **Reset** and get ready for the next lesson.

Session 20: Respect Certificates Lessons from the Field	
Warm-up Begin the PLUS Cycle (5 min.) • Session Overview • Reviewing Respect **Activity** Lessons from the Field (25-30 min.) • Sports Activity	**Cool-down** Continue the PLUS Cycle (5-10 min.) • Reflection • Goal-setting **Materials** Sports Equipment

Warm-up

Reviewing Respect

Ask players to think about the previous lesson. What can they do today to bring the Lessons from Literature into their work together in the sports activity?

Activity

Lessons from the Field
Sports Activity

Block I: Getting Started (5 min.)

Stand together in a circle for all Getting Started activities (except for jogging). Have players partner up, with one player doing the activity and the partner keeping count and giving encouragement. Be sure that players have their Portfolios handy so that they can record their progress. Players will try to improve upon their Past Personal Best (PPB) by achieving their Future Best Goal (FBG) and by tracking progress toward that goal in their Player Portfolios.

Encourage players to clap for and cheer on their teammates to create an enthusiastic environment. You also may choose to include music.

- **Measure resting heart rate (RHR)** — Spend a few minutes showing players how to find their pulses, either on their necks or wrists. Explain that you will be giving them a few seconds to count how many times their hearts beat. Take a moment for the players to sit quietly on the floor and to find their pulses. Give them 30 seconds to count their heartbeats.

- **Record, check in and set goals** — Allow a couple of minutes for players to record their RHRs in their Player Portfolios. Walk around the circle and help players double the number if needed.

- **Jog (2-3 min)** — This can be done as a lap or in place as a circle.

- **Stretch (2-3 min)** — Be sure to include stretches for the major muscle groups.

- **Strength/Endurance (1 min)** — Choose one or two of the Strength/Endurance activities (push-ups, sit-ups, lunges, calf raises). Players will work in pairs. One member of the pair will have 30 seconds to do as many of the activities as he or she can. Their partners will cheer them on and count for them.

- **Jump Rope (4 min)** — Again, players will work in pairs, with one person jumping and the other person counting and cheering. Players should have three to four sets of 30-45 seconds of jumping rope.

- **Track personal progress** — Have players record their totals for steps five and six in their Player Portfolios. These totals will represent players' Past Personal Bests (PPB). Players should check their progress from the previous session and set a Future Personal Best Goal (FBG) to work toward for next time. Be sure to remind players about setting realistic goals (for example, adding one or two to their PPB, as opposed to 10).

Block II: Structured Play (30 min.)

Skill Play (10 min.)

Choose one or two of the following activities to play today. You can refer back to the *Physical Activities Description Appendix* for instructions on how to run the activities. Encourage players to cheer for each other, and include music if you wish.

- Crab Walk Relay

- Jump Rope Race

- Dribble Relay

- Locomotion Relay

- Limbo

- Wheelbarrow Race

Sport Play (20 min.)

As a group, decide which sport you want to play today. Select from the sport list contained in the *Sports List Appendix*. Be sure to periodically

review with the group the Physical Activities Recommendations for Sport from Chapter Six.

Cool-down

If time permits, close the day with a few minutes of stretching while conducting the following R&R Huddle.

- **Recap** one or two key moments from the Lessons from the Field.

- **Reconnect** players back to the theme unit.

- **Reset** and transition players to the Cool-down, Reflection time.

    OR

- **Reflection**

Use this time to highlight teachable moments you observed during the day and to give players an opportunity to share their experiences about Sports PLUS. The following questions can serve as a guide:

- What did you like about today?

- What did you learn today?

- What are some ways you were respectful today?

- In what ways can we be more respectful next time?

Goal-setting

Use this time to track the group's progress toward their individual and team goals and to start the players thinking about one or two team goals related to Responsibility that will be set during the next session.

Session 20:
Respect Certificates
Lessons from Adventure

Warm-up	Cool-down
Begin the PLUS Cycle (5 min.)	Continue the PLUS Cycle (5-10 min.)
• Session Overview	• Reflection
• Respect Posters Revisited	• Presentation of Certificates
Activity	**Materials**
Lessons from Adventure (25-30 min.)	Respect Posters
• Respect Certificates	

Warm-up

Respect Posters Revisited

Take a brief tour of the respect posters that were created during the beginning of the theme unit. Stop at each poster and discuss what is represented and what it says about respect. Ask players to comment on how they think the group is doing with being respectful teammates to each other and with creating a good team. Draw upon what is on the posters to help players give specific examples of respect that they have noticed throughout the theme unit. Ask if anyone has anything they would like to add to the posters to update them (e.g., adding new insights and ideas they have learned over the course of the theme unit).

Activity

Lessons from Adventure
(see Player Portfolio)

Respect Certificates

During this activity, players will create a "Respect Certificate" to signify their completion of the second Sports PLUS theme unit. There are several ways this can be done, and players should have some voice in the decision. Possibilities include:

- Players could work in small groups to make certificates for other small groups.

- The whole team could work together to make one giant team certificate (e.g., making handprints to spell out Respect).

- Players could make individual certificates. (If this option is chosen, ask players to leave space on the certificates so the recipients' names can be filled in, before being distributed by the Masters of Ceremonies at the end of the day.)

Play

1. Gather the group into a circle, and explain the purpose of the next activity to the players — "To create certificates that signify our completion of this Sports PLUS theme unit."

2. Describe one or two possible ways this can be done, and ask players if they have any other ideas. As a group, decide what you are going to do, and create the certificate(s).

3. When the certificate(s) are finished, gather the group together to vote on the two people who have given their best effort to show Respect during this theme unit. Voting can be done either by a show of hands, applause for nominated candidates, or by writing names on slips of paper. (In the case of a tie, allow multiple winners.)

4. Once the decision has been made, explain that the players chosen will be the "Masters of Ceremonies" for the presentation of the Respect Certificate(s) at the end of the day.

- **R&R Huddle** (5 min.)

- **Recap** one or two points from the previous discussion about the Respect Posters.

- **Reconnect** players to the theme unit.

- **Reset** and transition to the next activity.

Cool-down

Reflection

Bring the group together for a brief go-round discussion about what the group thinks about the second unit of the Sports PLUS program. Does anyone have any questions? Is the group what you expected? What can we, teachers and staff, do to make it better? What can we all do to be more respectful toward each other? Use this discussion, as necessary, to set some goals and for continued discussion in the Warm-up to Unit Three.

Cool-down Ritual

Presentation of Respect Certificates

Have the two players chosen as Masters of Ceremonies (MC) present the certificates. If certificates were created for different small groups, the MCs should call each group up one by one and formally present the certificate with a handshake and congratulations. If the group decided on one giant certificate, the MCs can hang it up somewhere in the group meeting room. (You may need to help them accomplish this task.) Finally, if the group decided to create individual certificates, help the MCs fill out the names on each certificate before the ceremony. During the ceremony, the MCs should take turns calling each person to come up and receive their certificate.

CHAPTER TWELVE

Theme Unit 3: Rallying for Responsibility

The PLUS Youth Development Model
Responsibility

Session 21:
Responsibility Posters

Overview

Instructor's Notes: *Be sure to review this set of activities before starting this Sports PLUS Session. Directions for how to facilitate each activity are provided, but it is important that you become familiar with them so that you may more effectively lead the group.*

During group discussions, be sure to record all thoughts and ideas on a blackboard or newsprint. Remember that when students are working in their Player Portfolios, spelling, grammar, and penmanship are, relatively speaking, unimportant, so don't dwell on those details or you risk making Sports PLUS into MoreSchool.

The focus of this session is on transitioning to a new value, Responsibility, and defining it in relation to what the students have learned about Teamwork and Respect in earlier theme units.

The quote by Roberto Clemente emphasizes the importance of holding ourselves to a high standard and not making excuses. During the *Lessons from Literature,* students have an opportunity to think about making difficult choices. The *Responsibility Posters* activity challenges students to begin thinking about what responsibility means to them. Encourage them to consider what they hope to learn about responsibility during the next 10 Sports PLUS days.

Be sure to remind students to be on the look out for interesting stories and articles about responsibility that they can present at the end of the unit during *Sport Extras.* Remember that in addition to the activities and lesson plans, the way that you behave as the students' coach and role model, and the way that you demonstrate responsibility in your actions, will have a tremendous impact on what they learn about responsibility.

Session 21: **Responsibility Posters** **Lessons from Literature**	
Warm-up Begin the PLUS Cycle (10-15 min.) • Session Overview • Quote of the Week **Activity** Lessons from Literature (25-30 min.) • You Make the Call — *Jasmine's Choice*	**Cool-down** Continue the PLUS Cycle (5-10 min.) • Reflection **Materials** Copies of *Jasmine's Choice*

Instructor's note

You may want to begin this activity by talking about who Roberto Clemente was and what he did. You may either read the passage below, or describe Roberto Clemente's life more informally:

Roberto Clemente was a great right fielder who played baseball for the Pittsburgh Pirates from 1955 to 1972. During his 17-year career in the major leagues, Roberto Clemente was a 12 time all-star, having won 12 Golden Gloves and 4 National League batting titles. He hit his 3,000th hit on

September 30, 1972, and remains the all time Pirate leader in games, at bats, hits, singles, and total bases.

On New Year's Eve in 1972, Roberto Clemente boarded an airplane in Puerto Rico to help deliver supplies to earthquake victims in Nicaragua. His wife and friends begged him not to take the trip because of poor weather and an unstable cargo plane, but Roberto was determined to go. Frustrated that the previous supplies had not made it to the victims, Roberto decided to personally make sure that the victims received the much-needed supplies. Unfortunately, the plane went down off the coast of Puerto Rico, and all passengers on board were killed (http://www.robertoclemente21.com/Biography/biography.html).

In addition to being a great baseball player, Roberto Clemente was committed to giving back to his family, his community, his fans, and his country. People who remember Roberto remember him as much for his humanity and dedication to improving the lives of youth as for his hitting and fielding.

Roberto Clemente began his career in the major leagues just eight years after Jackie Robinson had become the first African American to be allowed to play in the major leagues. As a teenager, Roberto had played baseball in the Puerto Rican summer professional leagues, where many of the former Negro League players had played for years. During his major league career in the United States, Roberto had to fight prejudice against his skin color as well as prejudice against his ethnicity and nationality.

He was the first Latino ever inducted into the baseball Hall of Fame.

Warm-up

Quote of the Week

"If you have the opportunity to make things better, and you don't do that, you are wasting your time on earth."
— Roberto Clemente

Follow the five steps of the Quote of the Week Format (See the *Getting Started* chapter for additional explanation):

1. Write the Quote of the Week: Bring the group together into a circle, and write the Quote on the blackboard.

2. Think about the Quote as a group: Spend two or three minutes talking with the students about what they think the

quote means. Ask them to share answers to the group for the following questions:

3. What is it that Roberto Clemente wants people to do?

4. What do you think Roberto Clemente means when he says that you are wasting your time on earth if you don't make things better when you have the opportunity to do so?

5. Do you think working to make things better is related to responsibility? Why or why not?

6. Pair up to talk about the Quote: Have students separate into pairs. Ask them to spend about five minutes discussing the following questions with their partners. Explain that they will be sharing their answers with the whole group, so they may choose to write their answers in their Player Portfolios. (Be sure to walk around the groups, listen, and offer help where needed.):

7. What are one or two ways you can follow Roberto Clemente's example and act responsibly toward your Sports PLUS team? Toward your community?

8. What are one or two ways we can help our Sports PLUS teammates to make all of our responsibilities easier?

9. Share answers with the whole group: Come together as a large group and share the answers from each of the pair groups. Everyone who wants to should have an opportunity to share their answers.

10. Reflect individually about the Quote: Take two or three minutes for students to reflect individually by writing a response to the following Journal Prompts in their Player Portfolios:

11. One way I can follow Roberto Clemente's example and act responsibly toward my Sports PLUS team is by...

12. One way I can act responsibly toward my community is by...

Activity

Lessons from Literature
You Make the Call
One-on-One
(see Player Portfolio)

Key Concepts

- Dependability
- Decisionmaking
- Peer Presssure

Setup

Bring the group together to sit in a circle. If there is time, use one or two of the following questions to help set the tone before reading the story:

Sometimes we make a promise to do something, even though we would really like to do something else. Moments like these can present us with difficult decisions. Sometimes peer pressure can influence our decision-making process. Have you ever been faced with a difficult decision when peer pressure was being applied to make you do something you knew was wrong?

Read the story aloud and with enthusiasm to the whole group.

Discussion Questions:

Separate the students into groups by having them count off by threes (or fours depending on the group size). Spend a couple of minutes distributing students' Player Portfolios and pencils. Ask one or two volunteers to help.

Using their Player Portfolios, have students discuss and write answers to the following questions in their small groups. It is important to remember that spelling, grammar, and penmanship are NOT important during this activity.

1. Who is the main character?

2. What is the key problem the main character faces?

3. What are some possible ways Jasmine can solve her problem?

4. What would happen if she handled the problem this way?

5. How would Jasmine feel?

6. How would the team feel?

7. How would Coach Hernandez feel?

8. How would Jasmine's aunt feel?

9. If you were Jasmine, what are one or two ways that you might solve the problem?

10. What about your solution would be difficult to carry out?

11. What solution would you choose if you were Jasmine?

Group Share:

- After the small groups have had time to discuss each question, gather the groups together to sit in one large circle.

- Ask each small group to share their suggestions for solving the problem, using students' answers to number three above. (As suggestions are given, you or a volunteer should write them on poster paper for all to see.)

- Once all the different solutions have been laid out, spend a few minutes discussing the consequences of each solution, using students' answers to question number four as a guide.

- As a group, choose the best solution (i.e., the most good for the most people).

- Finally, as a group, complete the following two focus prompts on poster paper.

  1. One thing we can take from this story is that we should...

  2. We should be careful not to...

Additional Questions

Sometimes the hardest thing about being responsible is understanding where your responsibilities lie and then prioritizing them. Jasmine faced a difficult dilemma between her responsibility to her team and to her family. She had to decide which responsibility came first (took priority).

Think about the people in your life and the commitments or responsibilities you have to them and make a list of your responsibilities. Prioritize them and re-write them in order of their level of importance. (Note: Students can do this in their journals or you might write their responses on paper and then post them on a wall)

Cool-down

- **R&R Huddle** (5 min.)

- **Recap** using one or two key points that arose during the discussion.

- **Reconnect** students to theme unit by asking them to explain how they decided which of their responsibilities had the greatest importance.

- **Reset** and get ready for the next lesson.

Session 21: **Responsibility Posters** **Lessons from the Field**	
Warm-up Begin the PLUS Cycle (5 min.)	**Cool-down** Continue the PLUS Cycle (5-10 min.)
• Session Overview	• Reflection
• Reflecting on Responsibility	• Goal-setting
Activity Lessons from the Field (25-30 min.)	**Materials** Sports Equipment
• Sports Activity	

Warm-up

Reflecting on Responsibility (5 min.)

Ask students to think about the previous lesson. What can they do to bring the Lessons from Literature into their work together in the sports activity?

Activity

Lessons from the Field
Sports Activity

Block I: Getting Started (5 min.)

On the first day, players will learn how to measure their resting heart rates (RHR). They will also set baselines for their RHR, number of sit-ups/push-ups/lunges/calf raises, and number of jumps during jump rope. Each day they will try to improve upon their Past Personal Best (PPB) by achieving their Future Best Goal (FBG) and by tracking progress toward that goal in the physical activities progress chart located in the back of their Player Portfolios. Take one minute to make sure all participants turn to the back of their portfolios and locate the progress charts. Explain to them that they will be using this chart each time you meet to do physical activities. Be sure to emphasize the importance of keeping track of their progress by using the chart.

Stand together in a circle for all *Getting Started* activities (except jogging). Have players partner up, with one player doing the activity and the partner keeping count and giving encouragement. Be sure players have their Portfolios handy so that they can record their progress. Encourage them to clap and cheer for their teammates to create an enthusiastic environment. You may also choose to include music.

- **Measure resting heart rate (RHR)** — Spend a few minutes showing players how to find their pulses, either on their necks or wrists. Explain that you will be giving them a few seconds to count how many times their hearts beat. Take a moment to allow them to sit quietly on the floor and find their pulses. Give them 30 seconds to count their heartbeats.

- **Record, check in and set goals** — Allow a couple of minutes for players to record their RHRs in their Player Portfolios.

- **Jog (2-3 min.)** — This can be done as a lap or in place as a circle.

- **Stretch (2-3 min.)** — Be sure to include stretches for the major muscle groups.

- **Strength/Endurance (1 min.)** — On this first day, players will set baseline numbers for the four Strength/Endurance activities (push-ups, sit-ups, lunges, calf raises), but usually, you will only choose one or two. They will work in pairs. One member of the pair will have 30 seconds to do as many of the activities as they can. Their partner will cheer them on and count for them.

- **Jump Rope (4 min.)** — Again, players will work in pairs, with one person jumping and the other person counting and cheering. They should have three to four sets of 30-45 seconds of jumping rope.

- **Track personal progress** — Have players record their totals for steps five and six in their Player Portfolios. These totals will represent their baseline achievements, or their Past Personal Bests (PPB). Each day, players will check their progress from the previous session and will set a Future Personal Best Goal (FBG) to work toward for next time. Be sure to remind them about setting realistic goals (for example, adding one or two to their baseline, as opposed to 10).

Block II: Structured Play (30 min.)

Skill Play (10 min.)

Choose one or two of the following activities to play today. You can refer back to the *Physical Activities Description Appendix* for instructions on how to run the activities. Encourage players to cheer for each other, and include music if you wish.

- Jump Rope Games

- Sack Race

- Twister

- Beanbag Walk Relay

- Standing Broad Jump

- Backwards Run/Walk Relay

Sport Play (20 min.)

As a group, decide which sport you want to play today. Select from the sport list contained in the *Sports List Appendix*. Be sure to periodically review with the group the Physical Activities Recommendations for Sport from Chapter Six.

Cool-down

If time permits, close the day with a few minutes of stretching while conducting the following R&R Huddle.

- **Recap** one or two key moments from the Lessons from the Field.

- **Reconnect** players back to the theme unit.

- **Reset** and transition players to the Cool-down, Reflection time.

  OR

- **Reflection**

Use this time to highlight teachable moments you observed during the day and to give players an opportunity to share their experiences of Sports PLUS. The following questions can serve as a guide:

- What did you like about today?

- What did you learn today?

- What are some ways you were responsible today?

- In what ways can we be more responsible next time?

Session 21:
Introduction to Sports PLUS
Lessons from Adventure

Warm-up	Cool-down
Begin the PLUS Cycle (5 min.)	Continue the PLUS Cycle (5-10 min.)
• Session Overview	• Reflection
• Toe Tag	• Go-Round
Activity	**Materials**
Lessons from Adventure (25-30 min.)	2 poster-sized pieces of paper for each group of three or four players, different colored markers, one dictionary per group (if dictionaries are unavailable, write the definition of responsibility on a chalkboard or poster), magazines, newspapers for cutting, glue
• *Responsibility Posters*	

Warm-up

Toe Tag

Setup

Help each player find a partner. Say to players, "In this warm-up activity, you should think about what responsibility means and how you can practice it."

Play

Have players stand back to back. When you say, "Go," have the pairs turn and face each other. Each person attempts to "tag" the toe of his or her partner gently before getting tagged themselves.

1. Make sure that players are tagging each other's toes, not stomping or grinding!

2. Play several rounds, occasionally switching partners.

3. For a slightly calmer version, start the game by having partners face each other, with their hands on each other's shoulders.

Now players should try to tag each other's toes while keeping their hands on their partners' shoulders.

4. Reflection question: What did responsibility look like in this activity?

Activity

Lessons from Literature
Responsibility Posters
(see Player Portfolio)

Defining Responsibility

Begin by having a large group discussion of the meaning of the word Responsibility. This can be a brainstorming discussion, keeping track of ideas on a poster or chalkboard. Once you think the group has some ideas, form small groups of four or five players. Following the group discussion, this hands-on activity helps players come up with concrete examples of different aspects of responsibility and allows them to share with each other what they know about responsible behavior. The group also gathers many visual reminders of what they have agreed constitutes responsibility.

Setup

Separate the groups into teams of three or four. Give each team a table or some open space on the floor, poster paper, a dictionary if available, and some markers.

Play

1. Each group will use a dictionary to look up the meaning of responsibility. If dictionaries are unavailable, write the definition on the chalkboard.

2. Using this information, and their own understanding of responsibility, players will create a poster to share with the rest of the group. The poster can be anything the groups choose to represent responsibility. They can create a Being (see the Teamwork Unit) by tracing the outline of one of their bodies

on the poster paper, cut out pictures from magazines if you have a collection to use, or make their own drawing.

3. Groups should then write words and phrases around their drawings that give their definitions of responsibility. Players should use their own words to define responsibility, not the words from the dictionary. They should also write words or phrases on the outside of their Beings or drawings that show what the opposite of being responsible looks like and sounds like.

4. Remind the players that this is a team project and they should spend a few minutes planning what they, as a team, want to create and how they are going to create it. All members of the team should be actively involved in the planning, decision-making, and production of the poster. Allow 15–20 minutes for the small groups to work.

5. Once the teams have completed their posters, give each group a few minutes to present their posters to the larger group and to explain their definitions, drawings, words and phrases. If time permits, allow some discussion and questions for each group.

6. Hang the posters around the room and refer back to them as often as necessary throughout the program to reinforce and remind the players of their commitments. As the unit progresses, and players' understanding of responsibility increases, have them add new ideas, words, and phrases to their posters.

7. Hang the "Sports PLUS Leader to Detractor Poster" for Responsibility. Reflect on the 5-point scale and the connections between this scale and the players' posters. Utilize this scale to guide your reflections in all phases of the program.

- **R&R Huddle** (5 min.)

- **Recap** by asking for a few volunteers to comment about what they learned.

- **Reconnect** by highlighting a few important ideas from the activity and connecting their importance to the theme of responsibility.

- **Reset** and transition to the next activity.

Cool-down

Cool-down ritual

Impulse Go-Round

Do a quick, large group go-round using an impulse. Have the group hold hands, and as the impulse travels around the group, ask each player, and staff, to give a one-word example of responsibility as the hand-squeeze impulse reaches them. To make this into a game, see if the words can keep up with the impulse.

Homework Assignment

As a fun homework assignment, ask the players and staff to begin looking in local newspapers and magazines, and to listen for stories on the radio and television that show examples of responsibility. Ask everyone to bring these examples to group when they find them. The group will continue adding to the collection of articles and stories they gathered for the first two theme units and will use them at the end of the program.

Session 22:
Contract Renewal (with an Eye on responsibility)

Overview

Instructor's Notes: *Be sure to review this set of activities before starting this Sports PLUS Session. Directions for how to facilitate each activity are provided, but it is important that you become familiar with them so that you may more effectively lead the group.*

During group discussions, be sure to record all thoughts and ideas on a blackboard or newsprint. Remember that when students are working in their Player Portfolios, spelling, grammar, and penmanship are, relatively speaking, unimportant, so don't dwell on those details or you risk making Sports PLUS into MoreSchool.

This session focuses on helping players reflect on what they have already learned about teamwork and respect and to think critically about how they can apply those values toward understanding and living out responsibility.

The *Lessons from Literature* activity marks the first chapter-theme book. You might invite players who are particularly strong readers to take turns reading a chapter over the next five lessons.

Add On is a game that gets players thinking about how the Sports PLUS values relate to and support each other in a fun, interactive way. During the team-building activity, players learn a script for making good decisions that they can use in their daily lives.

You can impact the effectiveness of these activities by leading the group with a positive attitude and by encouraging players to view responsibility as a new, important value that will be exciting to explore together.

Session 22: Contract Renewal (with an Eye on Responsibility) Lessons from Literature	
Warm-up Begin the PLUS Cycle (10-15 min.) • Session Overview • Quote of the Week **Activity** Lessons from Literature (25-30 min.) • Theme Book — *Broadway Ball Players: Everybody's Favorite by Penny*	**Cool-down** Continue the PLUS Cycle (5-10 min.) • Reflection **Materials** Copies of *Broadway Ball Players: Everybody's Favorite by Penny*

Warm-up

Quote of the Week
(see Player Portfolio)

"If you are given a chance to be a role model, I think you should always take it because you can influence a person's life in a positive light, and that's what I want to do. That's what it's all about."

— Tiger Woods

Follow the 5 steps of the Quote of the Week Format (See the *Getting Started* chapter for additional explanation):

1. Write the Quote of the Week: Bring the group together into a circle, and write the Quote on the blackboard.

2. Think about the Quote as a group: Spend two or three minutes talking with the students about what they think the quote means. Ask students to share answers to the group for the following question:

3. Why do you think this quote was chosen to be part of the responsibility theme?

4. Pair up to talk about the Quote: Have students separate into pairs. Ask them to spend about five minutes discussing the following questions with their partners. Explain that they will be sharing their answers with the whole group, so they may choose to write them in their Player Portfolios. (Be sure to walk around the groups, listen, and offer help where needed.):

5. What is a role model?

6. Do you think it is important for famous athletes to be role models?

7. Share answers with the whole group: Come together as a large group and share the answers from each of the pair groups. Everyone who wants to should have an opportunity to share their answers.

8. Reflect individually about the Quote: Take two or three minutes for students to reflect individually by writing a response to the following Journal Question in their Player Portfolios:

9. Describe someone who is or could be your role model.

Activity

Lessons from Literature
Theme Book
Broadway Ball Players: Everybody's Favorite by Penny
(see Player Portfolio)

by Maureen Holohan

Lesson No. One: Chapters 1-3

Setup

Instructor's note

This story raises a number of issues, including the pressure that sometimes accompanies living up to the expectations of others, leadership, honesty, friendship, compassion, and fairness. There are also a number of adults in the story who act as both positive and negative role models. As students get into the story, challenge them to look for examples of the pressure Penny feels from others around her. Marvin, another character in the story, provides a perfect contrast to Penny — he is always in trouble, so people come to expect trouble from him. Ask students to pay attention to the actions and dialogue of the adults in the story and to look for clues about the way these adults treat students because of their expectations.)

Gather the students together into a circle and read the summary below.

This is the third book in the Broadway Ballplayers series that features a group of girls, ages 10-13, who live on the same street in an unnamed city. The girls are close friends and play a variety of sports together, but their differing personalities and competitive spirits sometimes lead to conflicts. Each book in the series is narrated by one of the girls. This helps readers to get to know each of the players, from their own and from others' perspectives.

Penny, this book's narrator and main character, is 12 years old and is considered to be the best all around athlete of the group. She is also an "A" student, snappy dresser, and often the peacemaker during conflicts. Everyone expects Penny to constantly perform above everyone else and to lead her team, whether in a jump rope contest or playing basketball. Penny feels this constant pressure and often wishes she could just play, unnoticed and not be singled out for all the attention and pressure to perform.

This book tells a story about what happens when they are invited to spend a week at a soccer camp. Before they can go, they must raise $375 in one week, so the girls decide to hold a bake sale, a jump rope tournament, and a car wash.

When the money they have collected disappears, it is Penny who must deal with the problem. The girls raise the needed money but Penny finds that the pressure on her to perform follows her to camp, where the story reaches a final conflict. Penny learns that regardless of the expectations of others, she must remain true to herself.

After reading the summary, you may want to spend a few minutes exploring different themes before beginning the book. A few suggestions are listed below:

1. Before beginning the book, ask students to read About the Author, beginning on page 157. Ask students to make some

general predictions about the story based on the cover, title and what they know about the author.

2. What sport do you think this story will involve?

3. From what we know about the author, what are some lessons this book might contain?

4. Who do you think the main character will be? Why?

5. Based on the title, can you think of any struggles or conflicts this character might have?

You also may choose to review some of the vocabulary below before beginning the story:

- faithful (p. 10)

- sarcastically (p. 11)

- humiliate (p.12)

- reputation (p. 15)

- dreaded (p. 17)

- embarrass (p. 18)

- frustrated (p. 19)

- scholarship (p. 24)

- compensation (p. 28)

Ask students to be on the look-out for words that are new to them as they read the story. They can write these words in their Player Portfolios.

Chapter-by-Chapter Summary

Read the first three chapters aloud and with enthusiasm to the whole group. Be sure to show pictures to the students as you read.

Chapter One

In this first chapter, we are introduced to Penny, the story's narrator. We learn that Penny is always expected to be the best and that she feels pressured to fulfill the expectations others put on her. We also meet the other Broadway Ballplayers and are briefly introduced to their neighborhood. The girls decide to enter a double-Dutch competition, even though jumping rope is something they don't usually do.

Chapter Two

The girls find that Molly, one of the group, is not very good at jumping rope, but she perseveres and her hard work pays off. We meet several other characters, including Mr. Gordon, the principal at the girls' school. We learn of Mr. Gordon's dedication and caring for his students. He tells the girls that they can attend a week-long soccer camp, but they must first raise $375 in one week. The girls make plans to raise the money and include the $50 they hope they'll win in the Double-Dutch competition. The chapter ends with a pick-up basketball game and Penny wondering just what her friends want from her.

Chapter Three

We meet Penny's family in this chapter, including her Grandmother, who helps the girls organize their bake sale to raise money for camp. We also learn something about Penny's life at home; she is expected to pitch in as a responsible family member. There are good lessons from her grandmother and we meet her father, who was also a great basketball player in his youth.

Discussion Questions

Spend a couple of minutes distributing students' Player Portfolios and pencils. (Ask for one or two volunteers to help.) Write the questions and focus prompts on a blackboard or newsprint.

Work together as a whole group to answer the following questions in a round-robin format:

- Who are some of the main characters so far in the story?

- What kind of competition are the Ballplayers going to enter at the Summer Fest?

- Why doesn't Penny want to enter?

- Who is Mr. Gordon?

- What kind of camp does he offer to the girls?

- How do the girls decide to make money for camp?

- Who organizes them and helps with baking?

- What are some of Penny's chores?

Additional questions

1. What does Penny mean when she says, "Our tight group of friends... always stuck together. It was an unwritten pact and unspoken promise among all of us." (p. 9)

2. Penny tells us her Grandmother always says, "Lucky things don't just happen by themselves." What do you think this means? (p. 13)

3. Find two examples where Penny feels pressure from her friends to perform and be the best? Does Penny like having these expectations placed on her? Why do you think she feels the way she does?

Cool-down

- **R&R Huddle** (5 min.)

- **Recap** one or two key points that arose during the discussion.

- **Reconnect** to the theme, Responsibility, using the questions below as a guide:

  – Have you ever been given a big responsibility? What was it?

  – Why was it challenging?

  – How did you feel when you completed it?

- **Reset** and transition to the next lesson.

Session 22: Contract Renewal (with an Eye on Responsibility) Lessons from the Field	

Warm-up
Begin the PLUS Cycle (5 min.)
  • Session Overview
  • Reflecting on Responsibility
	Cool-down
	Continue the PLUS Cycle (5-10 min.)
	  • Reflection
	  • Goal-setting

Activity Lessons from the Field (25-30 min.) • Sports Activity	**Materials** Sports Equipment

Warm-up

Reflecting on Responsibility (5 min.)

Ask students to think about the previous lesson. What can they do today to bring the Lessons from Literature into their work in the sports activity?

Activity

Lessons from the Field
Sports Activity

Block I: Getting Started (5 min.)

On the first day, players will learn how to measure their resting heart rates (RHR). They will also set baselines for their RHR, number of sit-ups/push-ups/lunges/calf raises, and number of jumps during jump rope. Each day they will try to improve upon their Past Personal Best (PPB) by achieving their Future Best Goal (FBG) and by tracking progress toward that goal in the physical activities progress chart located in the back of their Player Portfolios. Take one minute to make sure all participants turn to the back of their portfolios and locate the progress charts. Explain to them that they will be using this chart each time you meet to do physical activities. Be sure to emphasize the importance of keeping track of their progress by using the chart.

Stand together in a circle for all *Getting Started* activities (except for jogging). Have players partner up, with one player doing the activity and the partner keeping count and giving encouragement. Be sure that players have their Portfolios handy so that they can record their progress. Encourage them to clap and cheer for their teammates to create an enthusiastic environment. You may also choose to include music.

- **Measure resting heart rate (RHR)** — Spend a few minutes showing players how to find their pulses, either on their necks or wrists. Explain that you will be giving them a few seconds to count how many times their hearts beat. Take a moment to allow players to sit quietly on the floor and find their pulses. Give them 30 seconds to count their heartbeats.

- **Record, check in and set goals** — Allow a couple of minutes for players to record their RHRs in their Player Portfolios.

- **Jog (2-3 min.)** — This can be done as a lap or in place as a circle.

- **Stretch (2-3 min.)** — Be sure to include stretches for the major muscle groups.

- **Strength/Endurance (1 min.)** — On this first day, players will set baseline numbers for the four Strength/Endurance activities (push-ups, sit-ups, lunges, calf raises), but usually, you will only choose one or two. They will work in pairs. One member of the pair will have 30 seconds to do as many of the activities as they can. Their partner will cheer them on and count for them.

- **Jump Rope (4 min.)** — Again, players will work in pairs, with one person jumping and the other person counting and cheering. They should have three to four sets of 30-45 seconds of jumping rope.

- **Track personal progress** — Have players record their totals for steps five and six in their Player Portfolios. These totals will represent their baseline achievements, or their Past Personal Bests (PPB). Each day, players will check their progress from

the previous session and will set a Future Personal Best Goal (FBG) to work toward for next time. Be sure to remind them about setting realistic goals (for example, adding one or two to their baseline, as opposed to 10).

Block II: Structured Play (30 min.)

Skill Play (10 min.)

Choose one or two of the following activities to play today. You can refer back to the *Physical Activities Description Appendix* for instructions on how to run the activities. Encourage players to cheer for each other, and include music if you wish.

- Three-legged Race

- Water Balloon Toss

- Sprint/Stride Runs

- Gorilla Walk

- Rear-End Kick Relay

Sport Play (20 min.)

As a group, decide which sport you want to play today. Select from the sport list contained in the *Sports List Appendix*. Be sure to periodically review with the group the Physical Activities Recommendations for Sport from Chapter Six.

Cool-down

If time permits, close the day with a few minutes of stretching while conducting the following R&R Huddle.

- **Recap** one or two key moments from the Lessons from the Field.

- **Reconnect** players back to the theme unit.

- **Reset** and transition players to the Cool-down, Reflection time.

OR

- **Reflection**

Use this time to highlight teachable moments you observed during the day and to give players an opportunity to share their experiences about Sports PLUS during the day. The following questions can serve as a guide:

- What did you like about today?

- What did you learn today?

- What are some ways you were responsible today?

- In what ways can we be more responsible next time?

Goal-setting

Use this time to track the group's progress toward the team goals you set last time and to start the players thinking about one or two individual goals related to Responsibility that they would like to set during the next session.

Session 22: **Contract Renewal** **(with an Eye on Responsibility)** **Lessons from Adventure**	
Warm-up Begin the PLUS Cycle (5 min.) • Session Overview • Add On	**Cool-down** Continue the PLUS Cycle (5-10 min.) • Reflection • Contract Renewal
Activity Lessons from Adventure (25-30 min.) • Making Good Decisions	**Materials** None

Warm-up

Add On

The goal of this activity is to review the learning of past sessions and continue the new focus on Responsibility.

Setup

Bring the group together in a circle (sitting in chairs or on the floor). Say to the group, "Who can remember the two values we previously focused on? We have spent quite a bit of time discussing and learning about Teamwork and Respect. Let's take a few minutes to remember some of the things we have learned."

Play

1. Begin by explaining to the group that you will be playing a game called Add On. "If you can think of something to add to what the person speaking is saying, raise your hand. The speaker will finish what he or she is saying and give you a high five. Then it will be your turn to speak."

2. Next, ask the players to answer the following: "What are the two kinds of respect we have been talking about?"

3. Continue the game (with prompting from you). Encourage the group to think of the many activities and discussions they have had around the ideas of teamwork and respect.

4. Next, ask players to describe what they know so far about responsibility. "How do teamwork and respect relate to and support responsibility? What are some of the things that make living out the values difficult?"

5. Continue a large group discussion on the relationship of the values and how they work together. Ask players to be looking for examples from today's session that show all three values operating at the same time. These examples will be shared during today's Cool-down session.

Activity

Lessons from Adventure
Making Good Decisions

Helping youth to learn to take responsibility for their actions and behavior takes practice like anything else. Learning to make good decisions is a necessary part of any young person's development. But before players can develop good decision-making skills, they must be given opportunities to practice those skills. The cry of "You need to be more responsible!" is echoed in the classroom and in the home. One problem, however, is that our youth often do not have enough opportunities to make decisions for themselves in safe, controlled environments — environments within which players can take time to think through a situation, ask assistance if needed, and make mistakes that become learning opportunities rather than justification for criticism or even punishment. Without opportunities to practice making good decisions within such an environment, young people often have great difficulty when they are suddenly thrown into a situation in which they must make good decisions.

As an example, let us look at how children play sports. Much of a child's early sport experience is controlled by adults — we organize the leagues, make the teams, decide on the rules, call the plays and settle disputes. When these same young people attempt to run their own games or activities, they often get into disputes over teams, rules, positions, close plays, etc. All too often, when children regulate their own games they spend more time arguing than actually playing the game.

Making good decisions, like any other skill, should be practiced. The model presented below is taken from research into how people make moral choices when faced with a situation in which there are multiple options. Thomas Lickona, in his book *Educating for Character* (1991), gives us a process to follow. This process leads us to think about a situation, to make a decision, and then to act on that decision, using the following questions to get us started:

- What are my options?

- What are the probable consequences of different courses of action?

- Who will be affected by my decision?

- What course of action would most likely maximize the good consequences and be faithful to the important values at stake?

- How do I now act on my decision?

This thoughtful decision-making process can be divided into five action steps, which we call DSCCA (pronounced Deska). This process can be used to help players remember and internalize the steps.

Setup

Introducing DSCCA (pronounced Deska) Bring the group together into a circle. Briefly introduce the DSCCA Decision-Making Process by going through each step with the group. Explain what each step is and what it accomplishes. Next, discuss how each step of the model leads to the next step and, finally, to a solution.

Step 1 — Identify the Dilemma

The first step in DSCCA Decision-Making Process is to identify the dilemma or problem. Before a dilemma can be identified, an awareness of good and bad possibilities, of right and wrong choices, is necessary. The five Sports PLUS values help young people learn to recognize good behavior toward others and toward oneself. The broad themes of teamwork, respect and responsibility include many other desirable character values such as compassion, empathy, caring, kindness, self-discipline and integrity. In a decision-making process, the ability to understand the importance of these values comes into play. The more opportunities players have to read about, discuss, and practice these values, the better they will become at recognizing them and appreciating their importance.

Step 2 — Identify the Possible Solutions

The next step in making a good decision is to recognize the available solutions in a given situation. Depending on the specific situation, there may be few or many different courses of possible action.

Step 3 — Identify the Consequences of each Solution

Each possible solution will have direct consequences if taken. Thus, the next step in the decision-making process is to sort through and weigh the consequences of each solution. Making a good decision depends on an ability to recognize and feel emotionally which course of action represents right action and which represents wrong action (or for real-life situations, when things are rarely so clear-cut, which solutions represent better and worse actions).

Step 4 — Choose the most Responsible Solution

After sorting through and weighing the consequences of each alternative solution, a course of action must be chosen that represents the most good for the most people. This step is fundamental to good decision-making. The first three steps help us gather important information, but until this step is taken, no decision can be made. Thus, making good decisions requires an ability to understand the situation, to recognize alternatives for handling the dilemma, to sort through right and wrong options, to choose the best course of action, and then to take action.

Step 5 — Act on that Decision (or, Take Action)

This fifth, and final step, often is the most difficult part of the whole process. With practice, choosing the best course of action, recognizing "the right thing to do," may become fairly easy. Acting on that decision is often far more difficult. Peer pressure, self-defeat, honesty, possible punishment and a host of other influences and potential consequences may make the experience of acting on our decisions somewhat unpleasant. Having the courage to act on our convictions, to take action even though it may not be in our immediate best interest, requires tremendous self-confidence, self-discipline, and inner strength. It requires knowledge and emotional recognition of values like respect, responsibility, perseverance and fair play. The more opportunities youth have to practice using these values, the more they will recognize them as guidelines for good behavior and good decision-making. More importantly, with practice, young people can learn to rely on those values to help them take action when doing so is difficult.

(It's a good idea to make a poster of the model or to write the basic steps on a board.) Students also receive a copy of the model in their Player Portfolios, for quick reference and to use as a problem-solving worksheet.

D.S.c.c.a. Summary

Step 1:   Identify the Dilemma.

Step 2:   Identify the possible Solutions.

Step 3:   Identify the Consequences of each solution.

Step 4:   Choose the most responsible solution.

Step 5:   Act on that decision.

Play

After a brief overview of the DSCCA decision-making strategy and a review of each step, bring the group together in a circle to practice using DSCCA in the You Make the Call reading activity.

1. Spend a few minutes reviewing the story from the last session, Jasmine's Choice.

2. Next, take about five minutes to consider the following questions:

3. Have you ever been in a situation like the one described in the story we read last time?

4. What is something we learned today that would be helpful if you had to make a decision like the one in the story?

5. Divide the large group into four or five equally-sized, smaller groups. Ask each group to make up a situation similar to the one that happened in the story. Have players use the DSCCA decision-making strategy and the worksheet in their Player Portfolios to make a decision in the situation they create.

6. After 10-12 minutes bring the small groups back together into a circle. Ask each group to choose a delegate to share the dilemma and their DSCCA-solution with the entire group.

- **R&R Huddle** (5 min.)

- **Recap** one or two key points from the activity.

- **Reconnect** to the theme unit.

- **Reset** and transition to the next activity.

Cool-down

Cool-down Ritual

Player Contract Renewal

This is a good time to revisit the player contract that the players developed in the Teamwork Unit.

Have players take their contracts out of their Portfolios. The next value on the list is Responsibility. Spend some time in a whole group discussion reviewing what the group knows so far about responsibility and how it exists in their group. Refer to the posters created during this session. This would also be a good time for players to offer any examples they noticed of the values — Teamwork, Respect, and Responsibility — working together.

Move the discussion into what each player can do to be a responsible teammate. The following discussion questions are intended as suggestions to start and guide this discussion:

- What do you think responsibility means?

- Can anyone give an example of a responsible behavior they have seen in this group? At school? At home? In your neighborhood?

- Why is responsibility important to our group?

- What can each of us commit to in order to maintain a group of responsible teammates?

Once you think the group has a good understanding of why responsibility is important and how to be a responsible teammate, have a Player Contract Signing Ceremony. Remind players that by signing the Responsibility line on their contract, they are making a commitment to themselves and their teammates.

Session 23:
Responsibility Relay

Overview

> **Instructor's Notes:** *Be sure to review this set of activities before starting this Sports PLUS Session. Directions for how to facilitate each activity are provided, but it is important that you become familiar with them so that you may more effectively lead the group.*

> *During group discussions, be sure to record all thoughts and ideas on a blackboard or newsprint. Remember that when students are working in their Player Portfolios, spelling, grammar, and penmanship are, relatively speaking, unimportant, so don't dwell on those details or you risk making Sports PLUS into MoreSchool.*

One of the goals of this session is to continue players' thinking about how they are responsible for the well being of others — their family, their teammates, and their neighbors.

The *Quote of the Week* from Martin Luther King Jr. supports this idea. The theme book reading continues with *Everybody's Favorite*. The *Responsibility Relay* is an activity with which players will already be acquainted.

Session 23:
Responsibility Relay
Lessons from Literature

Warm-up Begin the PLUS Cycle (10-15 min.) • Session Overview • Quote of the Week **Activity** Lessons from Literature (25-30 min.) • Theme Book — *Broadway Ball Players: Everybody's Favorite by Penny*	**Cool-down** Continue the PLUS Cycle (5-10 min.) • Reflection **Materials** Copies of *Broadway Ball Players: Everybody's Favorite by Penny*

Instructor's note

You may wish to give some background on Martin Luther King, Jr. Although most students probably are probably somewhat aware of who Martin Luther King, Jr. was, it may be a good idea to spend a few minutes discussing the importance of King's life.

You may also wish to define some potentially difficult words for the students:

- Accomplice

- Well-being

- Ignore

Born in 1929, Martin Luther King, Jr. was an African-American Baptist minister and a key figure in the United States civil rights movement of the

1950s and '60s. King's emphasis on nonviolent demonstrations and his tremendous speaking ability inspired millions of supporters, both black and white, to join the fight for equality and made him famous worldwide. His significant contribution to the civil rights movement was recognized in 1964 when he was awarded the Nobel Peace Prize.

Despite his emphasis on nonviolence, King was frequently the target of violent attacks. His home was bombed; he was attacked physically on more than one occasion; and in 1968, at the age of 39, Martin Luther King, Jr. was killed by an assassin's bullet. Today, King is remembered for his eloquent speeches and his peaceful message, which eventually led to the abolishment of segregationist laws in the southern states. His birthday is a national holiday. The birthday of only one other person is observed as a national holiday, that of George Washington, the country's first president. (*World Book Encyclopedia:* Contributor: David J. Garrow, Ph.D., Presidential Distinguished Professor, Emory University).)

After explaining any complex words, you may wish to paraphrase the quote for the students into something such as "To not pay attention to evil is to take part in helping to make it worse," before they separate into pairs for the discussion questions.)

Warm-up

Quote of the Week

"How responsible am I for the well-being of my fellow men? To ignore evil is to become an accomplice to it."
— Martin Luther King, Jr.

Follow the 5 steps of the Quote of the Week Format (See the *Getting Started* chapter for additional explanation):

1. **Write the Quote of the Week:** Bring the group together into a circle, and write the Quote on the blackboard.

2. **Think about the Quote as a group:** Spend two or three minutes talking with the students about what they think the quote means. Ask students to share answers for the following questions:

3. What does it mean to ignore evil?

4. What does it mean to be an accomplice to something?

5. **Pair up to talk about the Quote:** Have students separate into pairs. Ask them to spend about five minutes discussing the following questions with their partners. Explain that they will be sharing their answers with the whole group, so they may choose to write their answers in their Player Portfolios. (Be sure to walk around the groups, listen, and offer help where needed.):

6. Why does being responsible mean that we cannot ignore bad things even if they don't directly affect us?

7. What are one or two ways that this applies to your own life?

8. What are one or two ways you can follow Martin Luther King's example and act responsibly toward your Sports PLUS team? Toward your community?

9. **Share answers with the whole group:** Come together as a large group and share the answers from each of the pair groups. Everyone who wants to should have an opportunity to share their answers.

10. **Reflect individually about the Quote:** Take two or three minutes for students to reflect individually by writing a response to the following Journal Question in their Player Portfolios:

    You may preface the journal question by asking students to think about things they think need improvement in their school or house.

11. One way I can show responsibility to my Sports PLUS teammates is by...

12. One way I can show responsibility to my family is by...

13. One way I can show responsibility to my school is by...

Activity

Lessons from Literature
Theme Book
Broadway Ball Players: Everybody's Favorite by Penny
(see Player Portfolio)

by Maureen Holohan

Lesson No. Two: Chapters 4-6

Setup

Gather the students into a circle and spend a few minutes discussing what has happened so far in the story. Ask students to summarize some of the action that has occurred and where they think the story might be headed in these next few chapters. The following questions will help get you started:

- Who are the characters we have met so far? Describe each of them.

- Summarize the story so far.

- What kind of a person do you think Penny is?

- From what you have read so far, why do you think Penny often feels pressure to perform?

You also may choose to review some of the vocabulary for today:

- pavilion (p. 30)

- leukemia (p. 31)

- incessantly (p. 32)

- homesick (p. 33)

- obnoxious (p. 34)

- compulsory (p. 37)

- averaged (p. 38)

- arrogantly (p. 39)

- pathetically (p. 43)

- dejectedly (p. 44)

- converged (p. 53)

- hysterically (p. 56)

Chapter-by-Chapter Summary

Read chapters four through seven aloud and with enthusiasm to the whole group.

Chapter Four

We finally get to the Summer Fest and the anticipated Double-Dutch contest. Here we learn that Wil, the smartest of the Ballplayers, is sensitive about her intelligence, and we get a glimpse of the personalities of several other Ballplayers. Problems with the money they collect from the bake sale are foreshadowed, and the jump rope competition finally begins. Once again, Penny feels pressure both to perform and to keep her team together mentally. Molly, the weakest jumper when they began practicing, performs well enough that the Ballplayers end the first round of the competition in first place.

Chapter Five

The second round of the Double Dutch tournament begins after some confusion which creates more stress for the girls. Wil complains of being sick from eating too many cupcakes. She performs poorly, leaving it up to Penny once again to save her team. There are several examples of internal dialogue from Penny where we see how she feels and handles the stress placed on her. Penny performs brilliantly and the Ballplayers win the competition.

Chapter Six

The jump rope contest is over but the girls get involved in a basketball game with several new characters. Much of the chapter is spent on this game and we get to know something about each of them, including Marvin, who will figure prominently in a coming conflict and provides a contrast to Penny's character. Penny's attitude about Marvin and his situation tells a lot about her. We also find out that Penny's father teaches a special education class. Penny is challenged to a one-on-one game with a high school boy in which she wins money. The chapter ends with the girls planning a car wash to raise the rest of the money needed for camp.

Discussion Questions

Spend a couple of minutes distributing students' Player Portfolios and pencils. (Ask for one or two volunteers to help.) Write the questions and focus prompts on a blackboard or newsprint.

Work together as a whole group to answer the following questions:

Questions one through seven should be answered in a round-robin format, with one student answering one question. Try to include students who may not always participate. (If answers for any of the questions are imprecise or need further elaboration, ask if anyone has anything to add.)

1. Which ballplayer gets teased for being so smart?

2. How do the girls make money for camp?

3. How does Molly do in the first round of the contest?

4. What's wrong with Wil as the second round is about to begin? Why?

5. Why do the students not trust Marvin?

6. At what game does Penny beat the high school boy?

7. How do the girls decide to raise the rest of the money for camp?

The following focus prompt should be answered in an exhaustive format. Continue letting students give responses until no new answers are given.

1. One way that Penny shows responsibility so far is by....

2. One example of how Penny feels pressure to perform in these chapters is....

Close the day by summarizing the following themes from today's reading:

"In these three chapters, we learn a bit more about some of the Ballplayers and are introduced to several other characters. We see the continued pressure Penny feels from her teammates and from just about everybody else. We also meet Marvin, who people also expect to act in certain ways, though quite opposite to Penny's behavior."

Cool-down

- **R&R Huddle** (5 min.)

- **Recap** one or two key points that arose during the discussion.

- **Reconnect** by asking volunteers to briefly share some responsibilities that they hold in their families right now.

- **Reset** and get ready for the next lesson.

Session 23: **Responsibility Relay** **Lessons from the Field**	
Warm-up Begin the PLUS Cycle (5 min.) • Session Overview • Reflecting on Responsibility **Activity** Lessons from the Field (25-30 min.) • Sports Activity	**Cool-down** Continue the PLUS Cycle (5-10 min.) • Reflection • Goal-setting **Materials** Sports Equipment

Warm-up

Reflecting on Responsibility (5 min.)

Ask students to think about the previous lesson. What can they do today to bring the Lessons from Literature into their work together in the sports activity?

Activity

Lessons from the Field
Sports Activity

Block I: Getting Started (5 min.)

On the first day, players will learn how to measure their resting heart rates (RHR). They will also set baselines for their RHR, number of sit-ups/push-ups/lunges/calf raises, and number of jumps during jump rope. Each day they will try to improve upon their Past Personal Best (PPB) by achieving their Future Best Goal (FBG) and by tracking progress toward that goal in the physical activities progress chart located in the back of their Player Portfolios. Take one minute to make sure all participants turn to the back of their portfolios and locate the progress charts. Explain to them that they will be using this chart each time you meet to do physical activities. Be sure to emphasize the importance of keeping track of their progress by using the chart.

Stand together in a circle for all *Getting Started* activities (except for jogging). Have players partner up, with one player doing the activity and the partner keeping count and giving encouragement. Be sure that they have their Portfolios handy so that they can record their progress. Encourage them to clap and cheer for their teammates to create an enthusiastic environment. You may also choose to include music.

- **Measure resting heart rate (RHR)** — Spend a few minutes showing players how to find their pulses, either on their necks or wrists. Explain that you will be giving them a few seconds to count how many times their hearts beat. Take a moment to allow the players to sit quietly on the floor and find their pulses. Give them 30 seconds to count their heartbeats.

- **Record, check in and set goals** — Allow a couple of minutes for players to record their RHRs in their Player Portfolios.

- **Jog (2-3 min.)** — This can be done as a lap or in place as a circle.

- **Stretch (2-3 min.)** — Be sure to include stretches for the major muscle groups.

- **Strength/Endurance (1 min.)** — On this first day, players will set baseline numbers for the four Strength/Endurance activities (push-ups, sit-ups, lunges, calf raises), but usually, you will only choose one or two. They will work in pairs. One member of the pair will have 30 seconds to do as many of the activities as they can. Their partner will cheer them on and count for them.

- **Jump Rope (4 min.)** — Again, players will work in pairs, with one person jumping and the other person counting and cheering. They should have three to four sets of 30-45 seconds of jumping rope.

- **Track personal progress** — Have players record their totals for steps five and six in their Player Portfolios. These totals will represent their baseline achievements, or their Past Personal Bests (PPB). Each day, players will check their progress from the previous session and will set a Future Personal Best Goal (FBG) to work toward for next time. Be sure to remind them about setting realistic goals (for example, adding one or two to their baseline, as opposed to 10).

Block II: Structured Play (30 min.)

Skill Play (10 min.)

Choose one or two of the following activities to play today. You can refer back to the *Physical Activities Description Appendix* for instructions on how to run the activities. Encourage players to cheer for each other, and include music if you wish.

- Tug o' War

- Long Distance Musical Chairs

- Star Jumps

- Leap Frog Relay

- Chinese Jump Rope

Sport Play (20 min.)

As a group, decide which sport you want to play today. Select from the sport list contained in the *Sports List Appendix.* Be sure to periodically review with the group the Physical Activities Recommendations for Sport from Chapter Six.

Cool-down

If time permits, close the day with a few minutes of stretching while conducting the following R&R Huddle.

- **Recap** one or two key moments from the Lessons from the Field.

- **Reconnect** players back to the theme unit.

- **Reset** and transition players to the Cool-down, Reflection time.

  OR

- **Reflection**

Use this time to highlight teachable moments you observed during the day and to give players an opportunity to share their experiences about Sports PLUS. The following questions can serve as a guide:

- What did you like about today?

- What did you learn today?

- What are some ways you were responsible today?

- In what ways can we be more responsible next time?

Goal-setting

Use this time to help players track progress toward their individually chosen goals, as well as toward team goals. As goals from earlier sessions are reached, guide players in setting additional individual and team goals related to Responsibility.

Session 23: **Responsibility Relay** **Lessons from Adventure**	

Warm-up
Begin the PLUS Cycle (5 min.)
 	
  • Session Overview
 	
  • Triangle Tag
	Cool-down
	Continue the PLUS Cycle (5-10 min.)
	
	  • Reflection
	
	  • Anonymous Put-Ups

Activity Lessons from Adventure (25-30 min.) • Responsibility Relay	**Materials** 4 large flip charts or sheets of poster paper hung around the room with the following headings on them — two that read "Responsibility for Yourself," and two that read "Responsibility for Others;" different colored markers at each station; cones or other objects to create a simple obstacle course

Warm-up

Triangle Tag

Setup

Find a creative way to separate the group into groups of four. Have each group of four designate one person to be "it."

Play

1. Ask the three players who are not "it" to form a circle by holding hands. The person who is "it" remains on the outside of the circle.

2. Now ask each group to choose one of the three in the circle to be the person being chased by the "tagger." When each group is ready to start, the person on the outside who is "it" tries to move around the outside of the circle and tag the designated person. The three people who are holding hands try to maneuver each other in a way that keeps the one being chased from being tagged.

3. Switch positions after someone gets tagged or after a few minutes.

4. For safety reasons, do not allow the players who are "it" to reach across the circle in an attempt to tag the "chasee."

Activity

Lessons from Adventure
Responsibility Relay
(see Player Portfolio)

Setup

The previous discussion should provide a good warm-up for this activity. Remind players that as they participate in the activity, they should also be practicing responsible behavior.

Before you begin, hang the four large pieces of poster or art paper in different parts of the room. Make sure that the players will be able to reach the paper to write on it. While there are four posters, there are only two statements. This is simply to speed up the activity and allow players time to be directly involved. Each team only visits two different posters. Set up the cones or other objects so that players will have a clear path to run around.

Divide the group into four smaller groups.

Play

1. Assign each team to one of the posters.

2. Each team will be given three to five minutes to write as many responses to complete the phrase "Responsibility for Yourself sounds like or looks like..." or "Responsibility to others looks like or sounds like..."

3. The team must work as a relay team — each person in the team has a turn with the marker and writes something on the poster. After writing a statement, each player must run around a cone before handing off the marker to a teammate. The team repeats the relay pattern until the time is up. Teammates can help each other if someone gets stuck.

4. After five minutes or so, yell "Switch!" at which point each team moves to a different poster with a different statement.

Discussion

Bring the players back together as a large group. Hang the posters in a place where everyone can see them. Spend some time discussing each poster. Create two new posters as a group with simple statements of what the group sees as the most important ideas about responsibility in the program. Finally, if time permits, allow the players an opportunity to decorate the posters.

Leave these posters hanging in the after-school space for the remainder of the program.

- **R&R Huddle** (5 minutes)

- **Recap** by highlighting one or two key discussion points.

- **Reconnect** with the following focus prompt: Responsibility is important because...

- **Reset** and transition to the next activity.

Cool-down

Cool-down Ritual

Anonymous Put-ups

Try this fun way for the group to offer anonymous put-ups to itself. Have players take out a piece of paper. Each player should write, in pen, a message to the group that describes why they are a good team, or how they show respect or responsibility. Give the group a few minutes to write, then have the players scrunch up their papers into a tight ball. On the count of three, the group members, standing close together, throw the balls of paper into the air. Everyone tries to catch one, preferably not the one they tossed. Have players open their balled-up papers and ask for volunteers to decipher and read the wrinkly messages.

Instructor's note

Remind players that it would be disrespectful to write something inappropriate. If a player finds something objectionable, use it as a teachable moment for a discussion on respect, teamwork, and responsibility.

Session 24:
Responsible Teammates

Overview

Instructor's Notes: *Be sure to review this set of activities before starting this Sports PLUS Session. Directions for how to facilitate each activity are provided, but it is important that you become familiar with them so that you may more effectively lead the group.*

During group discussions, be sure to record all thoughts and ideas on a blackboard or newsprint. Remember that when players are working in their Player Portfolios, spelling, grammar, and penmanship are, relatively speaking, unimportant, so don't dwell on those details or you risk making Sports PLUS into MoreSchool.

This session begins with a quote from Jackie Robinson that highlights the importance of respect. The *Lessons from Literature* continues with the theme book reading of *Everybody's Favorite*. The Lessons from Adventure continues with a trust activity called *Trust Chair*. It is an activity that requires that the group members both trust one another and are willing to make every effort to take care of one another. If, after reading the instructions, you don't think your group is ready for this activity, save it for another time.

The team-building activity, *Slot Machine,* challenges three groups to work together toward success. In addition to bringing up important topics, such as working together for the good of the whole team and respecting the team goal over individual accomplishments, this activity challenges players to create a symbol to represent their understanding of Responsibility.

The session closes with a Cool-down ritual that asks players to think about ways they can demonstrate responsibility in their communities.

Session 24:
Responsible Teammates
Lessons from Literature

Warm-up	Cool-down
Begin the PLUS Cycle (10-15 min.)	Continue the PLUS Cycle (5-10 min.)
• Session Overview	• Reflection
• Quote of the Week	**Materials**
Activity	Copies of *Teammates*
Lessons from Literature (25-30 min.)	
• Theme Book — *Teammates*	

Warm-up

Quote of the Week
(see Player Portfolio)

"Responsibility walks hand in hand with capacity and power."
— William Penn

Follow the 5 steps of the Quote of the Week Format (See the *Getting Started* chapter for additional explanation):

1. **Write the Quote of the Week:** Bring the group together into a circle, and write the Quote on the blackboard.

2. **Think about the Quote as a group:** Spend two or three minutes talking with the students about what they think the quote means. Ask students to share answers to the group for the following question:

3. What does 'capacity' mean in this quote?

4. **Pair up to talk about the Quote:** Have students separate into pairs. Ask them to spend about five minutes discussing the following questions with their partners. Explain that they will be sharing their answers with the whole group, so they may choose to write them in their Player Portfolios. (Be sure to walk around the groups, listen, and offer help where needed.):

5. How do you act if you are being responsible? What does being responsible look like?

6. Have you ever behaved irresponsibly with the team? Have you ever been a good teammate? How?

7. **Share answers with the whole group:** Come together as a large group and share the answers from each of the pair groups. Everyone who wants to should have an opportunity to share their answers.

8. **Reflect individually about the Quote:** Take two or three minutes for students to reflect individually by writing a response to the following Journal Question in their Player Portfolios:

9. Write about a time when you have acted responsibly with teammates or classmates or family.

Activity

Lessons from Literature
Theme Book

Broadway Ball Players: Everybody's Favorite by Penny
(see Player Portfolio)

by Maureen Holohan

Lesson No. Three: Chapters 7-9

Setup

Gather the students into a circle and spend a few minutes discussing what has happened so far in the story. Ask students to summarize some of the action that has occurred and where they think the story might be headed in the next few chapters. The chapters for today present a major conflict and dilemma for Penny.

You also may choose to review some of the vocabulary for today:

- circumstance (p. 60)

- defensively (p. 64)

- desperately (p. 67)

- stationary (p. 72)

- relationship (p. 78)

- mentor (p. 80)

- irked (p. 83)

- apprehensively (p. 85)

- humiliation (p. 89)

Chapter-by-Chapter Summary

Read chapters seven through nine aloud and with enthusiasm to the whole group.

Chapter Seven

This chapter begins with Penny and her family attending church. A quote from p. 60 ("Character, not circumstance, makes the person.") foreshadows a future conflict Penny will face. The main action revolves around the car wash the Ballplayers hold to continue raising money for camp. But when the box of money disappears, the girls decide to handle the situation themselves. Penny, who was supposed to be watching it, volunteers to talk to Marvin, whom everyone assumes took the money.

Chapter Eight

Penny struggles with how to deal with Marvin. She has a conversation with her grandmother in which we see how Penny's concern for Marvin affects her decisions. Penny's grandmother provides a contrast to Penny's thinking. Penny goes to Marvin's home early in the morning with a bag of groceries that her grandmother prepares. In a very caring and respectful way, Penny asks Marvin to give the money back. Marvin first denies having taken it, then hints that maybe he took it because he really needed it for "food and some clothes." Penny returns home thinking she failed, but Marvin's younger sister soon shows up with an envelope from Marvin.

Chapter Nine

This chapter opens with Penny telling her father about Marvin taking and returning the money. She asks her father to help Marvin find a job, and we learn some things about her father and the kind of person he is. The girls leave for soccer camp, and we see their apprehension about going someplace different and far from home. We find that Penny's reputation has preceded her and that the camp director is very strict. The chapter ends with a foreshadowing of a conflict.

Discussion Questions

Spend a couple of minutes distributing students' Player Portfolios and pencils. (Ask for one or two volunteers to help.) Write the questions and focus prompts on a blackboard or newsprint.

Work together as a whole group to answer the following questions:

Questions one through five should be answered in a round-robin format, with one student answering one question. Try to include students who may not always participate. (If any of the answers are imprecise or need further elaboration, ask if anyone has anything to add.)

1. What does Rev. James announce at church?

2. Who do the Ballplayers think took the money?

3. What does Penny take to Marvin's house when she talks to him about the missing money?

4. How does Penny get the missing money back?

5. Whose phone calls does Penny's grandmother want Penny to return?

6. The following focus prompt should be answered in an exhaustive format. Continue letting students give responses until no new answers are given.

7. One way Penny shows responsibility in these chapters is by....

For questions seven and eight, allow all students an opportunity to share their answers, regardless of whether or not the answers are original.

1. When would it be important in your life to show responsibility?

2. One thing that might make doing this difficult is...

Finally, ask students to write their responses to the following prompt in their Player Portfolios.

3. One way you can take responsibility even when it is difficult (as Penny did with the missing money) is by...

Additional Questions

- In chapter seven, what does Penny mean when she tells Rev. James, "I kept the faith." (p. 59)?

- What does the phrase that Reverend James quotes at church mean? "Character, not circumstance, makes the person" (p. 59)

- Why do you think Penny wonders what it would be like to play without everybody knowing who she is? (p. 62)

- Why does Angel think Penny may be the only one who can help Marvin? (p. 69)

- Why does Penny stop and think about calling herself Marvin's friend? (p. 74)

- When Penny approached Marvin about the money, she didn't yell, scream or shout at him. Do you think this was a good thing to do? Why or why not? (p. 77)

- In chapter 9, we find out something about Penny's father that tells what kind of person he is. What do we find out? (p. 80)

Cool-down

- **R&R Huddle** (5 min.)

- **Recap** one or two key points that arose during the discussion. The following suggestion will help get you started:

  – Penny tells Mr. O'Malley an untruth when he asks her about the money and afterward, she feels badly about it. Sometimes we do things that are not in our best character. We are not always going to be perfect, but the important thing is to do the right thing when we realize our mistake.

- **Reconnect** by asking volunteers to briefly share what they wrote in their Player Portfolios for question number nine above.

- **Reset** and get ready for the next lesson.

Session 24:
Responsible Teammates
Lessons from the Field

Warm-up	Cool-down
Begin the PLUS Cycle (5 min.)	Continue the PLUS Cycle (5-10 min.)
• Session Overview	• Reflection
• Reflecting on Responsibility	• Goal-setting
Activity	**Materials**
Lessons from the Field (25-30 min.)	Sports Equipment
• Sports Activity	

Warm-up
Reflecting on Responsibility (5 min.)

Ask students to think about the previous lesson. What can they do today to bring the Lessons from Literature into their work together in the sports activity?

Activity

Lessons from the Field
Sports Activity

Block I: Getting Started (5 min.)

On the first day, players will learn how to measure their resting heart rates (RHR). They will also set baselines for their RHR, number of sit-ups/push-ups/lunges/calf raises, and number of jumps during jump rope. Each day they will try to improve upon their Past Personal Best (PPB) by achieving their Future Best Goal (FBG) and by tracking progress toward that goal in the physical activities progress chart located in the back of their Player Portfolios. Take one minute to make sure all participants turn to the back of their portfolios and locate the progress charts. Explain to them that they will be using this chart each time you meet to do physical activities. Be sure to emphasize the importance of keeping track of their progress by using the chart.

Stand together in a circle for all *Getting Started* activities (except for jogging). Have players partner up, with one player doing the activity and the partner keeping count and giving encouragement. Be sure that they have their Portfolios handy so that they can record their progress. Encourage them to clap and cheer for their teammates to create an enthusiastic environment. You may also choose to include music.

- **Measure resting heart rate (RHR)** — Spend a few minutes showing players how to find their pulses, either on their necks or wrists. Explain that you will be giving them a few seconds to count how many times their hearts beat. Take a moment to allow the players to sit quietly on the floor and find their pulses. Give them 30 seconds to count their heartbeats.

- **Record, check in and set goals** — Allow a couple of minutes for players to record their RHRs in their Player Portfolios.

- **Jog (2-3 min.)** — This can be done as a lap or in place as a circle.

- **Stretch (2-3 min.)** — Be sure to include stretches for the major muscle groups.

- **Strength/Endurance (1 min.)** — On this first day, players will set baseline numbers for the four Strength/Endurance activities (push-ups, sit-ups, lunges, calf raises), but usually, you will only choose one or two. They will work in pairs. One member of the pair will have 30 seconds to do as many of the activities as they can. Their partner will cheer them on and count for them.

- **Jump Rope (4 min.)** — Again, players will work in pairs, with one person jumping and the other person counting and cheering. They should have three to four sets of 30-45 seconds of jumping rope.

- **Track personal progress** — Have players record their totals for steps five and six in their Player Portfolios. These totals will represent their baseline achievements, or their Past Personal Bests (PPB). Each day, players will check their progress from

the previous session and will set a Future Personal Best Goal (FBG) to work toward for next time. Be sure to remind them about setting realistic goals (for example, adding one or two to their baseline, as opposed to 10).

Block II: Structured Play (30 min.)

Skill Play (10 min.)

Choose one or two of the following activities to play with the players today. You can refer back to the *Physical Activities Description Appendix* for instructions on how to run the activities. Encourage players to cheer for each other, and include music if you wish.

- Beanbag Horseshoes

- Hula Hoop Challenge Course

- Shuttle Run Relay

- Clothes Relay

- Crab Walk

Sport Play (20 min.)

As a group, decide which sport you want to play today. Select from the sport list contained in the *Sports List Appendix*. Be sure to periodically review with the group the Physical Activities Recommendations for Sport from Chapter Six.

Cool-down

If time permits, close the day with a few minutes of stretching while conducting the following R&R Huddle.

- **Recap** one or two key moments from the Lessons from the Field.

- **Reconnect** players back to the theme unit.

- **Reset** and transition players to the Cool-down, Reflection time.

  OR

- **Reflection**

Use this time to highlight teachable moments you observed during the day and to give players an opportunity to share their experiences about Sports PLUS during the day. The following questions can serve as a guide:

- What did you like about today?

- What did you learn today?

- What are some ways you were responsible today?

- What are some examples of responsible behavior you noticed from your teammates?

- In what ways can we be more responsible next time?

Goal-setting

Use this time to help players track progress toward their individually chosen goals, as well as toward team goals. As goals from earlier sessions are reached, guide players in setting additional individual and team goals related to *Responsibility*.

Session 24: **Responsible Teammates** **Lessons from Adventure**	
Warm-up Begin the PLUS Cycle (5 min.) • Session Overview • Trust Chair	**Cool-down** Continue the PLUS Cycle (5-10 min.) • Reflection • Responsible Teammates
Activity Lessons from Adventure (25-30 min.) • Slot Machine	**Materials** None

Warm-up

Trust Chair

As stated earlier, if you don't think your players are able to take their responsibilities seriously enough to participate in this activity safely, don't use it at this time. Trust Chair asks that players make a commitment to take good care of one another and display respect for the safety of all members of the group. It is a good activity for exploring the concepts of making commitments to each other, trusting one another, and being responsible teammates.

Activity

1. Ask players to form a large circle, all facing the same direction (right or left, it doesn't matter).

2. Next, ask them to take two steps in, one more step, one more step...and so on until they are standing very close to each other.

3. On the count of three, ask everyone to sit down on the lap of the person behind them. When they are in close enough, they will form a tight circle, enabling each of them to sit on each other without expending much energy. Each person is

supported by the person behind them, forming a chair circle. This requires that everyone work together toward a common goal and illustrates how much stronger the group is as a whole than as individuals.

4. You may want to further illustrate this point by having the group first try sitting back on each other in pairs. Without the help of the group, this will be much more difficult, if not impossible to do.

R&R Huddle (5 minutes)

This activity provides lots of ideas and metaphors for both trust in our teammates and how we are responsible for our teammates. There are also the issues of safety and taking our obligations seriously to discuss.

Recap using one or two of the following questions:

1. What was hard about this activity?

2. Did it feel comfortable or uncomfortable?

3. Did you trust your teammates to take care of you?

Reconnect using one or two of the following focus prompts:

- One thing we did really well as a group was…

- One way we could have done better as a group is by…

- One thing we learned about responsibility is…

Reset and transition to the next activity.

Activity

Lessons from Adventure
Slot Machine
(see Player Portfolio)

This group problem-solving activity offers another opportunity for the group to work together to solve a problem.

You can do this activity in a classroom, but playing this game in your gym or outside on a field affords more options and creativity.

Bring the group together in a circle. Separate into three teams of three or more.

Play

1. The name of the game is Slot Machine. Like any slot machine player, the goal is to get three matching pictures.

2. Each team will go to a corner of the room and create a group gesture to represent responsibility, drawing from what they have learned about this value in previous sessions.

3. Once each team has a gesture, bring the group back together. Line the teams up in a triangle formation. Ask each team to show its gesture.

4. For the rest of the activity, there will be no talking among teams. The goal of the group is for you (the facilitator) to count to three, say "Go," and have all three teams show the same gesture.

5. Play one round — count to three and see what gesture each team shows. This round helps the group to understand the game. Now, send the teams back to their corners, allowing time for the teams to decide which gesture they will use.

6. Come back together. Count to three, and see what gestures are presented.

7. Repeat this process until all three groups get the same gesture (or the group tires of the game).

This problem can be more difficult than it appears:

1. The teams cannot speak to each other, yet they are all trying to do the same thing. They need to develop a system for non-verbal communication.

2. Sometimes one team forgets that the group's goal is to have everyone show the same gesture. This group may become unbending in showing any other gesture than their own (this can be OK if the rest of the teams use this group's gesture, but this doesn't always happen). If one team makes it impossible for the group as a whole to achieve its goal, stop the game and use this as a discussion topic — what responsibility does each small group have to the larger group in accomplishing its goal? What happens when a small group of people are not helping a team achieve its goal?

- **R&R Huddle** (5 minutes)

- **Recap** using the following focus prompt: The thing I enjoyed most about this activity was...

- **Reconnect** by asking players to complete the following sentence in their Player Portfolios: I learned that...

- **Reset** and transition to the next activity.

Cool-down

Cool-down Ritual
Responsible Teammates

In a large group, ask the players to think about ways that they can be responsible teammates at home, at school, and in the neighborhood. Next ask for volunteers to share their thoughts with the group. Ask them to come to the next session prepared to describe how they displayed responsible behavior in each of these areas.

Session 25:
Lending a Hand

Overview

Instructor's Notes: *Be sure to review this set of activities before starting this Sports PLUS Session. Directions for how to facilitate each activity are* *provided, but it is important that you become familiar with them so that you may more effectively lead the group.*

During group discussions, be sure to record all thoughts and ideas on a blackboard or newsprint. Remember that when players are working in their Player Portfolios, spelling, grammar, and penmanship are, relatively speaking, unimportant, so don't dwell on those details or you risk making Sports PLUS into MoreSchool.

Everyone needs a helping hand sometimes. Part of being responsible means both helping others who are in need and cooperating with others to accomplish a task. The *Quote of the Week* addresses these aspects of responsibility. The theme book reading of *Everybody's Favorite* continues. The teambuilding activity, *Wizards and Gelflings,* is an active game that involves a bit of imagination, acting, and being responsible for our teammates when they need help. The session concludes with an active, fun Cool-down ritual that gives players an opportunity to express their thoughts and feelings about Sports PLUS or events in their lives in general.

Session 25:
Lending a Hand
Lessons from Literature

Warm-up	**Cool-down**
Begin the PLUS Cycle (10-15 min.)	Continue the PLUS Cycle (5-10 min.)
• Session Overview	• Reflection
• Quote of the Week	**Materials**
Activity	Copies of *Broadway Ball Players: Everybody's Favorite by Penny*
Lessons from Literature (25-30 min.)	
• Theme Book — *Broadway Ball Players: Everybody's Favorite by Penny*	

Warm-up

Quote of the Week
(see Player Portfolio)

"If your neighbor can't smile, lend him yours."

— American Proverb

Instructor's note

You may want to ask the students if they have ever heard of a metaphor. Explain to them that this quote is a metaphor, and that a metaphor is something that helps us better understand something else.

Follow the five steps of the Quote of the Week Format (See the *Getting Started* chapter for additional explanation):

1. **Write the Quote of the Week:** Bring the group together into a circle, and write the Quote on the blackboard.

2. **Think about the Quote as a group:** Spend two or three minutes talking with the students about what they think the quote means. Ask students to share answers to the group for the following questions:

3. What do you think it means to lend someone your smile?

4. How does this quote relate to the theme of responsibility?

5. Do you think it's important to help your neighbor? Why or why not?

6. How is being a responsible neighbor similar to being a responsible teammate?

7. **Pair up to talk about the Quote:** Have students separate into pairs. Ask them to spend about five minutes discussing the following exercise with their partners. Explain that they will be sharing their ideas with the whole group, so they may want to make notes in their Player Portfolios. (Be sure to walk around the groups, listen, and offer help where needed.):

8. Ask students to plan a short skit (one or two minutes) that shows a way to help a teammate when he or she may be feeling badly.

9. **Share answers with the whole group:** Come together as a large group and share the ideas from each of the pair groups.

Everyone who wants to should have an opportunity to share their thoughts.

10. **Reflect individually about the Quote:** Take two or three minutes for students to reflect individually by writing a response to the following Journal Prompt in their Player Portfolios:

11. Tell about a time that you did something to lend a smile to your neighbor.

Activity

Lessons from Literature
Theme Book
Broadway Ball Players: Everybody's Favorite by Penny
(see Player Portfolio)

by Maureen Holohan

Lesson No. Four: Chapters 10-12

Setup

Gather the students into a circle and spend a few minutes discussing what has happened so far in the story. Ask students to summarize the plot, conflicts, and lessons they have encountered so far. The following questions will help them to get started:

- From what you know so far, what do you think might happen next?

- Penny travels quite far from home with the other Ballplayers. Have any of you ever gone away to camp? What was that like?

- Penny is faced with some difficult decisions to make while she's at home. Have you ever faced similar situations?

You also may choose to review some of the vocabulary for today:

- throw-in (p. 91)

- bleached (p. 91)

- furrowed (p. 92)

- obnoxious (p. 93)

- calculating (p. 94)

- bunions (p. 95)

- retaliate (p. 97)

- imprint (p. 100)

- dogged (p.103)

- lenient (p. 109)

- commotion (p. 111)

- assumed (p. 112)

Chapter-by-Chapter Summary

Read chapters 10-12 aloud and with enthusiasm to the whole group.

Chapter Ten

This chapter sets the stage for upcoming conflicts by introducing several new characters, including Kara, a girl who is described as the best soccer player at camp, but also as a snob. Penny meets several new girls who quickly begin treating her as their newfound friend. Penny is torn between this new group and the Ballplayers. Penny also discovers that Rita, one of the coaches, has high expectations of her and treats her as many people do at home. On the first page of this chapter, Penny again thinks to herself, "…I just wanted to be normal." The chapter ends with Penny being chosen as player of the day.

Chapter Eleven

The action in this chapter begins in the girls' cabin. Candi, known as Crazy Candi, dares anyone to cross the white line. At first, Molly agrees, but is dissuaded by the other Ballplayers. We also see Penny's caring nature when she tries to keep everyone quiet because Kara is sleeping. Hookman, a character out of a classic scary story at camp, is introduced. Penny and Kara realize that neither one of them can swim, which helps them become friends. The chapter concludes with a soccer match in which Penny's group plays another team with several other Ballplayers on it. Penny tries to pass the ball to her teammates, but Rita puts pressure on her to score. When Penny scores, however, her teammates seem to feel resentment toward Penny, which only causes more confusion and concern for her.

Chapter Twelve

This chapter sets the stage for an important, upcoming conflict. The chapter begins with the girls at dinner and a continuation of the Hookman story. Penny is then invited to visit another cabin without any Ballplayers. She goes, but this causes her to feel guilty about having fun without them. The character of Coach Oslo is revealed; to no one's surprise, we see that he plays favorites. We also learn more about Candi when she pulls out a suitcase full of candy and cigarettes. Several of the girls are nearly caught over the line at the boy's cabins. Some girls begin trouble by telling the Ballplayers that Penny is playing on their four-on-four team, while telling Penny the Ballplayers don't care. This begins a struggle for Penny to keep everyone happy while she is pulled in several directions, feeling lot of pressure from both her new and old friends. The chapter ends with a foreshadowing of a problem Penny faces that will come to a head in the next section.

Discussion Questions

Spend a couple of minutes distributing students' Player Portfolios and pencils. (Ask for one or two volunteers to help.) Write the questions and focus prompts on a blackboard or newsprint.

Work together as a whole group to answer the following questions:

Questions one through five should be answered in a round-robin format, with one student answering one question. Try to include students who may not always participate. (If any of the answers are imprecise or need further elaboration, ask if anyone has anything to add.)

1. What do Penny and Kara realize that they have in common?

2. Why is it hard for Penny to receive high expectations from the coaches at Soccer Camp and to be chosen as "Player of the Day"?

3. What happens to Penny during the soccer game? How does the coach's pressure to score create resentment from her teammates?

4. What happens when Penny visits Candi's cabin?

5. What happens to Penny when several of the girls cause trouble by telling the Ballplayers that Penny won't be playing on their 4-on-4 team?

The following focus prompt should be answered in an exhaustive format. Continue letting students give responses until no new answers are given.

6. One way Penny shows responsibility in these three chapters is by....

For question seven, allow all students an opportunity to share their answers, regardless of whether or not the answers are original.

7. As we see with Penny, responsibility can be very tough to live out, especially when people from different sides pull you in different directions. How can good teamwork help us to act responsibly?

Finally, ask students to write their responses to the following prompt in their Player Portfolios. (This is a complex, integrative question that may require some help from the facilitator to guide students' thinking)

8. One specific way I might show responsibility when there is a conflict between friends is by...

Cool-down

- **R&R Huddle** (5 min.)

- **Recap** one or two key points that arose during the discussion.

- **Reconnect** by asking volunteers to briefly share their responses to number eight above.

- **Reset** and get ready for the next lesson.

Session 25: Lending a Hand Lessons from the Field	
Warm-up Begin the PLUS Cycle (5 min.) • Session Overview • Reflecting on Responsibility **Activity** Lessons from the Field (25-30 min.) • Sports Activity	**Cool-down** Continue the PLUS Cycle (5-10 min.) • Reflection • Goal-setting **Materials** Sports Equipment

Warm-up
Reflecting on Responsibility (5 min.)

Ask students to think about the previous lesson. What can they do today to bring the Lessons from Literature into their work together in the sports activity?

Activity

Lessons from the Field
Sports Activity

Block I: Getting Started (5 min.)

On the first day, players will learn how to measure their resting heart rates (RHR). They will also set baselines for their RHR, number of sit-ups/push-ups/lunges/calf raises, and number of jumps during jump rope. Each day they will try to improve upon their Past Personal Best (PPB) by achieving their Future Best Goal (FBG) and by tracking progress toward that goal in the physical activities progress chart located in the back of their Player Portfolios. Take one minute to make sure all participants turn to the back of their portfolios and locate the progress charts. Explain to them that they will be using this chart each time you meet to do physical activities. Be sure to emphasize the importance of keeping track of their progress by using the chart.

Stand together in a circle for all *Getting Started* activities (except for jogging). Have players partner up, with one player doing the activity and the partner keeping count and giving encouragement. Be sure that they have their Portfolios handy so that they can record their progress. Encourage them to clap and cheer for their teammates to create an enthusiastic environment. You may also choose to include music.

- **Measure resting heart rate (RHR)** — Spend a few minutes showing players how to find their pulses, either on their necks or wrists. Explain that you will be giving them a few seconds to count how many times their hearts beat. Take a moment to allow the players to sit quietly on the floor and find their pulses. Give them 30 seconds to count their heartbeats.

- **Record, check in and set goals** — Allow a couple of minutes for players to record their RHRs in their Player Portfolios.

- **Jog (2-3 min.)** — This can be done as a lap or in place as a circle.

- **Stretch (2-3 min.)** — Be sure to include stretches for the major muscle groups.

- **Strength/Endurance (1 min.)** — On this first day, players will set baseline numbers for the four Strength/Endurance activities (push-ups, sit-ups, lunges, calf raises), but usually, you will only choose one or two. They will work in pairs. One member of the pair will have 30 seconds to do as many of the activities as they can. Their partner will cheer them on and count for them.

- **Jump Rope (4 min.)** — Again, players will work in pairs, with one person jumping and the other person counting and cheering. They should have three to four sets of 30-45 seconds of jumping rope.

- **Track personal progress** — Have players record their totals for steps five and six in their Player Portfolios. These totals will represent their baseline achievements, or their Past Personal Bests (PPB). Each day, players will check their progress from the previous session and will set a Future Personal Best Goal (FBG) to work toward for next time. Be sure to remind them about setting realistic goals (for example, adding one or two to their baseline, as opposed to 10).

Block II: Structured Play (30 min.)

Skill Play (10 min.)

Choose one or two of the following activities to play today. You can refer back to the *Physical Activities Description Appendix* for instructions on how to run the activities. Encourage players to cheer for each other, and include music if you wish.

- Bowling

- Sashay Relay

- Jump Rope Relay

- Water Fill Relay

- Hoop Monster

- Over, under, over, under

Sport Play (20 min.)

As a group, decide which sport you want to play today. Select from the sport list contained in the *Sports List Appendix*. Be sure to periodically review with the group the Physical Activities Recommendations for Sport from Chapter Six.

Cool-down

If time permits, close the day with a few minutes of stretching while conducting the following R&R Huddle.

- **Recap** one or two key moments from the Lessons from the Field.

- **Reconnect** players back to the theme unit.

- **Reset** and transition players to the Cool-down, Reflection time.

   OR

- **Reflection**

Use this time to highlight teachable moments you observed during the day and to give players an opportunity to share their experiences about Sports PLUS during the day. The following questions can serve as a guide:

- What did you like about today?

- What did you learn today?

Also, be sure to follow up the cool-down ritual from last time by asking players to share examples of how they were responsible in school, at home, and in the community.

Goal-setting

Use this time to help players track progress toward their individually chosen goals, as well as toward team goals. As goals from earlier sessions are reached, guide players in setting additional individual and team goals related to *Responsibility*.

Session 25: **Lending a Hand** **Lessons from Adventure**	
Warm-up Begin the PLUS Cycle (5 min.) • Session Overview • Me, You, Lisa	**Cool-down** Continue the PLUS Cycle (5-10 min.) • Reflection • Solving Problems
Activity Lessons from Adventure (25-30 min.) • Wizards and Gelflings	**Materials** Fleece or Nerf-type balls, boundary markers

Warm-up

Me, You, Lisa

Setup

Gather your group into a circle. Tell players that this is a fast-paced name review activity.

Play

1. Start by going around the circle, in order, and asking each player to say his or her name clearly so that everyone can hear them.

2. Next, ask players to make sure that they know the name of the person to their right and their left.

3. Tell players that each of them is to say three names in the following order: the person's to their right, their own name, and the person's to their left. After a person says the three names, the person to their left starts the same process, until each member of the group has said their three names.

4. Do a slow practice round, giving each person a chance to get a feel for saying the three names in the given order.

5. Ask players how quickly they think they can make it all the way around the circle. Do a few rounds, trying to improve their time with each round.

6. Consider doing a round or two in the opposite direction.

Activity

Lessons from Adventure
Wizards and Gelflings

This is a good game for having fun, moving around, and exploring the concept of responsibility to our teammates, even in the silliest of situations. You need a bit of room to move around, so depending on your classroom space, you may want to wait until the sport session to do this activity.

Play

Give the following instructions to the group. If you do this as a running game, remind players to play safe and take care physically of their teammates. Otherwise, make it a fast, walking-only activity.

1. "First of all, we have to use our imaginations a bit and transport ourselves to the kingdom of ...(let a volunteer come up with some goofy name for your kingdom.) In this kingdom, there are two kinds of creatures, Wizards and Gelflings. Now Wizards are grumpy, grouchy and crabby. They hate laughter, having fun, and they especially don't like Gelflings. Gelflings are very playful. They love to laugh, run around and have fun, and they especially enjoy making the Wizards lose their grouchy ways. The Wizards have made it their life's work to freeze all Gelflings with their magic."

2. You can make this a tag game or use fleece balls, Nerf-type balls or any other kind of very soft object. If you choose the latter, make a rule that only strikes below the shoulders count — head shots are not allowed. The object is for the Wizards to freeze Gelflings by tagging or hitting them with their magic orbs. Before you begin the game, lay out some boundary

markers creating an area large enough for players to run around in but not so big that cross-country chases take place. Have three or four Wizards for 20 Gelflings.

3. After designating the Wizards, on your signal of "Go!", the Wizards try to tag Gelflings or hit them with their magic orbs. In the first round, when a Gelfling is tagged, he or she has to remain frozen in place until all the other Gelflings have been tagged.

4. After only Wizards remain unfrozen, play the game again, but this time, whenever a Gelfling is tagged, he or she immediately freezes in place and begins to emit the universal Gelfling cry for help. This cry is accompanied by the gesture of one arm out, palm up and open. The other hand forms a fist with the thumb pointing up. Gelflings then strike their fist repeatedly on their palm and shout in a shrill and squeaky Gelfling voice, "Help me! Help Me! Help Me!"

5. In this second version, Gelflings can be freed whenever two other Gelflings join hands, with the frozen Gelfling between them, and shout, "Go free, little Gelfling, go free!" If a Wizard tags a Gelfling helping another Gelfling, the Gelfling who is helping is also frozen.

6. If Wizards get tired of being Wizards, they can tag a Gelfling and trade identities with them, giving players the chance to try out both roles. Play until players get tired of the game or just get tired from running.

- **R&R Huddle** (5 minutes)

- **Recap** using one or two of the following questions:

    - What were some of the differences between the two versions of the game?

    - Which version did you like better? Why?

- **Reconnect** with one or two of the following discussion questions:

  - How well did the Gelflings do in their responsibility to help their frozen teammates?

  - As a frozen Gelfling, did anyone feel ignored by their teammates?

  - What does it mean to be a responsible Gelfling? A responsible Wizard?

- **Reset** and transition to the next activity.

Cool-down

Cool-down Ritual

With the large group, ask for examples of circumstances when groups have to solve difficult problems like the activity presented earlier. How do you think sport teams solve problems together? What about professional teams where there are a lot of very good players? What kinds of things do you think those teams need to do to be able to work together? Where does leadership come from? What makes an effective leader?

This activity leads nicely into the next session when the players will make collages showing examples of stereotyping from magazines.

Session 26:
Trust and Responsibility

Overview

Instructor's Notes: *Be sure to review this set of activities before starting this Sports PLUS Session. Directions for how to facilitate each activity are provided, but it is important that you become familiar with them so that you may more effectively lead the group.*

During group discussions, be sure to record all thoughts and ideas on a blackboard or newsprint. Remember that when players are working in their Player Portfolios, spelling, grammar, and penmanship are, relatively speaking, unimportant, so don't dwell on those details or you risk making Sports PLUS into MoreSchool.

An important theme for this session is the relationship between trust and responsibility, and how we can live out responsibility when others trust and count on us.

The *Snake and the Eel* is a fun activity to warm up the group during the Adventure lesson. The teambuilding activity, *Stepping Stones,* helps players think about these issues in a fun and engaging way. To conclude the session, try using a reflective exercise that allows players to measurably express their success at practicing certain Sports PLUS values.

Session 26: **Trust and Responsibility** **Lessons from Literature**	

Warm-up
  Begin the PLUS Cycle (10-15 min.)
 	
  • Session Overview
 	
  • Quote of the Week
Activity
  Lessons from Literature (25-30 min.)
 	
  • Theme Book — *Broadway Ball Players: Everybody's Favorite by Penny*
	Cool-down
	  Continue the PLUS Cycle (5-10 min.)
	
	  • Reflection
	Materials
	  Copies of *Broadway Ball Players: Everybody's Favorite by Penny*

Warm-up

Quote of the Week

"No matter what accomplishments you make, somebody helps you."
— Wilma Rudolph

Follow the five steps of the Quote of the Week Format (See the *Getting Started* chapter for additional explanation):

1. **Write the Quote of the Week:** Bring the group together into a circle, and write the Quote on the blackboard.

2. **Think about the Quote as a group:** Spend two to three minutes talking with the students about what they think the quote means. Ask students to share their answers to the following question:

3. What does helping someone have to do with responsibility?

4. **Pair up to talk about the Quote:** Have students separate into pairs. Ask them to spend about five minutes discussing the following questions with their partners. Explain that they will be sharing with the whole group, so they may choose to write their answers in their Player Portfolios. (Be sure to walk around the groups, listen, and offer help where needed.):

5. The topic for this session is trust and responsibility. What does it mean to trust someone?

6. Think of an example that shows how trust is related to letting someone help you.

7. **Share answers with the whole group:** Come together as a large group and share the answers from each of the pair groups. Everyone who wants to should have an opportunity to share their answers.

8. **Reflect individually about the Quote:** Take two to three minutes for students to reflect individually by writing a response to the following Journal Question in their Player Portfolios:

9. What is an example of how you have been helped to make an accomplishment?

Activity

Lessons from Literature

Theme Book

Broadway Ball Players: Everybody's Favorite by Penny
(see Player Portfolio)

by Maureen Holohan

Lesson No. Five: Chapters 13-15

Setup

Gather the students together into a circle and spend a few minutes discussing what has happened so far in the story. Ask students to summarize some of the action that has occurred and where they think the story might be headed in these next few chapters. The following questions will help to get you started:

- The focus is on different characters now that the action of the story has moved to the soccer camp. What is different about the story now? Candi and Kara, in particular, are playing a bigger part in the action and the plot. How are these characters different from the Ballplayers?

- What are some of the conflicts among the Ballplayers and Penny that we read about last time?

- Although some things are different during this part of the story, some things are still the same for Penny. What are some examples of how things are different for Penny at camp, and some examples of how things have stayed the same for her?

You also may choose to review some of the vocabulary for today:

- snickers (p.116)

- momentum (p. 118)

- determined (p. 119)

- phonier (p. 120)

- calculate (p. 122)

- awkward (p. 125)

- stubborn (p. 130)

- virtually (p. 135)

Chapter-by-Chapter Summary

Read chapters 13-15 aloud and with enthusiasm to the whole group.

Chapter Thirteen

There is quite a bit of action in this chapter and most of it provides further examples of the pressure constantly put on Penny. It opens with another instance of Coach Oslo's obvious favoritism toward Penny — to the exclusion of others. Rita asks Penny to play in the counselor's scrimmage that evening and ignores Penny's request not to play. In one scene, Penny takes a leadership role when her camp's Olympics team argues over events. This provides a valuable glimpse into Penny's ability to lead her teammates and their respect for her. Chapter 13 ends with Rita acknowledging the concern Penny showed for the other campers who were not going to play in the scrimmage.

Chapter Fourteen

Chapter 14 is a pivotal chapter. Penny and Kara are pressured by Candi to go to the boys' cabins. Penny recognizes that she also pressures Kara to go. When they get to the cabin, cigarettes and beer quickly appear but before anything happens, they hear Coach Oslo. Penny gets out of the cabin, leaving Kara and the others behind. As this short chapter ends, we get a glimpse of the guilt Penny is feeling when she gets back to her cabin and lies to the Ballplayers about where she has been. It is interesting to note that Penny's greatest fear is what others will think of her if they find out what she has done.

Chapter Fifteen

The action picks up where we were left off in the previous chapter. Penny is obviously feeling very guilty, but she doesn't want anyone to find out what has happened, although she does tell Angel. Kara finally returns, but she will not speak to Penny when Penny tries to apologize. At breakfast the next morning, the rumors are flying, and Penny defends Kara to the other girls. Kara, Candi, and Lucy, who were all caught by Coach Oslo, have to run laps and wash dishes. Through all of the action, Penny continuously thinks about what Mr. Gordon and others will think of her if they find out she was involved. At the end of the chapter, we find that Kara would not tell Coach Oslo that Penny was with them. Although Candi and Lucy do tell on Penny, Coach Oslo refuses to believe them. Penny finally has to admit to the Ballplayers that she also was in the boys' cabin. The scene is set for the final action of the story, with Penny's team playing Kara's on the last day of camp for the camp championship.

Discussion Questions

Spend a couple of minutes distributing students' Player Portfolios and pencils. (Ask for one or two volunteers to help.) Write the questions and focus prompts on a blackboard or newsprint.

Work together as a whole group to answer the following questions. Questions one through five should be answered in a round-robin format, with one student answering one question. Try to include students who may not always participate. (If any of the answers are imprecise or need further elaboration, ask if anyone has anything to add.)

1. Penny doesn't want just her and Kara to play with the counselors. What does she want instead?

2. What do the boys have in their cabin that causes Penny to worry?

3. Whom does Penny confide in after getting away with being in the boys' camp?

4. What do Kara, Candi and Lucy have to do for their punishment?

5. Whom is Penny afraid to tell what she did?

The following focus prompt should be answered in an exhaustive format. Continue letting students give responses until no new answers are given.

6. One example of how Penny struggles to act responsibly in these chapters is when she ....

For question seven, allow all students an opportunity to share their answers, regardless of whether or not the answers are original.

7. Why is it difficult for Penny to show responsibility in these chapters?

Finally, ask students to write their responses to the following prompt in their Player Portfolios.

8. One way that I can help myself to act responsibly, even when pressure from parents, coaches, friends, and teachers makes it tough, is by....

Additional Questions

- On page 115, Coach Oslo greets Penny but ignores Molly. What Sports PLUS value is the coach not showing here? What do you think about Coach Oslo?

- Why do you think Penny doesn't want to play in the counselor's scrimmage? (p. 117)

- On page 120, Penny says, "No one would have ever guessed that we were undefeated by the way we treated each other in that game." What do you think Penny means by this?

- When all the girls are arguing, Penny takes charge of giving out the assignments for the Olympics. Why do you think the other girls listen to Penny? Do you think they are glad she stepped in? Why or why not? What Sports PLUS value is Penny demonstrating here? (p. 121)

- On page 125, Penny says she'll go to the boys' cabin if Kara will. What kind of pressure has Penny put on Kara here? Is this different from or the same as the pressure Penny often feels from others?

- At the end of Chapter 14, after Penny gets away, she feels pretty badly. Why do you think she feels this way even though she doesn't get caught?

- What are some things that happen to make Penny feel more and more guilty about not getting caught?

- Penny's greatest fear during these chapters is that others will think badly of her when they find out what she has done. Why do you think Penny has this fear? Have you ever felt a similar fear? What was that like?

Close the day by summarizing the following theme from today's reading:

"The theme of expectation and how Penny lives with what others expect of her is turned around a bit. The Ballplayers and Coach Oslo refuse to believe that Penny might have been involved until forced to face the truth. And Penny seems to be most concerned with keeping her involvement a secret. She is in a near panic over what people will think of her, including her parents, grandmother and Mr. Gordon. Penny has questioned her status throughout the entire book thus far, but now it seems that her overriding concern is the expectations of others. Facing this dilemma and resolving it for herself will occupy much of Penny's behavior over the last three chapters."

Cool-down

- **R&R Huddle** (5 minutes)

- **Recap** one or two key points that arose during the discussion.

- **Reconnect** by asking volunteers to briefly share what they wrote for question number eight above.

- **Reset** and get ready for the next lesson.

Session 26: Trust and Responsibility Lessons from the Field	
Warm-up Begin the PLUS Cycle (5 min.) • Session Overview • Reflecting on Responsibility **Activity** Lessons from the Field (25-30 min.) • Sports Activity	**Cool-down** Continue the PLUS Cycle (5-10 min.) • Reflection • Goal-setting **Materials** Sports Equipment

Warm-up
Reflecting on Responsibility (5 min.)

Ask students to think about the previous lesson. What can they do today to bring the Lessons from Literature into their work together in the sports activity?

Activity

Lessons from the Field
Sports Activity

Block I: Getting Started (5 min.)

On the first day, players will learn how to measure their resting heart rates (RHR). They will also set baselines for their RHR, number of sit-ups/push-ups/lunges/calf raises, and number of jumps during jump rope. Each day they will try to improve upon their Past Personal Best (PPB) by achieving their Future Best Goal (FBG) and by tracking progress toward that goal in the physical activities progress chart located in the back of their Player Portfolios. Take one minute to make sure all participants turn to the back of their portfolios and locate the progress charts. Explain to them that they will be using this chart each time you meet to do physical activities. Be sure to emphasize the importance of keeping track of their progress by using the chart.

Stand together in a circle for all *Getting Started* activities (except for jogging). Have players partner up, with one player doing the activity and the partner keeping count and giving encouragement. Be sure that they have their Portfolios handy so that they can record their progress. Encourage them to clap and cheer for their teammates to create an enthusiastic environment. You may also choose to include music.

- **Measure resting heart rate (RHR)** — Spend a few minutes showing players how to find their pulses, either on their necks or wrists. Explain that you will be giving them a few seconds to count how many times their hearts beat. Take a moment to allow the players to sit quietly on the floor and find their pulses. Give them 30 seconds to count their heartbeats.

- **Record, check in and set goals** — Allow a couple of minutes for players to record their RHRs in their Player Portfolios.

- **Jog (2-3 min.)** — This can be done as a lap or in place as a circle.

- **Stretch (2-3 min.)** — Be sure to include stretches for the major muscle groups.

- **Strength/Endurance (1 min.)** — On this first day, players will set baseline numbers for the four Strength/Endurance activities (push-ups, sit-ups, lunges, calf raises), but usually, you will only choose one or two. They will work in pairs. One member of the pair will have 30 seconds to do as many of the activities as they can. Their partner will cheer them on and count for them.

- **Jump Rope (4 min.)** — Again, players will work in pairs, with one person jumping and the other person counting and cheering. They should have three to four sets of 30-45 seconds of jumping rope.

- **Track personal progress** — Have players record their totals for steps five and six in their Player Portfolios. These totals will represent their baseline achievements, or their Past Personal Bests (PPB). Each day, players will check their progress from the previous session and will set a Future Personal Best Goal (FBG) to work toward for next time. Be sure to remind them about setting realistic goals (for example, adding one or two to their baseline, as opposed to 10).

Block II: Structured Play (30 min.)

Skill Play (10 min.)

Choose one or two of the following activities to play today. You can refer back to the *Physical Activities Description Appendix* for instructions on how to run the activities. Encourage players to cheer for each other, and include music if you wish.

- Circle Bonanza

- Water Balloon Volleyball

- Passing a Medicine Ball

- Jumping Distances

- Round and Round the Hoops Go

- Softball Throw

Sport Play (20 min.)

As a group, decide which sport you want to play today. Select from the sport list contained in the *Sports List Appendix*. Be sure to periodically review with the group the Physical Activities Recommendations for Sport from Chapter Six.

Cool-down

If time permits, close the day with a few minutes of stretching while conducting the following R&R Huddle.

- **Recap** one or two key moments from the Lessons from the Field.

- **Reconnect** players back to the theme unit.

- **Reset** and transition players to the Cool-down, Reflection time.

OR

- **Reflection**

Use this time to highlight teachable moments you observed during the day and to give players an opportunity to share their experiences about Sports PLUS. The following questions can serve as a guide:

- What did you like about today?

- What did you learn today?

- What are some ways you were responsible today?

- What are some examples of responsible behavior you noticed from your teammates?

- In what ways can we be more responsible next time?

Goal-setting

Use this time to help players track progress toward their individually chosen goals, as well as toward team goals. As goals from earlier sessions are reached, guide players in setting additional individual and team goals related to *Responsibility*.

Session 26: **Trust and Responsibility** **Lessons from Adventure**	
Warm-up Begin the PLUS Cycle (5 min.) • Session Overview • Snake and the Eel	**Cool-down** Continue the PLUS Cycle (5-10 min.) • Reflection • High Five
Activity Lessons from Adventure (25-30 min.) • Stepping Stones	**Materials** Cones or rope, one prop fewer than the number in the group (i.e., for 12 players you will need 11 props — props can be carpet squares, large pieces of cloth, pieces of wood, etc.), spot markers

Warm-up

The Snake and the Eel

Setup

Working as a group, set up a maze that resembles a narrow tunnel using cones or any other kind of marker to make boundaries. (Several jump ropes will work best.) Divide the group into two. Explain that one group is a snake and the other is an eel. They must travel through an underwater cave and pass each other without touching.

Play

Have the snake and the eel start at opposite ends of the underwater cave and attempt to get to the other hole and back without touching. Time the group's first effort. Any touching that occurs adds one second to the group's time. The first time is the New World Record. Give the group a couple of more attempts to break the record.

Activity

Lessons from Adventure
Stepping Stones

Setup

This is a great group activity that requires communication, concentration, and an ability to work together. This activity works best with 12 to 15 participants, so if you have a fairly large group, separate the players into two groups. You can even make a competition out of it. Read the instructions for working with two groups. Tell the players that they must listen very carefully to the instructions because there are ways to mess up that will make the activity more difficult. Before you begin, you will have to find an open stretch of your room or even a hallway. At minimum, the distance you choose should have at least two or three feet per person in the group, or enough distance that several of the props must be used twice.

Play

1. Tell the group that their task is fairly simple — they have to cross an open expanse of ground (use your imagination and make it an alligator-filled swamp or something equally uninviting) using only the props provided for the group.

2. There are a number of rules that govern the use of these props:

3. Props must remain in contact with someone at all times. If someone tosses a prop onto the floor and then steps on it, the group loses that prop.

4. Only two props can go backward. All others can only go forward.

5. Anyone who steps into the swamp must return to the starting point and be rescued. If the group is already in the middle of the swamp, they have to go back and get them.

6. Keep a close eye out for dropped props or players stepping into the swamp. You can also discuss the idea of the group being responsible for itself and having group members call their own infractions.

7. Successful completion is only possible if the group works together. Usually several people have to share a prop and the end person can support the person laying down the next prop by holding their hand. Offer few hints, but see what the group can come up with on their own.

8. If you are using two groups, have them begin from opposite sides. Don't say anything about a competition but watch to see if the groups naturally begin competing or if they figure out that they can share their resources, making both crossings easier.

9. One way to complete this activity is for people to shuffle across on the props, and then return to get others. Keeping the number of props that can go in backward to only a few usually cuts down on this solution, which relies more on individual work than on group cooperation.

There are a number of areas that are perfect for a group discussion, particularly how the group did working together as a team.

Questions for discussion

1. Did you complete the task?

2. If yes, how did you do it? If not, why not?

3. What is one thing that might have made this activity easier?

4. If you had to do it again, what would you do differently?

5. Did any leadership roles develop? If so, how did this happen?

- **R&R Huddle** (5 minutes)

- **Recap** one or two key points from the previous discussion.

- **Reconnect** by asking players the following question: What are some examples of the Sports PLUS values seen in this activity?

- **Reset** and transition to the next activity.

Cool-down

Cool-down Ritual
Go-round

Ask the players to form a circle with partners from the Come to Me activity standing next to each other. Do a go-round with each pair sharing how they think they did in the activity: Did they respect each other? Did they take the responsibility for their sightless partners seriously? What are some ways we can continue this same responsible behavior outside of this group?

Session 27:
Taking Responsibility

Overview

> *Instructor's Notes: Be sure to review this set of activities before starting this Sports PLUS Session. Directions for how to facilitate each activity are provided, but it is important that you become familiar with them so that you may more effectively lead the group.*

> *During group discussions, be sure to record all thoughts and ideas on a blackboard or newsprint. Remember that when players are working in their Player Portfolios, spelling, grammar, and penmanship are, relatively speaking, unimportant, so don't dwell on those details or you risk making Sports PLUS into MoreSchool.*

The *Quote of the Week* sets the tone for the session by raising the issue of adequate preparation. The Theme Book reading concludes today with the final section of *Everybody's Favorite* by Penny. Come to Me is a simple team-building activity that challenges teammates to trust each other and provides an opportunity for post-activity discussion. The day ends with a cool-down ritual that invites players to share "put-ups" with each other.

Session 27: **Taking Responsibility** **Lessons from Literature**	

Warm-up
  Begin the PLUS Cycle (10-15 min.)
  • Session Overview
  • Quote of the Week
Activity
  Lessons from Literature (25-30 min.)
  • Theme Book — *Broadway Ball Players: Everybody's Favorite by Penny*
	Cool-down
	  Continue the PLUS Cycle (5-10 min.)
	  • Reflection
	Materials
	  Copies of *Broadway Ball Players: Everybody's Favorite by Penny*

Warm-up

Quote of the Week

"It's better to look ahead and prepare than to look back and regret."
— Jackie Joyner Kersee

Follow the five steps of the Quote of the Week Format (See the *Getting Started* chapter for additional explanation):

1. **Write the Quote of the Week:** Bring the group together into a circle, and write the Quote on the blackboard.

2. **Think about the Quote as a group:** Spend two or three minutes talking with the students about what they think the quote means. Ask students to share their answers to the following questions:

3. How is preparation a way of being responsible?

4. One important way I can prepare myself before I have sports practice is by...

5. **Pair up to talk about the Quote:** Have students separate into pairs. Ask them to spend about five minutes discussing the following questions with their partners. Explain that they will

be sharing their answers with the whole group, so they may choose to write their answers in their Player Portfolios. (Be sure to walk around the groups, listen, and offer help where needed.):

6. What are one or two ways you can follow Jackie Joyner Kersee's example and act responsibly toward your Sports PLUS team? Toward your community?

7. **Share answers with the whole group:** Come together as a large group and share the answers from each of the pair groups. Everyone who wants to should have an opportunity to share their answers.

8. **Reflect individually about the Quote:** Take two or three minutes for students to reflect individually by writing a response to the following Journal Question in their Player Portfolios:

9. What are some of the challenges and tasks that you will face in the future? They could be in school, in sports or other areas of your life. Describe those challenges. Then, list three ways you can prepare yourself for those challenges.

10. One way I can prepare myself for [fill in a challenge] is by...

Activity

Lessons from Literature
Theme Book

Broadway Ball Players: Everybody's Favorite by Penny
(see Player Portfolio)

by Maureen Holohan

Lesson No. Six: Chapters 16-18

Setup

These final three chapters bring to conclusion the conflicts introduced throughout the book. Students should be familiar with the various characters and their personalities. Gather the students together in a circle and spend a few minutes discussing one or more of the suggestions below:

- What has happened so far in the story, especially as it relates to Penny and her current dilemma?

- Where do you think the story might be heading? Make some predictions about what you think will happen during the championship soccer match.

- What are some ways that Penny could resolve her dilemma? How do you think she will resolve the problem?

You also may choose to review some of the vocabulary for today:

- inevitable (p. 139)

- pursed (p. 141)

- humbly (p.142)

- hype (p. 142)

- sincerely (p. 147)

- dreadful (p. 151)

Chapter-by-Chapter Summary

Read chapters 16-18 aloud and with enthusiasm to the whole group.

Chapter Sixteen

The previous chapter ended with Penny finally confessing to several of the Ballplayers that she had been involved in the incident at the boys' cabin. This chapter depicts the long-awaited, end-of-camp championship soccer match. Penny is less than excited about playing Kara's team and begins the match playing half-heartedly. She also is feeling nervous and especially guilty because Mr. Gordon has arrived to bring them all home. Everyone is cheering for Penny, and even Kara yells for Penny to "...Just play!" With all the attention on Penny, she feels her teammates' resentment. Kara's team wins the game, but when the trophies are given out, Penny is named the most valuable player at camp. The chapter ends with Penny refusing the trophy and saying, "It belongs to Kara."

Chapter Seventeen

This chapter reveals many of the book's lessons. After giving the trophy for the most valuable player to Kara, Penny admits, in front of the whole camp that she also was in the cabin with Kara and the other girls. In a paragraph on page 146, Penny explains to the reader that she finally forgot what others thought and cared only about the truth. Mr. Gordon says, "After you did the wrong thing, you did the right thing..." He says that Penny was lucky to have had the chance to make up for her mistake. Penny and Kara recognize that they have become good friends, and even Candi and Lucy make up with Penny. The chapter ends with Penny realizing that she will still have to confront her parents and particularly her grandmother when she gets home.

Chapter Eighteen

In the final chapter of the book, Penny returns home. One of the book's most important lessons is underscored when she tells her grandmother what happened at camp. There is direct reference to an earlier quote from Rev. James regarding circumstance and character on page 152. The idea of staying true to one's self is one of the key lessons of the story. In the final scene of the book, we see Marvin working in a neighbor's yard helping to clean up. Penny has one final revelation about living up to, or not living up to, the expectations of others and recognizes that she and Marvin have this in common.

Discussion Questions

Spend a couple of minutes distributing students' Player Portfolios and pencils. (Ask for one or two volunteers to help.) Write the questions and focus prompts on a blackboard or newsprint.

Work together as a whole group to answer the following questions:

The following focus prompts should be answered in an exhaustive format. Continue letting students give responses until no new answers are given.

1. Some of Penny's teammates seem to become resentful of her in the championship game. On pages 142-43, her team loses the ball to Kara who scores the winning goal. Why do you think Penny's team isn't playing together? Why doesn't Denise pass the ball?

2. When Penny finally confesses that she also was at the boys' cabin the night the other girls got caught, she does so in front of the entire camp, including Mr. Gordon. Read the paragraph at the top of page 146 in which Penny explains why she did this. Can you explain what Penny means here? What do you think is the lesson, or lessons, that can be learned from this?

3. What does Penny mean on page 148 when she says of Coach Oslo, "He still didn't get it"?

4. Think again about the Booker T. Washington quote that is repeated on page 152. Why does Penny's grandmother remind her about this?

For questions five through seven, allow all students an opportunity to share their answers, regardless of whether or not the answers are original.

5. The relationship between Penny and Kara is resolved because of the way Penny handled her own dilemma, admitting she had been with the girls at the boys' cabin. When would it be important to admit a mistake?

6. In my life, I would find it difficult to admit a mistake if...

7. After reading this book, one thing I realize about being responsible is...

Additional Questions

In the final scene of the book Penny meets Marvin. She is surprised to find that she and Marvin actually have something in common. Reread the paragraph on page 156 when she realizes this.

- Can you explain what she means?

- When in your own life has something like this happened?

Cool-down

- **R&R Huddle** (5 minutes)

- **Recap** one or two key points that arose during the discussion.

- **Reconnect** by asking volunteers to briefly share what they think this book teaches us about responsibility.

- **Reset** and get ready for the next lesson.

Session 27: Taking Responsibility Lessons from the Field	
Warm-up Begin the PLUS Cycle (5 min.) • Session Overview • Reflecting on Responsibility	**Cool-down** Continue the PLUS Cycle (5-10 min.) • Reflection • Goal-setting
Activity Lessons from the Field (25-30 min.) • Sports Activity	**Materials** Sports Equipment

Warm-up

Reflecting on Responsibility (5 min.)

Ask students to think about the previous lesson. What can they do today to bring the Lessons from Literature into their work together in the sports activity?

Activity

Lessons from the Field
Sports Activity

Block I: Getting Started (5 min.)

On the first day, players will learn how to measure their resting heart rates (RHR). They will also set baselines for their RHR, number of sit-ups/push-ups/lunges/calf raises, and number of jumps during jump rope. Each day they will try to improve upon their Past Personal Best (PPB) by achieving their Future Best Goal (FBG) and by tracking progress toward that goal in the physical activities progress chart located in the back of their Player Portfolios. Take one minute to make sure all participants turn to the back of their portfolios and locate the progress charts. Explain to them that they will be using this chart each time you meet to do physical activities. Be sure to emphasize the importance of keeping track of their progress by using the chart.

Stand together in a circle for all *Getting Started* activities (except for jogging). Have players partner up, with one player doing the activity and the partner keeping count and giving encouragement. Be sure that they have their Portfolios handy so that they can record their progress. Encourage them to clap and cheer for their teammates to create an enthusiastic environment. You may also choose to include music.

- **Measure resting heart rate (RHR)** — Spend a few minutes showing players how to find their pulses, either on their necks or wrists. Explain that you will be giving them a few seconds to count how many times their hearts beat. Take a moment to allow the players to sit quietly on the floor and find their pulses. Give them 30 seconds to count their heartbeats.

- **Record, check in and set goals** — Allow a couple of minutes for players to record their RHRs in their Player Portfolios.

- **Jog (2-3 min.)** — This can be done as a lap or in place as a circle.

- **Stretch (2-3 min.)** — Be sure to include stretches for the major muscle groups.

- **Strength/Endurance (1 min.)** — On this first day, players will set baseline numbers for the four Strength/Endurance activities (push-ups, sit-ups, lunges, calf raises), but usually, you will only choose one or two. They will work in pairs. One member of the pair will have 30 seconds to do as many of the activities as they can. Their partner will cheer them on and count for them.

- **Jump Rope (4 min.)** — Again, players will work in pairs, with one person jumping and the other person counting and cheering. They should have three to four sets of 30-45 seconds of jumping rope.

- **Track personal progress** — Have players record their totals for steps five and six in their Player Portfolios. These totals will represent their baseline achievements, or their Past Personal Bests (PPB). Each day, players will check their progress from the previous session and will set a Future Personal Best Goal (FBG) to work toward for next time. Be sure to remind them about setting realistic goals (for example, adding one or two to their baseline, as opposed to 10).

Block II: Structured Play (30 min.)

Skill Play (10 min.)

Choose one or two of the following activities to play today. You can refer back to the *Physical Activities Description Appendix* for instructions on how to run the activities. Encourage players to cheer for each other, and include music if you wish.

- Balance Tag
- Ball Bowling

- High Skipping Relay

- Hopscotch

- Train

Sport Play (20 min.)

As a group, decide which sport you want to play today. Select from the sport list contained in the *Sports List Appendix*. Be sure to periodically review with the group the Physical Activities Recommendations for Sport from Chapter Six.

Cool-down

If time permits, close the day with a few minutes of stretching while conducting the following R&R Huddle.

- **Recap** one or two key moments from the Lessons from the Field.

- **Reconnect** players back to the theme unit.

- **Reset** and transition players to the Cool-down, Reflection time.

    OR

- **Reflection**

Use this time to highlight teachable moments you observed during the day and to give players an opportunity to share their experiences about Sports PLUS during the day. The following questions can serve as a guide:

- What did you like about today?

- What did you learn today?

- What are some ways you were responsible today?

- What are some examples of responsible behavior you noticed from your teammates?

- In what ways can we be more responsible next time?

Goal-setting

Use this time to help players track progress toward their individually chosen goals, as well as toward team goals. As goals from earlier sessions are reached, guide players in setting additional individual and team goals related to *Responsibility.*

<table>
<tr><td colspan="2">**Session 27:**
Taking Responsibility
Lessons from Adventure </td></tr>
<tr><td>**Warm-up**
Begin the PLUS Cycle (5 min.)

• Session Overview

• Moving from adventure</td><td>**Cool-down**
Continue the PLUS Cycle (5-10 min.)

• Reflection

• Put-Ups</td></tr>
<tr><td>**Activity**
Lessons from Adventure (25-30 min.)

• Come To Me</td><td>**Materials**
Boundary markers</td></tr>
</table>

Warm-up

Moving Without Touching

Setup

Create a play area that is approximately 20 feet by 20 feet for a group of about 15 students. Gather players there to hear the directions.

Play

1. Tell players that in this activity they will get a chance to practice what they have learned so far about being responsible toward other group members.

2. Tell players that the most important part of the activity is to move safely through the designated play area, making sure not to bump into anyone.

3. In this activity, players will move through the area at four different speeds, on your command.

The four different speeds, from least to greatest, are as follows:

- **Speed One:** Move as if they are stuck in molasses, where every step is slow and sticky.

- **Speed Two:** Move a bit faster, as if they are walking through deep sand.

- **Speed Three:** Move at a normal walk.

- **Speed Four:** Move at a quick walk, as if they are in a rush to get somewhere.

4. Call out the different speeds, watching as players maneuver their way around the play area.

5. Do a few rounds, each time pausing in between to ask players if they are demonstrating safety and responsibility. If they are not, what can they do differently to improve?

6. As a safety measure, ask players to travel through the space with "bumpers up:" both hands raised, palms out, in front of their chest.

Activity

Lessons from Adventure
Come To Me

This is a very simple activity that involves players pairing up. You can decide how to have players choose partners so that no one feels left out or unwanted. If you have an uneven number, have a staff member participate. Remind players that the safety of their partners and other teammates is important at all times. You will need some room to do this activity, although it involves relatively little movement and no running.

Play

Once players are paired up, tell them that this is an activity that tests our own sense of personal space and our comfort level for physical closeness. Remind players of their responsibility to the safety of their own partners and of other teammates near them.

1. Ask players to partner up. Once everyone has a partner, have each pair find a space to do the activity. They will need about ten feet between them, more if you have the space. There should be nothing between the partners.

2. On your signal of "Go!," one of the partners closes his or her eyes. The sighted partners then begin walking slowly toward their sightless teammates. When the players with their eyes closed think their partners are very close, they say, "Stop!," at which point they open their eyes and see how close their partners really are.

3. Play several rounds allowing each partner several turns being both sighted and sightless.

4. As a variation, have the sighted person try to sneak up on their partners. Sightless partners listen very carefully and try to figure out where their sighted partners are. Remind players to respect their sightless teammates — no teasing or making fun of people.

- **R&R Huddle** (5 minutes)

- **Recap** using one or two of the following discussion questions about how well players treated their sightless partners:

  - How did it feel not being able to see and knowing that someone was approaching?

  - Does anyone know what "personal space" refers to?

  - Did anyone stop their partners while they were still far away? Why do you think you did that?

- **Reconnect** players to the theme unit by pointing out the importance of being responsible toward and for each other during the activity.?

- **Reset** and transition to the next activity.

Cool-down

Cool-down Ritual
Put-ups

In a large group, have players shoot put-ups to one another across the circle. Players can pretend they have a basketball and as they take a shot toward a person, they give that person a put-up about some way that person acted respectfully or responsibly or as a good teammate. The receiver of the put-up thanks the giver and then passes the next put-up. Allow players to use a passing movement from any sport they choose — soccer, volleyball, tennis, golf, bowling, etc.

Session 28:
The Impact of Environment

Overview

> **Instructor's Notes:** *Be sure to review this set of activities before starting this Sports PLUS Session. Directions for how to facilitate each activity are provided, but it is important that you become familiar with them so that you may more effectively lead the group.*
>
> *During group discussions, be sure to record all thoughts and ideas on a blackboard or newsprint. Remember that when players are working in their Player Portfolios, spelling, grammar, and penmanship are, relatively speaking, unimportant, so don't dwell on those details or you risk making Sports PLUS into MoreSchool.*

Throughout the next few sessions, the players will explore two aspects of responsibility: (1) responsibility for ourselves and (2) responsibility toward others in our community. This session focuses on the environment and introduces players to the idea that when we see problems in our community, we have a responsibility to work to correct them. The day provides many opportunities for dialogue about how far our responsibility extends into the world, what responsibility we have for world problems that are not our fault, and what kinds of actions a responsible person should take toward solving such problems. It may be useful to make note of topics that arise. These can be brought up during future sessions.

The Bulldozers is a short story about taking initiative in our communities. It also shows that children can make a difference. *The Coming and Going of the Rain* is a fun, dynamic activity that contains a thoughtful metaphor and helps get players thinking about nature and the environment. The Environment Posters is designed to inform players about some of the threats to our environment. It also helps players to think about issues of pollution, conservation, and recycling more concretely.

Session 28: **The Impact of Environment** **Lessons from Literature**	

Warm-up
Begin the PLUS Cycle (10-15 min.)
    • Session Overview
    • Quote of the Week
Activity
Lessons from Literature (25-30 min.)
    • Sports Short — *The Bulldozers*
	Cool-down
	Continue the PLUS Cycle (5-10 min.)
	    • Reflection
	Materials
	Copies of *The Bulldozers*

Warm-up

Quote of the Week

"We all have dreams. But in order to make dreams into reality, it takes an awful lot of determination, dedication, self-discipline and effort."

— Jesse Owens

Follow the five steps of the Quote of the Week Format (See the *Getting Started* chapter for additional explanation):

1. **Write the Quote of the Week:** Bring the group together into a circle, and write the Quote on the blackboard.

2. **Think about the Quote as a group:** Spend two or three minutes talking with the students about what they think the

quote means. Ask students to share answers to the group for the following question:

3. What do you think this quote has to do with our theme of responsibility?

4. **Pair up to talk about the Quote:** Have students separate into pairs. Ask them to spend about five minutes discussing the following questions with their partners. Explain that they will be sharing their answers with the whole group, so they may choose to write them in their Player Portfolios. (Be sure to walk around the groups, listen, and offer help where needed.):

5. Describe what determination means. How can being determined help you to take responsibility?

6. Describe what dedication means. How can being dedicated help you to take responsibility?

7. **Share answers with the whole group:** Come together as a large group and share the answers from each of the pair groups. Everyone who wants to should have an opportunity to share their answers.

8. **Reflect individually about the Quote:** Take two or three minutes for students to reflect individually by writing a response to the following Journal Question in their Player Portfolios:

9. Reaching your dreams takes a lot of hard work. To reach your dreams you must be responsible to yourself. What do you think this means outside of sports?

Activity

Lessons from Literature
Sports Short

The Bulldozers
(see Player Portfolio)

Key Concepts

- Responsibility
- Initiative
- Teamwork

Setup

Bring the group together to sit in a circle. Use the following content to help facilitate a short, five or six minute discussion to help set the tone before reading the story. (Be sure to record students' answers on the board or on poster paper.)

"Sometimes when you want something badly, you may have to rely on yourself to get it. Complaining, blaming others, or waiting for someone else to do something for you, may mean that whatever it is you are waiting for will never happen. Someone once said, 'A lot can get accomplished when no one cares who gets the credit.'

- What do you think this means?

- How can wanting to get credit for doing something keep things from getting done?

The Story

Next, read the story aloud and with enthusiasm to the whole group.

Discussion Questions:

Spend a couple of minutes distributing students' Player Portfolios and pencils. (Ask for one or two volunteers to help.) Work together as a whole group to answer the following questions. Write the questions and focus prompts on a blackboard or newsprint.

Questions 1-4 should be answered in a round-robin format, with one student answering one question. Try to include students who may not always participate. (If answers for questions three and four are imprecise or need further elaboration, ask if anyone has anything to add.)

1. Who are the main characters?

2. What is the problem or challenge they face?

3. How does each character handle the problem?

4. What happened then?

The following focus prompt should be answered in an exhaustive format. Continue letting students give responses until no new answers are given.

5. The main characters learned that they should...

For questions six and seven, allow all students an opportunity to share their answers, regardless of whether or not the answers are original.

6. When would it be important in your life to... [insert answer from previous statement]?

7. One thing that might make doing this difficult is...

Finally, ask students to write their responses to the following prompt in their Player Portfolios.

8. One specific way I might show responsibility in my community is by...

Cool-down

- **R&R Huddle** (5 minutes)

- **Recap** one or two key points that arose during the discussion or by introducing one of the following ideas and questions:

  - Taking responsibility for our lives can mean a lot of different things. Sometimes taking responsibility for something can benefit a lot of other people. Have you ever been in a situation where something got done simply because of one person's actions? Have you ever been in a situation where nothing got done because no one took the initiative to take action?

    – Sometimes taking a leadership role involves a lot of work. Have you ever had this experience or seen someone else have take on the hard work of leadership?
- **Reconnect** by asking volunteers to briefly share what they wrote for question number eight.
- **Reset** and get ready for the next lesson.

Session 28: The Impact of Environment Lessons from the Field	

Warm-up
Begin the PLUS Cycle (5 min.)
  • Session Overview
  • Reflecting on Responsibility
Activity
Lessons from the Field (25-30 min.)
  • Sports Activity
	Cool-down
	Continue the PLUS Cycle (5-10 min.)
	  • Reflection
	  • Goal-setting
	Materials
	Sports Equipment

Warm-up

Reflecting on Responsibility (5 min.)

Ask students to think about the previous lesson. What can they do today to bring the Lessons from Literature into their work together in the sports activity?

Activity

Lessons from the Field
Sports Activity

Block I: Getting Started (5 min.)

On the first day, players will learn how to measure their resting heart rates (RHR). They will also set baselines for their RHR, number of sit-ups/push-ups/lunges/calf raises, and number of jumps during jump rope.

Each day they will try to improve upon their Past Personal Best (PPB) by achieving their Future Best Goal (FBG) and by tracking progress toward that goal in the physical activities progress chart located in the back of their Player Portfolios. Take one minute to make sure all participants turn to the back of their portfolios and locate the progress charts. Explain to them that they will be using this chart each time you meet to do physical activities. Be sure to emphasize the importance of keeping track of their progress by using the chart.

Stand together in a circle for all *Getting Started* activities (except for jogging). Have players partner up, with one player doing the activity and the partner keeping count and giving encouragement. Be sure that they have their Portfolios handy so that they can record their progress. Encourage them to clap and cheer for their teammates to create an enthusiastic environment. You may also choose to include music.

- **Measure resting heart rate (RHR)** — Spend a few minutes showing players how to find their pulses, either on their necks or wrists. Explain that you will be giving them a few seconds to count how many times their hearts beat. Take a moment to allow the players to sit quietly on the floor and find their pulses. Give them 30 seconds to count their heartbeats.

- **Record, check in and set goals** — Allow a couple of minutes for players to record their RHRs in their Player Portfolios.

- **Jog (2-3 min.)** — This can be done as a lap or in place as a circle.

- **Stretch (2-3 min.)** — Be sure to include stretches for the major muscle groups.

- **Strength/Endurance (1 min.)** — On this first day, players will set baseline numbers for the four Strength/Endurance activities (push-ups, sit-ups, lunges, calf raises), but usually, you will only choose one or two. They will work in pairs. One member of the pair will have 30 seconds to do as many of the activities as they can. Their partner will cheer them on and count for them.

- **Jump Rope (4 min.)** — Again, players will work in pairs, with one person jumping and the other person counting and cheering. They should have three to four sets of 30-45 seconds of jumping rope.

- **Track personal progress** — Have players record their totals for steps five and six in their Player Portfolios. These totals will represent their baseline achievements, or their Past Personal Bests (PPB). Each day, players will check their progress from the previous session and will set a Future Personal Best Goal (FBG) to work toward for next time. Be sure to remind them about setting realistic goals (for example, adding one or two to their baseline, as opposed to 10).

Block II: Structured Play (30 min.)

Skill Play (10 min.)

Choose one or two of the following activities to play today. You can refer back to the *Physical Activities Description Appendix* for instructions on how to run the activities. Encourage players to cheer for each other, and include music if you wish.

- Hula Hoop Marathon

- Slides

- Balloon-athon

- Pac-Man Tag

- Chase Ball

Sport Play (20 min.)

As a group, decide which sport you want to play today. Select from the sport list contained in the *Sports List Appendix*. Be sure to periodically review with the group the Physical Activities Recommendations for Sport from Chapter Six.

Cool-down

If time permits, close the day with a few minutes of stretching while conducting the following R&R Huddle.

- **Recap** one or two key moments from the Lessons from the Field.

- **Reconnect** players back to the theme unit.

- **Reset** and transition players to the Cool-down, Reflection time.

    OR

- **Reflection**

Use this time to highlight teachable moments you observed during the day and to give players an opportunity to share their experiences about Sports PLUS during the day. The following questions can serve as a guide:

- What did you like about today?

- What did you learn today?

- What are some ways you were responsible today?

- What are some examples of responsible behavior you noticed from your teammates?

- In what ways can we be more responsible next time?

Goal-setting

Use this time to help players track progress toward their individually chosen goals, as well as toward team goals. As goals from earlier sessions are reached, guide players in setting additional individual and team goals related to *Responsibility*.

Session 28: The Impact of Environment Lessons from Adventure	
Warm-up Begin the PLUS Cycle (5 min.) • Session Overview • Coming and Going of the Rain	**Cool-down** Continue the PLUS Cycle (5-10 min.) • Reflection • Go-Round
Activity Lessons from Adventure (25-30 min.) • Environment Posters	**Materials** Player Portfolios, poster board, markers, crayons

Warm-up

Coming and Going of Rain

Bring the whole group together into a circle. Explain that, in this activity, you will be creating a rainstorm. There should be no talking. Explain to the players that you will be walking around the circle doing a specific action. As you pass in front of each player, they should begin to follow your lead — do exactly what you are doing — and should continue that action until you come around again.

Place yourself in the center of the circle. Slowly approach one player, and looking him or her directly in the eyes, *begin rubbing together the palms of your hands,* creating a swishing noise. When the first player follows your lead, move sideways to the next one and continue slowly around the circle. When all the players are rubbing their palms together, return to the first one and begin *snapping your fingers.* Again, move around the circle until all players are snapping. Next, begin *clapping your hands* together. Move all the way around again until everyone is clapping. The next motion is to slap your thighs so as to make as much noise as possible. By this time, the storm is now at its full fury, with the whole group slapping their thighs.

Now reverse the motions by going from thigh slapping to clapping to snapping to palm rubbing. As you move around the circle for the last time, stop all noisemaking motion. As each player stops, the sound decreases to the point of returning to complete silence.

There is usually little need to discuss this activity except to remind players of their ability as a group to create their own culture. This activity recreates the sounds of a rainstorm and is a great opener for the discussion of the environment you will be having today.

Activity

Lessons from Adventure
Environment Posters
(see Player Portfo)

The following activity is designed to get players thinking about taking care of their earth. A sample discussion is described below, but you may want to spend some time researching air and water pollution, global warming, littering, deforestation, and any other topic you think would be important to cover.

Setup

Explain to the players that there are many different ways that our earth can become polluted and that our natural resources can be wasted (e.g., exhaust from cars pollutes the air, sewage can pollute our water, garbage pollutes our land). Talk with them about some possible solutions to the problem of pollution. For example, conservation — using less electricity by turning off lights and appliances when they are not being used, not wasting water while brushing teeth, etc. Recycling is also an important way to take care of our earth. Talk with players about the different kinds of materials — paper, plastic, aluminum, tin, glass — that can be recycled. Ask players for examples of each.

Play

Divide players into groups of three or four and ask each group to create an environment poster. You may choose to have each group do two posters: an illustration of what pollution can do to our earth, and a reactive poster that shows examples of recycling, conserving, etc. Alternatively, you may assign different groups to create different types of posters.

Discussion

Once players have finished their posters, bring the group together to describe what they have drawn. Engage players in brainstorming ideas for simple ways they can care for their earth. Ask them to complete the following focus prompts in their Player Portfolios:

- I think recycling is important because...

- One specific thing I can do at Sports PLUS to take better care of my earth is...

- One specific thing I can do at home to take better care of my earth is...

- **R&R Huddle** (5 minutes)

- **Recap** one or two key points from the previous discussion.

- **Reconnect** to the theme unit by focusing players' attention on their responsibility to care for their earth. If time permits, you may ask for volunteers to share what they wrote in their Player Portfolios.

- **Reset** and transition to the next activity.

Cool-down

Cool-down Ritual
Go-round

At the end of the day, have a short go-round to give players an opportunity to mention one thing they learned about the environment. Use the following focus prompts as a guide:

- One thing I learned about the environment today is...

- I believe it is important to be responsible for the environment because...

- One specific thing I can do to be more responsible for my environment is...

Session 29:

Personalizing Responsibility

Overview

Instructor's Notes: Be sure to review this set of activities before starting this Sports PLUS Session. Directions for how to facilitate each activity are provided, but it is important that you become familiar with them so that you may more effectively lead the group.

During group discussions, be sure to record all thoughts and ideas on a blackboard or newsprint. Remember that when players are working in their Player Portfolios, spelling, grammar, and penmanship are, relatively speaking, unimportant, so don't dwell on those details or you risk making Sports PLUS into MoreSchool.

In this session players begin by creating their own *Quote of the Week,* a great opportunity to personalize the lessons they have learned about Responsibility and to express their understanding of responsibility. The *Create Your Own Story* activity takes this opportunity a step further, giving players the chance to use their imaginations while drawing on their comprehension of how responsibility can be lived out. *Trust Wave* is an energetic activity that focuses on our responsibility for considering the safety and comfort of those around us.

Session 29: **Personalizing Responsibility** **Lessons from Literature**	
Warm-up Begin the PLUS Cycle (10-15 min.) • Session Overview • Quote of the Week **Activity** Lessons from Literature (25-30 min.) • Create Your Own Story	**Cool-down** Continue the PLUS Cycle (5-10 min.) • Reflection **Materials** Player Portfolios, paper, pencils, pens, crayons, markers

Warm-up

Create a Quote of the Week
(see Player Portfolio)

The goal of this activity is to allow students to engage their creativity, to work collectively, and to reflect upon the themes they have been learning.

Separate students into small groups and allow five to ten minutes for each group to create its own "Quote of the Week" about responsibility. Students can look through stories and previous quotes in their portfolios for ideas, but their quotes should be in their own words.

Encourage them to write their quotes on poster board that will then be hung on the wall. Make supplies, such as markers, available for decorating the poster because some students will find this part of the activity particularly enjoyable.

After they have finished, ask groups to take turns sharing their quotes with the large group.

Allow a few minutes to discuss each one, encouraging the students who are listening to ask questions once the presenting group has finished.

When the students have finished asking questions of the group, conclude the activity by asking questions of your own:

- What does your quote mean?

- When is it important to live this quote out?

- One way I can live out this quote during Sports PLUS is…

- One way I can live out this quote at school is…

- One way I can live out this quote at home is…

Activity

Lessons from Literature
Create Your Own Story
(see Player Portfolio)

The following activity encourages students' creativity and solidifies their understanding of responsibility. By having students create their own story involving responsibility, they will draw upon personal knowledge and examples of responsibility, as well as role models who exemplify responsibility. This activity also encourages students to understand the benefits of responsibility and to transfer that understanding into a new context. It is important to remember that spelling, grammar, and penmanship are NOT important during this activity.

Setup

Bring the group together into a circle and explain the next activity as you pass out students' Player Portfolios. Use the following description as a guide:

"Today during Lessons from Literature, we will be creating our own story about Responsibility. You may choose to work individually or with up to three other students. It may be helpful to create a story about some conflict or problem that is worked out using responsibility. Think of things that may have occurred on your own sports teams or during the Lessons from the Field this theme unit. You also may choose to write a story about some of the characters in an Instant Replay or to create a different ending for one of the stories we've read. Spend a few minutes looking back over your Player Portfolios to begin getting some ideas."

Play

Offer guidance as the students separate into groups. Make sure that no one feels left out, but do let the students choose their own groups. Walk around the room offering help and suggestions as needed.

Once students have finished writing, give them an opportunity to illustrate their stories if they choose to do so. (Some students may find it easier to draw a picture before writing an accompanying story. Let this be an option for those who want it.)

Explain to the students that they will have an opportunity to share their stories with the group on the next Sports PLUS day if they would like. Students can finish illustrating their stories at home if necessary.

Discussion Questions:

After students have had an opportunity to write and illustrate their stories, bring the whole group back together in a circle for a brief reflection on the following questions. Let everyone have an opportunity to share.

- What stories or examples of responsibility did you use to create your story?

- What are some of the problems that your main characters faced in your stories?

- How do your main characters solve their dilemmas?

Cool-down

- **R&R Huddle** (5 minutes)

- **Recap** one or two key points from the discussion.

- **Reconnect** students to the theme unit.

- **Reset** and get ready for the next lesson.

Session 29: **Personalizing Responsibility** **Lessons from the Field**	
Warm-up Begin the PLUS Cycle (5 min.) • Session Overview • Reflecting on Responsibility **Activity** Lessons from the Field (25-30 min.) • Sports Activity	**Cool-down** Continue the PLUS Cycle (5-10 min.) • Reflection • Goal-setting **Materials** Sports Equipment

Warm-up

Reflecting on Responsibility (5 min.)

Ask students to think about the previous lesson. What can they do today to bring the Lessons from Literature into their work together in the sports activity?

Activity

Lessons from the Field
Sports Activity

Block I: Getting Started (5 min.)

On the first day, players will learn how to measure their resting heart rates (RHR). They will also set baselines for their RHR, number of sit-ups/push-ups/lunges/calf raises, and number of jumps during jump rope. Each day they will try to improve upon their Past Personal Best (PPB) by achieving their Future Best Goal (FBG) and by tracking progress toward that goal in the physical activities progress chart located in the back of their Player Portfolios. Take one minute to make sure all participants turn to the back of their portfolios and locate the progress charts. Explain to them that they will be using this chart each time you meet to do physical activities. Be sure to emphasize the importance of keeping track of their progress by using the chart.

Stand together in a circle for all *Getting Started* activities (except for jogging). Have players partner up, with one player doing the activity and the partner keeping count and giving encouragement. Be sure that they have their Portfolios handy so that they can record their progress. Encourage them to clap and cheer for their teammates to create an enthusiastic environment. You may also choose to include music.

- **Measure resting heart rate (RHR)** — Spend a few minutes showing players how to find their pulses, either on their necks or wrists. Explain that you will be giving them a few seconds to count how many times their hearts beat. Take a moment to allow the players to sit quietly on the floor and find their pulses. Give them 30 seconds to count their heartbeats.

- **Record, check in and set goals** — Allow a couple of minutes for players to record their RHRs in their Player Portfolios.

- **Jog (2-3 min.)** — This can be done as a lap or in place as a circle.

- **Stretch (2-3 min.)** — Be sure to include stretches for the major muscle groups.

- **Strength/Endurance (1 min.)** — On this first day, players will set baseline numbers for the four Strength/Endurance activities (push-ups, sit-ups, lunges, calf raises), but usually, you will only choose one or two. They will work in pairs. One member of the pair will have 30 seconds to do as many of the activities as they can. Their partner will cheer them on and count for them.

- **Jump Rope (4 min.)** — Again, players will work in pairs, with one person jumping and the other person counting and cheering. They should have three to four sets of 30-45 seconds of jumping rope.

- **Track personal progress** — Have players record their totals for steps five and six in their Player Portfolios. These totals will represent their baseline achievements, or their Past Personal Bests (PPB). Each day, players will check their progress from the previous session and will set a Future Personal Best Goal (FBG) to work toward for next time. Be sure to remind them about setting realistic goals (for example, adding one or two to their baseline, as opposed to 10).

Block II: Structured Play (30 min.)

Skill Play (10 min.)

Choose one or two of the following activities to play today. You can refer to the *Physical Activities Description Appendix* for instructions on how to run the activities. Encourage players to cheer for each other, and include music if you wish.

- Line Jumping
- Jump Rope Relay
- Shuttle Run Relay
- Wheelbarrow Race
- Drum Major Walk

Sport Play (20 min.)

As a group, decide which sport you want to play today. Select from the sport list contained in the *Sports List Appendix*. Be sure to periodically review with the group the Physical Activities Recommendations for Sport from Chapter Six.

Cool-down

If time permits, close the day with a few minutes of stretching while conducting the following R&R Huddle.

- **Recap** one or two key moments from the Lessons from the Field.

- **Reconnect** players back to the theme unit.

- **Reset** and transition players to the Cool-down, Reflection time.

  OR

- **Reflection**

Use this time to highlight teachable moments you observed during the day and to give players an opportunity to share their experiences about Sports PLUS during the day. The following questions can serve as a guide:

- What did you like about today?

- What did you learn today?

- What are some ways you were responsible today?

- What are some examples of responsible behavior you noticed from your teammates?

- In what ways can we be more responsible next time?

Goal-setting

Use this time to help players track progress toward their individually chosen goals, as well as toward team goals. As goals from earlier sessions are reached, guide players in setting additional individual and team goals related to *Responsibility.*

Session 29: **Personalizing Responsibility Lessons from Adventure**	
Warm-up Begin the PLUS Cycle (5 min.) • Session Overview • Salt and Pepper	**Cool-down** Continue the PLUS Cycle (5-10 min.) • Reflection • Values
Activity Lessons from Adventure (25-30 min.) • Trust Wave	**Materials** Rope or tape

Warm-up

Salt and Pepper

This simple activity will help players get warmed up to listening to directions.

Setup

Create a line on the ground with a section of rope or tape. Ask players to stand on one side of the line, forming a single file line with each person standing with the rope to their side.

Play

1. Designate one side of the rope to be "salt" and the other to be "pepper." (Or, use any two distinctly different words.)

2. Tell players that when you call out one of the words, players should jump to the proper side of the line. If they are already on the proper side, they should stay put.

3. Mix up the order of what you call out. Keep them on their toes!

4. If someone jumps incorrectly or stays put when they should not, you can either have them become the new caller, or consider them "out."

Activity

Lessons from Adventure
Trust Wave

Setup

Explain to the group that being a responsible teammate involves taking care of our teammates both emotionally and physically. Have a group discussion before introducing the activity stressing the role of responsibility in taking care of teammates' safety.

You need a bit of room for this but not a lot. If your space is tight, save the activity for the sport session when you have more room.

Play

After a group discussion on the role of keeping teammates physically safe, read the following instructions to the group.

1. The group will form two lines, players facing each other, about an arms-length apart. (When players extend their arms they should overlap slightly with the person across from them.) These players are the spotters.

2. One player, called the runner, will start about six to ten feet away from the line of teammates. This runner, on the command of "Go!" runs between the two lines of teammates. As the runner approaches, the spotters, at the last moment, lift their arms to allow a wavelike opening for the runner to pass through.

3. After explaining the activity, stress again the importance of taking care of teammates' safety. The consequence for not being a respectful and responsible teammate is that someone may get hurt and, at the least, that may destroy the trust of that

person for his or her teammates. Ask the players to remember the Player Contracts they signed and what they committed to.

4. Create the two lines and ask for a volunteer to be the first runner. Try a few practice runs by having the first runner walk, then slowly jog through the spotters. This will also allow the spotters to test their timing so that their arms lift just before the runner gets to them. Only allow running through the line after a few practice runs.

5. Allow all players the opportunity to be a runner.

- **R&R Huddle** (5 minutes)

- **Recap** using a quick go-round that asks players to give one-word answers or short statements to describe how it felt to be a spotter and a runner.

- **Reconnect** using one or two of the following discussion questions:

  1. How did we, as a team, do in being responsible?

  2. Did we take our responsibilities seriously?

  3. What might happen if we didn't take our responsibilities seriously?

  4. Where else in our lives do we need our teammates to help take care of our safety?

- **Reset** and transition to the next activity.

Cool-down

Cool-down Ritual

Values

Ask for volunteers to give examples of the three values of teamwork, respect, and responsibility all working at the same time.

Session 30:

Responsibility Certificates

Overview

Instructor's Notes: *Be sure to review this set of activities before starting this Sports PLUS Session. Directions for how t o facilitate each activity are provided, but it is important that you become familiar with them so that you may more effectively lead the group.*

During group discussions, be sure to record all thoughts and ideas on a blackboard or newsprint. Remember that when players are working in their Player Portfolios, spelling, grammar, and penmanship are, relatively speaking, unimportant, so don't dwell on those details or you risk making Sports PLUS into MoreSchool.

This final Responsibility session follows the Sports PLUS format for the closing session of a unit. The *Responsibility Posters Revisited* activity allows players to revisit the commitments they made to themselves and each other in the beginning of the theme unit. In a larger sense, this activity affirms the value of responsibility by indirectly encouraging players to think about how responsible they were for living out the facets of responsibility that they included on their *Responsibility Posters*.

As much as possible, empower players to run the *Responsibility Certificates* and Sports Extras activities. By deciding how the activities are run and ensuring that they abide by their own rules, players practice living out the value of responsibility. Be sure to take notes on any issues that may arise (e.g., sharing). These issues may provide a valuable transition into the next theme unit, Fair Play.

Session 30: **Responsibility Certificates** **Lessons from Literature**	

Warm-up
Begin the PLUS Cycle (10-15 min.)
 	
  • Session Overview
 	
  • Quote of the Week
 	
Activity
Lessons from Literature (25-30 min.)
 	
  • Sports Extras
	Cool-down
	Continue the PLUS Cycle (5-10 min.)
	
	  • Reflection
	
	Materials
	Students' *Sports Extras* work

Warm-up

Quote of the Week

"The first thing is to love your sport. Never do it to please someone else. It has to be yours."

— Peggy Flemming

Follow the five steps of the Quote of the Week Format (See the *Getting Started* chapter for additional explanation):

5. **Write the Quote of the Week:** Bring the group together into a circle, and write the Quote on the blackboard.

6. **Think about the Quote as a group:** Spend two or three minutes talking with the students about what they think the quote means. Ask students to share answers to the group for the following question:

7. What does it mean to be responsible to your self?

8. **Pair up to talk about the Quote:** Have students separate into pairs. Ask them to spend about five minutes discussing the following questions with their partners. Explain that they will be sharing their answers with the whole group, so they may choose to write them in their Player Portfolios. (Be sure to walk around the groups, listen, and offer help where needed.):

9. What helps you be true to yourself?

10. How can being responsible to your own self get in the way of being responsible to others?

11. **Share answers with the whole group:** Come together as a large group and share the answers from each of the pair groups. Everyone who wants to should have an opportunity to share their answers.

12. **Reflect individually about the Quote:** Take two or three minutes for students to reflect individually by writing a response to the following Journal Question in their Player Portfolios:

13. What is an example of how you've been responsible to your self during Sports PLUS?

Activity

Lessons from Literature
Sports Extras

This is an important activity to conclude each theme unit. Students may work alone or in small groups. At the start of the unit, students were asked to look for actual events and stories of people in the news or in history who exemplify the core value for that theme unit. They should be reminded frequently throughout the theme unit to be on the lookout for examples of the core Sports PLUS values in magazines and newspapers. They can ask a parent or guardian for help if they are unsure where to find articles. If possible, provide students access during the Sports PLUS program to students' magazines, such as *Sports Illustrated for Kids*. A certain area of the room can be designated as the "Sports Extras Area," in which students can store their articles and stories as they find them.

Setup

1. Bring the group together to form a circle. Explain the next activity as you pass out the Player Portfolios and pencils. Use the following description as a guide:

   "Today you will have an opportunity to share a story about Responsibility with the rest of the group. You may choose either to share the article you brought in or to share the story you wrote during 'Create Your Own Story.'"

2. Ask students to spend a few minutes writing answers to the pre-work questions in their Player Portfolios:

3. Who is the main character in your story?

4. What happened to the main character? Or what did the main character do?

5. In what way is this story an example of Responsibility?

6. One lesson the main character learned is that he or she should...

7. This story teaches us that we should...

8. After students have had some time to answer the questions in their Portfolios, ask for volunteers to share their stories in their own words. Let everyone who wants to share do so.

Cool-down

- **R&R Huddle** (5 minutes)

- **Recap** by asking students: What do these articles teach us about Responsibility?

- **Reconnect** students to the theme unit using the following focus prompt: One way these examples of responsibility help us to be a better team is by...

- **Reset** and get ready for the next lesson.

Session 30: Responsibility Certificates Lessons from the Field	
Warm-up Begin the PLUS Cycle (5 min.)	**Cool-down** Continue the PLUS Cycle (5-10 min.)
• Session Overview	• Reflection
• Reflecting on Responsibility	• Goal-setting
Activity Lessons from the Field (25-30 min.)	**Materials** Sports Equipment
• Sports Activity	

Warm-up

Reflecting on Responsibility (5 min.)

Ask students to think about the previous lesson. What can they do today to bring the Lessons from Literature into their work together in the sports activity?

Activity

Lessons from the Field
Sports Activity

Block I: Getting Started (5 min.)

On the first day, players will learn how to measure their resting heart rates (RHR). They will also set baselines for their RHR, number of sit-ups/push-ups/lunges/calf raises, and number of jumps during jump rope. Each day they will try to improve upon their Past Personal Best (PPB) by achieving their Future Best Goal (FBG) and by tracking progress toward that goal in the physical activities progress chart located in the back of their Player Portfolios. Take one minute to make sure all participants turn to the back of their portfolios and locate the progress charts. Explain to them that they will be using this chart each time you meet to do physical activities. Be sure to emphasize the importance of keeping track of their progress by using the chart.

Stand together in a circle for all *Getting Started* activities (except for jogging). Have players partner up, with one player doing the activity and the partner keeping count and giving encouragement. Be sure that they have their Portfolios handy so that they can record their progress. Encourage them to clap and cheer for their teammates to create an enthusiastic environment. You may also choose to include music.

- **Measure resting heart rate (RHR)** — Spend a few minutes showing players how to find their pulses, either on their necks or wrists. Explain that you will be giving them a few seconds to count how many times their hearts beat. Take a moment to allow the players to sit quietly on the floor and find their pulses. Give them 30 seconds to count their heartbeats.

- **Record, check in and set goals** — Allow a couple of minutes for players to record their RHRs in their Player Portfolios.

- **Jog (2-3 min.)** — This can be done as a lap or in place as a circle.

- **Stretch (2-3 min.)** — Be sure to include stretches for the major muscle groups.

- **Strength/Endurance (1 min.)** — On this first day, players will set baseline numbers for the four Strength/Endurance activities (push-ups, sit-ups, lunges, calf raises), but usually, you will only choose one or two. They will work in pairs. One member of the pair will have 30 seconds to do as many of the activities as they can. Their partner will cheer them on and count for them.

- **Jump Rope (4 min.)** — Again, players will work in pairs, with one person jumping and the other person counting and cheering. They should have three to four sets of 30-45 seconds of jumping rope.

- **Track personal progress** — Have players record their totals for steps five and six in their Player Portfolios. These totals will represent their baseline achievements, or their Past Personal Bests (PPB). Each day, players will check their progress from the previous session and will set a Future Personal Best Goal (FBG) to work toward for next time. Be sure to remind them about setting realistic goals (for example, adding one or two to their baseline, as opposed to 10).

Block II: Structured Play (30 min.)

Skill Play (10 min.)

Choose one or two of the following activities to play today. You can refer to the *Physical Activities Description Appendix* for instructions on how to run the activities. Encourage players to cheer for each other, and include music if you wish.

- Water Fill Relay

- Beanbag Walk Relay

- Locomotion Relay

- Sack Race

- Clothes Relay

Sport Play (20 min.)

As a group, decide which sport you want to play today. Select from the sport list contained in the *Sports List Appendix*. Be sure to periodically review with the group the Physical Activities Recommendations for Sport from Chapter Six.

Cool-down

If time permits, close the day with a few minutes of stretching while conducting the following R&R Huddle.

- **Recap** one or two key moments from the Lessons from the Field.

- **Reconnect** players back to the theme unit.

- **Reset** and transition players to the Cool-down, Reflection time.

  OR

- **Reflection**

Use this time to highlight teachable moments you observed during the day and to give players an opportunity to share their experiences about Sports PLUS during the day. The following questions can serve as a guide:

- What did you like about today?

- What did you learn today?

- What are some ways you were responsible today?

- What are some examples of responsible behavior you noticed from your teammates?

- In what ways can we be more responsible next time?

Goal-setting

Use this time to track the group's progress toward their individual and team goals and to start the players thinking about one or two team goals related to *Fair Play* that will be set during the next session.

Session 30: **Responsibility Certificates** **Lessons from Adventure**	

Warm-up
Begin the PLUS Cycle (5 min.)
 	
   • Session Overview
 	
   • *Responsibility Posters* Revisited
	Cool-down
	Continue the PLUS Cycle (5-10 min.)
	
	   • Reflection
	
	   • Presentation of Certificates

Activity Lessons from Adventure (25-30 min.) • Responsibility Certificates	**Materials** *Responsibility Posters*

Warm-up

Responsibility Posters Revisited

Take a brief tour of the responsibility posters that were created during the beginning of the theme unit. Stop at each poster and discuss what is represented and what it says about responsibility. Ask players to comment on how they think the group is doing with being responsible teammates and with creating a good team. Draw upon the content of the posters for specific examples of responsibility that players noticed throughout the theme unit. Ask if anyone would like to update the posters (e.g., adding new insights and ideas they have learned over the course of the theme unit).

Activity

Lessons from Adventure
Responsibility Certificates
(see Player Portfolio)

During this activity, players will create Responsibility Certificates to signify their completion of the third Sports PLUS theme unit. There are several ways this can be done, and players should have some voice in the decision. Possibilities include:

- Players could work in small groups to make certificates for other small groups.

- The whole team could work together to make one giant team certificate (e.g., making handprints to spell out Responsibility).

- Players could make individual certificates. (If this option is chosen, ask players to leave space on the certificates so the recipients' names can be filled in, before being distributed by the Masters of Ceremonies at the end of the day.)

Play

1. Gather the group together into a circle, and explain the purpose of the next activity to the players — "To create certificates that signify our completion of this Sports PLUS theme unit."

2. Describe one or two possible ways this can be done, and ask players if they have any other ideas. As a group, the players decide what they are going to do, and create the certificate(s).

3. When the certificate(s) are finished, have the group gather to vote on the two players who have given their best effort to show Responsibility during this theme unit. Voting can be done either by a show of hands, applause for nominated candidates, or by writing names on slips of paper. (In the case of a tie, allow multiple winners.)

4. Once the decision has been made, explain that those who were chosen will be the "Masters of Ceremonies" for the presentation of the Responsibility Certificate(s) at the end of the day.

- **R&R Huddle** (5 minutes)

- **Recap** one or two points from the previous discussion about the Responsibility Posters.

- **Reconnect** players to the theme unit.

- **Reset** and transition to the next activity.

Cool-down

Reflection

Bring the group together for a brief go-round discussion about what they think of the third unit of the Sports PLUS program. Does anyone have any questions? Is the program what you expected? What can we, teachers and staff, do to make it better? What can we all do to be more responsible toward each other? Use this discussion, as necessary, to set some goals and for continued discussion in the Warm-up to Unit Four.

Cool-down Ritual
Presentation of Responsibility Certificates

Have the two players chosen as Masters of Ceremonies (MC) present the certificates. If certificates were created for different small groups, the MCs should call each group up one by one and formally present the certificate with a handshake and congratulations. If the group decided on one giant certificate, the MCs can hang it up somewhere in the group meeting room. (You may need to help them accomplish this task.) Finally, if the group decided to create individual certificates, help the MCs fill out the names on each certificate before the ceremony. During the ceremony, the MCs should take turns calling up each person to receive their certificate.

Chapter Thirteen

Theme Unit 4: Becoming a Fan of Fair Play

Session 31:
Fair Play Posters

Overview

Instructor's Notes: Be sure to review today's activities before the Sports PLUS Day begins. Directions for how to facilitate each activity are provided, but it is important that you become familiar with them so that you may more effectively lead the group.

During group discussions, be sure to record all thoughts and ideas on a blackboard or newsprint. Remember that when students are working in their Player Portfolios, spelling, grammar, and penmanship are, relatively speaking, unimportant, so don't dwell on those details or you risk making Sports PLUS into MoreSchool.

The focus of Session 31 is on transitioning to a new value, Fair Play, and defining it in the context of what the group has already learned about teamwork, respect, and responsibility.

The Quote of the Week initiates thought on Fair Play by contrasting how people sometimes see Fair Play at odds with winning. This is a theme you will visit often in the next 10 sessions. Students will create a poster that illustrates their understanding of Fair Play. The *You Make the Call* activity builds upon questions raised during the *Quote of the Week* by asking players to address problems that arise when a basic rule is broken in a baseball game. They will look at the ways rules make a game fair and more fun for everyone.

As always, be sure to remind students to be on the look out for articles and stories about Fair Play that they can present during Sports Extras.

Session 31: **Fair Play Posters** **Lessons from Literature**	

Warm-up
  Begin the PLUS Cycle (10-15 min.)
  • Session Overview
  • Quote of the Week
	Cool-down
	  Continue the PLUS Cycle (5-10 min.)
	  • Reflection

Activity
  Lessons from Literature (25-30 min.)
  • You Make the Call — *Out of Order Batter*
	Materials
	  Copies of *Out of Order Batter*

Warm-up

Quote of the Week

Some clubs want to win so much that they'll do anything to get it. Our approach has been just the opposite. We've tried to do things the right way. And by the right way I mean [following] the rules and regulations, and they are precisely what we go by. I may not like [the rules], but once they are in, we play by them.

— Don Shula, Former Head

Coach of the Miami Dolphins

Overview

Instructor's Notes: You may need to read this quote a second time and take extra time answering clarification questions because of its length. Focus the students' attention on the last part of the quote — *"I may not like them, but once they are in, we play by them."*

Follow the five steps of the Quote of the Week Format (See the *Getting Started* chapter for additional explanation):

1. Write the Quote of the Week: Bring the group together into a circle, and write the Quote on the blackboard.

2. Think about the Quote as a group: Spend two or three minutes talking with the students about what they think the quote means. Ask them to share answers to the group for the following questions:

   • What does Don Shula mean by the "right way" of doing things?

   • Why does Don Shula play by the "rules and regulations" even though he may not like them?

3. Pair up to talk about the Quote: Have students separate into pairs. Ask them to spend about five minutes discussing the following questions with their partners. Explain that they will be sharing their answers with the whole group, so they may choose to write them in their Player Portfolios. (Be sure to walk around the groups, listen, and offer help where needed.):

   • Why is it important to play by the rules even if you don't like them?

   • Why is it important to play by the rules even if you may lose?

   • Playing by the rules is sometimes hard because…

4. Share answers with the whole group: Come together as a large group and share the answers from each of the pair groups. Everyone who wants to should have an opportunity to share their answers.

5. Reflect individually about the Quote: Take two or three minutes for students to reflect individually by writing a response to the following question and prompt in their Player Portfolios:

    • Is playing by the rules important to you? Why or why not?

    • Sometimes playing by the rules is hard to do. One way to make playing by the rules easier is…

Activity

Lessons from Literature
You Make the Call
Out of Order Batter
(see Player Portfolio)

Key Concepts

- Following Rules
- Fairness
- Honesty
- Decision-making

Setup

Bring the group together to sit in a circle. If there is time, use one or two of the following questions to help set the tone before reading the story:

- What are some reasons that we have rules in a game?

- What would happen if some of the players didn't follow those rules?

- What would happen if we changed the rules whenever we wanted to win or gain an unfair advantage?

Encourage students to think about these issues as you read the story.

The Story

Read the story aloud and with enthusiasm to the whole group.

Discussion Questions:

Separate the students into groups by having them count off by threes (or fours depending on the group size). Spend a couple of minutes distributing students' Player Portfolios and pencils. Ask one or two volunteers to help.

Using their Player Portfolios, have students discuss and write answers to the following questions in their small groups. It is important to remember that spelling, grammar, and penmanship are NOT important during this activity.

1. Who is the main character in this story?

2. What is the key problem this character faces?

3. What are some possible ways that Ray can solve his problem?

4. What would happen if Ray handled the problem in this way?

   • How would Ray feel?

   • How would the rest of his team feel?

   • What about Kenny and the other team?

5. If you were Ray, what are two different ways you might solve the problem?

6. What might make your decision difficult?

7. If you were Ray, what solution would you choose?

Group Share

• After the small groups have had time to discuss each question, gather the groups together to sit in one large circle.

• Ask each small group to share their suggestions for solving the problem, using students' answers to number three above. (As suggestions are given, you or a volunteer should write them on poster paper for all to see.)

- Once all of the different solutions have been laid out, spend a few minutes discussing the consequences of each solution, using students' answers to question number four as a guide.

- As a group, choose the best solution (i.e., the most good for the most people).

- Finally, as a group, complete the following two focus prompts on poster paper.

  – One thing we can take from this story is that we should…

  – We should all be careful not to…

Cool-down

- *R&R Huddle* (5 min.)

- *Recap* using one or two key points from the previous discussion.

- *Reconnect* students using the following idea as a guide:

  – Doing the right thing and playing fair isn't always easy, especially when it makes the difference between winning and losing. When we face this dilemma, the question we have to ask ourselves is whether winning is so important or losing so bad that we would disrespect our values.

  – One thing I can do to make sure I stay true to my most important values during a game, even when it might impact winning or losing, is…

- *Reset* and get ready for the next lesson.

Session 31: **Fair Play Posters** **Lessons from the Field**	
Warm-up Begin the PLUS Cycle (5 min.) • Session Overview • Following Up on Fair Play **Activity** Lessons from the Field (25-30 min.) • Sports Activity	**Cool-down** Continue the PLUS Cycle (5-10 min.) • Reflection • Goal-setting **Materials** Sports Equipment

Warm-up

Following Up on Fair Play (5 min.)

Ask students to think about the previous lesson. What can they do today to bring the Lessons from Literature into their work together in the sports activity?

Activity

Lessons from the Field
Sports Activity

Block I: Getting Started (5 min.)

On the first day, players will learn how to measure their resting heart rates (RHR). They will also set baselines for their RHR, number of sit-ups/push-ups/lunges/calf raises, and number of jumps during jump rope. Each day they will try to improve upon their Past Personal Best (PPB) by achieving their Future Best Goal (FBG) and by tracking progress toward that goal in the physical activities progress chart located in the back of their Player Portfolios. Take one minute to make sure all participants turn to the back of their portfolios and locate the progress charts. Explain to them that they will be using this chart each time you meet to do physical activities. Be sure to emphasize the importance of keeping track of their progress by using the chart.

Stand together in a circle for all *Getting Started* activities (except for jogging). Have players partner up, with one player doing the activity and the partner keeping count and giving encouragement. Be sure that they have their Portfolios handy so that they can record their progress. Encourage them to clap and cheer for their teammates to create an enthusiastic environment. You may also choose to include music.

- **Measure resting heart rate (RHR)** — Spend a few minutes showing players how to find their pulses, either on their necks or wrists. Explain that you will be giving them a few seconds to count how many times their hearts beat. Take a moment to allow the players to sit quietly on the floor and find their pulses. Give them 30 seconds to count their heartbeats.

- **Record, check in and set goals** — Allow a couple of minutes for players to record their RHRs in their Player Portfolios.

- **Jog (2-3 min.)** — This can be done as a lap or in place as a circle.

- **Stretch (2-3 min.)** — Be sure to include stretches for the major muscle groups.

- **Strength/Endurance (1 min.)** — On this first day, players will set baseline numbers for the four Strength/Endurance activities (push-ups, sit-ups, lunges, calf raises), but usually, you will only choose one or two. They will work in pairs. One member of the pair will have 30 seconds to do as many of the activities as they can. Their partner will cheer them on and count for them.

- **Jump Rope (4 min.)** — Again, players will work in pairs, with one person jumping and the other person counting and cheering. They should have three to four sets of 30-45 seconds of jumping rope.

- **Track personal progress** — Have players record their totals for steps five and six in their Player Portfolios. These totals will represent their baseline achievements, or their Past Personal Bests (PPB). Each day, players will check their progress from the previous session and will set a Future Personal Best Goal

(FBG) to work toward for next time. Be sure to remind them about setting realistic goals (for example, adding one or two to their baseline, as opposed to 10).

Block II: Structured Play (30 min.)

Skill Play (10 min.)

Choose one or two of the following activities to play today. You can refer back to the *Physical Activities Description Appendix* for instructions on how to run the activities. Encourage players to cheer for each other, and include music if you wish.

- Sprint/Stride Runs

- Chinese Jump Rope

- Limbo

- Three-legged Race

- Beanbag Horseshoes

Sport Play (20 min.)

As a group, decide which sport you want to play today. Select from the sport list contained in the *Sports List Appendix.* Be sure to periodically review with the group the Physical Activities Recommendations for Sport from Chapter Six.

Cool-down

If time permits, close the day with a few minutes of stretching while conducting the following R&R Huddle.

- **Recap** one or two key moments from the Lessons from the Field.

- **Reconnect** players back to the theme unit.

- **Reset** and transition players to the Cool-down, Reflection time

OR

- **Reflection**

Use this time to highlight teachable moments you observed during the day and to give players an opportunity to share their experiences about Sports PLUS during the day. The following questions can serve as a guide:

- What did you like about today?

- What did you learn today?

- What are some ways you showed fair play today?

- How can we better show fair play next time?

Goal-setting

Keeping the S.M.A.R.T. goals script in mind, spend a few minutes working together as a group to set one or two team goals related to *Fair Play.*

Session 31: **Fair Play Posters** **Lessons from Adventure**	
Warm-up Begin the PLUS Cycle (5 min.) <ul><li>Session Overview</li><li>Everybody's It</li></ul> **Activity** Lessons from Adventure (25-30 min.) <ul><li>Fair Play Posters</li></ul>	**Cool-down** Continue the PLUS Cycle (5-10 min.) <ul><li>Reflection</li><li>Go-Round</li></ul> **Materials** 2 poster-sized pieces of paper for each group of 3 or 4 players, different colored markers, one dictionary per group (if dictionaries are unavailable, write definitions on the chalk board or poster paper), magazines, newspapers for cutting, glue

Warm-up

Everybody's It

Setup

Gather players to listen to the instructions. After the tag game, ask them to think about how fair play helped (or didn't) the game go smoothly. Why is fair play important?

Play

Tell players that in this tag game, everybody is it. When you say "Go," players try to tag one another, safely, below the shoulders. If someone gets tagged, they "take a knee." To get back in the game, a player who has been tagged raises both of their hands and waits for a free player to come by and give them a "high 10."

Activity

Lessons from Adventure
Fair Play Posters
(see Player Portfolio)

Defining Fair Play

Begin by having a large group discussion of the meaning of the term Fair Play. This can be a brainstorming discussion, keeping track of ideas on a poster or chalkboard. Once you think the group has some ideas, form small groups of four or five players. Following the group discussion, this hands-on activity helps players come up with concrete examples of different aspects of fair play and allows them to share with each other what they know about playing fair. The activity also provides many visual reminders of what they have agreed constitutes fair play.

Setup

Separate the groups into teams of three or four. Give each team a table or some open space on the floor, two pieces of poster-sized pieces of paper, a dictionary if available, and some markers.

Play

1. Each group will use a dictionary to look up the meaning of fair play. If dictionaries are unavailable, write the definition on the chalkboard.

2. Using this information, and their own understanding of fair play, players will create a poster to teach the rest of the group what fair play means to them. The poster can be anything the groups choose to represent fair play. They can create a Being (see the Teamwork Unit) by tracing the outline of one of their bodies on the poster paper, cut out pictures from magazines if you have a collection to use, or make their own drawing.

3. Groups should then write words and phrases around their drawing that gives their definition of fair play. Players should use their own words to define fair play, not the words from the dictionary. They should also write words or phrases on the outside of their Being or drawing that show what the opposite of playing fair looks and sounds like.

4. Remind the players that this is a team project and they should spend a few minutes planning what they, as a team, want to create and how they are going to create it. All members of the team should be actively involved in the planning, decision-making, and production of the poster. Allow 15–20 minutes for the small groups to work.

5. Once the groups have completed their posters, spend a few minutes presenting group posters to the large group and explaining definitions, drawings, words, and phrases. If time permits, allow some discussion and questions for each group.

6. Hang the posters around the room and refer back to them as often as necessary throughout the program to reinforce and remind players of their commitments. As the unit progresses, and players' understanding of fair play increases, have them add new ideas, words and phrases to their posters.

7. Hang the "Sports PLUS Leader to Detractor Poster" for Fair Play. Reflect on the 5-point scale and the connections between this scale and the players' posters. Utilize this scale to guide your reflections in all phases of the program.

- *R&R Huddle* (5 minutes)

- *Recap* one or two key points that arose during the discussion.

- *Reconnect* by asking players to share examples of Fair Play.

- *Reset* and transition to the next activity.

Cool-down

Cool-down Ritual

Impulse Go-Round

Do a quick large group go-round. Ask each player to offer a word or two describing what fair play looks like, sounds like, or feels like. They can draw from the Fair Play Posters they created during the first activity.

Homework Assignment

As a fun homework assignment, ask the players and staff to begin looking in local newspapers and magazines, and to listen for stories on the radio and television that show examples of fair play. Ask everyone to bring these examples to the group when they find them. The group will continue adding to the collection of articles and stories they gathered for the previous theme units and will use them at the end of the program.

Session 32: Fair Play Relay

Overview

Instructor's Notes: *Be sure to review this set of activities before starting this Sports PLUS Session. Directions for how to run each activity are provided, but it is important that you become familiar with them so that you may more effectively lead the group.*

During group discussions, be sure to record all thoughts and ideas on a blackboard or newsprint. Remember that when players are working in their Player Portfolios, spelling, grammar, and penmanship are, relatively speaking, unimportant, so don't dwell on those details or you risk making Sports PLUS into MoreSchool.

This session offers a powerful opportunity for players to discuss and experience fair play. The *Trust Walk* builds upon the team building and responsibility the group developed in earlier theme units. The *Fair Play Relay* is a fun and familiar activity that helps players explore their understanding of Fair Play. To conclude the session, players will review the principles and rules they have previously committed to and then sign the Fair Play line of the contract.

Session 32: Fair Play Relay Lessons from Literature	
Warm-up Begin the PLUS Cycle (10-15 min.) • Session Overview • Quote of the Week **Activity** Lessons from Literature (25-30 min.) • You Make the Call — *Play of the Week*	**Cool-down** Continue the PLUS Cycle (5-10 min.) • Reflection **Materials** Copies of *Play of the Week*

Warm-up

Quote of the Week
(see Player Portfolio)

It isn't hard to be good from time to time in sports. What is tough, is being good every day.
— Willie Mays

Follow the five steps of the Quote of the Week Format (See the *Getting Started* chapter for additional explanation):

1. Write the Quote of the Week: Bring the group together into a circle, and write the Quote on the blackboard.

2. Think about the Quote as a group: Spend two or three minutes talking with the students about what they think the quote means. Ask students to share answers to the group for the following question:

   • What does "being good" have to do with fair play?

3. Pair up to talk about the Quote: Have students separate into pairs. Ask them to spend about five minutes discussing the following questions with their partners. Explain that they will be sharing their answers with the whole group, so they may choose to write their answers in their Player Portfolios. (Be sure to walk around the groups, listen, and offer help where needed.):

   • Being "good" can either mean playing with great skill or following the rules. Give an example of how each meaning relates to playing fairly.

   • Why do you think it is important to play fair?

4. Share answers with the whole group: Come together as a large group and share the answers from each of the pair groups. Everyone who wants to should have an opportunity to share their answers.

5. Reflect individually about the Quote: Take two or three minutes for students to reflect individually by writing a response to the following Journal Question in their Player Portfolios:

Activity

Lessons from Literature
Sports Short
Play of the Week
(see Player Portfolio)

Setup

Bring the group together to sit in a circle. Use the following questions to help facilitate a short, five or six minute discussion to help set the tone before reading the story. (Be sure to record students' answers on the board or on poster paper.)

"Sometimes it's hard not to take an unfair advantage over an opponent when that advantage could lead to victory."

- If your teammates think it's OK for you to take an unfair advantage to help them win, does that make it easier or harder for you to play by the rules? Why?

- How might Fair Play and Teamwork be related?

The Story

Read the story aloud and with enthusiasm to the whole group.

Play of the Week

by Linda Berry

"Hey, Jennifer!"
"Good Pass!"
"Yippee!"
The voices from the soccer field usually made Allison hurry to join her teammates, not wanting to miss a minute. Today, instead, she inched her ball with her foot carefully around a bush and through the open gate onto the field. As she arrived, the coach was dividing the boys and girls into small group drills. Good. Allison didn't want to talk to anybody today. It was her fault that her team, the Roadrunners, had lost Saturday's game with the Jets.

Usually Allison enjoyed every minute of practice, but today she found herself watching her teammates to see if they were angry with her. Did Luis kick the one out of her reach on purpose?

Did Andy mean to bump into her like that? Why wouldn't Jennifer pass to her?

Allison had even thought of pretending to have a sore throat or stomachache or something to keep from coming to practice today. The funny thing was, she almost did have a stomachache from thinking about it. She hoped the stomachache would go away after she faced up to the team.

The coach's whistle interrupted her thoughts.

"OK, boys and girls. Oranges!" This call signaled to them that it was time to talk over practice and the last game.

Slowly Allison dribbled her ball over to the group. She tried some extra fancy juggling, almost hoping she'd miss and have to chase the ball far away from them.

"Good practice," the coach said after they had settled down on the grass and the oranges had been devoured.

Then, as usual, he checked his clipboard and made comments to each player. Allison braced herself.

"Erin, your dribbling is really improving. You're going to surprise those Fireballs Saturday! Allison, keep working on control. You're one of the strongest halfbacks."

Whoosh! Allison let out the breath she'd been holding. At least she was past that. Maybe the coach wouldn't say anything after all.

"Now, about last week's game."

Allison drew in another breath. It wasn't over yet.

"You looked good and played a good game. The Jets are a tough team. Let's see where we could have done better. Jennifer?

Jennifer laughed and said, "Man on man!" That was safe. They always needed to work on that. The coach agreed with her. "Right!! What else, Freddie?"

Freddie thought a bit and suggested, "Position. I know when I got out of position, the Jets got through and really put pressure on the goalie."

Again the coach agreed. "I'm glad you understand that. Good, Freddie."

"Now for the play of the week," the coach was saying. "Who has a suggestion?

This was something the boys and girls always enjoyed. Several hands waved.

"Erin?"

"I think it was when Luis went to cover the goal and blocked that shot close to the goal box."

There was a loud applause at this suggestion. The coach nodded. "Any other suggestions?"

Andy said, "I think the best play was Freddie's steal from that big guy on the Jets and then passing the ball to Jennifer to score."

The youngsters murmured approval. The coach said, "That was a beautiful play, and it shows how important teamwork is. Good! Any others?"

There was silence as the boys and girls thought. When nobody had any other suggestions the coach spoke again. "My recommendation for the play of the week isn't either of those." The teammates looked at one another in surprise. Those two plays had been the most dramatic of the game.

"Do you remember in the second half, when several players were bundled near our goal and the ball went out of bounds?"

They all remembered. That was just before the Jets made the goal that broke the tie and won the game. Allison began to squirm.

"Do you remember that the referee called it out on the Jets?

Yes, they remembered. Some of the athletes glanced at Allison. That stomachache was still there. "Do you remember that Allison raised her hand and corrected the ref, saying that she had knocked it out?"

How could they forget? That throw-in by the Jets led to a long pass and a strong kick and the winning goal. Even having Jessica in position in goal couldn't stop it! Now several boys and girls were looking at Allison more openly. She couldn't look up.

The coach continued. "You know, team, I call what Allison did the play of the year, not just the play of the week."

The boys and girls raised a questioning murmur.

The coach explained. "Winning a game unfairly or by mistake doesn't tell anything about how good a team we are. We play to do the best we can and see how we stack up against other teams. Right?"

The group was quiet now, most of them looking down at the grass. Several players nodded agreement. The coach wasn't quite through.

"Keeping the record straight and honest is the most important thing this team could ever learn about playing the game. I'm proud of Allison."

There was a pause, and then—"Let's hear it for Allison!" The whole team joined in with "Hip, hip, hooray!"

Funny about that stomachache... some back pounding and a few friendly words were just the medicine it needed.

Discussion Questions:

Spend a couple of minutes distributing students' Player Portfolios and pencils. (Ask for one or two volunteers to help.) Work together as a whole group to answer the following questions. Write the questions and focus prompts on a blackboard or newsprint.

Questions one through four should be answered in a round-robin format, with one student answering one question. Try to include students who may not always participate. (If answers for questions three and four are imprecise or need further elaboration, ask if anyone has anything to add.)

1. Who are the main characters in this story?

2. What is the problem or challenge they face?

3. How does Allison handle the problem?

4. What happened then?

The following focus prompt should be answered in an exhaustive format. Continue letting students give responses until no new answers are given.

5. Allison learned that she should…

For questions six and seven, allow all students an opportunity to share their answers, regardless of whether or not the answers are original.

6. When would it be important in your life to… [insert answer from previous statement]?

7. One thing that might make doing this difficult is…

Finally, ask students to write their responses to the following prompt in their Player Portfolios.

8. One specific way I might support my teammates who always want to play fair is…

Cool-down

- *R&R Huddle* (5 min.)

- **Recap** one or two key points that arose during the discussion.

- *Reconnect* by asking volunteers to briefly share what they wrote for question number eight.

- *Reset* and transition to the next lesson.

Session 32: **Fair Play Relay** **Lessons from the Field**	

Warm-up
  Begin the PLUS Cycle (5 min.)
    • Session Overview
    • Following Up on Fair Play
Activity
  Lessons from the Field (25-30 min.)
    • Sports Activity
	Cool-down
	  Continue the PLUS Cycle (5-10 min.)
	    • Reflection
	    • Goal-setting
	Materials
	  Sports Equipment

Warm-up

Following Up on Fair Play (5 min.)

Ask students to think about the previous lesson. What can they do today to bring the Lessons from Literature into their work together in the sports activity?

Activity

Lessons from the Field
Sports Activity

Block I: Getting Started (5 min.)

Stand together in a circle for all *Getting Started* activities (except for jogging). Have players partner up, with one player doing the activity and the partner keeping count and giving encouragement. Be sure that players have their Portfolios handy so that they can record their progress. Players will try to improve upon their Past Personal Best (PPB) by achieving their Future Best Goal (FBG) and by tracking progress toward that goal in their Player Portfolios.

Encourage players to clap for and cheer on their teammates to create an enthusiastic environment. You also may choose to include music.

Pick from the options below, making sure to include a cardio and a stretching warm-up.

- **Measure resting heart rate (RHR)** — Spend a few minutes showing players how to find their pulses, either on their necks or wrists. Explain that you will be giving them a few seconds to count how many times their hearts beat. Take a moment to allow the players to sit quietly on the floor and find their pulses. Give them 30 seconds to count their heartbeats.

- **Record, check in and set goals** — Allow a couple of minutes for players to record their RHRs in their Player Portfolios.

- **Jog (2-3 min.)** — This can be done as a lap or in place as a circle.

- **Stretch (2-3 min.)** — Be sure to include stretches for the major muscle groups.

- **Strength/Endurance (1 min.)** — On this first day, players will set baseline numbers for the four Strength/Endurance activities (push-ups, sit-ups, lunges, calf raises), but usually, you will only choose one or two. They will work in pairs. One member of the pair will have 30 seconds to do as many of the activities as they can. Their partner will cheer them on and count for them.

- **Jump Rope (4 min.)** — Again, players will work in pairs, with one person jumping and the other person counting and cheering. They should have three to four sets of 30-45 seconds of jumping rope.

- **Track personal progress** — Have players record their totals for steps five and six in their Player Portfolios. These totals will represent their baseline achievements, or their Past Personal Bests (PPB). Each day, players will check their progress from the previous session and will set a Future Personal Best Goal (FBG) to work toward for next time. Be sure to remind them about setting realistic goals (for example, adding one or two to their baseline, as opposed to 10).

Block II: Structured Play (30 min.)

Skill Play (10 min.)

Choose one or two of the following activities to play today. You can refer back to the *Physical Activities Description Appendix* for instructions on how to run the activities. Encourage players to cheer for each other, and include music if you wish.

- Circle Bonanza

- Backward Walk/Run Relay

- Shuttle Run Relay

- Bowling

- Standing Broad Jump

Sport Play (20 min.)

As a group, decide which sport you want to play today. Select from the sport list contained in the *Sports List Appendix*. Be sure to periodically review with the group the Physical Activities Recommendations for Sport from Chapter Six.

Cool-down

If time permits, close the day with a few minutes of stretching while conducting the following R&R Huddle.

- **Recap** one or two key moments from the Lessons from the Field.

- **Reconnect** players back to the theme unit.

- **Reset** and transition players to the Cool-down, Reflection time.

  OR

- **Reflection**

Use this time to highlight teachable moments you observed during the day and to give players an opportunity to share their experiences about Sports PLUS during the day. The following questions can serve as a guide:

- What did you like about today?

- What did you learn today?

- What are some ways you showed fair play today?

- How can we better show fair play next time?

Goal-setting

Use this time to track the group's progress toward the team goals you set last time and to start the players thinking about one or two individual goals related to Fair Play they would like to set during the next session.

Session 32: Fair Play Relay Lessons from Adventure	
Warm-up Begin the PLUS Cycle (5 min.) • Session Overview • Trust Walk **Activity** Lessons from Adventure (25-30 min.) • Fair Play Relay	**Cool-down** Continue the PLUS Cycle (5-10 min.) • Reflection • Contract Renewal **Materials** 4 large flip charts or sheets of poster paper hung around the room with the following headings on them— two that read "Fair Play in Sports," and two that read "Fair Play in Life;" different colored markers at each station; cones or other objects to create a simple obstacle course

Warm-up

Trust Walk

Setup

This activity challenges pairs to work together and to trust each other. You will need some space for players to walk around in. A classroom with desks will work well, but if you are in an open area, try setting up some cones or other objects for players to maneuver around. Each pair will need to follow a certain path. You may assign different routes for each pair. For example, "Johnny and Mary will go to the water fountain and back. Billy and Susie will walk around the desks." Or you can let the leader choose where to go if you feel that players can handle this responsibility.

Play

1. Ask players to partner up explaining that one person in each pair will be the leader and one person will be the follower. (The roles will switch in the next round.) Remind players that they each have a responsibility to take care of their teammates and that it is important that they take this responsibility seriously.

2. The follower must keep his or her eyes closed throughout the activity, while the leader must guide the sightless partner around the course. Leaders must walk with their partners, giving them verbal direction, but they may not touch their partners.

3. This activity challenges players to give good directions and to follow directions well. It may be difficult for followers to keep their eyes closed.

4. After each person has had a chance to play both roles, bring the group back together in a circle to talk about some of the challenges that came up during this activity. You may use some of the following questions as a guide:

    • What do you think was the hardest thing about being a follower? About being a leader?

- When you were a follower, did you open your eyes or feel tempted to open your eyes? Why do you think this was?

- Do you think this activity would have been easier or harder if we had done it on the first day of the program? Why do you think that is?

- Give an example of responsible behavior in this activity. Do you

Activity

Lessons from Adventure
Fair Play Relay
(see Player Portfolio)

Setup

Before you begin, hang the four large pieces of poster or art paper in different parts of the room. Make sure the players will be able to reach the paper. While there are four posters, there are only two statements. This is simply to speed up the activity and allow players time to be directly involved. Each team only visits two different posters. Set up the cones or other objects so that players will have a clear path to run around.

Divide the group into four smaller groups.

Play

1. Assign each team to one of the posters.

2. Each team will be given three to five minutes to write as many responses as they can to complete the phrase "Fair Play in Sports sounds like or looks like..." or "Fair Play in Life looks like or sounds like..."

3. The team must work as a relay team—each person in the team has a turn with the marker and writes something on the poster. After writing a statement, each player must run around a cone before handing off the marker to a teammate. The team repeats the relay pattern until the time is up. Teammates can help each other if someone gets stuck.

4. After five minutes or so, yell "Switch!" at which point each team moves to a different poster with a different statement.

Discussion

Bring the players back together as a large group. Hang the posters in a place where everyone can see them. Spend some time discussing each poster. Create two new posters as a whole group with simple statements for what the group sees as the most important ideas about fair play in the program. Finally, if time permits, allow the players an opportunity to decorate the posters.

Leave these posters hanging in the after-school space for the remainder of the program.

- **R&R Huddle** (5 minutes)

- **Recap** by highlighting one or two key discussion points.

- **Reconnect** with one or two of the following focus prompts: Fair Play is important because…

- **Reset** and transition to the next activity.

Cool-down

Cool-down Ritual

Player Contract Renewal

This is a good time to revisit the player contract that the players first developed in the Teamwork Unit.

Have players take their contracts out of their portfolios. The next value on the list is Fair Play. Spend some time in a whole group discussion reviewing what the group knows so far about fair play and how it exists in their group. Refer to the posters created during this session. This would also be a good time for players to offer any examples they noticed of the values—Teamwork, Respect, Responsibility, and Fair Play—working together.

Move the discussion into what each player can do to play fair. The following discussion questions are intended as suggestions to start and guide this discussion:

- What do you think fair play means?

- Can anyone give an example of playing fair from something they have seen in this group? At school? At home? In your neighborhood?

- Why is fair play important to our group?

- What can each of us commit to in order to maintain a fair play group environment?

Once you think the group has a good understanding of why fair play is important and how we can all be fair to our teammates, have a Player Contract Signing Ceremony. Remind players that by signing the Fair Play line on their contract, they are making a commitment to themselves and their teammates.

Session 33:
Make It, Take It

Overview

Instructor's Notes: *Be sure to review this set of activities before starting this Sports PLUS Session. Directions for how to run each activity are provided, but it is important that you become familiar with them so that you may more effectively lead the group.*

During group discussions, be sure to record all thoughts and ideas on a blackboard or newsprint. Remember that when players are working in their Player Portfolios, spelling, grammar, and penmanship are, relatively speaking, unimportant, so don't dwell on those details or you risk making Sports PLUS into MoreSchool.

The opening activity, the *Quote of the Week,* offers a simple, direct maxim that players can incorporate into their decision-making process. The *You Make the Call* activity challenges players' application of fairness in real life situations. Next, *Slot Machine* challenges three groups to work together toward success. In addition to bringing up important topics, such as working together for the good of the whole team and respecting the team goal over individual accomplishments, this activity challenges players to create a symbol to represent their understanding of Fair Play.

Session 33:
Make It Take It
Lessons from Literature

Warm-up	**Cool-down**
Begin the PLUS Cycle (10-15 min.)	Continue the PLUS Cycle (5-10 min.)
• Session Overview	
• Quote of the Week	• Reflection
Activity	**Materials**
Lessons from Literature (25-30 min.)	Copies of *Make It, Take It*
• You Make the Call — *Make It, Take It*	

Warup

Quote of the Week

(see Player Portfolio)

Honesty is the best policy.

– Maxim

Follow the five steps of the Quote of the Week Format (See the *Getting Started* chapter for additional explanation):

1. **Write the Quote of the Week:** Bring the group together into a circle, and write the Quote on the blackboard.

2. **Think about the Quote as a group:** Spend two or three minutes talking with the students about what they think the quote means. Ask students to share answers to the group for the following questions:

   • Why is honesty the best policy?

   • How is honesty related to fair play?

   • Why is honesty important for fair play?

3. **Pair up to talk about the Quote:** Have students separate into pairs. Ask them to spend about five minutes discussing the following questions with their partners. Explain that they will

be sharing their answers with the whole group, so they may choose to write them in their Player Portfolios. (Be sure to walk around the groups, listen, and offer help where needed.):

- Tell your partner about a time when being honest was difficult for you? What made being honest difficult?

- One thing that makes being honest hard is…

- One thing that might help us to be honest is…

4. **Share answers with the whole group:** Come together as a large group and share the answers from each of the pair groups. Everyone who wants to should have an opportunity to share their answers.

5. **Reflect individually about the Quote:** Take two or three minutes for students to reflect individually by writing a response to the following Journal Question in their Player Portfolios:

- The next time you play your favorite sport, one way you can demonstrate that you believe "honesty is the best policy" is by…

Activity

Lessons from Literature
Sports Short
Make It, Take It
(see Player Portfolio)

Key Concepts

- Problem-solving
- Generating Alternatives
- Fairness

Setup

Bring the group together to sit in a circle. If there is time, use one or two of the following questions to help set the tone before reading the story:

"All games have rules to make sure that neither side has an unfair advantage. But these rules usually do not say anything about the skill level of one team over another."

- Have you ever been in a game or situation where one team had a big advantage over the other because they were much better players?

- Was the game as much fun for the team who was losing?

- What are some things you could do in a situation like that to make the game fairer for everyone?

Read the story aloud and with enthusiasm to the whole group.

Make It, Take It

On Saturday morning, a group of six kids are shooting baskets at the basketball courts at Paintville Park. Rick is a fifth grader at the Roosevelt School where all the kids go and he is a good basketball player. He has been showing off his dribbling skills—behind his back, between his legs, switching hands. He doesn't mean to be a show-off, but he is not a very good student and likes the attention that his basketball skills give him. His sister Felicia, a sixth grader, is also a very good basketball player and often teams up with Rick to play two-on-two. But Felicia is not a show-off at all. In fact, she seems almost embarrassed by her skills. She also happens to be a top student.

Rick suggests that they form teams and play three-on-three. The other kids agree and Rick, Felicia and Stan form one team, while Tim, Henry and Lois form the other. Rick suggests that they play "Make It, Take It." This means that every time you score, your team gets the ball back on offense. They also decide to play to eleven by ones.

Rick and Tim shoot for first possession. Rick makes the shot and his team gets the ball first. Rick's team dominates the game. Rick is dribbling and passing well and he keeps feeding the ball inside to Felicia, who makes every shot. Stan is hot from the outside. Felicia fakes a couple of jumpers, passing to a wide-open Stan. Rick's team has yet to play defense, and they quickly build up an eight to nothing lead.

Tim and his teammates are getting more and more frustrated.

Lois finally grabs the ball and shouts, "Our team never gets the ball."

Stan says in return, "It's not our fault that your team can't stop us!"

"I'm not playing anymore. This is no fun," Henry remarks.

"I'm not either," echoes Lois. "This stinks."

"You guys are just sore losers," says Rick.

"You know Rick, it really doesn't seem very fair," Felicia says kind of quietly. "Maybe there's some way we can change the rules or switch teams to make it a more even game." All the other kids look at Felicia, wondering what she has in mind

---

Discussion Questions:

Separate the students into groups by having them count off by threes (or fours depending on the group size). Spend a couple of minutes distributing students' Player Portfolios and pencils. Ask one or two volunteers to help.

Using their Player Portfolios, have students discuss and write answers to the following questions in their small groups. It is important to remember that spelling, grammar, and penmanship are NOT important during this activity.

1. Who are the main characters in this story?

2. What is the main problem these characters face?

3. What is Felicia's suggestion for solving the problem?

4. Felicia suggests one way to solve the problem so that no one feels left out. What are some other ways that the situation might be handled?

5. What would happen if the situation were handled in that way?

    •   How would Felicia feel?

    •   How would Rick feel?

    •   How would Tim and Lois feel?

6. If you were Felicia, what are two different ways that you might solve the problem?

7. What might make your decision difficult?

8. What would you do if you were Felicia? What about if you were Lois?

Group Share:

- After the small groups have had time to discuss each question, gather the groups together to sit in one large circle.

- Ask each small group to share their suggestions for solving the problem, using answers to number four above. (As suggestions are given, you or a volunteer should write them on poster paper for all to see.)

- Once all of the different solutions have been laid out, spend a few minutes discussing the consequences of each solution, using students' answers to question number five as a guide.

- As a group, choose the best solution (i.e., the most good for the most people).

- Finally, as a group, complete the following two focus prompts on poster paper.

    - One lesson we can learn from this story is that we should be careful not to…

Cool-down

- *R&R Huddle* (5 min.)

- *Recap* one or two key points that arose during the discussion or ask students to respond to one of the following questions:

    - Is it as much fun to beat a team that is easy to beat as it is to beat an opponent that challenges your own skills? Why?

    - Aside from being fair to everyone playing, why would it be important to have teams with equal skill levels?

    - Is it easier to improve your skills by playing an easy

opponent or by playing an opponent who is better than you? Why?

- *Reconnect* students back to the theme unit.

- *Reset* and get ready for the next lesson.

Session 33: Make It Take It Lessons from the Field	
Warm-up Begin the PLUS Cycle (5 min.) • Session Overview • Following Up on Fair Play **Activity** Lessons from the Field (25-30 min.) • Sports Activity	**Cool-down** Continue the PLUS Cycle (5-10 min.) • Reflection • Goal-setting **Materials** Sports Equipment

Warm-up

Following Up on Fair Play (5 min.)

Ask students to think about the previous lesson. What can they do today to bring the Lessons from Literature into their work together in the sports activity?

Activity

Lessons from the Field
Sports Activity

Block I: Getting Started (4 min.)

Stand together in a circle for all *Getting Started* activities (except for jogging). Have players partner up, with one player doing the activity and the partner keeping count and giving encouragement. Be sure that players have their Portfolios handy so that they can record their progress. Players will try to improve upon their Past Personal Best (PPB) by achieving their

Future Best Goal (FBG) and by tracking progress toward that goal in their Player Portfolios.

Encourage players to clap for and cheer on their teammates to create an enthusiastic environment. You also may choose to include music.

Choose from the options below, making sure to include a cardio and a stretching warm-up.

- **Measure resting heart rate (RHR)** — Spend a few minutes showing players how to find their pulses, either on their necks or wrists. Explain that you will be giving them a few seconds to count how many times their hearts beat. Take a moment to allow the players to sit quietly on the floor and find their pulses. Give them 30 seconds to count their heartbeats.

- **Record, check in and set goals** — Allow a couple of minutes for players to record their RHRs in their Player Portfolios.

- **Jog (2-3 min.)** — This can be done as a lap or in place as a circle.

- Stretch (2-3 min.) — Be sure to include stretches for the major muscle groups.

- **Strength/Endurance (1 min.)** — On this first day, players will set baseline numbers for the four Strength/Endurance activities (push-ups, sit-ups, lunges, calf raises), but usually, you will only choose one or two. They will work in pairs. One member of the pair will have 30 seconds to do as many of the activities as they can. Their partner will cheer them on and count for them.

- **Jump Rope (4 min.)** — Again, players will work in pairs, with one person jumping and the other person counting and cheering. They should have three to four sets of 30-45 seconds of jumping rope.

- **Track personal progress** — Have players record their totals for steps five and six in their Player Portfolios. These totals will represent their baseline achievements, or their Past Personal Bests (PPB). Each day, players will check their progress from the previous session and will set a Future Personal Best Goal

(FBG) to work toward for next time. Be sure to remind them about setting realistic goals (for example, adding one or two to their baseline, as opposed to 10).

Block II: Structured Play (30 min.)

Skill Play (10 min.)

Choose one or two of the following activities to play today. You can refer back to the *Physical Activities Description Appendix* for instructions on how to run the activities. Encourage players to cheer for each other, and include music if you wish.

- Long Distance Musical Chairs

- Soft ball throw

- Twister

- Balance Tag

- Ball Bowling

Sport Play (20 min.)

As a group, decide which sport you want to play today. Select from the sport list contained in the *Sports List Appendix*. Be sure to periodically review with the group the Physical Activities Recommendations for Sport from Chapter Six.

Cool-down

If time permits, close the day with a few minutes of stretching while conducting the following R&R Huddle.

- **Recap** one or two key moments from the Lessons from the Field.

- **Reconnect** players back to the theme unit.

- **Reset** and transition players to the Cool-down, Reflection time.

OR

- **Reflection**

Use this time to highlight teachable moments you observed during the day and to give players an opportunity to share their experiences about Sports PLUS during the day. The following questions can serve as a guide:

- What did you like about today?

- What did you learn today?

- What are some ways you showed fair play today?

- How can we better show fair play next time?

Goal-setting

Use this time to track the group's progress toward your chosen team goals and to help players choose individual goals related to *Fair Play*.

Session 33: Make It Take It Lessons from Adventure	

Warm-up
Begin the PLUS Cycle (5 min.)
 	
   • Session Overview
 	
   • ESP
 	
Activity
Lessons from Adventure (25-30 min.)
 	
   • Slot Machine
	Cool-down
	Continue the PLUS Cycle (5-10 min.)
	
	   • Reflection
	
	   • Fair Play Cool-down
	
	Materials
	None

Warm-up

ESP

Setup

Help players to find partners. Have them stand in a circle, next to their partners, while listening to the follow directions. After the activity, ask students why it is important to be on the "same page" with team mates.

Play

1. Create full-body gestures to represent each of the four themes covered so far: teamwork, respect, responsibility and fair play

2. Demonstrate each gesture individually and have students practice the same motions.

3. After you are convinced that students know the four gestures, have them stand back-to-back with their partners. Tell students that they are to think of one of the four gestures. They are to try to read each other's minds…no talking!

4. At the sound of "E-S-P," students are to turn and face each other while displaying one of the four gestures.

5. If students are showing the same gestures, they should celebrate by giving each other a "high five."

6. Do several rounds.

Activity

Lessons from Adventure
Slot Machine

(see Player Portfolio)

This activity offers another opportunity for the group to work together to solve a problem.

This activity can work in a classroom, but using the gym or an outside field affords more options and creativity.

Bring the group together in a circle. Break into three teams of three or more.

Play

1. The name of the game is Slot Machine. Like any slot machine player, the goal is to get three matching pictures.

2. Each team will go to a corner of the room and create a group gesture to represent fair play, drawing on what they have learned about this value in previous sessions.

3. Once each team has a gesture, bring the group back together. Line the teams up in a triangle formation. Ask each team to show their gesture.

4. For the rest of the activity, there will be no talking among teams. The goal of the group is for you (the facilitator) to count to three, say go and have all three teams show the same gesture.

5. Play one round—count to three and see what gesture each team shows. This round helps the group to understand the game. Now, send the teams back to their corners, allowing time for the teams to decide which gesture they will use.

6. Come back together. Count to three, and see what gestures are presented.

7. Repeat this process until all three groups get the same gesture (or the group tires of the game).

R&R Huddle (5 minutes)

This problem can be more difficult than it appears:

1. The teams cannot speak to each other, yet they are all trying to do the same thing. They need to develop a system for non-verbal communication.

2. Sometimes one team forgets that the group's goal is to have everyone show the same gesture. This group may become unbending in showing any gesture other than their own (this can be OK if the rest of the teams use this group's gesture, but

this doesn't always happen). If one team makes it impossible for the group as a whole to achieve its goal, stop the game and use this as a discussion topic: What responsibility does each small group have to the larger group in accomplishing its goal? What happens when a small group of people are not helping a team achieve its goal?

- **Recap** using the following focus prompt: The best part of the activity was…

- **Reconnect** with the following sentence: I learned that…

- **Reset** and transition to the next activity.

Cool-down

Cool-down Ritual
Fair Play Cool-down

Bring the group together and ask for volunteers to describe a time when they experienced either fair play or unfair play. Let other players ask questions or offer suggestions about ways to improve situations like those described.

Session 34:
The Rules of the Game

Overview

Instructor's Notes: *Be sure to review this set of activities before starting this Sports PLUS Session. Directions for how to run each activity are provided, but it is important that you become familiar with them so that you may more effectively lead the group.*

During group discussions, be sure to record all thoughts and ideas on a blackboard or newsprint. Remember that when players are working in their

Player Portfolios, spelling, grammar, and penmanship are, relatively speaking, unimportant, so don't dwell on those details or you risk making Sports PLUS into MoreSchool.

The *You Make the Call* activity includes a short story that raises questions about peer pressure and how to handle the potential conflict between playing hard and demonstrating sportsmanship. This session's team-building activity encourages players' imaginations by asking them to create a game of their own with corresponding rules. It also provides them with a direct opportunity to shape their environment. Anonymous Put-ups closes the events of the day by asking players to share "put-ups" with one another, giving everyone an opportunity to feel known, needed, and cared about.

Session 34: **The Rules of the Game** **Lessons from Literature** 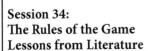	

Warm-up
   Begin the PLUS Cycle (10-15 min.)
 	
   • Session Overview
 	
   • Quote of the Week
Activity
   Lessons from Literature (25-30 min.)
 	
   • You Make the Call — *The Untied Shoe*
	Cool-down
	   Continue the PLUS Cycle (5-10 min.)
	
	   • Reflection
	Materials
	   Copies of *The Untied Shoe*

Warm-up

Quote of the Week
(see Player Portfolio)

It doesn't matter if you win or lose, it's how you play the game.
                                                                    – Unknown

Follow the five steps of the Quote of the Week Format (See the *Getting Started* chapter for additional explanation):

1. **Write the Quote of the Week:** Bring the group together into a circle, and write the Quote on the blackboard.

2. **Think about the Quote as a group:** Spend two or three minutes talking with the students about what they think the quote means. Ask students to share answers to the group for the following question:

   • Do you agree with this saying

3. **Pair up to talk about the Quote:** Have students separate into pairs. Ask them to spend about five minutes discussing the following questions with their partners. Explain that they will be sharing their answers with the whole group, so they may choose to write their answers in their Player Portfolios. (Be sure to walk around the groups, listen, and offer help where needed.):

   • What does "how you play the game" have to do with fair play?

   • Think of a specific example of when "how you play the game" might be more important than winning. Your example could be from a story we have read or from your own experience.

4. **Share answers with the whole group:** Come together as a large group and share the answers from each of the pair groups. Everyone who wants to should have an opportunity to share their answers.

5. **Reflect individually about the Quote:** Take two or three minutes for students to reflect individually by writing a response to the following Journal Question in their Player Portfolios:

   • Do you think everyone in this Sports PLUS group agrees with this quote? Why or why not?

Activity

Lessons from Literature
Sports Short
Make It, Take It
(see Player Portfolio)

Key Concepts

- Sportsmanship
- Playing Hard
- Playing Fiar
- Peer Pressure

Setup

Bring the group together to sit in a circle. If there is time, use one or two of the following questions to help set the tone before reading the story:

"We've talked a lot about Fair Play, about the rules of the game and the rules of conduct. The stories we have read so far have been pretty clear— someone broke the rules and played unfairly. But sometimes it is not so easy to decide whether something was fair or not."

- Can you think of a time when it was difficult to tell what was fair play and what wasn't?

The Story

Read the story aloud and with enthusiasm to the whole group.

The United Shoe

It is Saturday morning at the Eliot High School gym and the fifth grade basketball league has two games going on side by side. It is a noisy place... the sound of rubber-soled basketball shoes slapping the wooden floor mixes with whistles, shouts of "Over here, I'm open!" "Switch!" "You take him!", coaches yelling encouragement and instructions and parents cheering.

In one game, the score is tied in the last quarter. The Warriors are playing the Jazz in their second meeting of the season and the score has been close the whole game. Their first meeting ended in a two-point win for the Jazz.

The Jazz have the ball and, on a great pick and roll with the center and point guard, they go ahead by one basket. Avery, the Warriors' point guard and one of the best ball handlers on the team, takes the in-bound pass from his teammate Eric.

As Avery starts up the court, he sees Leo, one of the forwards on the Jazz, squatting down and frantically trying to tie his shoe. Avery slows up his dribbling, waiting for Leo to finish. Some of the other players shout for him to run up the court before Leo can get back into the play, giving the Warriors a brief advantage of five players to four. Even the coach screams from the sideline, "Run! Take advantage of him!"

But Avery remembers other things the coach has been saying all season— to play fair, never do something that goes against the spirit of the game, never take unfair advantage of a situation just to win. Avery thinks of all this in a flash. Watching Leo still struggling with his shoe, he slowly dribbles up court, wondering what to do.

Discussion Questions:

Separate the students into groups by having them count off by 3s (or 4s depending on the group size). Spend a couple of minutes distributing students' Player Portfolios and pencils. Ask one or two volunteers to help.

Using their Player Portfolios, have students discuss and write answers to the following questions in their small groups. It is important to remember that spelling, grammar, and penmanship are NOT important during this activity.

1. Who is the main character in this story?

2. What is the key problem this character faces?

3. What are some possible ways that Avery could handle this situation?

4. What would happen if he took these actions (discuss one by one)

   • How would Avery feel?

   • How would the rest of his team feel?

   • How would Leo feel?

   • How would the other team feel?

5. If you were Avery, what are two different ways you could handle this situation?

6. What might make your decision difficult?

7. If you were Avery, what would you choose to do? What if you were the coach?

Group Share:

- After the small groups have had time to discuss each question, gather them together to sit in one large circle.

- Ask each small group to share their suggestions for solving the problem, using students' answers to number three above. (As suggestions are given, you or a volunteer should write them on poster paper for all to see.)

- Once all the different solutions have been laid out, spend a few minutes discussing the con sequences of each solution, using students' answers to question number four as a guide.

- As a group, choose the best solution (i.e., the most good for the most people).

- Finally, as a group, complete the following two focus prompts on poster paper.

    - One thing we can take from this story is that we should….

    - We should all be careful not to….

Cool-down

- *R&R Huddle* (5 min.)

- *Recap* with one or two key points from the previous discussion.

- *Reconnect* by highlighting one or two responses to the two focus prompts above.

- *Reset* and get ready for the next lesson.

Session 34: The Rules of the Game Lessons from the Field	

Warm-up
Begin the PLUS Cycle (5 min.)
  • Session Overview
  • Following Up on Fair Play
Activity
Lessons from the Field (25-30 min.)
  • Sports Activity
	Cool-down
	Continue the PLUS Cycle (5-10 min.)
	  • Reflection
	  • Goal-setting
	Materials
	Sports Equipment

Warm-up

Following Through on Fair Play (5 min.)

Ask students to think about the previous lesson. What can they do today to bring Lessons from Literature into their work together in the sports activity?

Activity

Lessons from the Field
Sports Activity

Block I: Getting Started (5 min.)

Stand together in a circle for all *Getting Started* activities (except for jogging). Have players partner up, with one player doing the activity and the partner keeping count and giving encouragement. Be sure that players have their Portfolios handy so that they can record their progress. Players will try to improve upon their Past Personal Best (PPB) by achieving their Future Best Goal (FBG) and by tracking progress toward that goal in their Player Portfolios.

Encourage players to clap for and cheer on their teammates to create an enthusiastic environment. You also may choose to include music.

Choose from the options below, making sure to include a cardio and a stretching warm-up.

- **Measure resting heart rate (RHR)** — Spend a few minutes showing players how to find their pulses, either on their necks or wrists. Explain that you will be giving them a few seconds to count how many times their hearts beat. Take a moment to allow the players to sit quietly on the floor and find their pulses. Give them 30 seconds to count their heartbeats.

- **Record, check in and set goals** — Allow a couple of minutes for players to record their RHRs in their Player Portfolios.

- **Jog (2-3 min.)** — This can be done as a lap or in place as a circle.

- **Stretch (2-3 min.)** — Be sure to include stretches for the major muscle groups.

- **Strength/Endurance (1 min.)** — On this first day, players will set baseline numbers for the four Strength/Endurance activities (push-ups, sit-ups, lunges, calf raises), but usually, you will only choose one or two. They will work in pairs. One member of the pair will have 30 seconds to do as many of the activities as they can. Their partner will cheer them on and count for them.

- **Jump Rope (4 min.)** — Again, players will work in pairs, with one person jumping and the other person counting and cheering. They should have three to four sets of 30-45 seconds of jumping rope.

- **Track personal progress** — Have players record their totals for steps five and six in their Player Portfolios. These totals will represent their baseline achievements, or their Past Personal Bests (PPB). Each day, players will check their progress from the previous session and will set a Future Personal Best Goal (FBG) to work toward for next time. Be sure to remind them about setting realistic goals (for example, adding one or two to their baseline, as opposed to 10).

Block II: Structured Play (30 min.)

Skill Play (10 min.)

Choose one or two of the following activities to play today. You can refer back to the *Physical Activities Description Appendix* for instructions on how to run the activities. Encourage players to cheer for each other, and include music if you wish.

- Jump Rope Relay

- Slides

- Star Jumps

- Dribble Relay

- Hula Hoop Challenge Course

Sport Play (20 min.)

As a group, decide which sport you want to play today. Select from the sport list contained in the *Sports List Appendix*. Be sure to periodically review with the group the Physical Activities Recommendations for Sport from Chapter Six.

Cool-down

If time permits, close the day with a few minutes of stretching while conducting the following R&R Huddle.

- **Recap** one or two key moments from the Lessons from the Field.

- **Reconnect** players back to the theme unit.

- **Reset** and transition players to the Cool-down, Reflection time.

    OR

- **Reflection**

Use this time to highlight teachable moments you observed during the day and to give players an opportunity to share their experiences about Sports PLUS during the day. The following questions can serve as a guide:

- What did you like about today?

- What did you learn today?

- What are some ways you showed fair play today?

- How can we better show fair play next time?

- In what ways did your teammates show fair play today?

Goal-setting

Use this time to help players track progress toward their individually chosen goals, as well as toward team goals. As goals from earlier sessions are reached, guide players in setting additional individual and team goals related to *Fair Play*.

Session 34: **Fair Play Relay** **Lessons from Adventure**	

Warm-up
Begin the PLUS Cycle (5 min.)
  • Session Overview
  • Shoe Tie
Activity
Lessons from Adventure (25-30 min.)
  • The Game Game
	Cool-down
	Continue the PLUS Cycle (5-10 min.)
	  • Reflection
	  • Anonymous Put-Ups
	Materials
	Post paper, markers

Warm-up

Shoe Tie

Help each student find a partner. At least one person in each partnership needs to have shoes with laces. Explain to students that in this activity they will get to practice fair play and teamwork. Ask students to recall the short story, The Untied Shoe.

Play

1. With their partner, ask students to untie one of the four shoes belonging to the two of them.

2. Each person chooses one of their two hands. This is the only hand they can use in this activity.

3. Using one hand from each of the partners, ask students to attempt to tie the shoe.

4. Afterwards, ask students what helped them be successful at tying the shoe? What made it challenging?

Activity

Lessons from Adventure

The Game Game

This activity allows players to use their imaginations to create a game of their own and a poster that visually presents the game and its rules for play. You should use the games they invent as your sports component for today and the next few sessions so that all the groups have the opportunity to present and test them.

Keep your options open for using equipment. Let groups use anything available in your sports lockers or any other equipment available at your site.

Setup

Share with the group that they will be working in small teams to create their own new games. Have a discussion about the kinds of rules that make games fair, safe, and fun.

If you think the group can handle it, allow them to create their own teams. (If you think this may lead to some players feeling left out, create the groups yourself.)

Play

Once the small teams (three to five players) are set, give the following rules:

1. You will be creating a game for 15 people (or use the number of people in the group).

2. The game can have two teams competing against each other, more than two teams, or it can be a cooperative game.

3. The game will use any available equipment.

4. The game should have either a time limit or be played to a set number of points.

5. The game can be a running or walking type game.

6. Each team will also create a poster that in words and pictures explains their game and its rules of play.

7. Allow the groups 20 minutes to create their games. You will need to circulate among the groups. Encourage the students to be creative — the game could include rules about passing, rules about scoring, rules about the number of players who play at a time, etc.

8. Give each a group a chance to introduce and run their game during the Lessons from the Field. Take a break at the end of each game to talk about how the rules affected the play, whether the game was fun or not, and how the rules might be changed to make it better or more fair.

- ***R&R Huddle*** (5 minutes)

- ***Recap*** by asking players what kinds of rules they thought were important to include in their games.

- ***Reconnect*** the discussion to the Fair Play theme unit.

- ***Reset*** and transition to the next activity.

Cool-down

Cool-down Ritual

Anonymous Put-ups

Try this fun way for the group to offer anonymous put-ups to itself. Have players take out a piece of paper. Each player should write, in pen, a message to the group that describes why they are a good team, or how they show respect or responsibility. Give the group a few minutes to write, then have the players scrunch up their papers into a tight ball. On the count of three, the group, standing close together, throws the balls of paper into the air. Everyone tries to catch one, preferably not the one they tossed. Have players open their balled-up papers and ask for volunteers to decipher and read the wrinkly messages.

Session 35:
Friendly Rivals

Overview

> **Instructor's Notes:** *Be sure to review this set of activities before starting this Sports PLUS Session. Directions for how to run each activity are provided, but it is important that you become familiar with them so that you may more effectively lead the group.*
>
> *During group discussions, be sure to record all thoughts and ideas on a blackboard or newsprint. Remember that when players are working in their Player Portfolios, spelling, grammar, and penmanship are, relatively speaking, unimportant, so don't dwell on those details or you risk making Sports PLUS into MoreSchool.*

This session's *Quote of the Week* provides another useful maxim that students can learn to rely upon when facing difficult decisions. The *Theme Book* reading emphasizes the importance of playing fair. The team-building activity includes a fun relay race that requires fair play to ensure that neither team gains an unfair advantage. *Mental Video* offers students the chance to reflect on their recent experiences in the program and to relate those experiences to the rest of the group.

Session 35: **Friendly Rivals** **Lessons from Literature**	
Warm-up Begin the PLUS Cycle (10-15 min.) • Session Overview • Quote of the Week **Activity** Lessons from Literature (25-30 min.) • Theme Book — *The Greatest Sports Stories Never Told: The Friendly Rival*	**Cool-down** Continue the PLUS Cycle (5-10 min.) • Reflection **Materials** Copies of *The Greatest Sports Stories Never Told: The Friendly Rival*

Warm-up

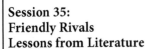

Quote of the Week
(see Player Portfolio)

It is better to be defeated on principle than to win on lies.
                                                    – Arthur Calwell

---

Overview

Instructor's Notes: You may wish to take time to explain and talk about the word "principle." Suggest that the students come up with synonyms for "principle," e.g. integrity, the right thing to do, honesty, not cheating, playing fairly.

Follow the five steps of the Quote of the Week Format (See the *Getting Started* chapter for additional explanation):

1. **Write the Quote of the Week:** Bring the group together into a circle, and write the Quote on the blackboard.

2. **Think about the Quote as a group:** Spend two or three minutes talking with the students about what they think the quote means. Next ask students to share answers to the group for the following questions:

   - What does it mean to be "defeated on principle?" How is this related to "playing fairly?"

   - What does it mean to "win on lies?" How is this related to "playing fairly?"

   - What is Arthur Calwell telling us about fair play?

3. **Pair up to talk about the Quote:** Have students separate into pairs. Ask them to spend about five minutes discussing the following questions with their partners. Explain that they will be sharing their answers with the whole group, so they may choose to write their answers in their Player Portfolios. (Be sure to walk around the groups, listen, and offer help where needed.):

   - What can happen to us when we "win on lies?"

   - Why is it important to win by playing fairly?

   - It can be hard to play by the rules and lose when you have a chance to not play fairly and win? What do you think makes this hard?

   - How can we help each other to play fairly?

4. **Share answers with the whole group:** Come together as a large group and share the answers from each of the pair groups. Everyone who wants to should have an opportunity to share their answers.

5. **Reflect individually about the Quote:** Take two or three minutes for students to reflect individually by writing a response to the following Journal Question in their Player Portfolios:

   • Sometimes the hardest thing to do isn't scoring more points or running faster than your opponent, but playing on principle (playing fairly). Write something that you can use to remind you and your teammates that it is always better to play on principle (play fair) than to win on lies (cheat).

Activity

Lessons from Literature
Theme Book
The Greatest Sports Stories Never Told:
The Friendly Rivals
(see Player Portfolio)

The Friendly Rival

by Bruce Nash and Allan Zullo

Track star Jesse Owens stared in disbelief at the flag signaling that he had fouled in his long jump attempt. It was his second miss, leaving the world-record holder only one more chance to qualify for the finals in the 1936 Olympics.

The distance was just 23 feet, 5 1/5 inches. Owens' world-record jump earlier that year was much longer – 26 feet, 8 1/4 inches. But in the Olympic preliminaries, he had failed twice at the shorter distance. One more miss and Owens would be eliminated from the long jump.

Then, just when things seemed darkest, help came from an unexpected source – his main competitor! He was Germany's Lutz Long, the only jumper in the field with a shot at beating Owens.

The dramatic meeting of the African-American and the German hero is one of the great untold stories of the 1936 Olympics held in Berlin, Germany. Back then, German dictator Adolf Hitler and his followers disliked blacks and believed that whites were superior. Hitler hoped that the Berlin Games would prove that white athletes were better than nonwhites.

But Owens, a student from Ohio State, proved the madman wrong. Jesse stunned Hitler and his Nazi followers by winning four gold medals in the 1936 Olympics. But without Lutz Long's unselfish sportsmanship, Owens would never have won a gold medal for the long jump.

Owens had entered the 200-meter race and the long jump even though both events were being held at about the same time. He started the day by running two qualifying heats for the 200-meter race. Still in his sweats, Owens then jogged to the infield section where the long-jump competition was just getting underway.

Because he was late in arriving, Owens was unaware that competitive jumping had already started. He took a practice run down the runway and half-heartedly leaped into the pit. To his shock, the officials in charge said he fouled and counted his warm-up jump as his first of three attempts to qualify.

Rattled by the officials' decision, and still winded from the 200-meter sprints he had just run, Owens tried too hard on his second attempt. He misjudged the takeoff spot – and fouled again! He was now one jump away from being eliminated in his best event.

That's when a tall, blond German tapped Owens on the shoulder and introduced himself, in English, as Lutz Long – the German long jumper who had already qualified for the afternoon finals. The black son of sharecroppers and the white German athlete chatted for a few minutes. Long, who didn't believe in Hitler's absurd theories on white superiority, then offered to help Owens.

"Something must be bothering you," Long told him. "You should be able to qualify with your eyes closed."

Owens explained that he hadn't known his first jump counted as a qualifying attempt and, in his eagerness to make up for the mistake, he overcompensated and missed his takeoff point on his second try.

"Since the distance you need to qualify isn't difficult, make a mark about a foot before you reach the foul line," Long told Jesse. "Use that as your jump-off point. That way you won't foul."

Owens thanked his rival. Jesse then dug a mark with his foot in the grass next to the runway about a foot short of the foul line. Minutes later, he soared into his third and final jump – and qualified by more than two feet.

But the drama wasn't over.

That afternoon, the American and the German dueled in a classic Olympic showdown for the long-jump gold medal.

Owens' first jump set an Olympic record of 25 feet, 5 1/5 inches. Then he bettered that mark with a leap of 25 feet, 10 inches. But Long responded to the challenge. On his next-to-last attempt, he thrilled thousands of fellow Germans in the huge stadium by matching Owens' record-setting jump.

Now it was Owens' turn. The American champion answered with another record-smashing leap, this time 26 feet, 3 3/4 inches. Long needed a superhuman last effort. Trying to put everything into his jump, Long overran the board and fouled. Jesse Owens had won the gold medal!

Owens still had another jump coming. He was so pumped up that he leaped 26 feet, 5 1/4 inches, breaking the Olympic record for the third time in three jumps.

With a scowling Adolf Hitler watching grimly from his box, the first person to throw his arms around Owens and congratulate him was Lutz Long.

Years later, Jesse recalled that moment when the two Olympic heroes stood arm in arm as friends: "You could melt down all the medals and cups I have and they wouldn't match the 24-carat friendship I felt for Lutz Long at that moment."

Long and Owens became good friends and wrote to each other even during World War II when Lutz was a lieutenant in the German army. In one battlefield letter to Owens in 1943, Long wrote, "I hope we can always remain best of friends despite the differences between our countries." It was the last letter Owens ever received from Lutz. Just days after it was written, Owen's good friend and track rival was killed in battle.

Owens stayed in touch with Long's family, and several years after the war, he received a touching letter from Lutz's son, Peter, who was now 22 years old. In his letter, Peter said he was getting married. "Even though my father can't be here to be my best man, I know who he would want in his place. He would want someone that he and his entire family admired and respected. He would want you to take his place. And I do, too."

So Jesse Owens flew to the wedding in Germany and proudly stood at the side of the son of Lutz Long – a great friend and Olympic athlete who placed sportsmanship ahead of winning.

(Used with Permission from Nash, Bruce & Allan Zullo. *The Greatest Sports Stories Never Told.* New York: Simon & Schuster, 1993.)

Setup

Ask students if they have ever made friends with a player from another team? How did that friendship come about? Why was/is it important to you?

The Story

Read the story aloud and with enthusiasm to the whole group.

Discussion Questions:

Spend a couple of minutes distributing students' Player Portfolios and pencils. (Ask for one or two volunteers to help.) Write the questions and focus prompts on a blackboard or newsprint.

Work together as a whole group to answer the following questions:

Questions one through four should be answered in a round-robin format, with one student answering one question. Try to include students who may not always participate. (If answers for questions three and four are imprecise or need further elaboration, ask if anyone has anything to add.)

1. Who is the main character in this story?

2. What is the problem or challenge he faces?

3. How is Jesse Owens helped with this problem?

4. What happened then?

The following focus prompt should be answered in an exhaustive format. Continue letting students give responses until no new answers are given.

5. One important lesson we learn from this story is that we should...

For questions six and seven, allow all students an opportunity to share their answers, regardless of whether or not the answers are original.

6. When would it be important in your life to... [insert answer from previous statement]?

7. One thing that might make doing this difficult is...

Finally, ask students to write their responses to the following prompt in their Player Portfolios.

8. One specific way I might show fair play by helping an opponent is by...

Cool-down

- *R&R Huddle* (5 min.)

- *Recap* one or two key points that arose during the discussion.

- *Reconnect* by asking volunteers to briefly share what they wrote for question number eight above.

- *Reset* and get ready for the next lesson.

Session 35: Friendly Rivals Lessons from the Field	
Warm-up Begin the PLUS Cycle (5 min.) • Session Overview • Following Up on Fair Play **Activity** Lessons from the Field (25-30 min.) • Sports Activity	**Cool-down** Continue the PLUS Cycle (5-10 min.) • Reflection • Goal-setting **Materials** Sports Equipment

Warm-up

Following Up on Fair Play (5 min.)

Ask students to think about the previous lesson. What can they do today to bring the Lessons from Literature into their work together in the sports activity?

Activity

Lessons from the Field
Sports Activity

Block I: Getting Started (5 min.)

Stand together in a circle for all *Getting Started* activities (except for jogging). Have players partner up, with one player doing the activity and the partner keeping count and giving encouragement. Be sure that players have their Portfolios handy so that they can record their progress. Players will try to improve upon their Past Personal Bests (PPB) by achieving their Future Best Goals (FBG) and by tracking progress toward that goal in their Player Portfolios.

Encourage players to clap for and cheer on their teammates to create an enthusiastic environment. You also may choose to include music.

Pick from the options below, making sure to include a cardio and a stretching warm-up.

- **Measure resting heart rate (RHR)** — Spend a few minutes showing players how to find their pulses, either on their necks or wrists. Explain that you will be giving them a few seconds to count how many times their hearts beat. Take a moment to allow the players to sit quietly on the floor and find their pulses. Give them 30 seconds to count their heartbeats.

- **Record, check in and set goals** — Allow a couple of minutes for players to record their RHRs in their Player Portfolios.

- **Jog (2-3 min.)** — This can be done as a lap or in place as a circle.

- **Stretch (2-3 min.)** — Be sure to include stretches for the major muscle groups.

- **Strength/Endurance (1 min.)** — On this first day, players will set baseline numbers for the four Strength/Endurance activities (push-ups, sit-ups, lunges, calf raises), but usually, you will only choose one or two. They will work in pairs. One member of the pair will have 30 seconds to do as many of the activities as they can. Their partner will cheer them on and count for them.

- **Jump Rope (4 min.)** — Again, players will work in pairs, with one person jumping and the other person counting and cheering. They should have three to four sets of 30-45 seconds of jumping rope.

- **Track personal progress** — Have players record their totals for steps five and six in their Player Portfolios. These totals will represent their baseline achievements, or their Past Personal Bests (PPB). Each day, players will check their progress from the previous session and will set a Future Personal Best Goal (FBG) to work toward for next time. Be sure to remind them about setting realistic goals (for example, adding one or two to their baseline, as opposed to 10).

Block II: Structured Play (30 min.)

Skill Play (10 min.)

Choose one or two of the following activities to play today. You can refer back to the *Physical Activities Description Appendix* for instructions on how to run the activities. Encourage players to cheer for each other, and include music if you wish.

- Over Under, Over Under

- Train

- Wheelbarrow Race

- Gorilla Walk

- Jumping Distances

Sport Play (20 min.)

As a group, decide which sport you want to play today. Select from the sport list contained in the *Sports List Appendix*. Be sure to periodically review with the group the Physical Activities Recommendations for Sport from Chapter Six.

Cool-down

If time permits, close the day with a few minutes of stretching while conducting the following R&R Huddle.

- ***Recap*** one or two key moments from the Lessons from the Field.

- ***Reconnect*** players back to the theme unit.

- ***Reset*** and transition players to the Cool-down, Reflection time.

  OR

- **Reflection**

Use this time to highlight teachable moments you observed during the day and to give players an opportunity to share their experiences about Sports PLUS during the day. The following questions can serve as a guide:

- What did you like about today?

- What did you learn today?

- What are some ways you showed fair play today?

- How can we better show fair play next time?

- In what ways did your teammates show fair play today?

Goal-setting

Use this time to help players track progress toward their individually chosen goals, as well as toward team goals. As goals from earlier sessions are reached, guide players in setting additional individual and team goals related to *Fair Play.*

Session 35:
Friendly Rivals
Lessons from Adventure

Warm-up	Cool-down
Begin the PLUS Cycle (5 min.)	Continue the PLUS Cycle (5-10 min.)
• Session Overview	• Reflection
• Look Up, Look Down	• Mental Video
Activity	**Materials**
Lessons from Adventure (25-30 min.)	2 balls (tennis ball size), 1 quarter or large coin for flipping
• Impulse Relay	

Warm-up

Look Up, Look Down

Tip!

It is always helpful to think of discussion questions before doing an activity. This strategy helps to keep the focus—allowing you to ask questions that lead the players to a point you are trying to make.

Play

1. Gather the group together in a circle.

2. The goal of this game is to be the last one in. Tell the players, "I am going to ask you to look down at your feet. When I say, 'Look up!' look up and directly into the face of someone in the group. If the person you looked at also looks at you, you both are out."

3. Each round continues until there are only two, or no players left in the circle.

4. Play a practice round, then play a few rounds for real. Let players move around to different places in the circle between rounds.

5. After playing a couple of rounds, bring the group back together to form a circle. Briefly discuss players' experiences during the game using the following questions as a guide:

- What did you like about this game? What did you not like?

- Did anyone cheat, or feel tempted to cheat, during the game by not really looking at someone so they wouldn't get out?

- Did anyone feel disappointed when they got out?

- Are there any ways to change this game to make it more fun for everyone?

Activity

Lessons from Adventure
Impulse Relay
(see Player Portfolio)

Bring the group together for this short relay game.

Setup

Separate the group into two teams. Teams should consist of about four to six people. Make more teams if you have a large group. Ask a team to sit on the floor, players side by side and close together. Have another team of an equal number sit opposite them, so that the two groups are facing each other. The two lines should be about two or three feet apart.

Play

1. Place a ball on the floor in front of the person at one end of each line.

2. Ask each team to hold hands. Have the two teams practice sending a hand-squeeze impulse beginning at the end of the line without the ball. When the person at the other end receives the squeeze, he should pick up the ball.

3. To play the game, the two people at the front of the lines will keep their eyes open. The rest of the group will have their eyes shut. No one should be touching the balls. To start the race, flip a coin so that it lands in front of the first two players who have their eyes open. They need to be able to see which way the coin lands because when the coin comes up heads, they start their impulse. The team to pick up the ball first (you'll be the judge) wins that round.

4. Rotate players—the person at the end comes to the beginning and all of the other players slide down. Play until everyone has had a turn at the beginning. The team that won the most rounds "wins"—but who's counting!

Variation

1. Instead of separating the large group into smaller teams, the whole group could be one big team racing against the clock. Team members could take turns keeping time for the group, which would give them a sense of responsibility.

Another possibility is to make this more of a physical activity by having multiple balls or different kinds of sport balls. For example, when the impulse reaches the end of the line, the last person picks up the ball and runs to put it in a basket, or has to dribble a basketball with his or her hands or a soccer ball with his or her feet for a short distance. After completing this task, the player runs to the beginning of the line and starts the next round of impulses.

- *R&R Huddle* (5 minutes)

- *Recap* by asking about players' experiences during the activity (e.g., "Was anyone tempted to cheat by starting the impulse early to catch up?").

- ***Reconnect*** with one or two of the following discussion questions: Do you think it's important to follow the rules in this situation? Why or why not? What would have happened if a team had cheated? Who would have been cheated?

- ***Reset*** and transition to the next activity.

Cool-down

Cool-down Ritual

Mental Video

For the cool-down today try the personal videotape activity. Ask players to sit on the floor (or just stay at their desks if this is easier) and close their eyes. "Imagine that you have a videotape of today's session in your head. Rewind your personal videotape and look for examples of the Sports PLUS values, especially fair play. Pause on those examples and reflect on how each was a positive or negative instance of the value and what you learned from it." If time allows, ask for volunteers to describe one of their examples.

Session 36:
Interacting Values

Overview

> **Instructor's Notes:** *Be sure to review this set of activities before starting this Sports PLUS Session. Directions for how to run each activity are provided, but it is important that you become familiar with them so that you may more effectively lead the group.*

> *During group discussions, be sure to record all thoughts and ideas on a blackboard or newsprint. Remember that when players are working in their Player Portfolios, spelling, grammar, and penmanship are, relatively speaking, unimportant, so don't dwell on those details or you risk making Sports PLUS into MoreSchool.*

The activities during this session provide ample opportunities for players to experience the interaction between the values of teamwork, respect, responsibility, and fair play. Visit the groups as they sort out roles for themselves and look for examples of fair play and the other Sports PLUS values in action. During the *Egg-Drop* activity, players must use creativity and teamwork to accomplish the goal of a group problem-solving activity. The closing *Go-Round* is a short, but effective way for players to reflect critically on the events of the session and to practice good listening skills.

Session 36:
Interacting Values
Lessons from Literature

Warm-up	Cool-down
Begin the PLUS Cycle (10-15 min.)	Continue the PLUS Cycle (5-10 min.)
• Session Overview	
• Quote of the Week	• Reflection
Activity	**Materials**
Lessons from Literature (25-30 min.)	Copies of *The Greatest Sports Stories Never Told: What Price Victory?*
• Theme Book — *The Greatest Sports Stories Never Told: What Price Victory?*	

Warm-up

Quote of the Week
(see Player Portfolio)

If you can react the same way to winning and losing, that's a big accomplishment. That quality is important because it stays with you the rest of your life, and there's going to be a life after tennis.

– Chris Evert

Follow the five steps of the Quote of the Week Format (See the *Getting Started* chapter for additional explanation):

1. **Write the Quote of the Week:** Bring the group together into a circle, and write the Quote on the blackboard.

2. **Think about the Quote as a group:** Spend two or three minutes talking with the students about what they think the quote means. Ask students to share answers to the group for the following question:

   • What does Chris mean, "there's going to be a life after tennis?"

3. **Pair up to talk about the Quote:** Have students separate into pairs. Ask them to spend about five minutes discussing the following questions with their partners. Explain that they will be sharing their answers with the whole group, so they may choose to write their answers in their Player Portfolios. (Be sure to walk around the groups, listen, and offer help where needed.):

   • How does learning about the theme of fair play help you outside of Sports PLUS?

   • Give at least two specific examples.

4. **Share answers with the whole group:** Come together as a large group and share the answers from each of the pair groups. Everyone who wants to should have an opportunity to share their answers.

5. **Reflect individually about the Quote:** Take two or three minutes for students to reflect individually by writing a response to the following Journal Question in their Player Portfolios:

   • What do fair play and sportsmanship have to do with each other?

Activity

Lessons from Literature
Theme Book
The Greatest Sports Stories Never Told
What Price Victory?
(see Player Portfolio)

What Price Victory?

by Bruce Nash and Allan Zullo

Ever since he was old enough to sail, Lawrence Lemieux dreamed of winning an Olympic medal.

At the 1988 Games in Seoul, South Korea, he had his chance. Racing off the coast in stormy seas in his one-man sailboat, Lemieux was in second place, gunning for the lead. Suddenly, he spotted a sailor draped over the hull of an over-turned boat and another sailor bobbing in the water.

Lemieux knew that if he veered off course to help the sailors, there was no chance of finishing first in the race. But he didn't even hesitate. He sacrificed his lifelong dream of winning an Olympic medal to save the lives of two fellow competitors.

Until that dramatic rescue, Lemieux's mind was focused on earning a medal. He was one of dozens of Olympic sailors competing in a series of races in different classes of boats that day.

Struggling against dangerous waves and fierce winds, Lemieux, a native of Edmonton, Alberta, Canada, kept his 14-foot Finn-class boat on course.

Suddenly, out of the corner of his eye, Lemieux spotted a sailor desperately clinging to the hull of a capsized boat. Then he saw another sailor floundering in the water. The strong current and wind were pushing both men and their boat farther out to sea, far from any Olympic safety vessels that patrolled the course. The two helpless sailors were from Singapore and competing in the 470-class race that had started before Lemieux's Finn-class event.

The skipper, Shaw Ciew, was holding onto the hull of his boat for dear life. But he had cut his hand in the accident and was rapidly losing strength from loss of blood. Meanwhile, his crewman, Joseph Clan, had fallen overboard and was fighting to stay afloat — while drifting farther away from the boat.

Lemieux could have sailed on and hoped that a rescue boat would come along to pick up the men, but he knew their lives depended upon him.

As that moment, a terrifying memory from Lemieux's own childhood flashed before his eyes. As a five-year-old, he was already crazy about boats. One day, he jumped into a small sailboat and set out for the middle of Lake Wabamun by himself — without a life jacket. A gust of wind capsized the craft, throwing the boy into the cold water. Swallowing the water and thrashing about, he was on the verge of drowning when he somehow managed to grab a rope from his boat and keep his head above water. Then he held on until one of his older brothers rescued him.

With the memory of his own near-drowning still in his mind, Lemieux made a bold attempt to save the sailors. At that moment, an Olympic medal didn't seem so very important. He turned his boat into the screaming wind and reversed his course, a highly dangerous maneuver.

Meanwhile, Chan was in danger of drowning. Despite the fact that he was wearing his life jacket, Chan was having trouble keeping his head above water because he was weighted down by his foul weather gear. "Please help me," Chan gasped. "I can't last much longer."

"Grab onto my boat when I come past you," said Lemieux.

"I can't, " cried Chan. "I hurt my back and I can't pull myself up into your boat."

With one hand on the tiller, Lemieux leaned over and grabbed the back of Chan's life jacket and tried to haul him aboard. Chan was halfway out of the water when the small boat — built to hold only one person — nearly capsized. There was no room in the cockpit, so Chan clutched the side of the boat.

"Just try to hold on until we get to your boat," Lemieux shouted to Chan.

Against all odds, Lemieux steered his overloaded, tilted boat through the crashing waves and reached the overturned boat. "You'll be safer on your hull than with me," he yelled at Chan. "If we all try to get in my boat, it will sink."

Chan scrambled onto the hull with his teammate, Ciew, who was about to slip into the water. But Lemieux tied up alongside the damaged craft and helped steady it so it wouldn't sink. After signaling for help, he stayed with the injured sailors until a patrol boat arrived.

Once the pair was safely aboard the rescue vessel, Lemieux set out to resume his race. But he'd fallen too far behind to catch up. He finished 21st out of a field of 33 racers. There would be no Olympic medal for Lemieux in 1988.

But his bravery and unselfishness did earn him an Olympic award. Lemieux was summoned to a special presentation by Juan Antonio Samaranch, the president of the International Olympic Committee. Samaranch praised Lemieux's heroism and gave him the Fair Play Award for the 1988 Olympic Games.

When Lemieux returned home, another meaningful ceremony awaited him. Members of the Northwood Presbyterian Church in Spokane, Washington, had a medal cast for him. As he stood on the platform with the gleaming medal draped around his neck, the Canadian national anthem was played.

Then a tearful Lemieux modestly thanked his American admirers. "You spend your whole lifetime trying to achieve a goal, and my goal was winning a gold medal," he told them. "I didn't win a gold medal, but I won something even more valuable — the love you've shown me here today."

(Used with Permission from Nash, Bruce & Allan Zullo. *The Greatest Sports Stories Never Told.* New York: Simon & Schuster, 1993.)

Overview

Instructor's Notes: For additional reading on the sport of sailing, students can try *Sailing* by Norman S. Barret (1987).

Setup

Bring the group together to sit in a circle. Use the following questions to help facilitate a short, five or six minute discussion to help set the tone before reading the story. (Be sure to record students' answers on the board or on poster paper.)

- Have you ever sacrificed one of your own goals to help someone else?

- Was the decision you made a difficult one?

- What were some of the factors that influenced your decision?

The Story

Read the story aloud and with enthusiasm to the whole group. Be sure to show the pictures to the students as you read.

Discussion Questions:

Spend a couple of minutes distributing students' Player Portfolios and pencils. (Ask for one or two volunteers to help.) Write the questions and focus prompts on a blackboard or newsprint.

Work together as a whole group to answer the following questions:

Questions one through four should be answered in a round-robin format, with one student answering one question. Try to include students who may not always participate. (If answers for questions three and four are imprecise or need further elaboration, ask if anyone has anything to add.)

1. Who is the main character in this story?

2. What is the problem or challenge he faces?

3. How does Lemieux decide to solve the problem?

4. What happened then?

The following focus prompt should be answered in an exhaustive format. Continue letting students give responses until no new answers are given.

5. One important lesson we can take from this story is that we should…

For questions six and seven, allow all students an opportunity to share their answers, regardless of whether or not the answers are original.

6. When would it be important in your life to… [insert answer from previous statement]?

7. One thing that might make doing this difficult is….

Finally, ask children to write their responses to the following prompt in their Player Portfolios.

8. One specific way I might show fair play by helping an opponent is by…

Cool-down

- *R&R Huddle* (5 min.)

- *Recap* one or two key points that arose during the discussion or ask students to explain what Lemieux meant when he said, "I didn't win a gold medal, but I won something even more valuable—the love you've shown me here today."

- *Reconnect* by asking volunteers to briefly share what they wrote for question number eight above.

- *Reset* and get ready for the next lesson.

Session 36: **Interacting Values** **Lessons from the Field**	
Warm-up Begin the PLUS Cycle (5 min.) • Session Overview • Following Up on Fair Play **Activity** Lessons from the Field (25-30 min.) • Sports Activity	**Cool-down** Continue the PLUS Cycle (5-10 min.) • Reflection • Goal-setting **Materials** Sports Equipment

Warm-up

Following Through on Fair Play (5 min.)

Ask students to think about the previous lesson. What can they do today to bring the Lessons from Literature into their work together in the sports activity?

Activity

Lessons from the Field
Sports Activity

Block I: Getting Started (5 min.)

Stand together in a circle for all *Getting Started* activities (except for jogging). Have players partner up, with one player doing the activity and the partner keeping count and giving encouragement. Be sure that players have their Portfolios handy so that they can record their progress. Players will try to improve upon their Past Personal Bests (PPB) by achieving their Future Best Goals (FBG) and by tracking progress toward those goals in their Player Portfolios.

Encourage players to clap for and cheer on their teammates to create an enthusiastic environment. You also may choose to include music.

Choose from the options below, making sure to include a cardio and a stretching warm-up.

- **Measure resting heart rate (RHR)** — Spend a few minutes showing players how to find their pulses, either on their necks or wrists. Explain that you will be giving them a few seconds to count how many times their hearts beat. Take a moment to allow the players to sit quietly on the floor and find their pulses. Give them 30 seconds to count their heartbeats.

- **Record, check in and set goals** — Allow a couple of minutes for players to record their RHRs in their Player Portfolios.

- **Jog (2-3 min.)** — This can be done as a lap or in place as a circle.

- **Stretch (2-3 min.)** — Be sure to include stretches for the major muscle groups.

- **Strength/Endurance (1 min.)** — On this first day, players will set baseline numbers for the four Strength/Endurance activities (push-ups, sit-ups, lunges, calf raises), but usually, you will only choose one or two. They will work in pairs. One member of the pair will have 30 seconds to do as many of the activities as they can. Their partner will cheer them on and count for them.

- **Jump Rope (4 min.)** — Again, players will work in pairs, with one person jumping and the other person counting and cheering. They should have three to four sets of 30-45 seconds of jumping rope.

- **Track personal progress** — Have players record their totals for steps five and six in their Player Portfolios. These totals will represent their baseline achievements, or their Past Personal Bests (PPB). Each day, players will check their progress from the previous session and will set a Future Personal Best Goal (FBG) to work toward for next time. Be sure to remind them about setting realistic goals (for example, adding one or two to their baseline, as opposed to 10).

Block II: Structured Play (30 min.)

Skill Play (10 min.)

Choose one or two of the following activities to play today. You can refer back to the *Physical Activities Description Appendix* for instructions on how to run the activities. Encourage players to cheer for each other, and include music if you wish.

- Jump Rope Games

- Sack Race

- Leap Frog Relay

- Backwards Walk/Run Relay

- Hopscotch

Sport Play (20 min.)

As a group, decide which sport you want to play today. Select from the sport list contained in the *Sports List Appendix*. Be sure to periodically review with the group the Physical Activities Recommendations for Sport from Chapter Six.

Cool-down

If time permits, close the day with a few minutes of stretching while conducting the following R&R Huddle.

- **Recap** one or two key moments from the Lessons from the Field.

- **Reconnect** players back to the theme unit.

- **Reset** and transition players to the Cool-down, Reflection time.

  OR

- **Reflection**

Use this time to highlight teachable moments you observed during the day and to give players an opportunity to share their experiences about Sports PLUS during the day. The following questions can serve as a guide:

- What did you like about today?

- What did you learn today?

- What are some ways you showed fair play today?

- How can we better show fair play next time?

- In what ways did your teammates show fair play today?

Goal-setting

Use this time to help players track progress toward their individually chosen goals, as well as toward team goals. As goals from earlier sessions are reached, guide players in setting additional individual and team goals related to *Fair Play*.

Session 36: **Interacting Values** **Lessons from Adventure**	
Warm-up Begin the PLUS Cycle (5 min.) • Session Overview • Everybody Up **Activity** Lessons from Adventure (25-30 min.) • Egg Drop	**Cool-down** Continue the PLUS Cycle (5-10 min.) • Reflection • Go-Round **Materials** 1 egg, 1 set of 15 drinking straws, 1 six-foot piece of masking tape, markers, 1 large, poster-size piece of paper, 1 chair, a couple of large plastic garbage bags

Warm-up

Everybody Up

Setup

This activity focuses on players working together — first in pairs, then in groups of four. If your classroom has a carpeted floor, safety should not be an issue. But as in other trust and personal responsibility types of activities, use your judgment regarding the players' ability to take care of one another. If necessary, wait to use an outdoor grassy area or the gym utilizing gym mats. Before you begin, remind players of their responsibilities to their partners and teammates.

Play

1. Have players partner up. The one criterion is that they choose a partner of approximately the same size and weight.

2. Once pairs are formed, give the following instructions:

    "Pairs will sit on the floor (or ground) facing each other. Sit near one another with your legs bent and knees close together and place the tips of your shoes together. Reach out and grasp hands tightly! Holding onto your partner as tightly as you can, pull with your arms and come to a standing position. Remember to hold on tightly. Don't yank at your partner; pull slowly, together, and you will soon be standing."

3. Try this a few times to be sure that players are working well together. Remove anyone who is not acting responsibly or stop and do a quick R&R huddle to address the problem.

4. If players are cooperating, try adding pairs together and standing with four people at once. This requires a little more effort, but working together, it can easily be accomplished.

5. If you have use of gym mats, or a grassy outside area, try the final attempt at Everybody Up. Bring the entire group together, with everyone scrunched in very close, feet in the middle. Have players grasp hands with someone in the group, relatively opposite from them, but there is usually such a mass

of hands in the middle that just holding on tightly to someone will work. When the whole group is ready, shout, "Everybody Up!" and see if the whole group can stand up together. This can sometimes result in players falling down, so remind them again to take care of one another's safety.

Variation

If the group has a lot of difficulty getting up in a circle, try forming two lines in which pairs work to get each other up. Another possibility is to have partners sit back-to-back with elbows locked.

- **R&R Huddle** (5 minutes)

- **Recap** by asking players about their experience during the activity: Did anyone feel unsafe at any time? Did we behave responsibly as partners? …as a group?

- **Reconnect** to the theme unit with one or two of the following questions: How well did we cooperate with one another? Can anyone think of a place or a time in our lives when two or more people have to rely on each other?

- **Reset** and transition to the next activity.

Activity

Lessons from Adventure
Egg Drop

Can an egg survive a six-foot drop? Perhaps, but only if the right protection system is designed! The players use this activity to think about the rules of conduct that surround games and see that it is these rules that keep players safe.

Setup

Separate your group into teams of three to five players.

Play

1. Each small team is responsible for coming up with a plan for protecting the egg from a six-foot drop. When making their plan, players can only use the straws and tape to protect their egg. Give the groups about 15 minutes to come up with their ideas.

2. At the end of the time, bring back together into a large group. Take a few minutes for groups to share the ideas they came up with. As a large group, decide how the task might best be accomplished. Players can choose the idea of one group in particular, or may come up with a variation of several ideas.

3. Once the group has made their decision, work as a team to construct the device with the egg safely inside.

4. Before dropping the egg, describe the following metaphor: "We are going to think of this egg as a player in a game. The game is the six-foot drop. What do the straws contribute? How is this like a team?" Give the players a few moments to think about the metaphor, and allow them to share their ideas. "We are going to think of the straws and tape that protect the egg during the drop as the rules of conduct that keep players safe during games."

5. After building the egg-protector, invite players to create a poster to describe why they think the player (egg) will be safe during the game (6-foot drop). For example, "Our player is surrounded on all sides by put-ups." Challenge players to think about how players should act during a game to keep the game fair and safe. The team can divide the jobs of creating the egg protector and designing the poster and presentation.

6. Get the group working on their project and move around the room answering questions and helping the students to understand the metaphor.

7. Finally, set a chair in the center of the room. Place the garbage bag on the floor in front of the chair. At the end of the construction time, drop the eggs.

Variation

You may want to have each small group make a poster before coming back to the larger group to discuss how to make the egg-protector. If the large group has a difficult time deciding on one strategy to protect the egg, you may consider trying a couple of different ways to see which work best. If you choose this option, be sure to spend some time after the activity discussing why the strategy worked or didn't work.

Discussion

After the activity, give the group a chance to talk about how they felt they worked together. Also, ask players to share why they think the egg protector worked or didn't work. The following questions can serve as a guide to get you started:

1. Did the device work? Why or why not?

2. What was hard about finding ways to protect such a fragile object?

3. How well do you think the group worked together? Were there certain things that didn't go so well?

4. What are some examples of how you worked well together?

5. If you think of the straws as the rules of games that protect players, what are some of the ways that rules help protect all players?

6. What are some of the different kinds of rules we need to keep us physically and emotionally safe during a game?

- ***R&R Huddle*** (5 minutes)

- ***Recap*** with one or two key points from the preceding discussion

- **Reconnect** to the theme unit by asking players to complete the following sentence: One thing I learned about fair play is…

- **Reset** and transition to the next activity.

Cool-down

Cool-down Ritual
Go-round
Do a large group go-round and ask each player to give one word or short phrase that represents fair play language.

Session 37:
Sticking to Your Beliefs

Overview

Instructor's Notes: *Be sure to review this set of activities before starting this Sports PLUS Session. Directions for how to run each activity are provided, but it is important that you become familiar with them so that you may more effectively lead the group.*

During group discussions, be sure to record all thoughts and ideas on a blackboard or newsprint. Remember that when players are working in their Player Portfolios, spelling, grammar, and penmanship are, relatively speaking, unimportant, so don't dwell on those details or you risk making Sports PLUS into MoreSchool.

As with all Sports PLUS sessions it is important to focus on building community—setting the tone for an emotionally and physically safe group, identifying behavioral expectations, and outlining the goals of the day and the sessions to follow. Give yourself a few minutes either before or after this session to reflect on all the hard and effective work you have done creating this community with your players. List the different challenges you have encountered and the creative ways you have negotiated them. Think about what a special, positive influence you have had in their lives. With fewer than one and a half units left, think about the values and principles of community you most want to emphasize with your players and then think of a plan to make it happen.

The *Theme Book* reading continues with another example of fair play. This session's team-building activity provides the group with some fun time together and a chance to get to know their teammates a little better. Feelings Impulse closes the day by challenging players to express how they are feeling.

<table>
<tr><td colspan="2">

Session 37:
Sticking to Your Beliefs
Lessons from Literature

</td></tr>
<tr><td>

Warm-up
  Begin the PLUS Cycle (10-15 min.)

  • Session Overview

  • Quote of the Week

Activity
  Lessons from Literature (25-30 min.)

  • Theme Book — *The Greatest
    Sports Stories Never Told: When
    Winning Took a Backseat*

</td><td>

Cool-down
  Continue the PLUS Cycle (5-10 min.)

  • Reflection

Materials
  Copies of *The Greatest Sports Stories
  Never Told: When Winning Took a
  Backseat*

</td></tr>
</table>

Warm-up

Quote of the Week
(see Player Portfolio)

*The most important decision I ever made in my career was to live
my life in sports as honestly and ethically as possible. Never having
compromised my values allows me to look back on my life with no regrets
and feel satisfaction in what I was able to accomplish.*

– Greg LeMond, three-time
winner of the Tour de France

Overview

> **Instructor's Notes:** Be sure that students know what the Tour de France
> is. If many do not, you can explain to them that it is the most competitive,
> difficult, and prestigious cycling race in the world. You may also wish to
> review a few vocabulary words such as ethically and *compromised*. You might
> explain to students what an ethical decision is and give a couple of examples.)

Follow the five steps of the Quote of the Week Format (See the *Getting
Started* chapter for additional explanation):

1. **Write the Quote of the Week:** Bring the group together into a
    circle, and write the Quote on the blackboard.

2. **Think about the Quote as a group:** Spend two or three minutes talking with the students about what they think the quote means. Ask students to share answers to the group for the following questions:

   - What does it mean to live a "life in sports as honestly and ethically as possible"?

   - What are some of the difficult choices Greg LeMond may have had to make in order to live honestly and ethically?

3. **Pair up to talk about the Quote:** Have students separate into pairs. Ask them to spend about five minutes discussing the following questions with their partners. Explain that they will be sharing their answers with the whole group, so they may choose to write their answers in their Player Portfolios. (Be sure to walk around the groups, listen, and offer help where needed.):

   - Why do you think living honestly and ethically gave Greg LeMond a feeling of great satisfaction?

   - Why do you think it is important to live honestly and ethically?

   - What are one or two ways you can follow Greg LeMond's example and live honestly and ethically?

4. **Share answers with the whole group:** Come together as a large group and share the answers from each of the pair groups. Everyone who wants to should have an opportunity to share their answers.

5. **Reflect individually about the Quote:** Take two or three minutes for students to reflect individually by writing a response to the following Journal Question in their Player Portfolios:

   - Sometimes it's hard to play fairly in sports because we want to win so badly. But when we make the decision to play fairly, we feel good about ourselves later on. Keeping that in mind, complete this sentence: One thing I can do to help myself choose to play fairly is to…

Activity

Lessons from Literature
Theme Book
The Greatest Sports Stories Nevr Told
When Winning Took a Backseat
(*see Player Portfolio*)

When Winning Took a Backseat

by Bruce Nash and Allan Zullo

Scott Bennett and Brad Howes grew up south of Salt Lake City in the fertile valley between the Jordan River and the towering Wasatch Mountains of Utah. The boys lived just far enough apart not to attend the same schools, but close enough to compete in the same leagues in baseball, football, and basketball.

No matter whose team won, Scott and Brad always shook hands and complimented each other on the way they played. The two didn't become close friends because they were always on opposite sides. But the boys grew up admiring each other's athletic skills.

And it was their childhood competition that forged a lasting friendship and set the stage for an extraordinary display of sportsmanship seldom seen in track and field.

It happened while the boys were members of school cross-country teams—Scott at Murray High and Brad at nearby Cottonwood High. During meets, as they pounded out mile after mile across the empty fields, Scott and Brad formed an unspoken bond. They learned to respect one another's competitive spirit and strengths. Brad liked to set a blistering pace early in the race, which wore down most other runners who tried to keep up with him. Scott, meanwhile, had a strong finishing kick, which had him breathing down the leader's neck on the final stretch.

Usually, the boys finished first and second when their schools competed. Sometimes Brad won; other times it was Scott who broke the tape first.

Their most memorable race—the one track and field coaches still talk about—occurred during the 1970 cross-country regional meet, with the winner going to the state finals. The event, held as part of cottonwood High's homecoming festivities, was run during halftime of the football game between Cottonwood and Murray. Since the schools were only about ten miles apart, the stands were jammed with rooters from both sides.

At halftime, Murray was leading by two touchdowns and threatening to spoil Cottonwood's homecoming. So when Scott and Brad took their places at the starting line, each knew there was a lot more at stake than just a race. Brad felt that by winning he could salvage some of Cottonwood's pride at homecoming. Scott wanted to win to prove that Murray was the best at everything.

There were three other runners in the race, but all eyes were on Scott and Brad when the starter's gun went off. The group circled the track that ringed the football field and headed out the exit for the 2.6 mile cross-country run.

As expected, Brad quickly took the lead in a race that went through the rolling, grassy hills of Sugarhouse Park bordering the school grounds. At the halfway point, Brad had pulled ahead of Scott by nearly 300 yards while the other runners had fallen out of contention.

Despite the gap, Scott wasn't worried. In past races, Brad usually grabbed the lead, but Scott, with his strong finish, often caught Brad on the final stretch. Sticking to his race strategy, Scott steadily gained on Brad. By the time the two reached the stadium, Scott was only a couple of steps behind.

When the pair dashed through the stadium tunnel and onto the track for the final lap, the capacity crowd rose to its feet to cheer the runners who were now racing stride for stride.

But coming around the final turn, Scott cut to the inside to pass Brad and get in position for a sprint down the stretch. Just then, Brad also moved inside and the runners' legs tangled. Both stumbled. Scott managed to keep his feet, but Brad sprawled headfirst onto the track.

Scott ran a few more paces. But suddenly, he became aware of an eerie silence. The crowd that had been shouting moments before fell deathly silent when Brad tripped and hit the ground. So Scott stopped and looked back at his lifelong rival. Brad, whose knees and hands were scraped and bleeding from falling on the cinders, was struggling to regain his feet.

Who won or lost the race no longer mattered to Scott. His friend and competitor was hurt. Scott knew what he had to do—he went back to help. "Give me your hand, Brad," said Scott. "Let me help you."

Brad looked up at Scott, smiled, and said, "Man, you're something else." Scott pulled his injured rival to his feet but Brad was hurting so badly that he couldn't run very well. So Scott put his arm around Brad and the two began trotting down the final stretch. The thousands of fans in the stands gasped when they saw Scott's gallant gesture and then erupted into thunderous applause.

Shocked by the unexpected spill, the track judges had dropped the tape that marked the finish line. "Get that tape back up!" a coach yelled. "They're coming in...together!"

With Brad limping the final 50 yards, and Scott helping him every step of the way, the two competitors crossed the finish line arm in arm. The coaches and the track judges then huddled over what to do about the incredibly unselfish act of sportsmanship they had just witnesses.

"One of the runners has to win, but that doesn't mean the other one has to lose," said Scott's coach, Same Moore. "I know Scott wouldn't want to have his victory tainted. I say we give both kids first place."

Moore's suggestion won unanimous approval from Brad's coach and the judges. The race was declared a dead heat.

"I have never seen such sportsmanship," said Moore. "I doubt if I ever will again."

(Used with Permission from Nash, Bruce & Allan Zullo. *The Greatest Sports Stories Never Told*. New York: Simon & Schuster, 1993.)

Set-up

Bring the group together to sit in a circle. Use the following questions to help facilitate a short, five or six minute discussion to help set the tone before reading the story. (Be sure to record students' answers on the board or on poster paper.)

- What does sportsmanship mean?

- How is sportsmanship related to fair play?

The Story

Read the story aloud and with enthusiasm to the whole group.

Discussion Questions:

Spend a couple of minutes distributing students' Player Portfolios and pencils. (Ask for one or two volunteers to help.) Work together as a group to answer the following questions. Write the questions and focus prompts on a blackboard or newsprint.

Questions one through five should be answered in a round-robin format, with one student answering one question. Try to include students who may not always participate. (If answers for questions three and four are imprecise or need further elaboration, ask if anyone has anything to add.)

1. Who are the main characters in this story?

2. What is their relationship like?

3. What happens to Brad in the final turn of the cross-country regional meet?

4. How does Scott handle this situation?

5. What happened then?

The following focus prompt should be answered in an exhaustive format. Continue letting students give responses until no new answers are given.

6. One important lesson this story teaches us is that we should...

For questions seven and eight, allow all students an opportunity to share their answers, regardless of whether or not the answer is original.

7. When would it be important in your life to... [insert answer from previous statement]?

8. One thing that might make doing this difficult is...

Finally, ask students to write their responses to the following prompt in their Player Portfolios.

9. One specific way I might show sportsmanship to another competitor while playing my favorite sport is...

Cool-down

- ***R&R Huddle*** (5 min.)

- ***Recap*** by asking students one of the following questions:

    - Is it possible to be competitive and want to win while still playing fair?

    - What does this story teach us about being competitive while playing fair?

- ***Reconnect*** to the theme unit by asking volunteers to share their responses to question number nine.

- ***Reset*** and get ready for the next lesson.

Session 37: **Sticking to Your Beliefs** **Lessons from the Field**	
Warm-up Begin the PLUS Cycle (5 min.) • Session Overview • Following Up on Fair Play **Activity** Lessons from the Field (25-30 min.) • Sports Activity	**Cool-down** Continue the PLUS Cycle (5-10 min.) • Reflection • Goal-setting **Materials** Sports Equipment

Warm-up

Following Up on Fair Play (5 min.)

Ask students to think about the previous lesson. What can they do today to bring the Lessons from Literature into their work together in the sports activity?

Activity

Lessons from the Field
Sports Activity

Block I: Getting Started (5 min.)

Stand together in a circle for all *Getting Started* activities (except for jogging). Have players partner up, with one player doing the activity and the partner keeping count and giving encouragement. Be sure that players have their Portfolios handy so that they can record their progress. Players will try to improve upon their Past Personal Bests (PPB) by achieving their Future Best Goals (FBG) and by tracking progress toward those goals in their Player Portfolios.

Encourage players to clap for and cheer on their teammates to create an enthusiastic environment. You also may choose to include music.

Choose from the options below, making sure to include a cardio and a stretching warm-up.

- **Measure resting heart rate (RHR)** — Spend a few minutes showing players how to find their pulses, either on their necks or wrists. Explain that you will be giving them a few seconds to count how many times their hearts beat. Take a moment to allow the players to sit quietly on the floor and find their pulses. Give them 30 seconds to count their heartbeats.

- **Record, check in and set goals** — Allow a couple of minutes for players to record their RHRs in their Player Portfolios.

- **Jog (2-3 min.)** — This can be done as a lap or in place as a circle.

- **Stretch (2-3 min.)** — Be sure to include stretches for the major muscle groups.

- **Strength/Endurance (1 min.)** — On this first day, players will set baseline numbers for the four Strength/Endurance activities (push-ups, sit-ups, lunges, calf raises), but usually, you will only choose one or two. They will work in pairs. One member of the pair will have 30 seconds to do as many of the activities as they can. Their partner will cheer them on and count for them.

- **Jump Rope (4 min.)** — Again, players will work in pairs, with one person jumping and the other person counting and cheering. They should have three to four sets of 30-45 seconds of jumping rope.

- **Track personal progress** — Have players record their totals for steps five and six in their Player Portfolios. These totals will represent their baseline achievements, or their Past Personal Bests (PPB). Each day, players will check their progress from the previous session and will set a Future Personal Best Goal (FBG) to work toward for next time. Be sure to remind them about setting realistic goals (for example, adding one or two to their baseline, as opposed to 10).

Block II: Structured Play (30 min.)

Skill Play (10 min.)

Choose one or two of the following activities to play today. You can refer back to the *Physical Activities Description Appendix* for instructions on how to run the activities. Encourage players to cheer for each other, and include music if you wish.

- Water Fill Relay

- Chase Ball

- Crab Walk

- Tug o' war

- High Skipping Relay

Sport Play (20 min.)

As a group, decide which sport you want to play today. Select from the sport list contained in the *Sports List Appendix*. Be sure to periodically review with the group the Physical Activities Recommendations for Sport from Chapter Six.

Cool-down

If time permits, close the day with a few minutes of stretching while conducting the following R&R Huddle.

- **Recap** one or two key moments from the Lessons from the Field.

- **Reconnect** players back to the theme unit.

- **Reset** and transition players to the Cool-down, Reflection time.

  OR

- **Reflection**

Use this time to highlight teachable moments you observed during the day and to give players an opportunity to share their experiences about Sports PLUS during the day. The following questions can serve as a guide:

- What did you like about today?

- What did you learn today?

- What are some ways you showed fair play today?

- How can we better show fair play next time?

- In what ways did your teammates show fair play today?

Goal-setting

Use this time to help players track progress toward their individually chosen goals, as well as toward team goals. As goals from earlier sessions are reached, guide players in setting additional individual and team goals related to *Fair Play*.

Session 37: **Sticking to Your Beliefs** **Lessons from Adventure**	

Warm-up
Begin the PLUS Cycle (5 min.)
   • Session Overview
   • Categories
Activity
Lessons from Adventure (25-30 min.)
   • Nonsense Numbers
	Cool-down
	Continue the PLUS Cycle (5-10 min.)
	   • Reflection
	   • Feelings Impulse
	Materials
	Pencil or pen for each person, Nonsense number worksheet (see below)

Warm-up

Categories

Setup

Gather students together to listen to the instructions. Mention to students that this activity will lead nicely into the next one, as both encourage students to learn about their commonalities as well as their differences.

Play

1. Tell students that you will call out a question or ask them to do something. Once they have listened to the "category" they are to find other students who do the same thing or respond to the question in a similar way. They should find ALL students who respond similarly and "clump" together with them.

2. Examples of questions or actions:

   - Fold your arms — which arm is on top, left or right?

   - Stand on one foot — which foot did you stand on?

   - Favorite pizza topping

   - Number of siblings

   - Number of pets (a group with no pets is fine)

   - Month in which you were born

3. In between each round, ask the different groups to shout out what their clump represents.

4. It is OK to have a "clump" of one.

Activity

Lessons from Adventure
Nonsense Numbers
(see Player Portfolio)

This is an activity that emphasizes fair play over winning.

Setup

Explain to the group that you are going to play a game where players earn points if they can answer yes to the different statements. Divide the group into teams using this silly method. Have all players line up at one end of the room. "If you are a boy, run to the other end of the room. If you have brown hair switch ends. If you have blue eyes, switch ends. If you are wearing blue pants, switch ends." Continue calling out appearance-related criteria until the two sides are approximately even.

Play

The activity is pretty self-explanatory. Each group will read the worksheet and assign themselves points based on the questions. Allow five minutes for the groups to complete the worksheet.

Bring the teams together and share final scores.

Nonsense Numbers Worksheet

- One point for each person who has red hair.

- One point for each person who has green eyes.

- Three points for each person whose last name begins with Z, Q, X or Y.

- One point for each person who has brown hair.

- One point for each person who has a pet.

- Five points for each person who went to kindergarten with someone in this room.

- Ten points for each person who loves to read.

- One point for each person who loves basketball

- One point for each person who loves gymnastics

- Three points for each person who likes to watch sports on TV.

- Two points for each person who likes to play sports.

- Five points for each person who has read a book this month.

- Ten points for each person who read a magazine or the newspaper this week.

- Five points for each person who has ever kept a journal.

- Five points for each person who has read any chapter book.

- Two points for each person who has read a chapter book about sports.

- One point for each person who plays on a sports team.

- Ten points for each person who knows what perseverance means.

- Ten points for each person who knows what fair play is.

- Ten points for each person who knows what respect means.

- Ten points for each person who knows what responsibility means.

- Ten points for each person who knows what teamwork means.

- Ten points for each person who can name everyone in this room.

- One point for each person who has exercised this week.

- One point for each person who knows how to play soccer.

Add up the final scores and see which team wins. Now, try it again, but this time, form the teams by counting off by threes. See who wins this time. This will help emphasize the point that the numbers really are Nonsense Numbers.

- **R&R Huddle** (5 minutes)

- **Recap** by asking players about their experience during the game: On how many questions did you tell the truth? How many people lied or stretched the truth on at least one question?

- **Reconnect** to the theme unit with the following discussion question: What happens to the game if we stretch the truth or lie about our answers?

- **Reset** and transition to the next activity.

Cool-down

Cool-down Ritual

Feelings Impulse

Using an impulse go-round, ask players to share one emotion word to describe how they are feeling today. After all players have had a turn, give anyone who wants to the opportunity to explain why they chose the word they did..

Session 38:
Picturing and Practicing Fair Play

Overview

Instructor's Notes: *Be sure to review this set of activities before starting this Sports PLUS Session. Directions for how to run each activity are provided, but it is important that you become familiar with them so that you may more effectively lead the group.*

During group discussions, be sure to record all thoughts and ideas on a blackboard or newsprint. Remember that when players are working in their Player Portfolios, spelling, grammar, and penmanship are, relatively speaking, unimportant, so don't dwell on those details or you risk making Sports PLUS into MoreSchool.

The activities for this session involve the attention and participation of every player and present an opportunity for players to take their understanding of Fair Play to a new level.

The *You Make the Call* challenges players to continue thinking about issues of fair play. The *Wall Mural* activity is not only an opportunity for artistic and creative players to express their talents. It also is an opportunity for players to govern themselves. Teachable moments are sure to occur. The *Go-Round* provides a simple recap for this session.

Session 38: **Picturing and Practicing Fair Play** **Lessons from Literature**	

Warm-up
Begin the PLUS Cycle (10-15 min.)
 	
  • Session Overview
 	
  • Quote of the Week
	Cool-down
	Continue the PLUS Cycle (5-10 min.)
	
	  • Reflection

Activity Lessons from Literature (25-30 min.) • You Make the Call — *In or Out*	**Materials** Copies of *In or Out*

Warm-up

Quote of the Week

It is reasonable that everyone who asks for justice should do justice.

– Thomas Jefferson

Follow the five steps of the Quote of the Week Format (See the *Getting Started* chapter for additional explanation):

1. **Write the Quote of the Week:** Bring the group together into a circle, and write the Quote on the blackboard.

2. **Think about the Quote as a group:** Spend two or three minutes talking with the students about what they think the quote means. Next ask students to share answers to the group for the following question:

   • What does this quote have to do with our theme of fair play?

3. **Pair up to talk about the Quote:** Have students separate into pairs. Ask them to spend about five minutes discussing the following questions with their partner. Explain that they will be sharing their answers with the whole group, so they may choose to write their answers in their Player Portfolios. (Be sure to walk around the groups, listen, and offer help where needed.):

- Give an example of how you can actively work toward fair play.

- Give an example of how you benefit from fair play.

4. **Share answers with the whole group:** Come together as a large group and share the answers from each of the pair groups. Everyone who wants to should have an opportunity to share their answers.

5. **Reflect individually about the Quote:** Take two or three minutes for students to reflect individually by writing a response to the following Journal Question in their Player Portfolios:

- How do you think you can "do justice" outside of Sports PLUS?

Activity

Lessons from Literature
You Make the Call
In or Out
(see Player Portfolio)

Key Concepts

- Fair Play
- Respect for Rules
- Teamwork
- Responsibility

Setup

Bring the group together to sit in a circle. If there is time, use the following paragraph to help set the tone before reading the story:

"In sports situations we often have to make decisions very quickly. Sometimes our decision can be influenced by how much we want to win, what we think our teammates want us to do, how we feel about our opponent, etc. The decision-making process can help, but it has to happen very quickly. This is one reason sports offer us so many valuable opportunities to practice the Sports PLUS values. If we can make good decisions in an emotional situation like sports, we are better prepared to make other decisions in our lives."

Read the story aloud and with enthusiasm to the whole group.

In or Out

Leo and Shatika are playing a doubles tennis match against Kenny and Li. The four sixth graders have been playing against each other for months and Leo and Shatika have won nearly every match. But this time, Kenny and Li are ahead by one game. If they can win the next game, they win the match. Li is really competitive and winning is very important to her.

Leo is serving and he and Shatika have been making some dumb mistakes. They are bickering and not playing well together. Leo has just double faulted to give Kenny and Li the advantage. If they win the next point, they win the match.

Leo serves to Kenny and the first serve is into the net. On his next serve, Leo puts a lot of spin on the ball, sending it wide toward the line. Kenny lunges for the ball, but it bounces and curves beyond his reach.

Li throws up her racket and yells, "That's out! We win!"

Shatika, who was playing the net yells back, "No way! The ball caught the line! It's deuce again."

Kenny is the only player who had a really good look at where the ball landed. He saw it catch the side of the line before it sailed off the court. He knows it was a good serve. But if he calls the ball in, they lose the point and may lose the game. Kenny also knows that Li will be furious if he calls the ball in. Within the rules, it is Kenny's call to make, and the three other players are looking at him, waiting for his call.

Discussion Questions:

Separate the students into groups by having them count off by threes (or fours depending on the group size). Spend a couple of minutes distributing students' Player Portfolios and pencils. Ask one or two volunteers to help.

Using their Player Portfolios, have students discuss and write answers to the following questions in their small groups. It is important to remember that spelling, grammar, and penmanship are NOT important during this activity.

1. Who are the main characters in this story?

2. What is the main problem these characters face?

3. What are some possible ways that Kenny can handle the problem?

4. What would happen if the problem were handled in this way?

   - How would Li feel?

   - How would Shatika and Leo feel?

   - How would Kenny feel?

5. If you were Kenny, what solution would you choose to handle the situation?

6. What might make your decision difficult?

7. If you were Shatika, how would you respond to Kenny? What about if you were Li?

Group Share:

- After the small groups have had time to discuss each question, gather them together to sit in one large circle.

- Ask each small group to share their suggestions for solving the problem, using students' answers to number three above. (As suggestions are given, you or a volunteer should write them on poster paper for all to see.)

- Once all the different solutions have been laid out, spend a few minutes discussing the consequences of each solution, using students' answers to question number four as a guide.

- As a group, choose the best solution (i.e., the most good for the most people).

- Finally, as a group, complete the following two focus prompts on poster paper.

     – One thing we can take from this story is that we should…

     – We should be careful not to…

Cool-down

- ***R&R Huddle*** (5 min.)

- ***Recap*** one or two key points that arose during the discussion.

- ***Reconnect*** using one of the following focus prompts:

     – Honesty is important because…

     – One way I lead by example as an honest player and person is by…

- ***Reset*** and get ready for the next lesson.

Session 38: **Picturing and Practicing Fair Play** **Lessons from the Field**	

Warm-up
Begin the PLUS Cycle (5 min.)
  • Session Overview
  • Following Up on Fair Play
Activity
Lessons from the Field (25-30 min.)
  • Sports Activity
	Cool-down
	Continue the PLUS Cycle (5-10 min.)
	  • Reflection
	  • Goal-setting
	Materials
	Sports Equipment

Warm-up

Following Through on Fair Play (5 min.)

Ask students to think about the previous lesson. What can they do today to bring the Lessons from Literature into their work together in the sports activity?

Activity

Lessons from the Field
Sports Activity

Block I: Getting Started (5 min.)

Stand together in a circle for all *Getting Started* activities (except for jogging). Have players partner up, with one player doing the activity and the partner keeping count and giving encouragement. Be sure that players have their Portfolios handy so that they can record their progress. Players will try to improve upon their Past Personal Bests (PPB) by achieving their Future Best Goals (FBG) and by tracking progress toward those goals in their Player Portfolios.

Encourage players to clap for and cheer on their teammates to create an enthusiastic environment. You also may choose to include music.

Choose from the options below, making sure to include a cardio and a stretching warm-up.

- *Measure resting heart rate (RHR)* — Spend a few minutes showing players how to find their pulses, either on their necks or wrists. Explain that you will be giving them a few seconds to count how many times their hearts beat. Take a moment to allow the players to sit quietly on the floor and find their pulses. Give them 30 seconds to count their heartbeats.

- *Record, check in and set goals* — Allow a couple of minutes for players to record their RHRs in their Player Portfolios.

- *Jog (2-3 min.)* — This can be done as a lap or in place as a circle.

- *Stretch (2-3 min.)* — Be sure to include stretches for the major muscle groups.

- *Strength/Endurance (1 min.)* — On this first day, players will set baseline numbers for the four Strength/Endurance activities (push-ups, sit-ups, lunges, calf raises), but usually, you will only choose one or two. They will work in pairs. One member of the pair will have 30 seconds to do as many of the activities as they can. Their partner will cheer them on and count for them.

- ***Jump Rope (4 min.)*** — Again, players will work in pairs, with one person jumping and the other person counting and cheering. They should have three to four sets of 30-45 seconds of jumping rope.

- ***Track personal progress*** — Have players record their totals for steps five and six in their Player Portfolios. These totals will represent their baseline achievements, or their Past Personal Bests (PPB). Each day, players will check their progress from the previous session and will set a Future Personal Best Goal (FBG) to work toward for next time. Be sure to remind them about setting realistic goals (for example, adding one or two to their baseline, as opposed to 10).

Block II: Structured Play (30 min.)

Skill Play (10 min.)

Choose one or two of the following activities to play today. You can refer back to the *Physical Activities Description Appendix* for instructions on how to run the activities. Encourage players to cheer for each other, and include music if you wish.

- Water Balloon Toss

- Line Jumping

- Round and Round the Hoops Go

- Passing Medicine Balls

- Locomotion Relay

Sport Play (20 min.)

As a group, decide which sport you want to play today. Select from the sport list contained in the *Sports List Appendix*. Be sure to periodically

review with the group the Physical Activities Recommendations for Sport from Chapter Six.

Cool-down

If time permits, close the day with a few minutes of stretching while conducting the following R&R Huddle.

- **Recap** one or two key moments from the Lessons from the Field.

- **Reconnect** players back to the theme unit.

- **Reset** and transition players to the Cool-down, Reflection time.

  OR

- **Reflection**

Use this time to highlight teachable moments you observed during the day and to give players an opportunity to share their experiences about Sports PLUS during the day. The following questions can serve as a guide:

- What did you like about today?

- What did you learn today?

- What are some ways you showed fair play today?

- How can we better show fair play next time?

- In what ways did your teammates show fair play today?

Goal-setting

Use this time to help players track progress toward their individually chosen goals, as well as toward team goals. As goals from earlier sessions are reached, guide players in setting additional individual and team goals related to *Fair Play*.

Session 38: **Picturing and Practicing Fair Play** **Lessons from Adventure**	
Warm-up Begin the PLUS Cycle (5 min.) • Session Overview • Human Knot **Activity** Lessons from Adventure (25-30 min.) • Wall Mural	**Cool-down** Continue the PLUS Cycle (5-10 min.) • Reflection • Go-Round **Materials** Player Portfolios, poster-board, markers, crayons

Warm-up

The Human Knot

This is a very simple activity involving the group and a moderate level of trust and responsibility. Read through it and decide if your group members can take their responsibility toward their teammates seriously and keep them safe at all times. And even though it is a simple activity, there are some good areas for discussion before and after the activity.

Setup

Begin by asking players if any of them have been involved with a group that seemed as if it was all knotted up. Problems arise even with the best of teams or groups and we sometimes have to slow down and work together to get the team unknotted.

Inform players that this is an activity where safety can be a concern. You might ask that everyone raise a hand and pledge to keep their teammates' safety in mind at all times during the activity. Ask if anyone thinks they can't make such a commitment and if anyone can't, have them help you monitor the activity.

You will need a bit of space for the activity, but not a lot.

Play

1. This activity works best with about 10–12 players. Depending on your group size, divide your large group in two.

2. Have each group stand in a very tight circle. Ask one person to reach across the circle and take the hand of two different teammates. The person next to them does the same and so on until everyone is holding hands with two different people. Make sure that no one is holding the hand of someone right next to them.

3. The goal is for the group to get itself unknotted. If you have two groups, this can be a competition. Better yet, make it a timed competition, where the groups work together to beat a specified time. Remind players not to force themselves or put too much pressure on other people's arms when trying to get untangled.

4. It usually takes a lot of communication and trial and error to get fully untangled and often people wind up facing different directions and even forming small separate circles. If they complete the activity quickly, have them try it again, but this time with the added challenge of not talking.

- ***R&R Huddle*** (5 minutes)

- ***Recap*** using one of the following questions as a guide:

  - What was frustrating about the activity?

  - Did you ever feel that the group was not taking care of its members in the effort to untangle itself?

  - Did anyone emerge as a leader?

- ***Reconnect*** using one of the following questions:

  - How well did you all communicate?

  - Can anyone give examples of the Sports PLUS values that occurred in the activity?

- Can anyone think of a time when a group you were in got all tangled up and had a hard time getting untangled? What happened?

- **Reset** and transition to the next activity.

Activity

Lessons from Adventure
The Wall Mural

Setup

In this activity, the whole group works together to create a mural that represents different examples of fair play, using articles, poems, stories, quotes, pictures, photographs, cartoons, or anything else the players suggest. Hang poster paper or mural paper on a long wall before the players arrive. If your room doesn't have a wall large enough to use, see if you can use a hallway just outside the classroom

Play

1. To encourage players' independent problem solving and cooperation skills, have them decide how to divide the space on the mural, with your guidance. They may decide to assign individuals to have their own spaces or they may choose to have groups share a space.

2. Working individually or in small groups, invite players to read through and collect articles, pictures, poems, quotations, cartoons, etc that illustrate different kinds of fair play in action. Players may also create their own pictures, poems, stories, quotations, or cartoons based on what they have learned about fair play during the theme unit.

   To help stimulate the players' thinking you may want to ask them questions that touch on the themes of fair play you have explored over the past few weeks:

- Why might someone cheat or play unfairly?

- How do people make sure they play by the rules even when that makes winning harder?

- What would your role model do when playing fairly might mean losing?

- What satisfaction or reward do you get from playing fairly?

3. Once players have found or created something they think demonstrates fair play, ask them to create a caption to briefly explain how or why that item represents fair play.

4. Finally, each person or group should hang their selections or creations on the mural along with their caption to explain why their item shows fair play in action.

5. When the mural is complete, bring the players back together in a circle. Thank them for their contributions and congratulate them on their good work.

6. Ask players to go around in a circle and share any "put-ups" they might have for each other, allowing players to pass if they wish.

7. Next, as a large group, take a "tour" of the mural. Ask each player or group to take a turn stepping out of the circle to point out their articles. Have players share with the whole group why they chose the item they did and how it illustrates fair play. Remind players that they will all have a chance to share and to be respectful of their teammates by listening to everyone.

8. You may ask the group to choose a name for its mural. Take everyone's suggestions; write them on a board or piece of paper; then vote on the one the team likes best.

Discussion

Encourage discussion about specific pieces of the mural and ask players to bring up issues that they have experienced in their own lives. You may not have time to use all discussion questions below, but they may help facilitate productive reflection.

1. What was your favorite part of making our mural?

2. In what ways was teamwork a part of this activity?

3. Did anyone find that sharing the articles, magazines, and materials was hard? Give one example of how you used teamwork to work things out?

4. Give one or two examples of why respect may have been important during this activity?

5. Were people respectful toward each other when sharing the space on the mural? What about sharing materials, such as scissors, pencils, or markers?

6. What would have happened if no one shared and if no one played by the rules during this activity?

- *R&R Huddle* (5 minutes)

- *Recap* one or two key points from the preceding discussion.

- Reconnect to the theme unit using one or two of the following focus prompts:

  - One way this mural activity can help us work with Fair Play during the rest of our time in Sports PLUS is…

  - One reason the mural we created shows how our Sports PLUS team works together is…

  - One thing I am proud of about our mural is…

- ***Reset*** and transition to the next activity.

Cool-down

Cool-down Ritual
Go-round

In a large group, ask players to give their favorite examples of fair play from the mural they made that day. If you have time, ask them to describe how they can learn from that example and how what they learned from that example can be used in their lives.

Session 39:
Getting Creative With Fair Play

Overview

    Instructor's Notes: *Be sure to review this set of activities before starting this Sports PLUS Session. Directions for how to run each activity are provided, but it is important that you become familiar with them so that you may more effectively lead the group.*

    During group discussions, be sure to record all thoughts and ideas on a blackboard or newsprint. Remember that when players are working in their Player Portfolios, spelling, grammar, and penmanship are, relatively speaking, unimportant, so don't dwell on those details or you risk making Sports PLUS into MoreSchool.

    In this session players begin by creating their own quote of the week. This is a great opportunity for them to personalize and own the lessons they have learned about fair play by creating a quote that expresses their understanding of fair play. The *Create Your Own Story* activity takes the learning opportunity of *Create Your Own Quote* a step further by giving players the chance to use their imagination while drawing on their comprehension of how fair play can be lived out. Pairs' Tag is a fun, high energy variation of the tag game children universally enjoy

Session 39: Getting Creative with Fair Play Lessons from Literature	
Warm-up Begin the PLUS Cycle (10-15 min.) • Session Overview • Create a Quote of the Week **Activity** Lessons from Literature (25-30 min.) • Create Your Own Story	**Cool-down** Continue the PLUS Cycle (5-10 min.) • Reflection **Materials** Player Portfolios, paper, pencils, pens, crayons

Warm-up

Create a Quote of the Week
(see Player Portfolio)

The goal of this activity is to allow students to engage their creativity, work collectively, and reflect upon the themes of fair play they have been learning.

Divide students into small groups and allow five or ten minutes for each group to create its own "Quote of the Week" about fair play. Students can look through stories and previous quotes in their portfolios for ideas, but their quotes should be in their own words.

Encourage them to write their quote on a piece of poster board that will then be hung on the wall. Make supplies, such as markers, available for decorating the posters because some students will find this part of the activity particularly enjoyable.

After students have finished, ask groups to take turns sharing their quotes with the group.

Allow a few minutes to discuss each one, during which you should encourage the students who are listening to ask questions once the group presenting has finished.

When the students have finished asking questions of the group, conclude the activity by asking three questions of your own:

- What does your quote mean?

- When is it important to live this quote?

- One way I can live this quote during Sports PLUS is… One way I can live this quote at school is… One way I can live this quote at home is…

Activity

Create Your Own Story

The following activity encourages students' creativity and solidifies their understanding of fair play. By having students create their own stories involving fair play, they will draw upon personal knowledge and examples of fair play, as well as role models that exemplify fair play. This activity also encourages students to understand the benefits of fair play and to transfer that understanding into a new context. It is important to remember that spelling, grammar, and penmanship are NOT important during this activity.

Setup

Bring the group together into a circle and explain the next activity as you pass out students' Player Portfolios. Use the following description as a guide:

"Today during Lessons from Literature, we will be creating our own story about Fair play. You may choose to work individually or with up to three other students. It may be helpful to create a story about some conflict or problem that is then worked out using fair play. Think of things that may have occurred on your own sports teams or during the Lessons from the Field this theme unit. You also may choose to write a story about some of the characters in an Instant Replay or to create a different ending for one of the stories we've read. Spend a few minutes looking back over your Player Portfolios to begin getting some ideas."

Play

Offer guidance as the students separate into groups. Make sure that no one feels left out, but do let the students choose their own groups. Walk around the room offering help and suggestions as needed.

Once students have finished writing, give them an opportunity to illustrate their stories if they choose to do so. (Some students may find it easier to draw a picture before writing a story. It may help to spur their imaginations. Let this be an option for those who want it.)

Explain to the students that they will have an opportunity to share their stories with the group on the next Sports PLUS day if they wish to do so. Students can finish illustrating their stories at home if necessary.

Discussion Questions:

After students have had an opportunity to write and illustrate their stories, bring the whole group back into a circle for a brief reflection on the following questions. Let everyone share who wants to do so.

- What stories or examples of fair play did you use to create your story?

- What are some of the problems that your main characters faced in your stories?

- How did your main characters solve their dilemma?

Cool-down

- ***R&R Huddle*** (5 min.)

- ***Recap*** one or two key points from the discussion.

- ***Reconnect*** students to the theme unit.

- ***Reset*** and get ready for the next lesson.

Session 39: **Getting Creative with Fair Play** **Lessons from the Field**	
Warm-up Begin the PLUS Cycle (5 min.) • Session Overview • Following Up on Fair Play **Activity** Lessons from the Field (25-30 min.) • Sports Activity	**Cool-down** Continue the PLUS Cycle (5-10 min.) • Reflection • Goal-setting **Materials** Sports Equipment

Warm-up

Following Up on Fair Play (5 min.)

Ask students to think about the previous lesson. What can they do today to bring the Lessons from Literature into their work together in the sports activity?

Activity

Lessons from the Field
Sports Activity

Block I: Getting Started (5 min.)

Stand together in a circle for all *Getting Started* activities (except for jogging). Have players partner up, with one player doing the activity and the partner keeping count and giving encouragement. Be sure that players have their Portfolios handy so that they can record their progress. Players will try to improve upon their Past Personal Bests (PPB) by achieving their Future Best Goals (FBG) and by tracking progress toward those goals in their Player Portfolios.

Encourage players to clap for and cheer on their teammates to create an enthusiastic environment. You also may choose to include music.

Choose from the options below, making sure to include a cardio and a stretching warm-up.

- **Measure resting heart rate (RHR)** — Spend a few minutes showing players how to find their pulses, either on their necks or wrists. Explain that you will be giving them a few seconds to count how many times their hearts beat. Take a moment to allow the players to sit quietly on the floor and find their pulses. Give them 30 seconds to count their heartbeats.

- **Record, check in and set goals** — Allow a couple of minutes for players to record their RHRs in their Player Portfolios.

- **Jog (2-3 min.)** — This can be done as a lap or in place as a circle.

- **Stretch (2-3 min.)** — Be sure to include stretches for the major muscle groups.

- **Strength/Endurance (1 min.)** — On this first day, players will set baseline numbers for the four Strength/Endurance activities (push-ups, sit-ups, lunges, calf raises), but usually, you will only choose one or two. They will work in pairs. One member of the pair will have 30 seconds to do as many of the activities as they can. Their partner will cheer them on and count for them.

- **Jump Rope (4 min.)** — Again, players will work in pairs, with one person jumping and the other person counting and cheering. They should have three to four sets of 30-45 seconds of jumping rope.

- **Track personal progress** — Have players record their totals for steps five and six in their Player Portfolios. These totals will represent their baseline achievements, or their Past Personal Bests (PPB). Each day, players will check their progress from the previous session and will set a Future Personal Best Goal (FBG) to work toward for next time. Be sure to remind them about setting realistic goals (for example, adding one or two to their baseline, as opposed to 10).

Block II: Structured Play (30 min.)

Skill Play (10 min.)

Choose one or two of the following activities to play today. You can refer back to the *Physical Activities Description Appendix* for instructions on how to run the activities. Encourage players to cheer for each other, and include music if you wish.

- Pac-Man/Ms. Pac-Man Tag

- Drum Major Walk

- Hoop Monster

- Jump Rope Relay

- Balloon-a-thon

Sport Play (20 min.)

As a group, decide which sport you want to play today. Select from the sport list contained in the *Sports List Appendix*. Be sure to periodically review with the group the Physical Activities Recommendations for Sport from Chapter Six.

Cool-down

If time permits, close the day with a few minutes of stretching while conducting the following R&R Huddle.

- **Recap** one or two key moments from the Lessons from the Field.

- **Reconnect** players back to the theme unit.

- **Reset** and transition players to the Cool-down, Reflection time.

  OR

- **Reflection**

Use this time to highlight teachable moments you observed during the day and to give players an opportunity to share their experiences about Sports PLUS during the day. The following questions can serve as a guide:

- What did you like about today?

- What did you learn today?

- What are some ways you showed fair play today?

- How can we better show fair play next time?

- In what ways did your teammates show fair play today?

Goal-setting

Use this time to help players track progress toward their individually chosen goals, as well as toward team goals. As goals from earlier sessions are reached, guide players in setting additional individual and team goals related to *Fair Play.*

Session 39: **Getting Creative with Fair Play** **Lessons from Adventure**	
Warm-up Begin the PLUS Cycle (5 min.) • Session Overview • Pairs Tag **Activity** Lessons from Adventure (25-30 min.) • Moonball	**Cool-down** Continue the PLUS Cycle (5-10 min.) • Reflection • Alphabet Go-Round **Materials** Boundary markers, 1 beach ball for each small group, Player Portfolios

Warm-up

Pairs Tag

This is a quick walking or running tag game to energize the group.

Setup

Mark off boundaries. If you have the space, make the boundaries large so the children can run. If you do not have much open space, this can still be a fun, challenging game if you keep the boundaries tight and make it a walking only game. Everyone should have their bumpers up—hands up, palms out at chest level acting as bumpers to avoid running into each other.

Play

1. Have players count off by threes. The ones will be a walking group, the twos will be a running group, and the threes will be a skipping group. Choose one number to be "It."

2. On the word, "Go!" the group who is "It" must try to tag the members of the other group. Once tagged, players must stand frozen.

3. When everyone has been tagged, play the game again, but this time, have players change places (the walkers become the runners, runners become skippers, and skippers become walkers). Play two more rounds so that everyone has an opportunity to experience each role

Variation

1. Everyone is in the same mode (all walk, all run, or all skip).
2. Form groups of three with one of each mode. The group will then work together to keep all group members in the game.

- *R&R Huddle* (5 minutes)

- *Recap* using one or two of the following questions: How did you like this game? Did you like it better when you were a walker or a runner? A skipper or a walker? Is it sometimes fun to play a game when you are at a disadvantage? Why or why not?

- **Reconnect** to the theme unit by asking players, How can this game be made more fair? (See variations below to get you started.)

- **Reset** and transition to the next activity.

Activity

Lessons from Adventure
Moonball

Setup

Separate the group into groups of six to eight students. Have an inflated beach ball ready for each group. Hand out the balls after giving instructions.

Play

1. Tell students that the goal is simple — to see how many times each group can hit the ball into the air without it touching the ground.

2. The following rules apply:

   - Each person may only hit the ball one time in a row. Some else must hit the ball before the first person can hit it again.

   - All students must be involved in some way.

   - If the ball hits the ground, the count goes back to zero.
3. Tell students that they are to keep track of their own scores.

4. Before beginning, ask students to think about what "fair play" will look like in this activity? How will they know if they are playing fair?

5. Encourage the groups to set a goal and work toward it.

- **R&R Huddle** (5 minutes)

- **Recap** using a quick go-round in which players give one-word or short statements to describe how it felt to be part of this activity.

- **Reconnect** using one or two of the following discussion questions:

  - As a team, how did we do about playing fair?

  - Did we take "fair play" seriously?

  - What might happen if we didn't take fair play seriously?

- **Reset** and transition to the next activity.

Cool-down

Cool-down Ritual

Alphabet Go-Round

Try this fun, creative way to do a group go-round. Form a circle with the whole group. You or a volunteer can begin the go-round. The catch here is that the group is trying to make a sentence or statement one word at a time, with each word coming from the next person in the circle. (Allow players to pass if they get stuck or ask for help in coming up with a word.) Each word offered must begin with the same letter of the alphabet as the players' first names. Don't worry about grammar or if the statement gets confused or nonsensical—the point is to have some fun in closing out the day.

Session 40:
Fair Play Certificates

Overview

> **Instructor's Notes:** *Be sure to review this set of activities before starting this Sports PLUS Session. Directions for how to run each activity are provided, but it is important that you become familiar with them so that you may more effectively lead the group.*
>
> *During group discussions, be sure to record all thoughts and ideas on a blackboard or newsprint. Remember that when players are working in their*

Player Portfolios, spelling, grammar, and penmanship are, relatively speaking, unimportant, so don't dwell on those details or you risk making Sports PLUS into MoreSchool.

This final Fair Play session follows the Sports PLUS format for the final session of a unit. The *Fair Play Posters* Revisited allows players to revisit the commitments they made to themselves and each other in the beginning of the theme unit.

As much as possible, empower players to run the *Fair Play Awards* and Sports Extras activities. By deciding how the activities are run and ensuring that they abide by their own rules, players practice living out the values. Be sure to take notes on any issues that may arise (e.g., sharing). These issues may provide a valuable transition into the next theme unit, Perseverance.

Session 40: Fair Play Certificates Lessons from Literature	
Warm-up Begin the PLUS Cycle (10-15 min.) • Session Overview • Quote of the Week **Activity** Lessons from Literature (25-30 min.) • Sports Extras	**Cool-down** Continue the PLUS Cycle (5-10 min.) • Reflection **Materials** What students bring in for Sports Extras

Warm-up

Quote of the Week
(see Player Portfolio)

I am not bound to win, but I am bound to be true.

– Abraham Lincoln

Follow the five steps of the Quote of the Week Format (See the *Getting Started* chapter for additional explanation):

1. **Write the Quote of the Week:** Bring the group together into a circle, and write the Quote on the blackboard.

2. **Think about the Quote as a group:** Spend two or three minutes talking with the kids about what they think the quote means. Next ask students to share answers to the group for the following question:

   • What do you think it means to 'be true'?

3. **Pair up to talk about the Quote:** Have students separate into pairs. Ask them to spend about five minutes discussing the following questions with their partners. Explain that they will be sharing their answers with the whole group, so they may choose to write them in their Player Portfolios. (Be sure to walk around the groups, listen, and offer help where needed.):

   • Can you think of an example from one of the stories that we have read where being true was more important than winning?

   • Can you give an example of when you have been true to your self — not necessarily in sports?

4. **Share answers with the whole group:** Come together as a large group and share the answers from each of the pair groups. Everyone who wants to should have an opportunity to share their answers.

5. **Reflect individually about the Quote:** Take two or three minutes for students to reflect individually by writing a response to the following Journal Question in their Player Portfolios:

   • If you were to describe

Activity

Lessons from Literature
Sports Extra

This is an important activity to conclude each theme unit. Students may work alone or in small groups. At the start of the unit, students were asked to look for actual events and stories of people in the news or in history who exemplify the core value for the theme unit. Students should be reminded frequently throughout the theme unit to be on the lookout for examples of the core Sports PLUS values in magazines and newspapers. They can ask a parent or guardian if they are unsure where to find an article. If possible, provide students access during the Sports PLUS program to students' magazines, such as Sports Illustrated for Kids. A certain area of the room can be designated as the "Sports Extras Area," in which students can store their articles and stories as they find them.

Setup

1. Bring the group together to form a circle. Explain the next activity as you pass out the Player Portfolios and pencils. Use the following description as a guide:

   "Today you will have an opportunity to share a story about Fair Play with the rest of the group. You may choose either to share the article you brought in or to share the story you wrote during 'Create Your Own Story.'"

2. Ask students to spend a few minutes writing answers to the pre-work questions in their Player Portfolios:

   • Who is the main character in your story?

   • What happened to the main character? Or what did the main character do?

   • In what way is this story an example of Fair Play?

   • One thing the main character learned is that he or she should…

   • This story teaches us that we should…

3. After students have had some time to answer the questions in their portfolios, ask for volunteers to share their stories in their own words. Let everyone who wants to share do so.

Cool-down

- *R&R Huddle* (5 min.)

- *Recap* by asking students: What do these articles teach us about Fair Play?

- *Reconnect* students to the theme unit using the following focus prompt: One way these examples of fair play help us be a better team is by...

- *Reset* and get ready for the next lesson.

Session 40: **Fair Play Certificates** **Lessons from the Field**	
Warm-up Begin the PLUS Cycle (5 min.) <ul><li>Session Overview</li><li>Following Up on Fair Play</li></ul>**Activity** Lessons from the Field (25-30 min.) <ul><li>Sports Activity</li></ul>	**Cool-down** Continue the PLUS Cycle (5-10 min.) <ul><li>Reflection</li><li>Goal-setting</li></ul>**Materials** Sports Equipment

Warm-up

Following Up on Fair Play (5 min.)

Ask students to think about the previous lesson. What can they do today to bring the Lessons from Literature into their work together in the sports activity?

Activity

Lessons from the Field
Sports Activity

Block I: Getting Started (5 min.)

Stand together in a circle for all *Getting Started* activities (except for jogging). Have players partner up, with one player doing the activity and the partner keeping count and giving encouragement. Be sure that players have their Portfolios handy so that they can record their progress. Players will try to improve upon their Past Personal Bests (PPB) by achieving their Future Best Goals (FBG) and by tracking progress toward those goals in their Player Portfolios.

Encourage players to clap for and cheer on their teammates to create an enthusiastic environment. You also may choose to include music.

Choose from the options below, making sure to include a cardio and a stretching warm-up.

- **Measure resting heart rate (RHR)** — Spend a few minutes showing players how to find their pulses, either on their necks or wrists. Explain that you will be giving them a few seconds to count how many times their hearts beat. Take a moment to allow the players to sit quietly on the floor and find their pulses. Give them 30 seconds to count their heartbeats.

- **Record, check in and set goals** — Allow a couple of minutes for players to record their RHRs in their Player Portfolios.

- **Jog (2-3 min.)** — This can be done as a lap or in place as a circle.

- **Stretch (2-3 min.)** — Be sure to include stretches for the major muscle groups.

- **Strength/Endurance (1 min.)** — On this first day, players will set baseline numbers for the four Strength/Endurance activities (push-ups, sit-ups, lunges, calf raises), but usually, you will only choose one or two. They will work in pairs. One member of the pair will have 30 seconds to do as many of the activities as they can. Their partner will cheer them on and count for them.

- **Jump Rope (4 min.)** — Again, players will work in pairs, with one person jumping and the other person counting and cheering. They should have three to four sets of 30-45 seconds of jumping rope.

- **Track personal progress** — Have players record their totals for steps five and six in their Player Portfolios. These totals will represent their baseline achievements, or their Past Personal Bests (PPB). Each day, players will check their progress from the previous session and will set a Future Personal Best Goal (FBG) to work toward for next time. Be sure to remind them about setting realistic goals (for example, adding one or two to their baseline, as opposed to 10).

Block II: Structured Play (30 min.)

Skill Play (10 min.)

Choose one or two of the following activities to play today. You can refer back to the *Physical Activities Description Appendix* for instructions on how to run the activities. Encourage players to cheer for each other, and include music if you wish.

- Circle Bonanza

- Hula Hoop Marathon

- Limbo

- Softball Throw

- Over, under, over, under

- Ball Bowling

Sport Play (20 min.)

As a group, decide which sport you want to play today. Select from the sport list contained in the *Sports List Appendix*. Be sure to periodically review with the group the Physical Activities Recommendations for Sport from Chapter Six.

Cool-down

If time permits, close the day with a few minutes of stretching while conducting the following R&R Huddle.

- *Recap* one or two key moments from the Lessons from the Field.

- Reconnect players back to the theme unit.

- *Reset* and transition players to the Cool-down, Reflection time.

    OR

- **Reflection**

Use this time to highlight teachable moments you observed during the day and to give players an opportunity to share their Sports PLUS experiences during this theme unit. The following questions can serve as a guide:

- What were some of your favorite things from this theme unit?

- What is one thing you learned about fair play during this theme unit?

- What are some examples of how we showed fair play during this theme unit?

- Were there any times when we didn't show fair play?

- How is fair play related to the other Sports PLUS values we've talked about—teamwork, respect, and responsibility?

Goal-setting

Use this time to track the group's progress toward their individual and team goals and to start the players thinking about one or two team goals related to Perseverance that will be set during the next session.

Session 40:
Fair Play Certificates
Lessons from Adventure

Warm-up	Cool-down
Begin the PLUS Cycle (5 min.)	Continue the PLUS Cycle (5-10 min.)
• Session Overview	• Reflection
• Fair Play Posters Revisited	• Presentation of Certificates
Activity	**Materials**
Lessons from Adventure (25-30 min.)	Fair Play posters
• Fair Play Certificates	

Warm-up

Fair Play Posters Revisited

Take a brief tour of the fair play posters that were created during the beginning of the theme unit. Stop at each poster and discuss what is represented on it and what it says about fair play. Ask players to comment on how they think the group is doing with playing fair and with creating a good team. Draw upon what is on the posters to help players come up with specific examples of fair play they noticed throughout the theme unit. Ask if anyone has anything they would like to add to the posters to update them (e.g., adding new insights and ideas they have learned over the course of the theme unit).

Activity

Lessons from Adventure
Fair Play Certificates
(see Player Portfolio)

During this activity, players will create a "Fair Play Certificate" to signify their completion of the fourth Sports PLUS theme unit. There are several ways this could be done, and players should have some voice in the decision. Possibilities include:

- Players could work in small groups to make certificates for other small groups.

- The whole team could work together to make one giant team certificate (e.g., making handprints to spell out Fair Play).

- Players could make individual certificates. (If this option is chosen, ask players to leave space on the certificates so the recipients' names can be filled in, before being distributed by the Masters of Ceremonies at the end of the day.)

Play

1. Gather the group together into a circle, and explain the purpose of the next activity to the players — "To create certificates that signify our completion of this Sports PLUS theme unit."

2. Describe one or two possible ways this can be done, and ask players if they have any other ideas. As a group, decide what you are going to do, and create the certificate(s).

3. When the certificate(s) are finished, gather the group together to vote on the two people who have given their best effort to show Fair Play during this theme unit. Voting can be done either by a show of hands, applause for nominated candidates, or by writing names on slips of paper. (In the case of a tie, allow multiple winners.)

4. Once the decision has been made, explain that the people chosen will be the "Masters of Ceremonies" for the presentation of the Fair Play Certificate(s) at the end of the day.

- ***R&R Huddle*** (5 minutes)

- ***Recap*** one or two points from the previous discussion about the Fair Play Posters.

- ***Reconnect*** players to the theme unit.

- ***Reset*** and transition to the next activity.

Cool-down

Cool-down Ritual

Presentation of Fair Play Certificates

Have the two players chosen as Masters of Ceremonies (MC) present the certificates. If certificates were created for different small groups, the MCs should call each group up one by one and formally present the certificate with a handshake and congratulations. If the group decided on one giant certificate, the MCs can hang it up somewhere in the group meeting room. (You may need to help them accomplish this task.) Finally, if the group decided to create individual certificates, help the MCs fill out the names on each certificate before the ceremony. During the ceremony, the MCs should take turns calling each person to receive their certificate.

CHAPTER FOURTEEN

Theme Unit 5: Practicing Perseverance

Session 41:
Perseverance Posters

Overview

Instructor's Notes: *Be sure to review today's activities before the Sports PLUS Day begins. Directions for how to run each activity are provided, but it is important that you become familiar with them so that you may more effectively lead the group.*

During group discussions, be sure to record all thoughts and ideas on a blackboard or newsprint. Remember that when players are working in their Player Portfolios, spelling, grammar, and penmanship are, relatively speaking, unimportant, so don't dwell on those details or you risk making Sports PLUS into MoreSchool.

The focus of this first session is on transitioning to the new value of Perseverance and defining this value in the context of what the group has already learned about the previous four values. This session is designed to help players understand the concept of perseverance and the reason it is an important character value.

The *Quote of the Week* introduces the idea of goal setting as a way to help players persevere. *Perseverance Posters* is a great activity to get players thinking about what perseverance means. Encourage players also to consider what they hope to learn about perseverance during the next 10 Sports PLUS sessions. The story of Wilma Rudolph during Lessons from Literature is a wonderful example of a person setting her sights on a challenging goal and persevering. This is an opportunity to invite someone into the group to read the story to the players.

Be sure to remind players to be on the look-out for interesting stories and articles about perseverance that they can present during *Sport Extras*. Remember that the way you carry yourself as the players' coach and role model, and the way you demonstrate perseverance in your own actions, will have a tremendous impact on what they learn about perseverance.

Session 41: **Perseverance Posters** **Lessons from Literature**	
Warm-up Begin the PLUS Cycle (10-15 min.) • Session Overview • Quote of the Week **Activity** Lessons from Literature (25-30 min.) • Theme Book — *Wilma Unlimited*	**Cool-down** Continue the PLUS Cycle (5-10 min.) • Reflection **Materials** Copy of *Wilma Unlimited*

Warm-up

Quote of the Week
(see Player Portfolio)

I like having a goal that's out there. Maybe I won't ever achieve it, but as long as I think I have a chance, then I will keep going

— Joan Benoit Samuelson,
Olympic Gold Medalist, Women's Marathon

Instructor's Note

Make sure that all students know what a marathon is. After you have explained, ask them to think about the longest distance they have ever run. Next, help students put into perspective how long a marathon is and why perseverance is important for completing one.

Follow the five steps of the Quote of the Week Format (See the Getting Started chapter for additional explanation):

1. **Write the Quote of the Week:** Bring the group together into a circle, and write the Quote on the blackboard.

2. **Think about the Quote as a group:** Spend two or three minutes talking with the students about what they think the quote means. Ask them to share answers to the following questions:

   - What does it mean to set a goal or to "have a goal that's out there"?

   - Why is it important to have "goals that are out there"?

3. **Pair up to talk about the Quote:** Have students separate into pairs. Ask them to spend about five minutes discussing the following questions with their partners. Explain that they will be sharing their answers with the whole group, so they may choose to write their answers in their Player Portfolios. (Be sure to walk around the groups, listen, and offer help where needed.):

   - How are goal setting and perseverance connected?

   - What are two or three things you can do to help yourself keep going when it looks as though you may not achieve your goal?

   - It is important to set goals and follow them because… (Give two or three reasons.)

4. **Share answers with the whole group:** Come together as a large group and share the answers from each of the pair

groups. Everyone who wants to should have an opportunity to share their answers.

5. **Reflect individually about the Quote:** Take two or three minutes for students to reflect individually by writing a response to the following Journal Prompts and Question in their Player Portfolios:

- Think of a goal you have in sports.

- Write that goal in your Player Portfolio.

- What is one thing you can do that will keep you trying the next time things get tough?

Activity

Lessons from Literature
Theme Book
Wilma Unlimited
(see Player Portfolio)

by Kathleen Krull

Setup

Gather the students into a circle and read the summary below:

"Wilma Unlimited is the story of Wilma Rudolph, who won three gold medals in track and field in a single Olympics. When Wilma was about five years old, she contracted polio which crippled one of her legs. Wilma Unlimited tells the tale of Wilma's determination and perseverance to overcome her disability and win Olympic gold."

Before reading the story, you may choose to review some of the vocabulary below:

- Polio

- Triumphant

- Scarlet fever

- Astonishment

- Outhouse

- Athletic scholarship

- Paralyzed

- Shimmering

- Twitchy with impatience

- Exhilarated

- Concentration

The Story

Read the story aloud and with enthusiasm to the whole group. Be sure to show the pictures to the students as you read.

Discussion Questions:

Spend a couple of minutes distributing students' Player Portfolios and pencils. (Ask for one or two volunteers to help.) Write the questions and focus prompts on a blackboard or newsprint.

Work together as a whole group to answer the following questions. Questions one through four should be answered in a round-robin format, with one student answering one question. Try to include students who may not always participate. (If answers for questions three and four are imprecise or need further elaboration, ask if anyone has anything to add.)

1. Who is the main character in this story?

2. What is the problem or challenge she faces?

3. How does the main character handle the problem?

4. What happens then?

The following focus prompt should be answered in an exhaustive format. Continue letting students give responses until no new answers are given.

5. Wilma Rudolph learned that she should…

For questions six and seven, allow all students an opportunity to share their answers, regardless of whether or not the answers are original.

6. When would it be important in your life to… [insert answer from previous statement]?

7. One thing that might make doing this difficult is…

Finally, ask students to write their responses to the following prompt in their Player Portfolios.

8. One specific way I might show perseverance in my life is by…

Ask for volunteers to share what they wrote. Be sure to let everyone who wants to share their responses.

Cool-down

- **R&R Huddle** (5 min.)

- **Recap** using one or two key points from the previous discussion.

- **Reconnect** by asking volunteers to briefly share what they wrote for question number eight.

- **Reset** and get ready for the next lesson.

Session 41: Perseverance Posters Lessons from the Field	

Warm-up
Begin the PLUS Cycle (5 min.)
  • Session Overview
  • Pondering about Perseverance
Activity
Lessons from the Field (25-30 min.)
  • Sports Activity
	Cool-down
	Continue the PLUS Cycle (5-10 min.)
	  • Reflection
	  • Goal-setting
	Materials
	Sports Equipment

Warm-up

Pondering Perseverance (5 min.)

Ask students to think about the previous lesson. What can they do today to bring the Lessons from Literature into their work together in the sports activity?

Activity

Lessons from Literature
Sports Activity

Block I: Getting Started (5 min.)

On the first day, players will learn how to measure their resting heart rates (RHR). They will also set baselines for their RHR, number of sit-ups/push-ups/lunges/calf raises, and number of jumps during jump rope. Each day they will try to improve upon their Past Personal Best (PPB) by achieving their Future Best Goal (FBG) and by tracking progress toward that goal in the physical activities progress chart located in the back of their Player Portfolios. Take one minute to make sure all participants turn to the back of their portfolios and locate the progress charts. Explain to them that they will be using this chart each time you meet to do physical activities. Be sure to emphasize the importance of keeping track of their progress by using the chart.

Stand together in a circle for all *Getting Started* activities (except for jogging). Have players partner up, with one player doing the activity and the partner keeping count and giving encouragement. Be sure that they have their Portfolios handy so that they can record their progress. Encourage them to clap and cheer for their teammates to create an enthusiastic environment. You may also choose to include music.

- **Measure resting heart rate (RHR)** — Spend a few minutes showing players how to find their pulses, either on their necks or wrists. Explain that you will be giving them a few seconds to count how many times their hearts beat. Take a moment to allow the players to sit quietly on the floor and find their pulses. Give them 30 seconds to count their heartbeats.

- **Record, check in and set goals** — Allow a couple of minutes for players to record their RHRs in their Player Portfolios.

- **Jog (2-3 min.)** — This can be done as a lap or in place as a circle.

- **Stretch (2-3 min.)** — Be sure to include stretches for the major muscle groups.

- **Strength/Endurance (1 min.)** — On this first day, players will set baseline numbers for the four Strength/Endurance activities (push-ups, sit-ups, lunges, calf raises), but usually, you will only choose one or two. They will work in pairs. One member of the pair will have 30 seconds to do as many of the activities as they can. Their partner will cheer them on and count for them.

- **Jump Rope (4 min.)** — Again, players will work in pairs, with one person jumping and the other person counting and cheering. They should have three to four sets of 30-45 seconds of jumping rope.

- **Track personal progress** — Have players record their totals for steps five and six in their Player Portfolios. These totals will represent their baseline achievements, or their Past Personal Bests (PPB). Each day, players will check their progress from the previous session and will set a Future Personal Best Goal (FBG) to work toward for next time. Be sure to remind them about setting realistic goals (for example, adding one or two to their baseline, as opposed to 10).

Block II: Structured Play (30 min.)

Skill Play (10 min.)

Choose one or two of the following activities to play today. You can refer back to the *Physical Activities Description Appendix* for instructions on how to run the activities. Encourage players to cheer for each other, and include music if you wish.

- Clothes Relay

- Hula Hoop Challenge Course

- Dribble Relay

- Standing Broad Jump

- Balance Tag

Activity

Sport Play (20 min.)

As a group, decide which sport you want to play today. Select from the sport list contained in the *Sports List Appendix*. Be sure to periodically review with the group the Physical Activities Recommendations for Sport from Chapter Six.

Cool-down

If time permits, close the day with a few minutes of stretching while conducting the following R&R Huddle.

- **Recap** one or two key moments from the Lessons from the Field.

- **Reconnect** players back to the theme unit.

- **Reset** and transition players to the Cool-down, Reflection time.

  OR

- **Reflection**

Use this time to highlight teachable moments you observed during the day and to give players an opportunity to share their experiences about Sports PLUS during the day. The following questions can serve as a guide:

- What did you like about today?

- What did you learn today?

- What are some ways you persevered today?

- How can we better show perseverance next time?

Goal-setting

Keeping the *S.M.A.R.T. goals* script in mind, spend a few minutes working together as a group to set one or two team goals related to Perseverance.

Session 41: **Perseverance Posters** **Lessons from Adventure**	
Warm-up Begin the PLUS Cycle (5 min.) • Session Overview • Secret Agent **Activity** Lessons from Adventure (25-30 min.) • Perseverance Posters	**Cool-down** Continue the PLUS Cycle (5-10 min.) • Reflection • Go-Round **Materials** 2 poster-sized pieces of paper for each group of 3 or 4 players, different colored markers, one dictionary per group (if dictionaries are unavailable, write the definition of perseverance on a chalkboard or poster), magazines, newspapers for cutting, glue

Warm-up

Secret Agent

Setup

Gather players for the instructions. After the tag game, ask players to think about how they demonstrated perseverance. How could perseverance help you in this activity?

Play

1. Ask players to choose one player, without acknowledging that person, to be their "guardian angel."

2. Ask players to then choose a different player, again without letting anyone know who they selected, to be their "secret agent."

3. Explain to players that the good news is that their guardian angel is there to protect them, but the bad news is that their secret agent is actually a double agent and is giving away secrets about them.

4. In this activity, players are to try to keep their guardian angel between them and their secret agent. In order to do this, each player has to follow their guardian angel wherever he or she goes.

5. End the activity after a few minutes of "chaos" as players jockey to keep their guardian angels between them and their secret agents.

6. Play a few more rounds. Ask players to change guardian angels and secret agents each time. Between each round, ask players to walk around and acknowledge their guardian angels and their secret agents.

7. Finally, ask players to think about the role perseverance plays in this activity.

Activity

Lessons from Adventure
Perseverance Posters
(see Player Portfolio)

Defining Perseverance

Begin by having a large group discussion of the meaning of the word Perseverance. This can be a brainstorming discussion, keeping track of ideas on a poster or chalkboard. Once you think the group has some ideas, form small groups of three or four players. Following the group discussion, this hands-on activity helps players come up with concrete examples of different aspects of perseverance and allows them to share what they know. The group now has many visual reminders of what they have agreed constitutes perseverance

Setup

Separate the groups into teams of three or four. Give each team a table or some open space on the floor, two pieces of poster-sized pieces of paper, a dictionary if available, and some markers.

Play

1. Each group will use a dictionary to look up the meaning of perseverance. If dictionaries are unavailable, write the definition on the chalkboard.

2. Using this information, and their own understanding of perseverance, players will create a poster to teach the rest of the group what perseverance means to them. The poster can be anything the groups choose to represent perseverance. They can create a Being (see the Teamwork Unit) by tracing the outline of one of their bodies on the poster paper, cut out pictures from magazines if you have a collection to use, or make their own drawing.

3. Groups should then write words and phrases around their drawing that gives their definition of perseverance. Players should use their own words to define perseverance, not the words from the dictionary. They should also write words or phrases on the outside of their Being or drawing that show what the opposite of perseverance looks and sounds like.

4. Remind the players that this is a team project and they should spend a few minutes planning what they, as a team, want to create and how they are going to create it. All members of the team should be actively involved in the planning, decision-making, and production of the posters. Allow 15-20 minutes for the small groups to work.

5. Once the groups have completed their posters, spend a few minutes presenting group posters to the group and explaining

definitions, drawings, words, and phrases. If time permits, allow some discussion and questions for each group.

6. Hang the posters around the room and refer back to them as often as necessary throughout the program to reinforce and remind players of their commitments. As the unit progresses, and players' understanding of perseverance increases, have them add new ideas, words and phrases to their posters.

7. Hang the "Sports PLUS Leader to Detractor Poster" for Perseverance. Reflect on the 5-point scale and the connections between this scale and the players' posters. Utilize this scale to guide your reflections in all phases of the program.

- **R&R Huddle** (5 minutes)

- **Recap** one or two key points that arose during the discussion.

- **Reconnect** by asking players to share examples of perseverance.

- **Reset** and transition to the next activity.

Cool-down

Cool-down Ritual

Go-Round

In a large group circle, ask for volunteers to provide their own examples of when someone told them they could not achieve something because they were too small, too young, not smart enough, etc. How did they react? Do they think they have learned anything about perseverance from today's activities and the story of Wilma Rudolph that might make them react differently if this happens again?

Homework Assignment

As a fun homework assignment, ask the players and staff to begin looking in local newspapers and magazines, and to listen for stories on the radio and television that show examples of perseverance. Ask everyone to bring these examples to the group when they find them. The group will continue adding to the collection of articles and stories they gathered for the previous theme units and will use them at the end of the program.

Session 42:
Perseverance Relay

Overview

Instructor's Notes: *Be sure to review this set of activities before starting this Sports PLUS Session. Directions for how to run each activity are provided, but it is important that you become familiar with them so that you may more effectively lead the group.*

During group discussions, be sure to record all thoughts and ideas on a blackboard or newsprint. Remember that when players are working in their Player Portfolios, spelling, grammar, and penmanship are, relatively speaking, unimportant, so don't dwell on those details or you risk making Sports PLUS into MoreSchool.

Today is the first day of a five-session theme book. *Hang Tough, Paul Mather* is the story of a boy's perseverance in the face of a life-threatening disease. The first activity from the Lessons from Adventure, *Twizzle*, is a mildly competitive activity with many rules. Depending on how much space you have in your classroom, you may want to play it in the gym or outside. The *Perseverance Relay* is a fun and familiar activity that helps players explore their understanding of perseverance. To conclude the session, players will review the principles and rules they have previously committed to and then sign the Perseverance line of the Player Contract.

Session 42: Perseverance Relay Lessons from Literature	

Warm-up
Begin the PLUS Cycle (10-15 min.)
 	
   • Session Overview
 	
   • Quote of the Week
 	
Activity
Lessons from Literature (25-30 min.)
 	
   • Theme Book — *Hang Tough, Paul Mather*
	Cool-down
	Continue the PLUS Cycle (5-10 min.)
	
	   • Reflection
	
	Materials
	Copies of *Hang Tough, Paul Mather*

Warm-up

Quote of the Week

The Six W's: Work will win when wishing won't."

— Todd Blackledge

Follow the five steps of the Quote of the Week Format (See the *Getting Started* chapter for additional explanation):

1. **Write the Quote of the Week:** Bring the group together into a circle, and write the Quote on the blackboard.

2. **Think about the Quote as a group:** Spend two or three minutes talking with the students about what they think the quote means. Ask students the following question:

   • What do hard work and perseverance have in common?

3. **Pair up to talk about the Quote:** Have students separate into pairs. Ask them to spend about five minutes discussing the following questions with their partners. Explain that they will be sharing their answers with the whole group, so they may choose to write their answers in their Player Portfolios. (Be sure to walk around the groups, listen, and offer help where needed.):

   • Can you imagine why Todd, who played college football and then went on to the NFL, might have believed in this quote?

   • Think of an example from your Sports PLUS time when this quote came true.

4. **Share answers with the whole group:** Come together as a large group and share the answers from each of the pair groups. Everyone who wants to should have an opportunity to share their answers.

5. **Reflect individually about the Quote:** Take two or three minutes for students to reflect individually by writing a

response to the following Journal Question in their Player Portfolios:

- How do the six W's play out in life outside of sports? Give an example.

Activity

Lessons from Literature
Theme Book
Hang Tough, Paul Mather
(see Player Portfolio)

by Alfred Slote

Instructor's Note

> This book was originally published in 1973. Some things may seem strange to students (e.g., Paul and his brother going home from school for lunch), and some of the language may seem dated. In addition, many medical advances have been made since 1973 in treating childhood leukemia. These points can serve as discussion items to help students put the book into context as they read it.

Perspective

This story is Paul's story as told by himself. The present tense section of the story takes place with Paul in the hospital. Paul's doctor gives him a tape recorder, and Paul subsequently recounts the events that happened before he entered the hospital. Chapters two, three, four, six, seven, and eight are "flashbacks" as Paul tells his story. Drawing a timeline may help students to follow the order of events as Paul recounts them.

Gather the students together into a circle and read the summary below:

Hang Tough, Paul Mather is the story of a boy's perseverance in the face of a life-threatening disease. Paul Mather is a sixth-grader, who has leukemia. He and his family have just moved from California to Arborville so that a specialist can treat him.

The one thing that Paul loves more that anything is baseball. He was a star pitcher on his last team in California, but has been forbidden by his parents and doctors to play baseball because of his illness. As soon as his family pulls into their new town, however, he is recruited by some neighborhood kids to be on their baseball team.

Paul's determination to play baseball lands him in trouble, but it also reveals his determination to hang tough, and to succeed."

After reading the summary, you may want to spend a few minutes exploring different themes before beginning the book. A couple of suggestions are listed below:

Ask students to examine the book: look at the title page and table of contents, read the headings and the summary at the back of the book. Ask students to predict what they think will happen in the story.

- The central theme is Paul's fight against his illness. Ask students if they, or someone they know, have had to stay in the hospital for a long period of time. (Note: Be aware that this may be a sensitive subject area for children. Keep this in mind when reading the book and facilitating discussion.)

Chapter-by-Chapter Summary

Read the story aloud and with enthusiasm to the whole group. The following chapter summary will act as a guide as you make your way through the book.

Chapter One: *The Tape Recorder*

In chapter one, we meet Paul Mather and his doctor, Tom Kinsella. Paul is in the hospital, and is just getting to know his new doctor. We begin to learn about where Paul lived before he came to Arborville.

Chapter Two: *Arrival in Arborville*

In chapter two, Paul recounts his very first impressions of Arborville as he arrives with his father, mother and brother. We are introduced to Paul's younger brother Larry, whom Paul refers to alternately as "Pest" and "Punk." We are told that this is the family's second move, and that the reason they have had to move is because of Paul's illness. As soon as they have arrived at their new house, Larry strikes up a conversation with some neighborhood boys and brags about Paul's pitching skills.

Chapter Three: Pitch in a Winding Lane

The neighborhood kids play for a baseball team that is in need of a good pitcher. With Larry boasting about his pitching abilities, Paul allows himself to be drawn in to demonstrating his skills to the boys. The boys try to convince Paul that they could use him on their team. Paul's father watches and calls them to come inside.

Before reading the story, you may choose to review some of the vocabulary below:

- abrupt (p.18)

- blow your stack (p.18)

- consequences (p. 23)

- determined (p. 18)

- grimace (p.27)

- lob (p.20)

- punctuate (p.16)

- tempt (p.24)

Discussion Questions

Spend a couple of minutes distributing students' Player Portfolios and pencils. (Ask one or two volunteers to help.) Write the questions and focus prompts on a blackboard or newsprint.

Work together as a whole group to answer the following questions:

Questions one through eight should be answered in a round-robin format, with one student answering one question. Try to include students who may not always participate. (If answers for any of the questions are imprecise or need further elaboration, ask if anyone has anything to add.)

1. Who is the main character?

2. What is his favorite pastime or sport?

3. Is he good at this pastime? How do we know?

4. What are the names of Paul's family members?

5. What happens to his family?

6. What is Paul's nickname for his little brother?

7. What is the problem or challenge Paul faces?

8. What does Paul do to get himself into trouble with Monk, Tip, and Abels?

Close the activity by passing a baseball around the circle, and let each student have a turn holding it. Ask students to close their eyes and examine the ball when it is their turn. Feel the seams; squeeze the ball; toss it from hand to hand. What does the ball feel like? What words would they use to describe the baseball and the way it feels in their hands?

Cool-down

- **R&R Huddle** (5 min.)

- **Recap** one or two key points that arose during the discussion.

- **Reconnect** by asking students to share examples of perseverance and the other Sports PLUS values they noticed in the first three chapters.

- **Reset** and transition to the next lesson.

Session 42: **Perseverance Relay** **Lessons from the Field**	

Warm-up
    Begin the PLUS Cycle (5 min.)
      • Session Overview
      • Pondering Perseverance
Activity
    Lessons from the Field (25-30 min.)
      • Sports Activity
	Cool-down
	    Continue the PLUS Cycle (5-10 min.)
	      • Reflection
	      • Goal-setting
	Materials
	    Sports Equipment

Warm-up

Pondering Perseverance (5 min.)

Ask students to think about the previous lesson. What can they do today to bring the Lessons from Literature into their work together in the sports activity?

Activity

Lessons from the Field
Sports Activity

Block I: Getting Started (5 min.)

On the first day, players will learn how to measure their resting heart rates (RHR). They will also set baselines for their RHR, number of sit-ups/push-ups/lunges/calf raises, and number of jumps during jump rope. Each day they will try to improve upon their Past Personal Best (PPB) by achieving their Future Best Goal (FBG) and by tracking progress toward that goal in the physical activities progress chart located in the back of their Player Portfolios. Take one minute to make sure all participants turn to the back of their portfolios and locate the progress charts. Explain to them that they will be using this chart each time you meet to do physical activities. Be sure to emphasize the importance of keeping track of their progress by using the chart.

Stand together in a circle for all *Getting Started* activities (except for jogging). Have players partner up, with one player doing the activity and the partner keeping count and giving encouragement. Be sure that they have their Portfolios handy so that they can record their progress. Encourage them to clap and cheer for their teammates to create an enthusiastic environment. You may also choose to include music.

Choose from the options below, making sure to include a cardio and a stretching warm-up.

- **Measure resting heart rate (RHR)** — Spend a few minutes showing players how to find their pulses, either on their necks or wrists. Explain that you will be giving them a few seconds to count how many times their hearts beat. Take a moment to allow the players to sit quietly on the floor and find their pulses. Give them 30 seconds to count their heartbeats.

- **Record, check in and set goals** — Allow a couple of minutes for players to record their RHRs in their Player Portfolios.

- **Jog (2-3 min.)** — This can be done as a lap or in place as a circle.

- **Stretch (2-3 min.)** — Be sure to include stretches for the major muscle groups.

- **Strength/Endurance (1 min.)** — On this first day, players will set baseline numbers for the four Strength/Endurance activities (push-ups, sit-ups, lunges, calf raises), but usually, you will only choose one or two. They will work in pairs. One member of the pair will have 30 seconds to do as many of the activities as they can. Their partner will cheer them on and count for them.

- **Jump Rope (4 min.)** — Again, players will work in pairs, with one person jumping and the other person counting and cheering. They should have three to four sets of 30-45 seconds of jumping rope.

- **Track personal progress** — Have players record their totals for steps five and six in their Player Portfolios. These totals will represent their baseline achievements, or their Past Personal Bests (PPB). Each day, players will check their progress from

the previous session and will set a Future Personal Best Goal (FBG) to work toward for next time. Be sure to remind them about setting realistic goals (for example, adding one or two to their baseline, as opposed to 10).

Block II: Structured Play (30 min.)

Skill Play (10 min.)

Choose one or two of the following activities to play today. You can refer back to the *Physical Activities Description Appendix* for instructions on how to run the activities. Encourage players to cheer for each other, and include music if you wish.

- Three-legged race
- Water Balloon Toss
- Sprint/Stride Runs
- Chinese Jump Rope
- Kick Up Your Heels Relay

Sport Play (20 min.)

As a group, decide which sport you want to play today. Select from the sport list contained in the *Sports List Appendix*. Be sure to periodically review with the group the Physical Activities Recommendations for Sport from Chapter Six.

Cool-down

If time permits, close the day with a few minutes of stretching while conducting the following R&R Huddle.

- **Recap** one or two key moments from the Lessons from the Field.
- **Reconnect** players back to the theme unit.
- **Reset** and transition players to the Cool-down, Reflection time.

OR

- **Reflection**

Use this time to highlight teachable moments you observed during the day and to give players an opportunity to share their experiences about Sports PLUS during the day. The following questions can serve as a guide:

- What did you like about today?

- What did you learn today?

- What are some ways you persevered today?

- How can we better show perseverance next time?

Goal-setting

Use this time to track the group's progress toward the team goals you set last time and to start the players thinking about one or two individual goals related to Perseverance.

Session 42: Perseverance Relay Lessons from Adventure	
Warm-up Begin the PLUS Cycle (5 min.) • Session Overview • Twizzle **Activity** Lessons from Adventure (25-30 min.) • Perseverance Relay	**Cool-down** Continue the PLUS Cycle (5-10 min.) • Reflection • Contract Renewal **Materials** 4 large flip charts or sheets of poster paper hung around the room with the following headings — 2 that read *Perseverance in Sports,* and two that read *Perseverance in Life;* different colored markers at each station; cones or other objects to create a simple obstacle course

Warm-up

Twizzle

This is a game that requires concentration and has a lot of rules. The object is for the players to use the various game movements to get from point A to point B within a certain amount of time.

Play

1. Have the group form a line with everyone facing you at the front of the line. All players should be at arm's-length from each other. Review the commands and movements so that all players know what to do.

2. Explain that, on your command, everyone should begin walking toward you.

3. When you give any of the following commands, participants must perform the appropriate movement.

   GO — Walk in a synchronized way in the direction you are facing.

   STOP — Stop moving and freeze!

   TURN — Make a half turn to your right, step big with your left foot, slide both feet together and freeze!

   JUMP — Jump and make a half turn in the same direction and freeze!

   TWIZZLE — Jump and make a full (360°) turn and freeze!

4. Challenge the players to move together as a group, remaining as synchronized as possible with you being the judge. Each

time a major infraction occurs (i.e., the group is out of sync) the whole group must take five to ten steps back.

5. If the group gets really good, try combining the moves to make it even more challenging.

Variation

You may choose to engage players in choosing the commands and actions before the game begins. Allow them to make suggestions for new movements and incorporate them into the next round of play.

Activity

Lessons from Adventure
Perseverance Relay
(see Player Portfolio)

Setup

Before you begin, hang the four large pieces of poster or art paper in different parts of the room. Make sure that the players will be able to reach the paper to write on it. While there are four posters, there are only two statements. This is simply to speed up the activity and allow players time to be directly involved. Each team only visits two different posters. Set up the cones or other objects so that players will have a clear path to run around.

Divide the group into four smaller groups. Remind players that as they participate in the activity, they should also be practicing behavior that represents perseverance and the other Sports PLUS values.

Play

1. Assign each team to one of the posters.

2. Each team will be given three to five minutes to write as many responses to complete the phrase "Perseverance in Sports sounds like or looks like…" or "Perseverance in My Life looks like or sounds like…"

3. The team must work as a relay team — each player on the team has a turn with the marker and writes something on the poster. After writing a statement, each player must run around a cone before handing off the marker to a teammate. The team repeats the relay pattern until the time is up. Teammates can help each other if someone gets stuck.

4. After five minutes or so, yell "Switch!" Each team then moves to a different poster with a different statement.

Discussion

Have the players gather again as a large group. Hang the posters in a place where everyone can see them. Spend some time discussing each poster. Create two new posters as a group with simple statements for what the group sees as the most important ideas about perseverance in the program. Finally, if time permits, allow the players an opportunity to decorate the posters.

Leave these posters hanging in the after-school space for the remainder of the program.

- **R&R Huddle** (5 minutes)

- **Recap** by highlighting one or two key discussion points.

- **Reconnect** with the following focus prompt: Perseverance is important because...

- **Reset** and transition to the next activity.

Cool-down

Cool-down Ritual

Player Contract Renewal

This is a good time to revisit the contract that the players first developed in the Teamwork Unit.

Have players take their contracts out of their portfolios. The last value on the list is perseverance. Spend some time in a whole group discussion reviewing what the group has learned so far about perseverance and how it exists in their group. Refer to the posters created during this session. This would also be a good time for players to offer any examples they noticed of the values — Teamwork, Respect, Responsibility, Fair Play, and Perseverance — working together.

Move the discussion to what each player can do to persevere in difficult situations. The following discussion questions are intended as suggestions to start and guide this discussion:

- What do you think perseverance means?

- Can anyone give an example of perseverance from something they have seen in this group? At school? At home? In your neighborhood?

- Why is perseverance important to you as an individual? Why is it important for our group?

- What can each of us commit to in order to better persevere?

Once you think the group has arrived at a good understanding of why perseverance is important, have a Player Contract Signing Ceremony. Remind players that by signing the Perseverance line on their contract, they are making a commitment to themselves and their teammates.

Session 43:
Hanging Tough

Overview

Instructor's Notes: *Be sure to review this set of activities before starting this Sports PLUS Session. Directions for how to run each activity are provided, but it is important that you become familiar with them so that you may more effectively lead the group.*

During group discussions, be sure to record all thoughts and ideas on a blackboard or newsprint. Remember that when players are working in their Player Portfolios, spelling, grammar, and penmanship are, relatively speaking, unimportant, so don't dwell on those details or you risk making Sports PLUS into MoreSchool.

This session's *Quote of the Week* is a straightforward, practical maxim that can help players live out perseverance. The theme book reading continues with *Hang Tough, Paul Mather.* Next, *Slot Machine* challenges three groups to work together toward success. In addition to bringing up important topics, such as working together for the good of the whole team and respecting the team goal over individual accomplishments, this activity challenges players to create a symbol to represent their understanding of perseverance. The session ends with another look at the Perseverance Posters.

Session 43:
Hanging Tough
Lessons from Literature

Warm-up	Cool-down
Begin the PLUS Cycle (10-15 min.)	Continue the PLUS Cycle (5-10 min.)
• Session Overview	• Reflection
• Quote of the Week	**Materials**
Activity	Copies of *Hang Tough, Paul Mather*
Lessons from Literature (25-30 min.)	
• Theme Book — *Hang Tough, Paul Mather*	

Warm-up

Quote of the Week
(see Player Portfolio)

When in doubt, try your best.

— Anonymous

Follow the five steps of the Quote of the Week Format (See the Getting Started chapter for additional explanation):

1. **Write the Quote of the Week:** Bring the group together into a circle, and write the Quote on the blackboard.

2. **Think about the Quote as a group:** Spend two or three minutes talking with the students about what they think the quote means. Ask students to share answers to the group for the following questions:

   • What is this quote telling us?

   • Why do you think it is important to "try your best" even when you are not sure of the outcome?

3. **Pair up to talk about the Quote:** Have students separate into pairs. Ask them to spend about five minutes discussing the following questions with their partners. Explain that they will be sharing their answers with the whole group, so they may choose to write their answers in their Player Portfolios. (Be sure to walk around the groups, listen, and offer help where needed.):

   • One way to try your best when in doubt is to…

   • One way to help your teammates try their best when in doubt is to…

4. **Share answers with the whole group:** Come together as a large group and share the answers from each of the pair groups. Everyone who wants to should have an opportunity to share their answers.

5. **Reflect individually about the Quote:** Take two or three minutes for students to reflect individually by writing responses to the following Journal Question in their Player Portfolios:

   • Think of something in school that is difficult for you or may not be your favorite subject. One way you can make sure to try your best when working with that subject or activity is to….

Activity

Lessons from Literature
Theme Book
Hang Tough, Paul Mather
(see Player Portfolio)

by Alfred Slote

Lesson No. Two: Chapter 4-6

Setup

Gather the students into a circle and discuss the themes below:

- Ask students if they have ever experienced moving to a new place. How old were they? What was it like to start a new school and make new friends? In the book, Paul seemed to make friends quickly because he was a good pitcher. What are some of the other ways that students can connect and make friends when they are in a new environment?

- The most difficult part for Paul about being sick is that he has been forbidden to even throw a baseball. Has there ever been a time when you weren't able to do something you enjoyed doing? What is it like to not be able to do something you love doing?

Ask students to keep these issues in mind as they continue reading the book.

Chapter-by-Chapter Summary

Read chapters four through six aloud and with enthusiasm to the whole group.

Chapter Four: Ball Park Detour

Paul's parents are angry with him for pitching the baseball; Paul wishes that his Dad would understand how badly he wants to play. Paul's parents do not want him to exert himself at all, and even refuse to let him help carry in luggage; Paul is frustrated. The family goes out to get some dinner, and

Larry leads them past the baseball park where the neighborhood students are playing a game. The coach comes over and asks Paul to be on the team. Angry, Paul's parents say "no" and drive away.

Chapter Five: Time Out #1

Paul is back in the hospital; he interrupts the telling of his story for a conversation with Dr. Kinsella. Dr. Kinsella tells Paul that his medicine dosage must be increased. Paul tells Dr. Kinsella that he knows the name of his disease, which his parents have not wanted to tell him. Paul confesses his fear that there is no cure. Dr. Kinsella lets him cry and comforts him with more optimistic news of the chances for a cure.

Chapter Six: Coach Comes Recruiting

Paul resumes his narration of his story about Arborville before the hospital. The same evening they arrive in town, the local coach comes to Paul's house to recruit him for the team. Paul's parents tell him Paul is sick but give no details of his illness. Paul urges his parents to ask the doctor to move up his doctor's appointment so that he can get permission to play, but his parents are cautious. The coach is persistent and leaves the registration card for the baseball league; Paul ends up with it in his hands.

Before reading the story, you may choose to review some of the vocabulary below:

- assert (p.50)

- curve ball (p.44)

- disastrous (p.58)

- dosage (p.42)

- grim (p.49)

- instinct (p.48)

- reluctantly (p.49)

- stealing his signs (p.42)

- thrive (p.51)

- transfusion (p.42)

Discussion Questions

Spend a couple of minutes distributing students' Player Portfolios and pencils. (Ask for one or two volunteers to help.) Write the questions and focus prompts on a blackboard or newsprint.

Work together as a whole group to answer the following questions:

Questions one through seven should be answered in a round-robin format, with one student answering one question. Try to include students who may not always participate. (If answers for any of the questions are imprecise or need further elaboration, ask if anyone has anything to add.)

1. Who is the Coach of Wilson Dairy?

2. Why do you think Larry, Paul's younger brother, led his parents past the ball park on their way to dinner?

3. Who is Dr. Kinsella?

4. What does Dr. Kinsella mean when he tells Paul he "plays it safe"?

5. Do you think Paul wants to play it safe? Why or why not?

6. What does Paul tell Dr. Kinsella he is afraid of ?

7. Paul cried in front of Dr. Kinsella. What do you think about this? Do you think it was a sign of weakness or of strength? Why?

The following focus prompt should be answered in an exhaustive format. Continue letting students give responses until no new answers are given.

8. One way that Paul has shown perseverance is by...

Cool-down

- **R&R Huddle** (5 min.)

- **Recap** one or two key points that arose during the discussion. You might consider asking:

– Larry continues to encourage Paul to play baseball despite his illness. Do you think this encouragement helps motivate Paul or do you think it makes him sadder?

- **Reconnect** to theme unit. Consider asking the following question:

  – Why do you think Paul has a hard time telling Dr. Kinsella about his fears?

- **Reset** and get ready for the next lesson.

Session 43: **Hanging Tough** **Lessons from the Field**	
Warm-up Begin the PLUS Cycle (5 min.) • Session Overview • Pondering Perseverance **Activity** Lessons from the Field (25-30 min.) • Sports Activity	**Cool-down** Continue the PLUS Cycle (5-10 min.) • Reflection • Goal-setting **Materials** Sports Equipment

Warm-up

Pondering Perseverance (5 min.)

Ask students to think about the previous lesson. What can they do today to bring the Lessons from Literature into their work together in the sports activity?

Activity

Lessons from the Field
Sports Activity

Block I: Getting Started (5 min.)

On the first day, players will learn how to measure their resting heart rates (RHR). They will also set baselines for their RHR, number of sit-ups/push-ups/lunges/calf raises, and number of jumps during jump rope. Each day they will try to improve upon their Past Personal Best (PPB) by achieving their Future Best Goal (FBG) and by tracking progress toward that goal in the physical activities progress chart located in the back of their Player Portfolios. Take one minute to make sure all participants turn to the back of their portfolios and locate the progress charts. Explain to them that they will be using this chart each time you meet to do physical activities. Be sure to emphasize the importance of keeping track of their progress by using the chart.

Stand together in a circle for all *Getting Started* activities (except for jogging). Have players partner up, with one player doing the activity and the partner keeping count and giving encouragement. Be sure that they have their Portfolios handy so that they can record their progress. Encourage them to clap and cheer for their teammates to create an enthusiastic environment. You may also choose to include music.

Choose from the options below, making sure to include a cardio and a stretching warm-up.

- **Measure resting heart rate (RHR)** — Spend a few minutes showing players how to find their pulses, either on their necks or wrists. Explain that you will be giving them a few seconds to count how many times their hearts beat. Take a moment to allow the players to sit quietly on the floor and find their pulses. Give them 30 seconds to count their heartbeats.

- **Record, check in and set goals** — Allow a couple of minutes for players to record their RHRs in their Player Portfolios.

- **Jog (2-3 min.)** — This can be done as a lap or in place as a circle.

- **Stretch (2-3 min.)** — Be sure to include stretches for the major muscle groups.

- **Strength/Endurance (1 min.)** — On this first day, players will set baseline numbers for the four Strength/Endurance activities (push-ups, sit-ups, lunges, calf raises), but usually, you will only choose one or two. They will work in pairs. One member of the pair will have 30 seconds to do as many of the activities as they can. Their partner will cheer them on and count for them.

- **Jump Rope (4 min.)** — Again, players will work in pairs, with one person jumping and the other person counting and cheering. They should have three to four sets of 30-45 seconds of jumping rope.

- **Track personal progress** — Have players record their totals for steps five and six in their Player Portfolios. These totals will represent their baseline achievements, or their Past Personal Bests (PPB). Each day, players will check their progress from the previous session and will set a Future Personal Best Goal (FBG) to work toward for next time. Be sure to remind them about setting realistic goals (for example, adding one or two to their baseline, as opposed to 10).

Block II: Structured Play (30 min.)

Skill Play (10 min.)

Choose one or two of the following activities to play today. You can refer back to the *Physical Activities Description Appendix* for instructions on how to run the activities. Encourage players to cheer for each other, and include music if you wish.

- Tug o' war

- Sashay Relay

- Star Jumps

- Twister

- Train

Sport Play (20 min.)

As a group, decide which sport you want to play today. Select from the sport list contained in the *Sports List Appendix.* Be sure to periodically review with the group the Physical Activities Recommendations for Sport from Chapter Six.

Cool-down

If time permits, close the day with a few minutes of stretching while conducting the following R&R Huddle.

- **Recap** one or two key moments from the Lessons from the Field.

- **Reconnect** players back to the theme unit.

- **Reset** and transition players to the Cool-down, Reflection time.

    OR

- **Reflection**

Use this time to highlight teachable moments you observed during the day and to give players an opportunity to share their experiences about Sports PLUS during the day. The following questions can serve as a guide:

- What did you like about today?

- What did you learn today?

- What are some ways you persevered today?

- How can we better show perseverance next time?

- In what ways did your teammates persevere today?

Goal-setting

Use this time to track the group's progress toward your chosen team goals and to help players choose individual goals related to Perseverance.

Session 43:
Hanging Tough
Lessons from Adventure

Warm-up	Cool-down
Begin the PLUS Cycle (5 min.)	Continue the PLUS Cycle (5-10 min.)
• Session Overview	• Reflection
• Psychic Handshake	• Poster Tour
Activity	**Materials**
Lessons from Adventure (25-30 min.)	None
• Slot Machine	

Warm-up

Psychic Handshake

Setup

This activity will end with either three or four groups, depending on the number of groups you want for Slot Machine. Gather students to hear the instructions.

Play

1. Tell players to silently, without telling anyone, pick a number between one and three (or one and four if you want to have four groups).

2. Demonstrate how players will silently approach each other: shake hands "pumping" the number of times that equals the number you picked. For example, if I picked three, I would try to "pump" hands three times. However, if the player with whom I am shaking hands picked one, then they will try to hold fast at one "pump," creating resistance for me.

3. If both players pump the same number of times, they should stay together and try to find other players who picked the same number.

4. This quick activity ends when everyone is in a group.

5. You may need to even out the group

Activity

Lessons from Adventure
Slot Machine
(see Player Portfolio)

This group problem-solving activity offers another opportunity for the group to work together to solve a problem.

You can do this activity in a classroom, but playing in your gym or outside on a field affords more options and creativity.

Bring the group together in a circle. Separate into three teams of three or more.

Play

1. The name of the game is Slot Machine. The goal is to get three matching pictures.

2. Each team will go to a corner of the room and create a group gesture to represent perseverance, drawing from what they have learned about this value in previous sessions.

3. Once each team has a gesture, bring the group back together. Line the teams up in a triangle formation. Ask each team to show its gesture.

4. For the rest of the activity, there will be no talking among teams. The goal of the group is for you (the facilitator) to count to three, say "Go," and have all three teams show the same gesture.

5. Play one round — count to three and see what gesture each team shows. This round helps the group to understand the game. Now, send the teams back to their corners, allowing time for the teams to decide which gesture they will use.

6. Come back together. Count to three, and see what gestures are presented.

7. Repeat this process until all three groups get the same gesture (or the group tires of the game).

- **R&R Huddle** (5 minutes)

- **Recap** — at this point, the group has played this game during each session of the Sports PLUS program. Using one or two of the following questions, engage players in a brief reflection of the team's progress toward working together:

  - What are some differences between the first time we played this game and this last time?

  - Was it easier or more difficult? What was easier? Was anything more challenging this time around?

- **Reconnect** by asking players to complete one or two of the following sentences:

  - As a team, we were (successful/unsuccessful) during Slot Machine because…

  - This time, playing Slot Machine was (easier/ more difficult) because…

  - I learned that…

- **Reset** and transition to the next activity.

Cool-down

Cool-down Ritual

Poster Tour

To reinforce the idea of perseverance, take a brief tour of the posters created at the beginning of this theme unit and ask if anyone has anything they would like to add to the posters. Remind players to continue looking for articles in the news and stories that provide examples of the Sports PLUS values in action, especially examples of perseverance.

Session 44:
S.M.A.R.T. Goals

Overview

> **Instructor's Notes:** *Be sure to review this set of activities before starting this Sports PLUS Session. Directions for how to run each activity are provided, but it is important that you become familiar with them so that you may more effectively lead the group.*
>
> *During group discussions, be sure to record all thoughts and ideas on a blackboard or newsprint. Remember that when players are working in their Player Portfolios, spelling, grammar, and penmanship are, relatively speaking, unimportant, so don't dwell on those details or you risk making Sports PLUS into MoreSchool.*

During the Lessons from Literature, students continue their theme book reading about Paul Mather. This session's Adventure lesson begins with an activity that seems simple enough, but is really quite challenging. *Count Off* will require the group to work together and to persevere if they are to succeed.

S.M.A.R.T. Goals reviews the script students can use when setting goals. Finally, students end the session with Mental Video to help them reflect on their experiences in the program over the past few days.

Session 44: S.M.A.R.T. Goals Lessons from Literature	
Warm-up Begin the PLUS Cycle (10-15 min.) • Session Overview • Quote of the Week **Activity** Lessons from Literature (25-30 min.) • Theme Book — *Hang Tough, Paul Mather*	**Cool-down** Continue the PLUS Cycle (5-10 min.) • Reflection **Materials** Copies of *Hang Tough, Paul Mather*

Warm-up

Quote of the Week

My motto was always to keep swinging. Whether I was in a slump or feeling badly or having trouble off the field, the only thing to do was keep swinging.

— Hank Aaron

Follow the five steps of the Quote of the Week Format (See the Getting Started chapter for additional explanation):

1. ***Write the Quote of the Week:*** Bring the group together into a circle, and write the Quote on the blackboard.

2. ***Think about the Quote as a group:*** Spend two or three minutes talking with the students about what they think the quote means. Ask students to share answers to the group for the following question:

   • What does Hank mean by "keep swinging?"

3. ***Pair up to talk about the Quote:*** Have students separate into pairs. Ask them to spend about five minutes discussing the following questions with their partners. Explain that they will be sharing their answers with the whole group, so they may choose to write their answers in their Player Portfolios. (Be sure to walk around the groups, listen, and offer help where needed.):

   • What do "keeping swinging" and persevering have in common?

   • What are some common things that happen that get in the way of "keeping swinging?"

4. ***Share answers with the whole group:*** Come together as a large group and share the answers from each of the pair groups. Everyone who wants to should have an opportunity to share their answers.

5. ***Reflect individually about the Quote:*** Take two or three minutes for students to reflect individually by writing a response to the following Journal Question in their Player Portfolios:

- How does perseverance help you succeed?

Activity

Lessons from Literature
Theme Book
Hang Tough, Paul Mather
(see Player Portfolio)

by Alfred Slote

Lessons No. Three: Chapters 7-9

Setup

Ask students to look over the chapter titles for Chapters 7-9. What predictions can you make about what is going to happen?

Before reading the story, you may choose to review some of the vocabulary below

- deadpan (p.75)

- eligible (p.92)

- fighting chance (p.89)

- flabbergasted (p.63)

- forfeit (p.89))

- geology (p.64)

- hesitate (p.76)

- manufacture (p.65)

- nimble (p.61)

- nausea (p.83)

- unimpressive (p.89)

Chapter-by-Chapter Summary

Read Chapters seven through nine aloud and with enthusiasm to the whole group.

Chapter Seven: False Entry

The next day Paul and Larry register at school, even though there are only two weeks left in the school year. On the playground, Larry joins in the sports games that are being played. In the classroom, Paul is surprised to find that news of his pitching ability has spread and kids already know who he is. Back at home, Paul realizes that his parents do not want to make an earlier doctor's appointment. They are preoccupied with other things and Paul is still not allowed to help out. He decides to take matters into his own hands and forges his father's signature on the baseball entry card.

Chapter Eight: Spotted

The next day at school Paul gives the entry card to his new friend Monk Lawler to turn in for him and agrees to meet Monk at his house to get a uniform and a ride to the game. Paul has no trouble avoiding his parents later and heading off to Monk's house, but on the way to the game, Paul and the rest of the team pass through Paul's neighborhood. Larry watches them pass. Monk realizes that Paul has forged the entry card and does not really have permission to play.

Chapter Nine: Time Out #2

In the hospital, Paul receives medication from Nurse Brophy, and we learn that Paul's medication makes him feel ill. In this scene, Paul has been in the hospital for a month; he remembers the game he tried to play without permission, and thinks about trying to be healthy enough to play with the team again in 12 days.

Discussion Questions

Spend a couple of minutes distributing students' Player Portfolios and pencils. (Ask for one or two volunteers to help.) Write the questions and focus prompts on a blackboard or newsprint.

Work together as a whole group to answer the following questions:

Questions one through four should be answered in a round-robin format, with one student answering one question. Try to include students who may not always participate. (If answers for questions three and four are imprecise or need further elaboration, ask if anyone has anything to add.)

- What is the main problem Paul is facing at this point in the story?

- How does Paul handle this problem?

- What happened then?

- Do you think Paul's decision was the right one? Why or why not?

The following focus prompt should be answered in an exhaustive format. Continue letting students give responses until no new answers are given.

1. When Monk found out about Paul's forged permission card he should have…

For questions six and seven, allow all students an opportunity to share their answers, regardless of whether or not the answers are original.

2. When would it be important in your life to… [insert answer from previous statement]?

3. One thing that might make doing this difficult is…

Finally, ask students to write their responses to the following prompt in their Player Portfolios.

4. One way that I can use the D.S.C.C.A. decision-making model to help me do the right thing in a tough dilemma is by…

Cool-down

- **R&R Huddle** (5 min.)

- **Recap** one or two key points that arose during the discussion. You may choose to focus on students' responses to questions five through seven.

- **Reconnect** by asking volunteers to briefly share what they wrote for question number eight.

- **Reset** and transition to the next activity.

Session 44: S.M.A.R.T. Goals Lessons from the Field	

Warm-up
Begin the PLUS Cycle (5 min.)
  • Session Overview
  • Pondering Perseverance
Activity
Lessons from the Field (25-30 min.)
  • Sports Activity
	Cool-down
	Continue the PLUS Cycle (5-10 min.)
	  • Reflection
	  • Goal-setting
	Materials
	Sports Equipment

Warm-up

Pondering Perseverance (5 min.)

Ask students to think about the previous lesson. What can they do today to bring the Lessons from Literature into their work together in the sports activity?

Activity

Lessons from the Field
Sports Activity

Block I: Getting Started (5 min.)

On the first day, players will learn how to measure their resting heart rates (RHR). They will also set baselines for their RHR, number of sit-ups/push-ups/lunges/calf raises, and number of jumps during jump rope. Each day they will try to improve upon their Past Personal Best (PPB) by achieving their Future Best Goal (FBG) and by tracking progress toward that goal in the physical activities progress chart located in the back of their Player Portfolios. Take one minute to make sure all participants turn to the back of their portfolios and locate the progress charts. Explain to them that they will be using this chart each time you meet to do physical activities. Be sure to emphasize the importance of keeping track of their progress by using the chart.

Stand together in a circle for all *Getting Started* activities (except for jogging). Have players partner up, with one player doing the activity and the partner keeping count and giving encouragement. Be sure that they have their Portfolios handy so that they can record their progress. Encourage them to clap and cheer for their teammates to create an enthusiastic environment. You may also choose to include music.

Choose from the options below, making sure to include a cardio and a stretching warm-up.

- **Measure resting heart rate (RHR)** — Spend a few minutes showing players how to find their pulses, either on their necks or wrists. Explain that you will be giving them a few seconds to count how many times their hearts beat. Take a moment to allow the players to sit quietly on the floor and find their pulses. Give them 30 seconds to count their heartbeats.

- **Record, check in and set goals** — Allow a couple of minutes for players to record their RHRs in their Player Portfolios.

- **Jog (2-3 min.)** — This can be done as a lap or in place as a circle.

- **Stretch (2-3 min.)** — Be sure to include stretches for the major muscle groups.

- **Strength/Endurance (1 min.)** — On this first day, players will set baseline numbers for the four Strength/Endurance activities (push-ups, sit-ups, lunges, calf raises), but usually, you will only choose one or two. They will work in pairs. One member of the pair will have 30 seconds to do as many of the activities as they can. Their partner will cheer them on and count for them.

- **Jump Rope (4 min.)** — Again, players will work in pairs, with one person jumping and the other person counting and cheering. They should have three to four sets of 30-45 seconds of jumping rope.

- **Track personal progress** — Have players record their totals for steps five and six in their Player Portfolios. These totals will represent their baseline achievements, or their Past Personal Bests (PPB). Each day, players will check their progress from the previous session and will set a Future Personal Best Goal (FBG) to work toward for next time. Be sure to remind them about setting realistic goals (for example, adding one or two to their baseline, as opposed to 10).

Block II: Structured Play (30 min.)

Skill Play (10 min.)

Choose one or two of the following activities to play today. You can refer back to the *Physical Activities Description Appendix* for instructions on how to run the activities. Encourage players to cheer for each other, and include music if you wish.

- Wheelbarrow Race

- Jump Rope Games

- Beanbag Horseshoes

- Beanbag Walk Relay

- Gorilla Walk

- Slides

Sport Play (20 min.)

As a group, decide which sport you want to play today. Select from the sport list contained in the *Sports List Appendix*. Be sure to periodically review with the group the Physical Activities Recommendations for Sport from Chapter Six.

Cool-down

If time permits, close the day with a few minutes of stretching while conducting the following R&R Huddle.

- **Recap** one or two key moments from the Lessons from the Field.

- **Reconnect** players back to the theme unit.

- **Reset** and transition players to the Cool-down, Reflection time.

  OR

- **Reflection**

Use this time to highlight teachable moments you observed during the day and to give players an opportunity to share their experiences about Sports PLUS during the day. The following questions can serve as a guide:

- What did you like about today?

- What did you learn today?

- What are some ways you persevered today?

- How can we better show perseverance next time?

- In what ways did your teammates persevere today?

Goal-setting

Use this time to help players track progress toward their individually-chosen goals, as well as toward team goals. As goals from earlier sessions are reached, guide players in setting additional individual and team goals related to Perseverance.

<table>
<tr>
<td colspan="2">Session 44:
S.M.A.R.T. Goals
Lessons from Adventure </td>
</tr>
<tr>
<td>

Warm-up
  Begin the PLUS Cycle (5 min.)

  - Session Overview

  - Count Off

Activity
  Lessons from Adventure (25-30 min.)

  - S.M.A.R.T. Goals

</td>
<td>

Cool-down
  Continue the PLUS Cycle (5-10 min.)

  - Reflection

  - Mental Video

Materials
  Poster paper, markers

</td>
</tr>
</table>

Warm-up

Count Off

This is a deceptively difficult activity. The rules of play are simple — the group has to count off to ten, or up to the number of players in the group. The catch is that the group cannot speak (except to say a number) or make any non-verbal signs to one another or communicate in any way.

Play

1. If you have a large group, divide it in two. You want about 10-12 players in each group.

2. Tell the players that they simply have to count to 10 (or, up to whatever the number of participants in the group) in order, with each group member saying one number.

3. They may not talk except to count off a number.

4. They may not make any non-verbal signs to each other or communicate in any way with their teammates.

5. If two or more players say a number at the same time, the group must start over.

6. Before you start playing, let the group set either a time goal or a number of rounds to play before they are successful.

7. If the group is unsuccessful at meeting their goal, allow a 20-second time-out for players to regroup and come up with a strategy.

Variation

If the group is pretty successful at counting off together, try having players count up. With this variation, the goal is simply to count as high as possible, to see how well the group can work together.

This activity can get very frustrating for a group. Because the players cannot communicate with each other, two or three people will often say a number at the same time, forcing the group to begin again. Watch for players getting frustrated and stop the game if you think they need to discuss what is going on. Occasionally a group will very quickly count through their sequence without any difficulties. If this happens, they may think it was too easy. Let them try it again and do it with their eyes closed.

- **R&R Huddle** (5 min.)

- **Recap** using one or two of the following discussion questions:

  - How did you feel when the group was working well? How did you feel when it was not working well? Provide specific words to describe your feelings.

  - What was hard about this activity?

  - Did you get frustrated? How did that feel?

  - Did you want to quit? What kept you going?

- **Reconnect** to the theme unit by asking players to respond to one or two of the following questions:

  – How is perseverance important for this activity?

  – How is this game similar to other kinds of group efforts?

  – How does a game like this help a group develop teamwork?

- **Reset** and transition to the next activity.

Activity

Lessons from Adventure
(see Player Portfolio)

S.M.A.R.T. Goals

Goal-setting has been an important process throughout the Sports PLUS program, but it is especially relevant in the Perseverance Theme Unit. Learning how to set and work toward goals is an important personal skill for anyone to have. Having a goal keeps us on task, gives us a clear direction, and helps us monitor our progress. By continuing to persevere as we strive to reach our goals, we draw closer to achieving them.

As with the other skill-building lessons included in the Sports PLUS program — the T.E.A.M. Problem-Solving Model and the D.S.C.C.A. Good Decision-Making method — setting goals has a step-by-step process to help guide us. This activity reviews the S.M.A.R.T. *goal-setting* process, which provides an easy and understandable way to assess our goal-setting strategies.

- Specific

- Measurable

- Achievable

- Relevant

- Timely

Specific

First, a goal should be specific so that it is clear what needs to be accomplished. A basketball player who wants to be a better defender should carefully define his or her goal by choosing specific aspects of the game to improve. For example, holding the player he or she is guarding to under eight points or making three steals per game are specific ways to be a better defender. A student who wants to be a better reader should choose specific goals like finishing a challenging book or making a grade of B or better on the next reading quiz.

Measurable

Second, goals should be measurable. Using the example of the basketball player above, keeping track of the opponent's points or counting the number of steals made in a game are ways to measure progress. When choosing a goal, ask yourself, "What are the ways I will be able to measure your progress?"

Achievable

Third, goals should be achievable — setting goals that have little or no likelihood of being met will only lead to frustration and probably giving up. A beginning reader who sets a goal of reading Tolstoy's War and Peace will likely fail. A beginning runner has little chance of completing a marathon, or running a mile in less than four minutes. The key to goal setting is to set goals that are neither impossible to reach nor too easily met. Goals should be challenging enough that they require hard work to achieve them, but they should not be so high that accomplishing them is unrealistic. In short, goals should be challenging, yet attainable. When choosing a goal, ask yourself, "Will accomplishing this goal be a challenge for me?" and "Can I realistically expect to achieve this goal?"

Relevant

Fourth, goals should be relevant. In keeping with the Sports PLUS values, goals must be worthy of our time and effort and should in some way make us better at what we do. Setting goals that do little to help us develop as people or that have negative consequences (e.g., learning how to hot-wire a car) are unworthy of our time and effort. When choosing a goal, ask yourself, "Is the goal I am setting relevant and meaningful to me? Is it a worthwhile pursuit?"

Timely

Finally, when setting goals, keep in mind the time frame within which it should be accomplished. Some have argued that goals are dreams with a timeline. Having a time frame to work within helps us to track progress toward achieving our goal and enables us to measure our true success. For example, setting a goal to read a book is very different than setting a goal to complete a book in one month. Someone whose goal is to read a challenging book within a month will benefit from tracking their progress through the book as the days and weeks go by to ensure they are on schedule and are likely to achieve success. When choosing a goal, ask yourself, "How much time will it take to achieve my goal?" "When, specifically, will I take time to work on it?" and, "When can I reasonably expect to complete my goal?"

Play

1. After reviewing each component of the

2. S.M.A.R.T. *goal-setting* process, spend a few moments giving players an opportunity to dis cuss each one. Is each guideline clear? Are there any questions? Does anyone have something to add?

3. Next, ask players to spend some time coming up with goals for themselves in each of the following categories using the S.M.A.R.T. *goal-setting* process:

   - Fun/adventure (things you want to try or do)

   - Family

   - Reading/education

   - Career

   - Service to others

   - Teamwork

- Respect

- Responsibility

- Fair Play

- Perseverance

4. Ask players to choose the three or four goals that are most important to them.

5. Finally, ask them to write a few short sentences in their Player Portfolios about their number one goal. R&R Huddle (5 minutes)

- **Recap** by asking for a few volunteers to share one of their goals.

- **Reconnect** S.M.A.R.T. goals to Perseverance.

- **Reset** and transition to the next activity.

Cool-down

Cool-down Ritual

Mental Video

For the cool-down today, try the personal videotape activity. First, ask for volunteers to name the five steps of setting S.M.A.R.T. goals. Next, ask players to sit on the floor (or just stay at their desks if this is easier) and close their eyes. "Imagine that you have a videotape of your life in your head. Rewind your personal videotape and look for examples of goals that you have set for yourself at different times in your life. Pause on those examples and think about how well those goals matched up with the five guidelines for the goal-setting process. Were you able to achieve your goals? Why or why not?" If time allows, ask for volunteers to describe one of their examples.

Session 45:
Playing Big

Overview

Instructor's Notes: *Be sure to review this set of activities before starting this Sports PLUS Session. Directions for how to run each activity are provided, but it is important that you become familiar with them so that you may more effectively lead the group.*

During group discussions, be sure to record all thoughts and ideas on a blackboard or newsprint. Remember that when players are working in their Player Portfolios, spelling, grammar, and penmanship are, relatively speaking, unimportant, so don't dwell on those details or you risk making Sports PLUS into MoreSchool.

This session's *Quote of the Week* is by Spud Webb, a 5' 5" former NBA basketball player who won the slam dunk contest. Help students understand how tall 5' 5" is by pointing out that Spud Webb was no taller than many of them. You may be able to find a picture of Spud Webb on the Internet. This session continues with the theme book, *Hang Tough, Paul Mather.* Shoe Sort is a challenging game that will require students to use Teamwork and Respect in order to practice Perseverance. Draw attention to this before beginning. The session ends with a simple *Go-Round,* which asks students to share one or two words that express what perseverance means to them.

Session 45: Playing Big **Lessons from Literature**	
Warm-up Begin the PLUS Cycle (10-15 min.) • Session Overview • Quote of the Week **Activity** Lessons from Literature (25-30 min.) • Theme Book — *Hang Tough, Paul Mather*	**Cool-down** Continue the PLUS Cycle (5-10 min.) • Reflection **Materials** Copies of *Hang Tough, Paul Mather*

Warm-up

Quote of the Week
(see Player Portfolio)

I don't play small. You have to go out and play with what you have.
I admit I used to want to be tall. But I made it in high school, and now
in the pros, so it doesn't matter.

— Spud Webb, former 5' 5" NBA player
and Slam Dunk Champion.

Follow the five steps of the Quote of the Week Format (See the Getting
Started chapter for additional explanation):

1. **Write the Quote of the Week:** Bring the group together into a
    circle, and write the Quote on the blackboard.

2. **Think about the Quote as a group:** Spend two or three
    minutes talking with the students about what they think the
    quote means. Ask students to share answers to the group for
    the following questions:

    •   What kinds of challenges do you think Spud Webb had to
        face because of his size?

    •   Why do you think he says that being tall "doesn't matter"
        anymore?

    •   Do you think Spud Webb had to face people who didn't
        think he could play basketball? What are some ways he
        might have handled this?

    •   When you are trying something new, do you think it is
        better to listen to people who don't think you can do it or
        to listen to those who believe in you? Why?

3. **Pair up to talk about the Quote:** Have students separate into
    pairs. Ask them to spend about five minutes discussing the
    following questions with their partners. Explain that they will
    be sharing their answers with the whole group, so they may
    choose to write their answers in their Player Portfolios. (Be

sure to walk around the groups, listen, and offer help where needed.):

- Can you think of something you would like to try but are afraid to? Complete this sentence: Something I would like to try but am afraid to because I might not be good at it is…

- What are one or two ways we can help our Sports PLUS teammates to persevere in trying this new challenge.

4. Share answers with the whole group: Come together as a large group and share the answers from each of the pair groups. Everyone who wants to should have an opportunity to share their answers.

5. Reflect individually about the Quote: Give students an opportunity to reflect individually by taking two or three minutes to write a response to the following Journal Questions in their Player Portfolios:

- Think of the goal you set during our last "quote of the week" discussion. What was it?

- Think of what you said you would like to try. What is one thing you can do that will help you to believe in yourself?

Activity

Lessons from Literature
Theme Book
Hang Tough, Paul Mather
(see Player Portfolio)

by Alfred Slote

Lesson No. Four: Chapters 10-22
Setup

Gather students in a circle and discuss one or more of the following questions:

- How do you like the story so far? What do you think about Paul's struggle and his decision to lie to his parents and teammates just to play baseball?

- Using what you have read so far and looking ahead at the next several chapter titles, what kinds of predictions can you make about what might happen next in the story?

Before reading the story, you may choose to review some of the vocabulary below

- bluff (p.105)

- dispute (p.98)

- fluke (p.105)

- rile (p.102)

- wince (p.105)

Chapter-by-Chapter Summary

Read Chapters seven through nine aloud and with enthusiasm to the whole group.

Chapter Ten: Big Game

Paul resumes his story about what happened when he tried to play baseball with the Wilson Dairy team. He convinces Monk that forging his dad's signature was the right thing to do. At the game, players from both teams are clearly impressed with Paul's pitching just watching him warm up. The coach from the other team comes over to make sure that Paul is registered properly.

Chapter Eleven: From Hero to Goat

The game begins, and Paul impresses both teams with his confidence and skill as a pitcher. Paul also spots weakness in the other pitcher's concentration. Because of Paul's great pitching, Wilson Dairy is winning the game in the second inning when Paul comes up to bat. He hits an infield ground ball, and struggles to run to first base, colliding with the first baseman. Paul's father appears; he is angry and tells the coach he never signed the entry card.

Chapter Twelve: The Short Season

When the other team discovers that Paul's entry card is forged, they force Wilson Dairy to forfeit the game. The team is angry at Monk because he knew Paul's secret. Paul learns that Larry did indeed tell his parents that he saw Paul. His father says they are going directly to the doctor's office. Paul convinces his father to sign his card officially before they leave; Paul is weaker than he realizes and needs help standing up.

Discussion Questions

Spend a couple of minutes distributing students' Player Portfolios and pencils. (Ask one or two volunteers to help.) Write the questions and focus prompts on a blackboard or newsprint.

Work together as a whole group to answer the following questions:

Questions one through five should be answered in a round-robin format, with one student answering one question. Try to include students who may not always participate. (If answers for any of the questions are imprecise or need further elaboration, ask if anyone has anything to add.)

1. How does Paul convince Monk that forging his father's signature was the right thing to do? What do you think about this?

2. What happens while Paul is warming up at the baseball field?

3. What happens later when Paul comes up to bat?

4. What happens to Monk? To the Wilson Dairy team? Between the two coaches? To Paul?

5. Do you think Paul acted responsibly or irresponsibly toward his teammates by forging the card? Why?

The following focus prompt should be answered in an exhaustive format. Continue letting students give responses until no new answers are given

6. Paul shows perseverance by...

7. Paul shows (does not show) responsibility by...

8. For question eight, allow all students an opportunity to share their answers, regardless of whether or not the answers are original

9. Sometimes it takes courage to do the right thing, especially when you want to do something else. What are some examples of when it might take courage to do the right thing?

Finally, ask students to write their responses to the following prompt in their Player Portfolios.

10. One specific way I can help my teammates to persevere is to...

Cool-down

- **R&R Huddle** (5 min.)

- **Recap** one or two key points that arose during the discussion. You may try using the following prompts:

  - Can you imagine a situation where you might be tempted to break the rules as Paul did?

  - How might you prepare yourself to face this situation and still do the right thing?

- **Reconnect** by asking volunteers to briefly share what they wrote for question number nine above.

- **Reset** and get ready for the next lesson.

Session 45: Playing Big Lessons from the Field	
Warm-up Begin the PLUS Cycle (5 min.) • Session Overview • Pondering Perseverance **Activity** Lessons from the Field (25-30 min.) • Sports Activity	**Cool-down** Continue the PLUS Cycle (5-10 min.) • Reflection • Goal-setting **Materials** Sports Equipment

Warm-up

Pondering Perseverance (5 min.)

Ask students to think about the previous lesson. What can they do today to bring the Lessons from Literature into their work together in the sports activity?

Activity

Lessons from the Field
Sports Activity

Block I: Getting Started (5 min.)

On the first day, players will learn how to measure their resting heart rates (RHR). They will also set baselines for their RHR, number of sit-ups/push-ups/lunges/calf raises, and number of jumps during jump rope. Each day they will try to improve upon their Past Personal Best (PPB) by achieving their Future Best Goal (FBG) and by tracking progress toward that goal in the physical activities progress chart located in the back of their Player Portfolios. Take one minute to make sure all participants turn to the back of their portfolios and locate the progress charts. Explain to them that they will be using this chart each time you meet to do physical activities. Be sure to emphasize the importance of keeping track of their progress by using the chart.

Stand together in a circle for all *Getting Started* activities (except for jogging). Have players partner up, with one player doing the activity and the partner keeping count and giving encouragement. Be sure that they have their Portfolios handy so that they can record their progress. Encourage them to clap and cheer for their teammates to create an enthusiastic environment. You may also choose to include music.

Choose from the options below, making sure to include a cardio and a stretching warm-up.

- Measure resting heart rate (RHR) — Spend a few minutes showing players how to find their pulses, either on their necks or wrists. Explain that you will be giving them a few seconds to count how many times their hearts beat. Take a moment to allow the players to sit quietly on the floor and find their pulses. Give them 30 seconds to count their heartbeats.

- Record, check in and set goals — Allow a couple of minutes for players to record their RHRs in their Player Portfolios.

- Jog (2-3 min.) — This can be done as a lap or in place as a circle.

- Stretch (2-3 min.) — Be sure to include stretches for the major muscle groups.

- Strength/Endurance (1 min.) — On this first day, players will set baseline numbers for the four Strength/Endurance activities (push-ups, sit-ups, lunges, calf raises), but usually, you will only choose one or two. They will work in pairs. One member of the pair will have 30 seconds to do as many of the activities as they can. Their partner will cheer them on and count for them.

- Jump Rope (4 min.) — Again, players will work in pairs, with one person jumping and the other person counting and cheering. They should have three to four sets of 30-45 seconds of jumping rope.

- Track personal progress — Have players record their totals for steps five and six in their Player Portfolios. These totals will represent their baseline achievements, or their Past Personal Bests (PPB). Each day, players will check their progress from

the previous session and will set a Future Personal Best Goal (FBG) to work toward for next time. Be sure to remind them about setting realistic goals (for example, adding one or two to their baseline, as opposed to 10).

Block II: Structured Play (30 min.)

Skill Play (10 min.)

Choose one or two of the following activities to play today. You can refer back to the *Physical Activities Description Appendix* for instructions on how to run the activities. Encourage players to cheer for each other, and include music if you wish.

- Log Rolling

- Balloon-a-thon

- Passing Medicine Balls

- Hoop Monster

- Hopscotch

Sport Play (20 min.)

As a group, decide which sport you want to play today. Select from the sport list contained in the *Sports List Appendix*. Be sure to periodically review with the group the Physical Activities Recommendations for Sport from Chapter Six.

Cool-down

If time permits, close the day with a few minutes of stretching while conducting the following R&R Huddle.

- **Recap** one or two key moments from the Lessons from the Field.

- **Reconnect** players back to the theme unit.

- **Reset** and transition players to the Cool-down, Reflection time.

    OR

- **Reflection**

Use this time to highlight teachable moments you observed during the day and to give players an opportunity to share their experiences about Sports PLUS during the day. The following questions can serve as a guide:

- What did you like about today?

- What did you learn today?

- What are some ways you persevered today?

- How can we better show perseverance next time?

- In what ways did your teammates persevere today?

Goal-setting

Use this time to help players track progress toward their individually chosen goals, as well as toward team goals. As goals from earlier sessions are reached, guide players in setting additional individual and team goals related to Perseverance.

Session 45: Playing Big Lessons from Adventure	

Warm-up
Begin the PLUS Cycle (5 min.)
 	
  • Session Overview
 	
  • Grouplets
 	
Activity
Lessons from Adventure (25-30 min.)
 	
  • Shoe Sort
	Cool-down
	Continue the PLUS Cycle (5-10 min.)
	
	  • Reflection
	
	  • Go-Round
	
	Materials
	None

Warm-up

Grouplets

Play

1. Tell students that you will be calling out a number between one and eight (your highest number should reflect an accurate amount based on the number of people in your group).

2. When students hear the number, they are to "clump" together as quickly as possible with the number of students that is equal to the number that was called out.

3. Keep the game moving by quickly calling out another number.

4. Each time, most likely, some students will be left out. You could "eliminate" these students, but to keep spirits up, just keep calling out new numbers and watch the flurry of movement as students quickly try to get into clumps.

Activity

Lessons from Adventure Shoe Sort

Setup

This seemingly simple activity can cause a considerable amount of frustration and requires a lot of teamwork to complete. Before beginning, gather players together to review the main rules and talk about how to proceed in a way that will ensure everyone's safety. You may choose to divide the large group into smaller groups.

Play

1. Explain to the group or groups that this activity will be done with everyone's eyes closed and in silence.

2. The goal is simple — the group, with eyes closed and no talking — must line up, in order of shoe size. That's it.

3. Teachers and staff should be with the group or groups to keep players from bumping heads or wandering off.

4. Remind players to be aware of safety and to move slowly, especially when bending down to feel someone's shoes. Taking care of our teammates' safety is our first priority.

5. When the group thinks they are in order, they should open their eyes. Of course, figuring out when they think they are in order without being able to verbally communicate is part of the problem.

Once you have given the simple instructions and safety reminders, have the players bunch up together and say, "Go," at which point everyone closes their eyes and cannot talk until they think they are in order by shoe size. Be on the alert for players not behaving in a safe manner or not taking care of their teammates. Stop the activity if necessary and have a discussion of safety. If players open their eyes and are not yet in order, give them a few minutes to plan some strategy and maybe to create signals before tackling the task again.

- **Recap** by asking players how well they took care of each other and worked together.

- **Reconnect** to the theme units with one or two of the following questions:

  - Was anyone tempted to cheat and open their eyes? How is this activity related to Perseverance? How is this related to Fair Play?

  - Are Respect and/or Responsibility important in this activity? Why or why not?

- **Reset** and transition to the next activity.

Cool-down

Cool-down Ritual

Go-round

Do a large group go-round and ask players to give one or two word examples of what perseverance means in their classroom. If time permits, ask for volunteers to offer examples of perseverance from their own lives.

Session 46:
Quick, Line Up

Overview

Instructor's Notes: *Be sure to review this set of activities before starting this Sports PLUS Session. Directions for how to run each activity are provided, but it is important that you become familiar with them so that you may more effectively lead the group.*

During group discussions, be sure to record all thoughts and ideas on a blackboard or newsprint. Remember that when players are working in their Player Portfolios, spelling, grammar, and penmanship are, relatively speaking, unimportant, so don't dwell on those details or you risk making Sports PLUS into MoreSchool.

This session opens with a *Quote of the Week* and then continues with the theme book reading of *Hang Tough, Paul Mather.* Quick, *Line Up* is a high-energy game that focuses on teamwork and perseverance. Many variations are offered so that you can adjust the challenge according to the team's ability, and the session ends with Pat on the Back to promote team-bonding and to boost team morale.

Session 46: Quick, Line Up Lessons from Literature	
Warm-up Begin the PLUS Cycle (10-15 min.) • Session Overview • Quote of the Week **Activity** Lessons from Literature (25-30 min.) • Theme Book — *Hang Tough, Paul Mather*	**Cool-down** Continue the PLUS Cycle (5-10 min.) • Reflection **Materials** Copies of *Hang Tough, Paul Mather*

Warm-up

Quote of the Week

The greatest glory in living lies not in never failing, but in rising every time we fall.

— Nelson Mandela

Instructor's Note

Spend a few minutes making sure students know who Nelson Mandela is and the context in which he may have said this quote.

Follow the five steps of the Quote of the Week Format (See the Getting Started chapter for additional explanation):

1. **Write the Quote of the Week:** Bring the group together into a circle, and write the Quote on the blackboard.

2. **Think about the Quote as a group:** Spend two or three minutes talking with the students about what they think the quote means. Ask students to share their answers to the following question:

   • What does this quote have to do with perseverance?

3. **Pair up to talk about the Quote:** Have students separate into pairs. Ask them to spend about five minutes discussing the following questions with their partners. Explain that they will be sharing their answers with the whole group, so they may choose to write them in their Player Portfolios. (Be sure to walk around the groups, listen, and offer help where needed.):

   • Why is it important to learn from our mistakes?

   • How can your teammates help you rise when you fall?

4. **Share answers with the whole group:** Come together as a large group and share the answers from each of the pair groups. Everyone who wants to should have an opportunity to share their answers.

5. **Reflect individually about the Quote:** Allow two or three minutes for students to reflect individually by writing a response to the following Journal Question in their Player Portfolios:
   How will rising each time you fall help you and your teammates?

Activity

Lessons from Literature
Theme Book
Hang Tough, Paul Mather
(see Player Portfolio)

by Alfred Slote

Lesson No. Five: Chapter 13-15

Setup

Ask students to look over the chapter titles for Chapters 13-15. What predictions can you make about what is going to happen?

Before reading the story, you may choose to review some of the vocabulary below:

   • collision (p.117)

- dobber (p.126)

- remission (p.120)

- unstable (p.120)

The Story

Read Chapters 13-15 aloud and with enthusiasm to the whole group.

Chapter-by-Chapter Summary

Chapter 13: No Pep Talks for This Patient

The final chapters of the book take place in the hospital. It has been a month since the baseball game incident, and Paul has been in the hospital ever since. Paul gets to know Dr. Kinsella better. Paul learns that the doctor is young, friendly, and used to play catcher on a baseball team in college. He understands Paul's love of baseball. The Wilson Dairy team also comes to visit Paul.

Chapter 14: Return of a Uniform

Paul has been trying to get well enough to play in Wilson Dairy's rematch against Ace Appliance since he went into the hospital. Despite the objections of the nurse, Dr. Kinsella tells Paul's mother to bring Paul's uniform to the hospital and arranges for Paul to leave the hospital for the game. Paul is very excited about being able to play in the game, but when Dr. Kinsella brings a wheelchair for him into the room, Paul realizes he has been kidding himself about playing in the game. He finally admits to himself that he has lost a lot of weight and is in no condition to play anything.

Chapter 15: Return of a Ball Player

On the way out of the hospital Paul receives many stares and much attention from the doctors, nurses and others in the hospital. On the way to the game, Paul's dad drives around the town, giving Paul a little tour because he's been in the hospital so long. At the baseball field, Paul is greeted with some discomfort and then excitement by the team. The Ace team also welcomes Paul warmly. Larry shows leadership and is protective of Paul's energy. Paul watches Red, the opposing pitcher, and tries to remember his weaknesses so that he can tell his teammates and help his team win.

Discussion Questions

Spend a couple of minutes distributing students' Player Portfolios and pencils. (Ask one or two volunteers to help.) Write the questions and focus prompts on a blackboard or newsprint.

Work together as a whole group to answer the following questions. Questions one through five should be answered in a round-robin format, with one student answering one question. Try to include students who may not always participate. (If answers are imprecise or need further elaboration, ask if anyone has anything to add.)

- How does Dr. Kinsella help Paul?

- Why does Dr. Kinsella like Paul so much? *(p. 124)*

- Why does Paul want to go to the baseball game?

- Why do you think Dr. Kinsella allows him to go?

- How do Paul's teammates react when they see him in a wheelchair?

The following focus prompt should be answered in an exhaustive format. Continue letting students give responses until no new answers are given.

1. Paul shows perseverance in these chapters by...

For questions seven and eight, allow all students an opportunity to share their answers, regardless of whether or not the answers are original.

2. Why do you think it is so hard for Paul to accept that he is not strong enough to play in the baseball game?

3. How does Paul show courage and perseverance when he goes to the game to support his teammates?

Finally, ask students to write their responses to the following prompt in their Player Portfolios. (This is a complex, integrative question that may require some mental boosts from the facilitator to guide students' thinking)

4. Paul realizes he cannot play in the baseball game, yet he does not give in and feel sorry for himself. Instead, he is encouraged by the knowledge that he can help his team just by showing up to the game. One specific way I might show perseverance, as Paul does, when faced with a difficult situation is by...

Cool-down

- **R&R Huddle** (5 min.)

- **Recap** one or two key points that arose during the discussion.

- **Reconnect** by asking volunteers to briefly share what they wrote for question number nine above.

- **Reset** and get ready for the next lesson.

<table>
<tr><td colspan="2">Session 46:
Quick, Line Up
Lessons from the Field </td></tr>
<tr><td>Warm-up
Begin the PLUS Cycle (5 min.)
• Session Overview
• Pondering Perseverance
Activity
Lessons from the Field (25-30 min.)
• Sports Activity</td><td>Cool-down
Continue the PLUS Cycle (5-10 min.)
• Reflection
• Goal-setting
Materials
Sports Equipment</td></tr>
</table>

Warm-up

Pondering Perseverance (5 min.)

Ask students to think about the previous lesson. What can they do today to bring the Lessons from Literature into their work together in the sports activity?

Activity

Lessons from the Field
Sports Activity

Block I: Getting Started (5 min.)

On the first day, players will learn how to measure their resting heart rates (RHR). They will also set baselines for their RHR, number of sit-ups/push-ups/lunges/calf raises, and number of jumps during jump rope. Each day they will try to improve upon their Past Personal Best (PPB) by achieving their Future Best Goal (FBG) and by tracking progress toward that goal in the physical activities progress chart located in the back of their Player Portfolios. Take one minute to make sure all participants turn to the back of their portfolios and locate the progress charts. Explain to them that they will be using this chart each time you meet to do physical activities. Be sure to emphasize the importance of keeping track of their progress by using the chart.

Stand together in a circle for all *Getting Started* activities (except for jogging). Have players partner up, with one player doing the activity and the partner keeping count and giving encouragement. Be sure that they have their Portfolios handy so that they can record their progress. Encourage them to clap and cheer for their teammates to create an enthusiastic environment. You may also choose to include music.

Choose from the options below, making sure to include a cardio and a stretching warm-up.

- *Measure resting heart rate (RHR)* — Spend a few minutes showing players how to find their pulses, either on their necks or wrists. Explain that you will be giving them a few seconds to count how many times their hearts beat. Take a moment to allow the players to sit quietly on the floor and find their pulses. Give them 30 seconds to count their heartbeats.

- **Record, check in and set goals** — Allow a couple of minutes for players to record their RHRs in their Player Portfolios.

- **Jog (2-3 min.)** — This can be done as a lap or in place as a circle.

- **Stretch (2-3 min.)** — Be sure to include stretches for the major muscle groups.

- **Strength/Endurance (1 min.)** — On this first day, players will set baseline numbers for the four Strength/Endurance activities (push-ups, sit-ups, lunges, calf raises), but usually, you will only choose one or two. They will work in pairs. One member of the pair will have 30 seconds to do as many of the activities as they can. Their partner will cheer them on and count for them.

- **Jump Rope (4 min.)** — Again, players will work in pairs, with one person jumping and the other person counting and cheering. They should have three to four sets of 30-45 seconds of jumping rope.

- **Track personal progress** — Have players record their totals for steps five and six in their Player Portfolios. These totals will represent their baseline achievements, or their Past Personal Bests (PPB). Each day, players will check their progress from the previous session and will set a Future Personal Best Goal (FBG) to work toward for next time. Be sure to remind them about setting realistic goals (for example, adding one or two to their baseline, as opposed to 10).

Block II: Structured Play (30 min.)

Skill Play (10 min.)

Choose one or two of the following activities to play today. You can refer back to the *Physical Activities Description Appendix* for instructions on how to run the activities. Encourage players to cheer for each other, and include music if you wish.

- Chase Ball

- Bowling

- High Skipping Relay

- Crab Walk

- Locomotion Relay

Activity

Sport Play (20 min.)

As a group, decide which sport you want to play today. Select from the sport list contained in the *Sports List Appendix*. Be sure to periodically review with the group the Physical Activities Recommendations for Sport from Chapter Six.

Cool-down

If time permits, close the day with a few minutes of stretching while conducting the following R&R Huddle.

- **Recap** one or two key moments from the Lessons from the Field.

- **Reconnect** players back to the theme unit.

- **Reset** and transition players to the Cool-down, Reflection time.

  OR

- **Reflection**

Use this time to highlight teachable moments you observed during the day and to give players an opportunity to share their experiences about Sports PLUS during the day. The following questions can serve as a guide:

- What did you like about today?

- What did you learn today?

- What are some ways you persevered today?

- How can we better show perseverance next time?

- In what ways did your teammates persevere today?

Goal-setting

Use this time to help players track progress toward their individually chosen goals, as well as toward team goals. As goals from earlier sessions are reached, guide players in setting additional individual and team goals related to Perseverance.

Session 46: **Quick, Line Up** **Lessons from Adventure**	
Warm-up Begin the PLUS Cycle (5 min.) • Session Overview • Yurt Circle **Activity** Lessons from Adventure (25-30 min.) • Quick, Line Up	**Cool-down** Continue the PLUS Cycle (5-10 min.) • Reflection • Pat on the Back **Materials** None

Warm-up

Yurt Circle Setup

Explain to the group: "There are many times when you need to be able to depend on the people you are with in a group and know that you can work well together. Let's see how well this group can work together."

Play

1. Ask players to hold hands in a circle and to move outward until everyone feels some pull on their arms from the people

to their left and right. Starting anywhere, ask the group to count off by twos all the way around the circle.

2. Encouraging the group to move slowly and deliberately, ask all the "ones" to lean toward the center of the circle and all the "twos" to lean out (without bending at the waist). Each player should have his or her feet placed about shoulder width and in line with the circumference of the circle.

3. For this activity to be successful, it's important that the players not bend at the waist. If they cooperate with one another, each player can exert quite a strong pull on their supporting partners and accomplish a remarkable forward or backward lean. It may take several tries to get to this point, as it takes a lot of trust and cooperation.

4. After some practice and increased proficiency, ask the "ones" and "twos" to try reversing positions (backward to forward and vice versa). This is not easy to do and will require a few attempts. Even if the group never succeeds, it's good for a few laughs and some unselfconscious hand-holding.

Activity

Lessons from Adventure
Quick, Line Up

Setup

You'll need a clean, open area in the room to allow players to move freely.

Activity

1. Ask the group to stand in a circle in the middle of the open space. You will stand in the center of the circle.

2. From the circle, create a square with four relatively equal length lines. Each side of the square will constitute a team.

3. Ask each line to remember the order of their line — who they are standing next to and how they are aligned (i.e., facing their front, right or left side, or back).

4. You are going to spin around. Once you have stopped, you will call, "Quick, Line Up!" Once you have said this, the teams must move as quickly as they can to line up in the same order and in the same alignment with you as before. To signal that their line is finished, each team should raise their hands and call out, "Quick, Line Up!"

5. Play one round for practice and then introduce one or more of the variations described below.

6. For safety's sake, this is a walking only game. Have players walk with their bumpers up. Let them have some fun, but keep chaos controlled.

- **R&R Huddle** (5 min.)

- **Recap** with one or two of the following questions:

   - How did you communicate without using words?

   - How did you feel when someone didn't understand what you were trying to tell them?

   - Were you frustrated or angry? Did it make you laugh?

   - Did you give up or keep trying?

- **Reconnect** to Perseverance by emphasizing the importance of continuing to try in the face of adversity.

- **Reset** and transition to the next activity.

Variation

1. Time the whole group. Have them work together, competing against the clock to complete the square with an improved overall time.

2. Challenge players to complete the task without talking with one another. This will give them an opportunity to work on their non-verbal communication skills.

3. Mix up the teams so that some of the players face the front of the circle, while others have their backs to it.

Finally, try using additional shapes — triangle, rectangle, pentagon, hexagon, etc. — or different criteria — birthdates, heights — to determine the order of the line-up. Players could be timed, and this variation could be paired with the "no-talking" variation described above.

Cool-down

Cool-down Ritual

Pat on the Back

Try a group pat on the back today, especially if the group did a good job respecting and taking care of one another. Form a large circle. Have everyone put their arms over the shoulders of the players next to them. On your signal, everyone will give the two players next to them a pat on the back and offer a couple of respectful comments to the group.

Session 47:

Practicing Perseverance

Overview

Instructor's Notes: *Be sure to review this set of activities before starting this Sports PLUS Session. Directions for how to run each activity are provided, but it is important that you become familiar with them so that you may more effectively lead the group.*

During group discussions, be sure to record all thoughts and ideas on a blackboard or newsprint. Remember that when players are working in their Player Portfolios, spelling, grammar, and penmanship are, relatively speaking, unimportant, so don't dwell on those details or you risk making Sports PLUS into MoreSchool.

Today's session begins with a *Quote of the Week* that offers another practical saying that students can use to help them practice perseverance in their daily lives. Students finish reading *Hang Tough, Paul Mather* during the Lessons from Literature. *Have You Ever?* is a hands-on, team-building activity that helps students talk about how it feels to be left out, what to do if they're feeling left out, and how to help others not to feel left out. The session ends with Anonymous Put-ups to give students an opportunity to share what they've been enjoying about the program.

Session 47: **Practicing Perseverance** **Lessons from Literature**	
Warm-up Begin the PLUS Cycle (10-15 min.) • Session Overview • Quote of the Week **Activity** Lessons from Literature (25-30 min.) • Theme Book — *Hang Tough, Paul Mather*	**Cool-down** Continue the PLUS Cycle (5-10 min.) • Reflection **Materials** Copies of *Hang Tough, Paul Mather*

Warm-up

Quote of the Week
(see Player Portfolio)

You can do anything if you put your mind to it.

— Anonymous

Follow the five steps of the Quote of the Week Format (See the Getting Started chapter for additional explanation):

1. **Write the Quote of the Week:** Bring the group together into a circle, and write the Quote on the blackboard.

2. **Think about the Quote as a group:** Spend two or three minutes talking with the students about what they think the quote means. Ask students to share their responses to the following question:

    *   Using your own words, what do you think this quote means?

3. **Pair up to talk about the Quote:** Have students separate into pairs. Ask them to spend about five minutes discussing the following questions with their partners. Explain that they will be sharing their answers with the whole group, so they may choose to write them in their Player Portfolios. (Be sure to walk around the groups, listen, and offer help where needed.):

    *   What was the hardest thing you have ever done? How did you manage to do it?

    *   Why do you think is it important to "put your mind to it" when pursuing your goals and dreams?

4. **Share answers with the whole group:** Come together as a large group and share the answers from each of the pair groups. Everyone who wants to should have an opportunity to share their answers.

5. **Reflect individually about the Quote:** Take two or three minutes for students to reflect individually by writing a response to the following Journal prompt in their Player Portfolios:

    *   Think about what you have learned about perseverance and determination during the Sports PLUS program. Obstacles will sometimes make it hard for you to accomplish your goals and realize your dreams, but as the quote says, "you can do anything if you put your mind to it."

    *   List three things that you have learned from your Sports PLUS experience that help you to overcome obstacles and meet your goals.

Activity

Lessons from Literature
Theme Book
Hang Tough, Paul Mather
(see Player Portfolio)

by Alfred Slote

Lesson No. Five: Chapters 16-17

Read Chapters 16-17 aloud and with enthusiasm to the whole group.

Chapter 16: Winner in a Wheelchair

The game is uneventful for a couple of innings, until Paul remembers Red's weakness: Red easily loses his focus. By calling out at strategic moments, Paul knows how to exploit Red's weakness and distract him. Red's pitching is off, and the Wilson Dairy batters get enough hits to score and win the game. The yelling took all of Paul's energy, and he is extremely weak, but feels good. He knows he was able to contribute to the victory. After the game, Red congratulates Paul as if he had played the game. Going back to the hospital, Paul is happy.

Chapter 17: Hang Tough, Paul Mather

Back at the hospital, Paul's nurse has been waiting past her regular duty hours for him to return. He feels weak and sick from being out, but is elated with his memories of the day at the game. Paul knows that he has a long way to go to fight his illness, but he ends the story on an optimistic note, echoing Dr. Kinsella's words of encouragement to "hang tough."

Discussion Questions

Questions one through four should be answered in an exhaustive format. Continue letting students give responses until no new answers are given.

1. Paul expected to be able to help his team win against Ace Appliance by pitching again, but he was too sick to pitch. What other way does Paul find to help Wilson Dairy in their re-match against Ace Appliance?

2. What do you think of the way Paul chooses to help his team? Was it respectful? Did he show fair play? Why or why not?

3. Do you think you might use a solution like Paul used to help his team if you were in a similar situation? Why or why not?

4. When Paul returns to the hospital he does not want to take off his uniform. Why do you think this is?

For questions five through seven, allow all students an opportunity to share their answers, regardless of whether or not the answers are original.

5. Usually when we talk about perseverance, we are talking about the need to continue doing something until we find success: continue shooting the basketball at the basket, continue throwing the football down the field, continue kicking the soccer ball into the net. But Paul Mather has to persevere by not doing things: he is not allowed to carry suitcases in from the car or to help his dad put up a backboard; he is not even allowed to throw a baseball.

   Why do you think it is difficult to not be able to do things?

6. In which situation do you think it is more difficult to persevere: to keep on doing something or to not do something?

7. One way I can apply Paul's example of perseverance to help me deal with a challenge I am facing in my own life is by...

Additional Discussion Points

If time allows, consider introducing the following statement:
   "It's not how many times you get knocked down that counts; it's how many times you get back up."

- How does this saying apply to Paul?

- In what ways is it related to what you've learned about perseverance?

- How might this saying apply to you?

Cool-down

- **R&R Huddle** (5 min.)

- **Recap** one or two key points that arose during the discussion.

- **Reconnect** by asking volunteers to briefly share what they wrote for question number seven.

- **Reset** and get ready for the next lesson.

Session 47: **Practicing Perseverance** **Lessons from the Field**	
Warm-up Begin the PLUS Cycle (5 min.) <ul><li>Session Overview</li><li>Pondering Perseverance</li></ul>**Activity** Lessons from the Field (25-30 min.) <ul><li>Sports Activity</li></ul>	**Cool-down** Continue the PLUS Cycle (5-10 min.) <ul><li>Reflection</li><li>Goal-setting</li></ul>**Materials** Sports Equipment

Warm-up

Pondering Perseverance (5 min.)

Ask students to think about the previous lesson. What can they do today to bring the Lessons from Literature into their work together in the sports activity?

Activity

Lessons from the Field
Sports Activity

Block I: Getting Started (5 min.)

On the first day, players will learn how to measure their resting heart rates (RHR). They will also set baselines for their RHR, number of sit-ups/push-ups/lunges/calf raises, and number of jumps during jump rope. Each day they will try to improve upon their Past Personal Best (PPB) by achieving their Future Best Goal (FBG) and by tracking progress toward that goal in the physical activities progress chart located in the back of their Player Portfolios. Take one minute to make sure all participants turn to the back of their portfolios and locate the progress charts. Explain to them that they will be using this chart each time you meet to do physical activities. Be sure to emphasize the importance of keeping track of their progress by using the chart.

Stand together in a circle for all *Getting Started* activities (except for jogging). Have players partner up, with one player doing the activity and the partner keeping count and giving encouragement. Be sure that they have their Portfolios handy so that they can record their progress. Encourage them to clap and cheer for their teammates to create an enthusiastic environment. You may also choose to include music.

Choose from the options below, making sure to include a cardio and a stretching warm-up.

- **Measure resting heart rate (RHR)** — Spend a few minutes showing players how to find their pulses, either on their necks or wrists. Explain that you will be giving them a few seconds to count how many times their hearts beat. Take a moment to allow the players to sit quietly on the floor and find their pulses. Give them 30 seconds to count their heartbeats.

- **Record, check in and set goals** — Allow a couple of minutes for players to record their RHRs in their Player Portfolios.

- **Jog (2-3 min.)** — This can be done as a lap or in place as a circle.

- **Stretch (2-3 min.)** — Be sure to include stretches for the major muscle groups.

- **Strength/Endurance (1 min.)** — On this first day, players will set baseline numbers for the four Strength/Endurance activities (push-ups, sit-ups, lunges, calf raises), but usually, you will only choose one or two. They will work in pairs. One member of the pair will have 30 seconds to do as many of the activities as they can. Their partner will cheer them on and count for them.

- **Jump Rope (4 min.)** — Again, players will work in pairs, with one person jumping and the other person counting and cheering. They should have three to four sets of 30-45 seconds of jumping rope.

- **Track personal progress** — Have players record their totals for steps five and six in their Player Portfolios. These totals will represent their baseline achievements, or their Past Personal Bests (PPB). Each day, players will check their progress from the previous session and will set a Future Personal Best Goal (FBG) to work toward for next time. Be sure to remind them about setting realistic goals (for example, adding one or two to their baseline, as opposed to 10).

Block II: Structured Play (30 min.)

Skill Play (10 min.)

Choose one or two of the following activities to play today. You can refer back to the *Physical Activities Description Appendix* for instructions on how to run the activities. Encourage players to cheer for each other, and include music if you wish.

- Circle Bonanza

- Round and Round the Hoops Go

- Pac Man/Ms. Pac Man Tag

- Limbo

- Jump Rope Relay

- Jumping Distances

Sport Play (20 min.)

As a group, decide which sport you want to play today. Select from the sport list contained in the *Sports List Appendix*. Be sure to periodically review with the group the Physical Activities Recommendations for Sport from Chapter Six.

Cool-down

If time permits, close the day with a few minutes of stretching while conducting the following R&R Huddle.

- **Recap** one or two key moments from the Lessons from the Field.

- **Reconnect** players back to the theme unit.

- **Reset** and transition players to the Cool-down, Reflection time.

  OR

- **Reflection**

Use this time to highlight teachable moments you observed during the day and to give players an opportunity to share their experiences about Sports PLUS during the day. The following questions can serve as a guide:

- What did you like about today?

- What did you learn today?

- What are some ways you persevered today?

- How can we better show perseverance next time?

- In what ways did your teammates persevere today?

Goal-setting

Use this time to help players track progress toward their individually chosen goals, as well as toward team goals. As goals from earlier sessions are reached, guide players in setting additional individual and team goals related to *Perseverance*.

Session 47: **Practicing Perseverance** **Lessons from Adventure**	
Warm-up Begin the PLUS Cycle (5 min.) • Session Overview • Have You Ever? **Activity** Lessons from Adventure (25-30 min.) • Human Bridge	**Cool-down** Continue the PLUS Cycle (5-10 min.) • Reflection • Anonymous Put-Ups **Materials** 1 place-marker per person — carpet square, scraps of paper or masking tape X's on the floor

Warm-up

Have You Ever?

Play

1. Bring the group together in a circle. Ask each player to stand on their place-marker. If you don't have any markers, have each player mark his or her spot with a masking tape X. You are It and will not have a space.

2. Begin the game by asking a "Have you ever…?" question about behaviors related to the Sports PLUS values. For example, "Have you ever been part of a team that worked together?"

3. Those players who can answer yes to the question need to find a new spot. Since there is one more player than there are spots, one person will be left out. That player now asks a new "Have you ever…"

4. The player asking, "Have you Ever…?" needs to ask a question that he or she can answer yes to. In other words, if you have not ever been part of a team that worked together, you would not ask that question.

5. Sometimes the player in the middle has trouble thinking of a question. If you think that may happen with your group, help by calling out some questions. This will keep the game moving.

Sample questions: Have you ever...

- ...gotten better at something?

- ...learned how to ride a bike?

- ...used a dictionary at home?

- ...remembered to do your homework?

- ...held the door open for someone?

- ...felt like giving up when things were tough?

- ...told a lie?

- ...apologized for something you did wrong?

- ...felt left out of a game?

- ...been told you couldn't play?

- ...told someone else they couldn't play?

- ...included someone who was new?

- ...made a new friend?

Discussion

During the discussion, ask players to reflect on their experience. Did everyone have a chance to move at least once? Did anyone move when they weren't supposed to? How did you feel when you hadn't done some of the things that were mentioned?

Next, ask players to share more about some of their responses. For example, what was something you tried and got better at? What was one time you felt like giving up? How did it feel to be left out of a game? The point is to get players thinking about how honest they were in their responses and to invite them to share their experiences with the whole group. You may want to start the conversation by sharing some of your own experiences.

- **R&R Huddle** (5 min.)

- **Recap** one or two key points from the previous discussion.

- **Reconnect** by asking players to complete the sentence: I learned…

- **Reset** and transition to the next activity.

Activity

Lessons from Adventure
Human Bridge

Setup

It is important in this activity to remind players to be safe, and as they persevere and try their best, to be responsible for themselves and their partners. Gather players for the instructions. Help each player find a partner.

Play

1. Explain that players are going to work with their partners to form a human bridge.

2. Demonstrate the way to make this bridge as sturdy as possible: both partners raise their hands over their heads and connect by putting palms to palms. With a straight and outstretched body, students try to walk their feet backwards, pressing in toward their partners.

3. The goal is for each pair to create the widest bridge they can.

4. Make sure that players stay within their limits and stay safe while pushing themselves to go further.

5. After a short time, ask players to try again with new partners.

- ***R&R Huddle*** (5 min.)

- *Recap* by asking players about their experience during the game: How did perseverance help them be successful?

- *Reconnect* to the theme unit with the following discussion question: What happens to the game if we do not persevere?

- *Reset* and transition to the next activity.

Cool-down

Cool-down Ritual

Anonymous Put-ups

Try this fun way for the group to offer anonymous put-ups to itself. Have players take out a piece of paper. Each player should write, in pen, a message to the group that describes why they are a good team, or how they show respect or responsibility or perseverance. Give the group a few minutes to write, then have the players scrunch up their papers into a tight ball. On the count of three, the group, standing close together, throws the balls of paper into the air. Everyone tries to catch one, preferably not the one they tossed. Have players open their balled-up papers and ask for volunteers to decipher and read the wrinkly messages.

Instructor's Note

Remind players that it would be disrespectful to write something inappropriate. If a player finds something objectionable, save it for a discussion on respecting the group.

Session 48:
Poetry in Motion

Overview

Instructor's Notes: *Be sure to review this set of activities before starting this Sports PLUS Session. Directions for how to run each activity are provided, but it is important that you become familiar with them so that you may more effectively lead the group.*

During group discussions, be sure to record all thoughts and ideas on a blackboard or newsprint. Remember that when players are working in their Player Portfolios, spelling, grammar, and penmanship are, relatively speaking, unimportant, so don't dwell on those details or you risk making Sports PLUS into MoreSchool.

This session presents students with an opportunity to explore poetry and experiment with creativity, all the while learning about perseverance.

The Langston Hughes' poem Dreams dovetails nicely with what students have been learning about goal setting. Students also will have a chance to create their own, individual poems. *Pass the Shoe* is a simple game that engages students in a fun rhyming pattern. During *Team Poetry,* students work together to create a team poem. The session closes with a simple go-round.

Session 48: **Poetry in Motion** **Lessons from Literature**	
Warm-up Begin the PLUS Cycle (10-15 min.) • Session Overview • Quote of the Week **Activity** Lessons from Literature (25-30 min.) • Create Your Own Poem	**Cool-down** Continue the PLUS Cycle (5-10 min.) • Reflection **Materials** Copies of *Dreams*

Warm-up

Dreams
(see Player Portfolio)

by Langston Hughes

Do you have dreams about what you hope to do and what kind of person you hope to become? Ask students to write one or two of their dreams in their Player Portfolios. Then, give them an opportunity to share these dreams with the group.

The Story

Ask students to read the poem silently before reading it aloud as a group.

Discussion Questions

Spend a couple of minutes distributing students' Player Portfolios and pencils. (Ask one or two volunteers to help.) Write the questions and focus prompts on a blackboard or newsprint.

Work together as a whole group to answer the following questions. Questions one through four should be answered in an exhaustive format. Continue letting students give responses until no new answers are given.

1. What is this poem about?

2. How could dreams die?

3. How can you hold onto your dreams?

4. According to this poem, what happens when you lose your dreams?

For questions five and six, allow all students an opportunity to share their answers, regardless of whether or not the answers are original.

5. When would it be important in your life to hold onto your dreams?

6. One thing that might make doing this difficult is…

Finally, ask students to write their responses to the following prompt in their Player Portfolios.

7. One specific way I might hold onto my dreams is by…

- **R&R Huddle** (5 min.)

- **Recap** by asking students to finish the following focus prompt. Dreams are important because…

- **Reconnect** by asking volunteers to briefly share what they wrote for question number seven.

- **Reset** and transition to the next activity.

Dreams

by Langston Hughes

Hold fast to your dreams
For if dreams die
Life is a broken-winged bird
That cannot fly.
Hold fast to your dreams
For when dreams go Life
is a barren field Frozen
with snow.

Activity

Lessons from Literature
(see Player Portfolio)

Create Your Own Poem

The following activity enables students to use their creative writing abilities while exploring themselves through the creation of a poem.

Have the group sit together in a circle and spend a few minutes passing out Player Portfolios and pencils. Ask students to work individually to complete the statements in their Player Portfolios. Give them approximately 10 minutes to work on their poems, allowing more time if needed. Remind them that spelling, penmanship, and grammar are NOT important during this activity. Walk around the room to provide assistance as needed.

With some students you may need to give a front-loading pep talk. Encourage students who seem reluctant to partake in this activity by letting them know that you take their hopes and dreams very seriously, and this is a chance for them to express who they are — which is a very important opportunity — and, therefore, they should take themselves seriously by taking this activity seriously.

When students have completed the activity, ask for volunteers to share their poems with the group. Students may wish to hang their poems around the room or to take them home. (*Source:* Robert Tisdale, New Hampton School.)

I AM

1. I am… (two special qualities, that describe you)

2. I hope… (something you actually hope for)

3. I will try… (something you really will make an effort to do)

4. I want to be… (something you want to become)

5. I am… (repeat first line of the poem again)

Cool-down

- **R&R Huddle** (5 min.)

- **Recap** by asking students to respond aloud to the following focus prompt: One thing I learned from this activity is…

- **Reconnect** by asking students to share responses to the following focus prompt: Perseverance is important in helping me to become who I want to be because…

- **Reset** and get ready for the next lesson.

Session 48: Poetry in Motion Lessons from the Field	
Warm-up Begin the PLUS Cycle (5 min.) • Session Overview • Pondering Perseverance **Activity** Lessons from the Field (25-30 min.) • Sports Activity	**Cool-down** Continue the PLUS Cycle (5-10 min.) • Reflection • Goal-setting **Materials** Sports Equipment

Warm-up

Pondering Perseverance (5 min.)

Ask students to think about the previous lesson. What can they do today to bring the Lessons from Literature into their work together in the sports activity?

Activity

Lessons from the Field
Sports Activity

Block I: Getting Started (5 min.)

On the first day, players will learn how to measure their resting heart rates (RHR). They will also set baselines for their RHR, number of sit-ups/push-ups/lunges/calf raises, and number of jumps during jump rope. Each day they will try to improve upon their Past Personal Best (PPB) by achieving their Future Best Goal (FBG) and by tracking progress toward that goal in the physical activities progress chart located in the back of their Player Portfolios. Take one minute to make sure all participants turn to the back of their portfolios and locate the progress charts. Explain to them that they will be using this chart each time you meet to do physical activities. Be sure to emphasize the importance of keeping track of their progress by using the chart.

Stand together in a circle for all *Getting Started* activities (except for jogging). Have players partner up, with one player doing the activity and the partner keeping count and giving encouragement. Be sure that they have their Portfolios handy so that they can record their progress. Encourage them to clap and cheer for their teammates to create an enthusiastic environment. You may also choose to include music.

Choose from the options below, making sure to include a cardio and a stretching warm-up.

- **Measure resting heart rate (RHR)** — Spend a few minutes showing players how to find their pulses, either on their necks or wrists. Explain that you will be giving them a few seconds to count how many times their hearts beat. Take a moment to allow the players to sit quietly on the floor and find their pulses. Give them 30 seconds to count their heartbeats.

- **Record, check in and set goals** — Allow a couple of minutes for players to record their RHRs in their Player Portfolios.

- **Jog (2-3 min.)** — This can be done as a lap or in place as a circle.

- **Stretch (2-3 min.)** — Be sure to include stretches for the major muscle groups.

- **Strength/Endurance (1 min.)** — On this first day, players will set baseline numbers for the four Strength/Endurance activities (push-ups, sit-ups, lunges, calf raises), but usually, you will only choose one or two. They will work in pairs. One member of the pair will have 30 seconds to do as many of the activities as they can. Their partner will cheer them on and count for them.

- **Jump Rope (4 min.)** — Again, players will work in pairs, with one person jumping and the other person counting and cheering. They should have three to four sets of 30-45 seconds of jumping rope.

- **Track personal progress** — Have players record their totals for steps five and six in their Player Portfolios. These totals will represent their baseline achievements, or their Past Personal Bests (PPB). Each day, players will check their progress from the previous session and will set a Future Personal Best Goal (FBG) to work toward for next time. Be sure to remind them about setting realistic goals (for example, adding one or two to their baseline, as opposed to 10).

Block II: Structured Play (30 min.)

Skill Play (10 min.)

Choose one or two of the following activities to play today. You can refer back to the *Physical Activities Description Appendix f*or instructions on how to run the activities. Encourage players to cheer for each other, and include music if you wish.

- Water Fill Relay

- Leap Frog Relay

- Drum Major Walk

- Hula Hoop Marathon

- Shuttle Run Relay

Sport Play (20 min.)

As a group, decide which sport you want to play today. Select from the sport list contained in the *Sports List Appendix.* Be sure to periodically review with the group the Physical Activities Recommendations for Sport from Chapter Six.

Cool-down

If time permits, close the day with a few minutes of stretching while conducting the following R&R Huddle.

- **Recap** one or two key moments from the Lessons from the Field.

- **Reconnect** players back to the theme unit.

- **Reset** and transition players to the Cool-down, Reflection time.

  OR

- **Reflection**

Use this time to highlight teachable moments you observed during the day and to give players an opportunity to share their experiences about Sports PLUS during the day. The following questions can serve as a guide:

- What did you like about today?

- What did you learn today?

- What are some ways you persevered today?

- How can we better show perseverance next time?

- In what ways did your teammates persevere today?

Goal-setting

Use this time to help players track progress toward their individually chosen goals, as well as toward team goals. As goals from earlier sessions are reached, guide players in setting additional individual and team goals related to Perseverance.

Session 48: Poetry in Motion Lessons from Adventure	

Warm-up
Begin the PLUS Cycle (5 min.)
    • Session Overview
    • Pass the Shoe
Activity
Lessons from Adventure (25-30 min.)
    • Slot Machine
	Cool-down
	Continue the PLUS Cycle (5-10 min.)
	    • Reflection
	    • Go-Round
	Materials
	Paper and writing utensils

Warm-up

Pass the Shoe

This seemingly simple rhythmic passing game is actually more difficult than you might think. The game is simple and fun, but it will test the teamwork, patience, and perseverance of your group. See if your group can persevere to reach its goal!

Setup

Ask the group to sit on the floor in a nice, tight circle. Each person will remove one shoe. Tell the group that they will play a game that will test their teamwork, respect, and perseverance.

Play

You'll begin by teaching a pattern and poem for passing the shoes around the circle. The poem is this: "I pass the shoe from me to you. Respect! It's what we do. Teamwork! Teamwork! That's what it's all about. Teamwork! Teamwork! Let's give a shout! (Shout)."

After teaching players the simple poem, show them how the shoes are passed. The shoes are passed according to the poem as follows:

Say...	as you...
"I pass!"	Pass the shoe to the RIGHT
"The shoe!"	Pass the shoe to the RIGHT
"From me!"	Pass the shoe to the RIGHT
"To you!"	Pass the shoe to the RIGHT
"Respect"	Pass the shoe to the RIGHT
"It's what!"	Pass the shoe to the RIGHT
"We do!"	Pass the shoe to the RIGHT
"Teamwork!"	Pass the shoe to the LEFT
"Teamwork!"	Pass the shoe to the LEFT
"That's what!"	Pass the shoe to the LEFT
"It's all about!"	Pass the shoe to the LEFT
"Teamwork!"	Pass the shoe to the LEFT
"Teamwork!"	Pass the shoe to the LEFT
"Let's give!"	Pass the shoe to the LEFT
"A shout!"	Hold onto the shoe
EVERYONE	Tap the shoe in front of
CHEERS!!!	yourself

Practice saying the poem together a few times before passing the shoes. Once you think the group has learned the poem, start to slowly recite it together, passing the shoe as the directions indicate. The first difficult part will be remembering to pass the shoe to the LEFT on "Teamwork." When you reach "A shout," everyone should hold his or her shoe. Then, everyone taps the shoe in their hand or on the floor in front of themselves and cheers (you may have players cheer something such as "Sports PLUS!" or you may just let them make up their own cheers.) Once you complete the cycle, continuously start over with "I pass...." Start slowly at first.

After you have tried the game a few times, have the group set a goal. This goal might be to complete the poem one or two times with no mistakes or to complete the poem within a certain time limit. Play the game until the goal is accomplished or the group gets tired.

Variation

If the game seems too difficult, feel free to modify it by having the players only pass the shoes in one direction. You may also decide to have the group recite only half of the poem.

Activity

Lessons from Adventure
Team Poetry

Setup

Is there a rule anywhere that says a poem has to be written by only one person? This is a fun group exercise in creativity and vocabulary. Depending on the size of your group, you may want to separate into two groups, but it works best if you have at least 10 to a group.

Play

Working together as a team, you are going to create your own poem about teamwork, perseverance, or any of the other Sports PLUS values you have been talking about. At least we hope it will come out that way! In this activity, we are going to create a poem as a poetry team, with each member of the team contributing different words.

The rules are simple — members of the team contribute words to create a poem based on the order of the alphabet. Start the poem by asking for a word that begins with the letter A. The next word of the poem must begin with the letter B, the next C and so on all the way to Z. You don't have to begin with the letter A; you could begin with the letter F and go through the alphabet until you get back to F, as long as you use all the letters in order. Use some of the same guidelines as a brainstorming session — there are no wrong answers. Also remind players to at least attempt to find a word that makes some sense and keeps the poem going.

You can have players proceed in a certain order, or you can leave it open and let anyone shout out the next word. If you do this, remind the group to be respectful of all ideas in case two players offer different words simultaneously. In this case you will need to have a way to choose which word to use, or even use both if they work — it's your game after all.

Ask for a volunteer or two to write the words in order and read the poem when it's completed. This should be worth a few laughs for the group.

Variation

> If you choose to go around the circle so that all players have a turn, you may want to have a dictionary on hand so that players can look up words if they get stuck.

- **R&R Huddle** (5 min.)

- **Recap** by asking players to rate their experience during the activity using their thumbs: Thumbs-up means "GREAT!" Thumbs-down means "not so good." Thumbs-sideways means "somewhere in between."

- **Reconnect** the poem to the theme unit.

- **Reset** and transition to the next activity.

Cool-down

Cool-down Ritual

Go-round

This variation of a go-round can be a bit more challenging — and funny. Have the group form a circle and explain that as a group we are going to create a statement about how we did today as a team. Begin the statement yourself by saying "Thank..." The person to your right then says a word (which will probably be, "you..."), then the person to their right continues, and so on all the way around the circle and back to you. If someone gets stuck, let them pass, but then they have to offer a word after the last person in the circle. Don't worry about making total sense, as long as the players are making a good effort to construct a coherent thought and are having fun.

Session 49:
Putting It Out There

Overview

Instructor's Notes: *Be sure to review this set of activities before starting this Sports PLUS Session. Directions for how to run each activity are provided, but it is important that you become familiar with them so that you may more effectively lead the group.*

During group discussions, be sure to record all thoughts and ideas on a blackboard or newsprint. Remember that when players are working in their Player Portfolios, spelling, grammar, and penmanship are, relatively speaking, unimportant, so don't dwell on those details or you risk making Sports PLUS into MoreSchool.

This session, the second-to-last, follows the routine of previous theme units with *Create Your Own Quote* of the Week and *Create Your Own Story*. The team building activity, Toss Up, challenges the group to set goals and to persevere. Students should begin to feel a strong sense of accomplishment as they discover how much more effectively they live out the Sports PLUS values in comparison with when the program first began.

Session 49: Putting It Out There **Lessons from Literature**	
Warm-up Begin the PLUS Cycle (10-15 min.) • Session Overview • Quote of the Week **Activity** Lessons from Literature (25-30 min.) • Create Your Own Story	**Cool-down** Continue the PLUS Cycle (5-10 min.) • Reflection **Materials** Player Portfolios, paper, pencils, pens, crayons

Warm-up

Create a Quote of the Week

(see Player Portfolio)

The goal of this activity is to allow students to engage their creativity, work collectively, and reflect on the themes of respect they have been learning.

Separate students into small groups and allow five to ten minutes for each group to create its own "Quote of the Week" about perseverance. Students can look through stories and previous quotes in their portfolios for ideas, but their quotes should be in their own words.

Encourage them to write their quotes on poster board that will then be hung on the wall. Make supplies, such as markers, available for decorating the poster because some students will find this part of the activity particularly enjoyable.

After students have finished, ask groups to take turns sharing their quotes with the group.

Allow a few minutes to discuss each one. Encourage the students who are listening to ask questions once the group presenting has finished.

When the students have finished asking questions of the group, conclude the activity by asking three questions of your own:

- What does your quote mean?

- When is it important to live out this quote?

- One way I can live out this quote during Sports PLUS is… One way I can live out this quote at school is… One way I can live out this quote at home is…

Activity

Lessons from Adventure
(see Player Portfolio)

Create Your Own Story

The following activity encourages students' creativity and solidifies their understanding of perseverance. By having students create their own stories involving perseverance, they will draw upon personal knowledge as well as role models who exemplify perseverance. This activity also encourages students to understand the benefits of perseverance and to transfer that understanding into a new context. It is important to remember that spelling, grammar, and penmanship are NOT important during this activity.

Setup

Bring the group together into a circle and explain the next activity as you circulate students' Player Portfolios. Use the following description as a guide:

"Today during Lessons from Literature, we will be creating our own stories about Perseverance. You may choose to work individually or with up to three other students. It may be helpful to create a story about some conflict or problem that is worked out using perseverance. Think of things that may have occurred on your own sports teams or during the Lessons from the Field this theme unit. You also may choose to write a story about some of the characters in an Instant Replay or to create a different ending for one of the stories we've read. Spend a few minutes looking back over your Player Portfolios to begin getting some ideas."

Play

Offer guidance as the students separate into groups. Make sure that no one feels left out, but do let the students choose their own groups. Walk around the room offering help and suggestions as needed.

Once students have finished writing, give them an opportunity to illustrate their stories if they choose to do so. (Some students may find it easier to draw a picture before writing an accompanying story. Let this be an option for those who want it.)

Explain to the students that they will have an opportunity to share their stories with the group on the next Sports PLUS day if they wish to do so. Students can finish illustrating their stories at home if necessary.

Discussion Questions:

After students have had an opportunity to write and illustrate their stories, bring the whole group together in a circle for a brief reflection on the following questions. Let everyone share who wants to do so.

- What stories or examples of perseverance did you use to create your story?

- What are some of the problems that the main characters faced in your stories?

- How do your main characters solve their dilemma?

Cool-down

- **R&R Huddle** (5 min.)

- **Recap** one or two key points from the discussion.

- **Reconnect** students to the theme unit.

- **Reset** and get ready for the next lesson.

Session 49: **Putting It Out There** **Lessons from the Field**	

Warm-up
Begin the PLUS Cycle (5 min.)
  • Session Overview
  • Pondering Perseverance
Activity
Lessons from the Field (25-30 min.)
  • Sports Activity
	Cool-down
	Continue the PLUS Cycle (5-10 min.)
	  • Reflection
	  • Goal-setting
	Materials
	Sports Equipment

Warm-up

Pondering Perseverance (5 min.)

Ask students to think about the previous lesson. What can they do today to bring the Lessons from Literature into their work together in the sports activity?

Acrivity

Sports Activity

Block I: Getting Started (5 min.)

On the first day, players will learn how to measure their resting heart rates (RHR). They will also set baselines for their RHR, number of sit-ups/push-ups/lunges/calf raises, and number of jumps during jump rope. Each day they will try to improve upon their Past Personal Best (PPB) by achieving their Future Best Goal (FBG) and by tracking progress toward that goal in the physical activities progress chart located in the back of their Player Portfolios. Take one minute to make sure all participants turn to the back of their portfolios and locate the progress charts. Explain to them that they will be using this chart each time you meet to do physical activities. Be sure to emphasize the importance of keeping track of their progress by using the chart.

Stand together in a circle for all *Getting Started* activities (except for jogging). Have players partner up, with one player doing the activity and the partner keeping count and giving encouragement. Be sure that they have their Portfolios handy so that they can record their progress. Encourage them to clap and cheer for their teammates to create an enthusiastic environment. You may also choose to include music.

Choose from the options below, making sure to include a cardio and a stretching warm-up.

- **Measure resting heart rate (RHR)** — Spend a few minutes showing players how to find their pulses, either on their necks or wrists. Explain that you will be giving them a few seconds to count how many times their hearts beat. Take a moment to allow the players to sit quietly on the floor and find their pulses. Give them 30 seconds to count their heartbeats.

- **Record, check in and set goals** — Allow a couple of minutes for players to record their RHRs in their Player Portfolios.

- **Jog (2-3 min.)** — This can be done as a lap or in place as a circle.

- **Stretch (2-3 min.)** — Be sure to include stretches for the major muscle groups.

- **Strength/Endurance (1 min.)** — On this first day, players will set baseline numbers for the four Strength/Endurance activities (push-ups, sit-ups, lunges, calf raises), but usually, you will only choose one or two. They will work in pairs. One member of the pair will have 30 seconds to do as many of the activities as they can. Their partner will cheer them on and count for them.

- **Jump Rope (4 min.)** — Again, players will work in pairs, with one person jumping and the other person counting and cheering. They should have three to four sets of 30-45 seconds of jumping rope.

- **Track personal progress** — Have players record their totals for steps five and six in their Player Portfolios. These totals will represent their baseline achievements, or their Past Personal Bests (PPB). Each day, players will check their progress from the previous session and will set a Future Personal Best Goal (FBG) to work toward for next time. Be sure to remind them about setting realistic goals (for example, adding one or two to their baseline, as opposed to 10).

Block II: Structured Play (30 min.)

Skill Play (10 min.)

Choose one or two of the following activities to play today. You can refer back to the *Physical Activities Description Appendix* for instructions on how to run the activities. Encourage players to cheer for each other, and include music if you wish.

- Softball Throw

- Backward Run/Walk Relay

- Over, Under, Over, Under

- Sack Race

- Wheelbarrow Race

Sport Play (20 min.)

As a group, decide which sport you want to play today. Select from the sport list contained in the *Sports List Appendix*. Be sure to periodically review with the group the Physical Activities Recommendations for Sport from Chapter Six.

Cool-down

If time permits, close the day with a few minutes of stretching while conducting the following R&R Huddle.

- **Recap** one or two key moments from the Lessons from the Field.

- **Reconnect** players back to the theme unit.

- **Reset** and transition players to the Cool-down, Reflection time.

  OR

- **Reflection**

Use this time to highlight teachable moments you observed during the day and to give players an opportunity to share their experiences about Sports PLUS during the day. The following questions can serve as a guide:

- What did you like about today?

- What did you learn today?

- What are some ways you persevered today?

- How can we better show perseverance next time?

- In what ways did your teammates persevere today?

Goal-setting

Use this time to help players track progress toward their individually chosen goals, as well as toward team goals. As goals from earlier sessions are reached, guide players in setting additional individual and team goals related to Perseverance.

Session 49: **Putting It Out There** **Lessons from Adventure**	
Warm-up Begin the PLUS Cycle (5 min.) • Session Overview • Catch Up **Activity** Lessons from Adventure (25-30 min.) • Toss Up	**Cool-down** Continue the PLUS Cycle (5-10 min.) • Reflection • Feelings Impulse **Materials** Lots of soft objects — fleece balls, foam balls, stuffed animals, etc., at least 1 per player

Warm-up

Catch Up?

This activity will get players ready for working on teambuilding.

Setup

Ask the group to stand in a circle. Invite four players to enter the center of the circle and face out toward the other group members. Imagining a clock, the four players in the middle should stand roughly at 12, three, six and nine o'clock. Give each of these players in the middle a soft, tossable object.

Play

1. The activity begins with all four players tossing their items to the players across from them. The receiving players throw the objects back. The player in the middle then rotates slightly to the player to his or her right and repeats the same type of tossing, each time exchanging a toss with the next player.

2. The four players in the middle are "working" their part of the circle. Have players start tossing to evenly spread outer circle group members.

3. The goal is for each of the players in the middle to try to catch up to the tossing of the player next to them. If one of the four players in the middle does catch up, the round ends.

4. Make sure to rotate players through the middle.

Activity

Lessons from Adventure
Toss Up

Setup

This is a fun and pretty simple activity — at least it looks simple. The theme of perseverance plays out well here, as does setting goals. Be sure to remind players of their commitments to each other and to respect their teammates at all times.

Play

1. If you have a large group, 18 or more, you might want to think about separating the group in two for a few practice runs. Have the group form a cluster with players close together but not bumping into each other. Each player gets one soft, throwable object.

2. The instructions are simple: on the count of three, everyone throws their objects up into the air. The goal is for the group to catch as many of the objects as possible. The rules are that a player cannot catch the object they threw and the objects cannot be thrown directly to another person — they must be tossed as high as your space allows.

3. Allow a bit of discussion time for the group to set an initial goal of how many of the objects they think they can catch. Allow a couple of attempts and count the number of objects caught. Then let the group set a new goal, either more or less than they originally thought they could catch.

- **R&R Huddle** (5 min.)

- **Recap** by asking players how they felt during the activity: Did anyone feel frustrated?

- **Reconnect** to the theme unit by asking players, "How is perseverance important for this activity?" and transition to the next activity.

Cool-down

Cool-down Ritual

Feelings Impulse

Using an impulse go-round, ask players to share a feeling word to describe how they are feeling about the Sports PLUS program right now. If time permits, ask for volunteers to share why they chose the word they did. Also, you may want to ask players to compare their feelings about the program now with how they felt at the beginning. For example, do they feel happier because they know everyone in the group better now?

Session 50:
Perseverance Certificates

Overview

> **Instructor's Notes:** *Be sure to review this set of activities before starting this Sports PLUS Session. Directions for how to run each activity are provided, but it is important that you become familiar with them so that you may more effectively lead the group.*
>
> *During group discussions, be sure to record all thoughts and ideas on a blackboard or newsprint. Remember that when players are working in their Player Portfolios, spelling, grammar, and penmanship are, relatively speaking, unimportant, so don't dwell on those details or you risk making Sports PLUS into MoreSchool.*

This final Perseverance theme unit follows the Sports PLUS format for the closing session of a unit. The *Perseverance Posters Revisit* allows players to revisit the commitments they made to themselves and each other in the beginning of the theme unit. Challenge players to think not only about what they have learned about Perseverance, but also about the values from previous units.

As much as possible, empower players to run the *Perseverance Awards and Sports Extras* activities. By deciding how the activities are run and ensuring that they abide by their own rules, players practice living the values. The

Sports PLUS program concludes with a special awards ceremony and closing ritual that allows the group to end the program with a strong sense of closure and accomplishment.

Session 50: **Perseverance Certificates** **Lessons from Literature**	
Warm-up Begin the PLUS Cycle (10-15 min.) • Session Overview • Quote of the Week **Activity** Lessons from Literature (25-30 min.) • Sports Extras	**Cool-down** Continue the PLUS Cycle (5-10 min.) • Reflection **Materials** Student-found items for Sports Extras

Warm-up

Quote of the Week

The triumph can't be had without the struggle.

— Wilma Rudolph

Overview

Share some background information on Wilma Rudolph's life and athletic career. Revisit the short story read during the Perseverance unit.

Follow the five steps of the Quote of the Week Format (See the Getting Started chapter for additional explanation):

1. **Write the Quote of the Week:** Bring the group together into a circle, and write the Quote on the blackboard.

2. **Think about the Quote as a group:** Spend two or three minutes talking with the students about what they think the quote means. Ask students to share answers to the group for the following question:

- Do you agree with Wilma's quote? Why or why not?

3. **Pair up to talk about the Quote:** Have students separate into pairs. Ask them to spend about five minutes discussing the following questions with their partners. Explain that they will be sharing their answers with the whole group, so they may choose to write them in their Player Portfolios. (Be sure to walk around the groups, listen, and offer help where needed.):

- Why do you think Wilma made this statement?

- Think of what you have accomplished in Sports PLUS. What accomplishments have come your way via challenging situations?

4. **Share answers with the whole group:** Come together as a large group and share the answers from each of the pair groups. Everyone who wants to should have an opportunity to share their answers.

5. **Reflect individually about the Quote:** Take two or three minutes for students to reflect individually by writing their responses to the following Journal Question in their Player Portfolios::

- What is one thing you have struggled with during Sports PLUS? What helped you to get through?

Activity

Sports Extras

This is an important activity for the conclusion of each theme unit. Students may work alone or in small groups. At the start of the unit, students were asked to look for actual events and stories of people in the news or in history who exemplify the core value for that theme unit. Students should be reminded frequently throughout the theme unit to be on the lookout for examples of the core Sports PLUS values in magazines and newspapers. They can ask a parent or guardian if they are unsure of where to find an article. If possible, provide access during the Sports

PLUS program to students' magazines, such as Sports Illustrated for Kids. A certain area of the room can be designated as the "Sports Extras Area," in which students can store their articles and stories as they find them.

Setup

1. Bring the group together to form a circle. Explain the next activity as you pass out the Player Portfolios and pencils. Use the following description as a guide:

   "Today you will have an opportunity to share a story about Perseverance with the rest of the group. You may choose either to share the article you brought in or to share the story you wrote during 'Create Your Own Story.'"

2. Ask students to spend a few minutes writing answers to the pre-work questions in their Player Portfolios:

   - Who is the main character in your story?

   - What happened to the main character? Or what did the main character do?

   - In what way is this story an example of Perseverance?

   - One thing the main character learned is that he or she should…

   - This story teaches us that we should…

3. After students have had some time to answer the questions in their Portfolios, ask for volunteers to share their stories in their own words. Let everyone who wants to share do so.

Cool-down

- **R&R Huddle** (5 min.)

- **Recap** by asking students: What do these articles teach us about Perseverance?

- **Reconnect** students to the theme unit using the following focus prompt: One way these examples of perseverance help us be a better team is by…

- **Reset** and get ready for the next lesson.

Session 50: **Perseverance Certificates** **Lessons from the Field**	

Warm-up
   Begin the PLUS Cycle (5 min.)
   • Session Overview
   • Pondering Perseverance
Activity
   Lessons from the Field (25-30 min.)
   • Sports Activity
	Cool-down
	   Continue the PLUS Cycle (5-10 min.)
	   • Reflection
	   • Goal-setting
	Materials
	   Sports Equipment

Warm-up

Pondering Perseverance (5 min.)

Ask students to think about the previous lesson. What can they do today to bring the Lessons from Literature into their work together in the sports activity?

Activity

Sports Activity

Block I: Getting Started (5 min.)

On the first day, players will learn how to measure their resting heart rates (RHR). They will also set baselines for their RHR, number of sit-ups/push-ups/lunges/calf raises, and number of jumps during jump rope. Each day they will try to improve upon their Past Personal Best (PPB) by achieving their Future Best Goal (FBG) and by tracking progress toward that goal in the physical activities progress chart located in the back of their Player Portfolios. Take one minute to make sure all participants turn to the back of their portfolios and locate the progress charts. Explain to them that they will be using this chart each time you meet to do physical activities. Be sure to emphasize the importance of keeping track of their progress by using the chart.

Stand together in a circle for all *Getting Started* activities (except for jogging). Have players partner up, with one player doing the activity and the partner keeping count and giving encouragement. Be sure that they have their Portfolios handy so that they can record their progress. Encourage them to clap and cheer for their teammates to create an enthusiastic environment. You may also choose to include music.

Choose from the options below, making sure to include a cardio and a stretching warm-up.

- **Measure resting heart rate (RHR)** — Spend a few minutes showing players how to find their pulses, either on their necks or wrists. Explain that you will be giving them a few seconds to count how many times their hearts beat. Take a moment to allow the players to sit quietly on the floor and find their pulses. Give them 30 seconds to count their heartbeats.

- **Record, check in and set goals** — Allow a couple of minutes for players to record their RHRs in their Player Portfolios.

- **Jog (2-3 min.)** — This can be done as a lap or in place as a circle.

- **Stretch (2-3 min.)** — Be sure to include stretches for the major muscle groups.

- **Strength/Endurance (1 min.)** — On this first day, players will set baseline numbers for the four Strength/Endurance activities (push-ups, sit-ups, lunges, calf raises), but usually, you will only choose one or two. They will work in pairs. One member of the pair will have 30 seconds to do as many of the activities as they can. Their partner will cheer them on and count for them.

- **Jump Rope (4 min.)** — Again, players will work in pairs, with one person jumping and the other person counting and cheering. They should have three to four sets of 30-45 seconds of jumping rope.

- **Track personal progress** — Have players record their totals for steps five and six in their Player Portfolios. These totals will represent their baseline achievements, or their Past Personal Bests (PPB). Each day, players will check their progress from the previous session and will set a Future Personal Best Goal (FBG) to work toward for next time. Be sure to remind them about setting realistic goals (for example, adding one or two to their baseline, as opposed to 10).

Block II: Structured Play (30 min.)

Skill Play (10 min.)

Choose one or two of the following activities to play today. You can refer back to the *Physical Activities Description Appendix* for instructions on how to run the activities. Encourage players to cheer for each other, and include music if you wish.

- Dribble Relay

- Ball Bowling

- Limbo

- Hula Hoop Challenge Course

- Water Balloon Volleyball

Sport Play (20 min.)

As a group, decide which sport you want to play today. Select from the sport list contained in the *Sports List Appendix*. Be sure to periodically review with the group the Physical Activities Recommendations for Sport from Chapter Six.

Cool-down

If time permits, close the day with a few minutes of stretching while conducting the following R&R Huddle.

- **Recap** one or two key moments from the Lessons from the Field.

- **Reconnect** players back to the theme unit.

- **Reset** and transition players to the Cool-down, Reflection time.

Session 50: Perseverance Certificates Lessons from Adventure	
Warm-up Begin the PLUS Cycle (5 min.) • Session Overview • Perseverance Posters Revisited **Activity** Lessons from Adventure (25-30 min.) • Perseverance Certificates	**Cool-down** Continue the PLUS Cycle (5-10 min.) • Reflection • Presentation of Certificates **Materials** Parting Sports PLUS item, such as a t-shirt, Frisbee, basketball, bandanna, etc.; bracelets (optional, but recommended); Perseverance Certificates created during the session; perseverance posters

Warm-up

Perseverance Posters Revisited

Take a brief tour of the perseverance posters that were created at the beginning of the theme unit. Stop at each poster and discuss what is represented on it and what it says about perseverance. Ask players to comment on how they think the group has done with persevering this unit and with creating a good team. Draw upon what is on the posters to help players give specific examples of perseverance they noticed throughout the theme unit. Ask if anyone has anything they would like to add to the posters to update them (e.g., adding new insights and ideas they have learned over the course of the theme unit).

Activity

Lessons from Adventure
(see Player Portfolio)

Perseverance Certificates

During this activity, players will create a "Perseverance Certificate" to signify their completion of the final Sports PLUS theme unit. Players should make individual certificates, with a blank space for names. These certificates will then be distributed by the Masters of Ceremonies at the end of the day.

Play

1. Gather the group into a circle, and explain the purpose of the next activity "To create certificates that signify our completion of this Sports PLUS theme unit."

2. Describe one or two possible ways this can be done, and ask players if they have any other ideas. As a group, decide what you are going to do, and create the certificate(s).

3. When the certificate(s) are finished, gather the group together to vote on the two people who have given their best effort to show Perseverance during this theme unit. Voting can be done either by a show of hands, applause for nominated candidates, or by writing names on slips of paper. (In the case of a tie, allow multiple winners.)

4. Once the decision has been made, explain that the students chosen will be the "Masters of Ceremonies" for the presentation of the Perseverance Certificate(s) at the end of the day.

- **Recap** one or two points from the previous discussion about the Perseverance Posters.

- **Reconnect** players back to the theme unit.

- **Reset** and transition to the next activity.

Cool-down

Reflection and Cool-down Ritual

Setup

Before the players enter, set up the room in which the closing ceremony will be held. Each player should have a designated place, with their personal parting Sports PLUS keepsake from the program (e.g., a Frisbee, shirt, basketball, bandanna, certificate, etc.). The places should form a circle.

Play

When the setup is complete, lead the players to their places. Ask them to sit on the floor, close their eyes, and think about moments from their journey through the Sports PLUS program. Lead them on a guided reflection about their time in the Sports PLUS program to help them recall important experiences. The following can be used as a guide:

"Keeping your eyes closed, imagine that you have a videotape of your entire Sports PLUS experience playing in your head. As I remind you of specific events, replay the video in your mind so that you can see and remember."

This reflection should be kept very brief. (One to two minutes should be plenty of time.)

> After the players open their eyes, take a few seconds to share a few parting words with the group. Next, ask the two players chosen as Masters of Ceremonies (MC) to come up to present the Perseverance Certificates. (Be sure to help the MC's fill out the names on each certificate before the ceremony.) MC's should call each player by name and have them come to the front of the room to receive their certificates. Players may choose to take this opportunity to say a few parting words to the group.

If you're using bracelets, ask them to pick up their bracelets once everyone has had a chance to speak. Have them ask one person who was special to them during the program to tie on their bracelet for them. *PLUS into MoreSchool.*

REFERENCES

Bandura, A. (1991). "Social cognitive theory of moral thought and action." In W. M. Kurtines and J. L. Gewirtz (Eds.) *Handbook of moral behavior and development: Volume 1: Theory.* Hillsdale, NJ, Lawrence Erlbaum Associates, pp. 45-103.

Beedy, J. P. and Gough, R. W. (2000). *Guidelines for effective character education through sports.* Washington, DC, Character Education Partnership.

Beedy, J. (1997). *Sports Plus: ositive Learning Using Sports: Developing Youth Sports Programs That Teach Positive Values.* Hamilton, MA, Project Adventure, Inc.

Beedy J.P. (1988). *Understanding the interpersonal world of youth sports.* Unpublished Dissertation. Cambridge, MA: Harvard University.

Beedy J.P. (2003). *PLUS systems model: A holistic, community-wide approach to maximizing the development potential of sport.* (In Press). New

Hampton, NH: New Hampton School.

Biro, B.D. (1997). *Beyond success: The 15 secrets to effective leadership based on legendary Coach John Wooden's pyramid of success.* New York: Penguin Publishing.

Boiselle, E. Hussar, K. Noam, G. & Schwartz, S. (2008). Toward a Systematic Evidence-Base for Science in Out-of-School Time: The Role of Assessment. Cambridge, MA: Harvard University & PEAR.

Brennan, M. A., & Barnett, R. V. (2009). "Bridging community and youth development: Exploring theory, research, and application." *Community Development,* 40, 305-310.

Brennan, M. A., Barnett, R. V., & Baugh, E. (2007). "Youth involvement in community development: Implications and possibilities for extension." *Journal of Extension,* 45 (4), 203-213.

Brennan, M. A., Barnett, R. V., & Lesmeister, M. (2007). "Enhancing local capacity and youth involvement in the community development process." *Journal of Community Development,* 38 (4), 13-27.

Bukowski, W.M., Newcomb, A.F., and Hartup, W. (1996). *The company they keep: Friendship in childhood and adolescence.* Cambridge: Cambridge University Press.

Coyne, Daniel, Talent Code

Davidson, M.L., (2002). "Character Education: Our Timeless Quest. Past Progress and Future Challenges." *The Hamptonia Magazine,* 118, 1.

Davidson, M.L., & Khmelkov, V.T., (2002). A global portrait of social and moral health for youth & adults. [Is this a book?]

Davidson, M.L., Moran-Miller, K.E., Beedy, J.P. (2002). *Performance and Moral Character: A Blueprint for Developing Character in Competitive*

Contexts. Cortland: Center for the 4th and 5th Rs (Respect and Responsibility).

Davidson, M.L., Moran-Miller, K.E., Beedy, J.P., Bredemeier, B.L., Power, F.C., Shields, D.L., (2002). *An Ethnographic Study of Character Development in An Elite Prep-School Basketball Program.* Notre Dame: Mendelson Center for Sport, Character & Culture.

Davidson, M.L., Moran-Miller, K.E., Beedy, J.P., Bredemeier, B.L., Power, F.C., Shields, D.L., (2002). *Relationships are the rule: Cultivating character and community in elite sports.* Unpublished Report. New Hampton, NH: New Hampton School.

Davidson, M.L., (2001). Schoolwide approaches for teaching values through literature. In A.W. Pailliotet & P. Schmidt (Eds.), *Exploring values across the curriculum with literature and mass media.* International Reading Association.

Posey, J., & Davidson, M.L. (2001). *Character education evaluation toolkit: A user-friendly and practical evaluation guide for educators and administrators.* Alexandria, VA: Character Education Partnership.

Davidson, M.L., (Fall, 2000). Concept mapping and character education: New directions in character education planning and evaluation. *International Journal of Research in Education,* 10(1)34-42.

Damon, W. (1995). *Greater expectations: Overcoming the culture of indulgence in our homes and schools.* New York, Free Press.

Dewey, John, (1938) Experience and Education

Duda, J. L. and J. G. Nicholls (1992). "Dimensions of achievement motivation in schoolwork and sport." *Journal of Educational Psychology,* 84(3): 290-299.

Etnier, J.L., Salazar, W., Landers, D.M., Petruzzello, S.J., Han, M., Nowell, P. (1997). "The influence of physical fitness and exercise upon cognitive functioning: A meta-analysis." *Journal of Sport and Exercise Psychology,* 19 (3), 249-277.

Eyre, R. and Eyre L. (1993). *Teaching your children values.* New York: Fireside.

Friedman, Thomas L., (2005), *The World Is Flat: A Brief History of the Twenty-first Century.* Farrar, Straus and Giroux.

"Front runners: proof that sports-based youth development programs work". Up2Us Center for Sports-Based Youth Development. Up2Us.org

Goleman, D. (1995). *Emotional intelligence: Why it can matter more than IQ.* New York, Bantam Books.

Harackiewicz, J. M. and A. J. Elliot (1993). "Achievement goals and intrinsic motivation." *Journal of Personality and Social Psychology* 65: 904-915.

Harwood, Chris. (2008). "Developmental consulting in a professional football academy: the 5Cs coaching efficacy program". *The Sports Psychologist.* 22, 109- 133.

Hellison, Don. (2009): "Engaging urban youths", *Journal of Physical Education,* Recreation & Dance, 80:8, 27-34.

Hellison, Don and Parker, Melissa. (2001): "Teaching responsibility in physical education: standards, outcomes, and beyond", *Journal of Physical Education,* Recreation & Dance, 72:9, 25-27.

Kohn, A. (1993). Punished by rewards: The trouble with gold stars, incentive plans, A's, praise and other bribes. New York, Houghton Mifflin Company.

Lauer, H., (2002). *Sports participation and youth development programs.* Unpublished report for the Edna McConnell Clark Foundation.

Lickona, T. (1991). *Educating for character: How our schools can teach respect and responsibility.* New York, Bantam.

Lickona, T. (1983). *Raising good children: From birth through the teenage years.* New York, Bantam.

Kropp, P. (1996). *How to make your child a reader for life.* Canada: Random House of Canada.

Molden, D. C. and C. S. Dweck (2000). *Meaning and motivation. Intrinsic and extrinsic motivation: The search for optimal motivation and performance.* C. Sansone and J. M. Harackiewicz. New York, Academic Press: 131-159.

Moore, Adrienne. (2001) "Sports-based youth development:using sports as an intentional solution for the real issues that young people face". OSPI Conference Presentation. May 18, 2001. Narvaez, D., T. Gleason, et al. (1999). "Moral theme comprehension in children." *Journal of Educational Psychology* 91(3): 477-487.

Nicholls, J. G. (1984). "Achievement motivation: Conceptions of ability, subjective experience, task choice, and performance." *Psychological Review* 91: 328-346.

North American Youth Sport Institute, (1997). *Kidits,* Vol. IV, p. 9. http://naysi.com/kidbits/KB09.htm" \t "_blank" http://naysi.com/kidbits/KB09.htm.

Perkins, Daniel, Ph.D. and Wechsler, Cory. "Quality components of sports-based youth development programs". Up2Us Center for Sports-Based Youth Development. Up2Us.org

Perkins, Daniel, Ph.D., Madsen, Kristine, and Wechsler, Cory. "Sports-based youth development". Up2Us Center for Sports-Based Youth Development. Up2Us.org

Perkins, Daniel, and Noam, G. (2007). "Characteristics of Sports-Based

Youth Development Programs." *New Directions for Youth Development,* Number 115, 75–84, Fall 2007.

Perkins, Daniel, and Le Menestrel, Suzanne. "Sports-Based Youth Development" *New Directions for Youth Development.* Number 115, Fall 2007.

Perkins, D. F. (2009). "Community Youth Development," in J. Wood & J. Hine (Eds.), *Working with Young People* (104-113). London: Sage.

Presidents Council on Physical Fitness and Sports (2000, Dec.). *Research Digest,* 3(12), 1-8.

Resnick, M. D., P. S. Bearman, et al. (1997). "Protecting adolescents from harm: Findings from the National Longitudinal Study on Adolescent Health." *Journal of the American Medical Association* 278(10): 823-832.

Ryan, R. M. and E. L. Deci (2000). *When rewards compete with nature: The undermining of intrinsic motivation and self-regulation. Intrinsic and extrinsic motivation: The search for optimal motivation and performance.* C. Sansone and J. M. Harackiewicz. New York, Academic Press: 13-54.

Schaps, E., M. Watson, et al. (1996). "A sense of community is key to effectiveness in fostering character education." *Journal of Staff Development* 17(2): 42-47.

Schorr, L. & Schorr, D. (1989). *Within Our Reach: Breaking the Cycle of Disadvantage.* New York: Doubleday.

Schwinner, J.B., Burwinkle, T.M., and Varni, J.W. (2003). Health-related quality of life of severely obese children and adolescents. *Journal of the American Medical Association,* 289 (14), pp. 1813-1818.

Selman, R.L., and Kwok, J. Counting hearts and eye-balls: How to help adolescents make better decisions using entertainment and new media (and know that you have succeeded). Mind, work, and life: A Festschrift on the occasion of Howard Gardner's 70th birthday (Vol. Two, pp. 372-398). Cambridge, MA: The Offices of Howard Gardner.,(2014)

Shields, D. L. (2001). *Opponents or enemies: Rethinking the nature of competition. Sport Character and Culture: Promoting Social and Moral Development Through Sport,* University of Notre Dame.

Shields, D. L. and B. J. L. Bredemeier (1995). *Character development and physical activity.* Champaign, IL, Human Kinetics.

Siegel, D., (2002). *Reconceptualizing and recreating youth sports in Boston.* Unpublished report for the Barr Foundation.

Siegel, Donald. (2007): "Relating physical education and activity levels to academic achievement in children". *Journal of Physical Education,* Recreation & Dance, 78:1, 10.

Stevenson, C. L. (1985). "College athletics and "character": The decline and fall of socialization research." *Sport and Higher Education.* D. B. Chu, J. O. Segrave and B. Becker. Champaign, IL, Human Kinetics: 249-266.

Strauss, R., Pollack, H.S. (2001). "Epidemic increase in childhood overweight, 1986-1998." *Journal of American Medical Association,* 286(22), pp. 2845-2848.

Wagner, Tony, (2015) *Most Likely to Succeed: Preparing Our Kids for the Innovation Era.*

Wagner, Tony, (2012) *Creating Innovators.* Scribner. A Division of Simon and Schuster, Inc. New York, NY.

Weiss, Maureen R., Ph.D. and Wiese-Bjornstal, Diane M., Ph.D. (2009) "Promoting positive youth development through physical activity". President's Council on Physical Fitness and Sports Research Digest, Series 10, No. 3. September 2009.

Wiggins, Grant,   (2005) Association for Supervision and Curriculum Development, 1703 N. Beauregard St. Alexandra, VA 22311-1714 USA. Understanding by Design

ABOUT THE AUTHOR

Jeff Beedy is the pioneer and leader in sport-based education. Jeff's original doctoral thesis in the early 1980's charted the cartography of a new domain — sports as moral pedagogy, built on a foundation of research and experience.

At Harvard University Jeff Beedy studied with renowned child psychologists Carol Gilligan, Lawrence Kohlberg, Robert Selman, and Sesame Street founder Gerald Lesser. Jeff taught "Social Reflections of Literature" for Pulitzer Prize winner Dr. Robert Coles.

Jeff's PLUS (Positive Learning Using Sports) is used around the globe, including in China, South Korea, and throughout the United States and Canada.

Jeff's PLUS model for child development was used in conjunction with a U.N. grant and the Olympic Doves Movement to bridge peace between Greek and Turkish children on the island of Cyprus.

In 2010, Jeff became the founding head of Korea International School, the first boarding school to open in South Korea's $2 billion Global Education City on Jeju Island.

Jeff is currently, working on a new book titled *The Other Classroom: Reframing Children's Sports to Teach Survival Skills.*

In his earlier years, Jeff played in the Cape Cod Baseball league, and skied in the freestyle tour. Jeff and his wife Karyn are musicians and play professionally as the Nadia and Jocko Band.

Matt Davidson

Aiding in my research has been Matt Davidson, Ph.D. He is an original Founder and the current President of the Institute for Excellence & Ethics (IEE), a 501 (c) (3) non-profit organization. Find out more about IEE by visiting the IEE website http://www.excellenceandethics.org, IEE Facebook page https://www.facebook.com/excellenceandethics, or by following Matt Davidson on Twitter at twitter.com/mdavidsonatiee.